THE HISTORY OF
THE MAZRU'I DYNASTY OF
MOMBASA

UNION ACADÉMIQUE INTERNATIONALE
FONTES HISTORIAE AFRICANAE
Series Arabica XI

THE HISTORY OF THE MAZRU'I DYNASTY OF MOMBASA

by
SHAYKH AL-AMIN BIN 'ALI AL MAZRU'I

Translated and annotated
by
J. McL. Ritchie

Published *for* THE BRITISH ACADEMY
by OXFORD UNIVERSITY PRESS

Oxford University Press, Walton Street, Oxford OX2 6DP

Oxford New York
Athens Auckland Bangkok Bombay
Calcutta Cape Town Dar es Salaam Delhi
Florence Hong Kong Istanbul Karachi
Kuala Lumpur Madras Madrid Melbourne
Mexico City Nairobi Paris Singapore
Taipei Tokyo Toronto

and associated companies in
Berlin Ibadan

British Library Cataloguing in Publication Data
Data available

ISBN 0–19–726158–2

Phototypeset by Intype, London
Printed in Great Britain
on acid-free paper by
Bookcraft (Bath) Ltd.
Midsomer Norton, Avon

Contents

Preface

The Manuscript of the Arabic Text of this work, written by the Author in lead pencil on foolscap paper, was entrusted to me for translation in the year 1965 by its custodian, the Chief Qadi of Kenya, Shaykh Muhammad b. Qasim al-Mazru'i. The aim of the present translation and edition is to make it available to the non-Arabic-speaking public, and to set it alongside other documents and accounts relating to 18th Century Mombasa and its rulers, so that it may provide a further measure by which the history of the period may be evaluated, and the details of the picture of events filled out. It is important in that it is the only document about the Mazru'i dynasty of Liwalis which can be said to come in any degree 'from within' the situation, that is, from within the East African population, the Swahili-speaking community and the Mazru'i family itself. There are many references to the Mazru'i family and its rulers, but none from quite so intimate a source as this.

In subjects such as the one dealt with in this work one may expect a certain amount of bias: but bias on the part of one who writes from within must be set against the inevitable bias, smaller or greater, of those who write 'from without', whatever may be the motive of the writer, or the occasion which caused him to write, or the interest — strategic, scientific, commercial or other — which he has in view. The editing and comments on this work therefore, by entailing a comparison with other available accounts, will, it may be hoped, make easier the defining of the balance of bias, and thus help the historian to arrive at a knowledge of the events as near the truth as it may be possible to get.

Acknowledgements

My thanks are due to the Chief Qadi of Kenya, now unfortunately deceased, for his help in checking the translation as well as for the short biographical account of the Author which I have set before the Arabic text as given to me, and have translated as an introduction to the English Translation. I also thank Shaykh Haydar al-Kindi, through whom I was put into contact with the MS in the first place, and the late Mr. James Kirkman of Fort Jesus National Park, whose friendly assistance and humour have been an encouragement in various frustrations. Mr. F. J. Berg, lecturer in East African History in Colgate College, U.S.A., has provided me with the sources of several of the items of information which appear in the comments and appendices, in particular, the note regarding the tribal alignments in the City of Mombasa and its vicinity, and the genealogies in Appendix No. 1. Professor G. S. P. Freeman-Grenville has been a kind and helpful adviser all along, and it is largely due to his encouragement and interest that this work is appearing at all. I would lastly like to record my thanks to the late Mr. John T. H. Allen, who was working for a time in the University of Dar-es-Salaam, for his interest and the help he gave in supplying the text of the two Swahili poems relevant to the subject of this work, together with the Library references, which appear in Appendix No. 5. I also acknowledge with thanks the permission of the Kenya Survey for the use of their Maps in the production of some of the Sketch Maps in Appendix No. 2.

Finally, a word of special gratitude to Miss Mary Anne Stravens of Mombasa who typed and duplicated the original translation which is the basis of this edition, and to a number of people, too numerous to mention all by name, who have given material help in various ways.

James McL. Ritchie
Edinburgh 1993

A Note on the Transliteration of Arabic Words and Names

The Arabic Words and Proper Names in the English text of this Edition, with the exception of some common words which have so passed into current usage that they may be regarded as English words, are transliterated in accordance with the following table:

Arabic Letter	English Equivalent	Arabic Letter	English Equivalent
Alif	'	Dad	D
Ba	B	Ta	T
Ta	T	Za	Z
Tha	TH	'Ayn	'
Jim	J	Ghayn	GH
Ha	H	Fa	F
Kha	KH	Qaf	Q
Dal	D	Kaf	K
Dhal	DH	Lam	L
Ra	R	Mim	M
Zai	Z	Nun	N
Sin	S	Ha	H
Shin	SH	Waw	W
Sad	S	Ya	Y

	Short	Long
Vowels	A	A
	I	I
	U	U

(The consonantal part of the long vowel is not written).

Diphthongs	AY	AU

The Definite Article is always written 'Al-', except in Arabic phrases.

In passages quoted from other authors and sources, however, I have left the orthography as printed in the original even when it does not conform with the above scheme.

INTRODUCTION

A Biographical Sketch of the Author

The author of this work was Shaykh Al-Amin b. 'Ali b. 'Abdullah b. Nafi' b. Mazru' b. 'Abdullah b. Khamis b. 'Ali b. 'Abdullah b. 'Ali Al-Mazru'i, Teacher, Imam and Scholar.

This 'Abdullah b. Khamis is the seventh lineal ancestor of the fourteen lineages of the Mazari'a who emigrated to the Swahili Coast, as mentioned in the First Chapter of this book. His grandfather, the Scholar Shaykh 'Abdullah b. Nafi' was the first of the Mazari'a to adopt the Shafi'i School.

Shaykh Al-Amin, God rest[1] his soul, was born in the Town of Mombasa on 15 Jumada Al-Akhira A.H. 1308, or 27th January A.D. 1891, and his father died when he was four years old. So he was brought up in the care of his relative the learned Shaykh Sulayman b. 'Ali b. Khamis Al-Mazru'i, the former Chief Qadi of Kenya. From him he received most of his proficiency in the Religious Sciences.

He used frequently to visit Zanzibar to study under the Scholars Sayyid Ahmad b. Abi Bakr b. Sumyat and Shaykh 'Abdullah b. Muhammad Ba Kathir.[2] He made a wide and deep study of the Sciences and excelled his fellows, and the 'Ulama'[3] began to go to him from Zanzibar, Tanga and Lamu and other regions of East Africa to gather a little from the abundance of his knowledge.

Among his pupils were the excellent and learned Ma'mun b. Sulayman b. 'Ali Al-Mazru'i, previous Qadi of Mombasa, and the excellent and learned Shaykh 'Abdullah b. Salih Al-Farsi, present Qadi of Zanzibar, and the excellent and learned Teacher Shaykh Muhammad b. Ahmad Al-Burayki, the Teacher Hajj Shaykh Ahmad b. Ibrahim b. Ahmad al-Kukni, and the Teacher Hajj Shaykh Sa'id b. Ahmad Sa'id Al-Qumri, and the late Teacher Shaykh Muhammad 'Abdullah Ghazali, and the late Teacher Shaykh Rashid b. Qasim Al-Mazru'i, and the humble writer of this account.

---

[1] **God rest his soul.** In Arabic *"Rahamahu 'llahu"*.

[2] **Ba Kathir.** This name suggests that the Shaykh who bore it was a member of the Royal family of Sayyun who ruled in what was until recently the Fifth Governorate of the People's Democratic Republic of Yemen, formerly the Hadhramaut.

[3] ***'Ulama.*** This term is the plural of the word *'Alim*, the word used to describe one who has a recognised status as a scholar and teacher of Religion among Muslims.

The late learned Shaykh 'Ali b. Humayd Al-Buhri,[4] former Qadi of Tanga, used to boast that he was one of the late Shaykh's pupils.

He loved the Muslims in general and his own people in particular. He started libraries and Schools of Religion for them, and spent the best part of his time in instruction and teaching and writing books on Religion, which had a great influence in spreading Islam in the country. He was the first to write books on religion in the Swahili language. Even if there were no book to his credit but that entitled *The Children's Guide*, which is read in all the mosques and schools of East Africa and beyond, it would suffice as a mark of his influence in this world, and as a treasure laid up for the next.[5]

When he understood the great benefit of Newspapers he desired them for his own folk, and issued on 4 Jumada Al-Akhira A.H. 1349, (25th January A.D. 1930) a paper in the Swahili language which dealt with political, social and religious questions, especially the spreading of the Sunna, and rejection of heresies.

His people showed violent hostility to him, but he was patient under their injuries relying upon God, the most faithful in His saying, may He be exalted, "Answer their injuries with patience and rely upon God. God certainly loves those who rely on Him".[6] Much of the truth has spread to the praise of God, and much of what is useless has perished. He used to write the books with his own hand, and duplicate them and distribute them free.

Then on 22 Shawwal A.H. 1350 (29th February A.D. 1932) he published a weekly newspaper in Arabic and Swahili which he called *Al-Islah* (Reform), issued with the Qur'anic verse: "I can only desire reform as far as I am able. My attainment of it is in God only. I rely on Him and to Him I turn patiently".[7] Its fame spread throughout East Africa.

He then became Qadi of Mombasa in Ramadan A.H. 1351 (December A.D. 1932). He performed this office with distinction, and was a model of justice and equity. Then in Rabi' Al-Awwal A.H. 1356 (June A.D. 1937) he became Chief Qadi,[8] and performed this office with aptitude and worthi-

---

[4] *'Ali b. Humayd Al-Buhri*. This man, according to a verbal report I received from Mr. John Allen, was regarded by Dr. Schacht, the Great Authority on Islamic Law, as one of the most learned, if not the most learned, in the Science of Islamic Jurisprudence of all the Scholars he had met.

[5] It may be noted here that Scholarship in Islam is a meritorious activity which goes towards a man's credit in the Day of Judgment.

[6] "Answer their injuries . . ." The writer has given this as a verse from the Qur'an, but in fact it is either a misquotation or a saying made up from Qur'anic phrases which have come together in his memory. I can find no actual verse in these terms.

[7] "*I only desire . . .* " Qur'an Sura 11, vs. 90 (Fluegel).

[8] Sc. Chief Qadi of Kenya, at that time a Crown Colony.

ness, and was a good example for his successors. His duties as Qadi and Mufti did not prevent him writing, teaching and travelling to many East African regions to preach Islam and give leadership.

He died in the afternoon of Tuesday 8 Jumada Al-Awla A.H. 1366 (? April 1947), leaving great grief and deep sorrow in the hearts of Muslims. May God sheathe him in His Mercy and Good Pleasure, and cause him to dwell in the spaciousness of His Paradise with the Prophets, the faithful, the Martyrs and the righteous to whom He has been gracious, and may he be a worthy companion to them.

The late Shaykh Al-Amin left as male offspring Shaykh Harith b. Al-Amin Al-Mazru'i, who was Liwali[9] of Lamu, and Dr.'Ali b. Al-Amin Al-Mazru'i, Professor of Political Science in Makerere University.

Shaykh Muhammad b. Qasim Al-Mazru'i Mombasa

The Mazru'i State of Mombasa — Its Historical Background and Context

The Portuguese, after a century of almost undisputed supremacy in the Indian Ocean, together with a nearly complete commercial monopoly, were in the 17th Century growing exhausted, and becoming increasingly challenged by other forces, while at the same time the Arabian State of 'Uman, which had, after a long period of disruption and internecine strife, become consolidated and unified under the Ya'rubi Dynasty of Imams, founded by Nasir b. Murshid, was beginning to make itself felt as an international power in the Indian Ocean.

Since the terrain of 'Uman was at that time so little able to afford a viable livelihood to the majority of its population, it sought to extend its commerce as its political power increased. The arbitrary and occasionally oppressive rule of Portugal had, whatever may be said in mitigation of their blame, estranged the local population of East Africa, and forced them to look for a deliverer; and this they found, or thought they had found, in the Yar'ubi Imam; for in a coastal country with no hinterland, such as the East African Littoral prior to the late 19th Century, the people are forced to seek help from across the sea.

The Town of Mombasa petitioned 'Uman for help against the Portu-

---

[9] **Liwali**. I have used the term Liwali throughout the translation for the Arabic Wali, since this is the accepted title for the office in East Africa. It is in fact a corruption of the Arabic word with the definite article — Al-Wali.

guese in 1649,[1] and the result of this, and of similar contacts between the other parts of the coast, was a confrontation between the Portuguese and 'Uman. A struggle ensued which lasted in all over 80 years (A.D. 1649 – A.D. 1729), and ended with the final expulsion of the Portuguese from all the East African Coast north of Cape Delgado. As far as Mombasa was concerned, they had been driven out of the Town and the Fort in the year A.D. 1698, after over two and a half years' siege, but they returned for a short period in A.D. 1728–9 before being finally driven out.[2]

The withdrawal of the Portuguese was not however followed by an immediate and absolute substitute of 'Umani rule and administration. The Imam appointed governors (Arabic — Wali; Swahili — Liwali)[3] in important centres such as Pate, Lamu, Mombasa, Zanzibar and Kilwa, and these were received at first gladly by the local population as deliverers and bringers of stability and security; but other factors had begun to operate.

First of all, the Ya'rubi Dynasty began to suffer from the almost universal malady of Islamic ruling families, namely dynastic quarrels. These plunged the country once more into civil war. Secondly, the expanding power of Iran had sought to strengthen its grasp on the Arabian Gulf by interfering in the 'Umani power struggle. Thirdly, at the end of the 18th and beginning of the 19th Centuries, the Wahhabis of the Arabian Peninsula tried to extend their area of rule to 'Uman and Masqat, so that the 'Umani rulers were faced with a threat from the landward side as well as from across the Gulf.

This all meant that 'Uman was not able properly to attend to its political and administrative commitments in East Africa, a task difficult at the best and most peaceful of times owing to the dependance of communications on the seasonal Monsoons, but rendered doubly hard when the Imam, or whoever was in the best position to use the power of the Imam, was fighting a rearguard action as well, which constantly diverted his attention from his overseas dependencies.

The result of all this was a power vacuum in East Africa during the 18th Century, and the first decades of the 19th. It was specially pronounced in the periods A.D. 1700–1730 and 1830–1839. At the end of the first period the Portuguese had been finally expelled after the momentary come-back referred to above. In spite of various tentative and abortive

---

[1] Freeman-Grenville: The French at Kilwa Island, p. 11. The uncertainty of much of the dating is seen in the fact that the same author, in the Oxford Dictionary of East Africa, p. 141, puts the rise of 'Uman in 1650, after which, he states, the people of Mombasa petitioned the Imam.
[2] Oxford History of East Africa: p. 142.
[3] See Note No. 9 in the Introduction.

moves, such as that of La Bourdonnais as early as A.D. 1734[4] to persuade the French Government to commence commercial operations, and signs of other activity by private individuals such as the mysterious Mr. Cook referred to by Shaykh Al-Amin, neither the British nor the French had yet entered the area in force, since they tended to regard East Africa at that time as a rather unhealthy cul-de-sac, or backwater, offering no advantage to the merchant which would justify their seeking to gain a firm and permanent footing there. It took the strategic needs of the Napoleonic War to arouse within the British and French minds any true idea of the importance of East Africa.

In A.D. 1749 the Ya'rubi Dynasty finally gave place to the rule of Ahmad b. Sa'id, who was appointed Imam in that year, and became the first ruler of the Bu Sa'idi Dynasty. Yet he had a tough fight to establish his position, and was only able to give intermittent attention to East Africa. Under his successor, Sa'id b. Ahmad, his grandson Hamid b. Sa'id had caused a sudden and unexpected visit to be made to Mombasa by a mysterious person who forced the Mazru'i Liwali to sign a paper saying that he held his position by authority of the 'Umani Imam, but he had then disappeared without further action. According to an as yet unpublished document, a photographic copy of which is in my possession,[5] this visitor had the rather suggestive nickname of "Hubub Al-Ghabash" which so far as I have been able to make out means "The Blast of the Dark", or possibly "A Blast from the Dark", which seems to describe very fittingly not so much the man as the nature of his visit.

It is just in such circumstances as these that small petty states rise and for a time flourish in the vacuum. As Israel and Judah, Syria and Phoenicia had flourished when Egypt and Assyria were weak; as the Kingdom of Palmyra had grown to temporary strength in the Third Century A.D. when Rome was weakened by unrest in high places; as even pirates had made for themselves evanescent kingdoms in the West Indies because of the power struggle between the expanding colonial powers; so Mombasa, the strongest and most important city and port on the East African Coast, was able to exist as an independent political entity for about 102 years (c. A.D. 1735–1837) under its own rulers.

These rulers were the Mazru'i Family, or clan, known by their Arabic plural as Mazari'a. They were Liwalis of Mombasa for a period of 139 years in all, apart from a few years at the start of that period when others held office. They came first as Liwalis for 'Uman in A.D. 1698 after the long siege which ended the Portuguese rule. They remained representatives

[4] Freeman-Grenville: The French at Kilwa Island, p. 12.
[5] Entitled "Kawkab al-Dhurriya" by Shaykh Fadil b. 'Umar al-Bawri.

of the Imam until Ahmad b. Saʿid became effective ruler, when Muhammad b. ʿUthman, Liwali of Mombasa, also assumed independent status. This happened some time after his installation as Liwali, but as we attempt to make clear in the textual notes, there is considerable uncertainty as to the actual time when his Liwaliship commenced. The only thing that we can say with any degree of probability is that his assumption of independent status was sometime after A.D. 1735; for Ahmad b. Saʿid had possessed effective power for some years before he was made Imam, while the Yaʿrubi Imamate had suffered schism before it finally came to an end.

Muhammad b. ʿUthman thus took advantage of the power vacuum and ruled as a sovereign on the Swahili Coast from Ngomeni to Tanga, together with the Island of Pemba. He and his successors held their own until A.D. 1837. The ʿUmani power was however consolidated and increased again, and gradually cut away the districts surrounding Mombasa from the Mazruʿi authority and control. The Island of Pemba was captured from them by the Amir Hamad, Commander of the Army and Fleet of Sayyid Saʿid b. Sultan in A.D. 1823, and the Sayyid also managed to win over to his side the anti-Mazruʿi faction in Mombasa itself. He failed however to conquer the rulers in open battle, and in the end seems to have got the better of them by base treachery.

But the Mazariʿa were not defeated only by Sayyid Saʿid's treachery. As long as they remained in the Fort,[6] they could defy him. There were however other factors against them. They could not latterly be sure of the loyalty and support of the Swahili population who were in theory their subjects. It further appears on careful study that they only ruled by a sort of *Concordat*, or covenant, between themselves and the Swahili Tribes,[7] a restriction which tied their hands and hampered the execution of their policies; and they really, in spite of Shaykh Al-Amin's liberal estimate of the depth of their mainland territory as being 60 miles, had no hinterland within the area of their rule. It is true they fled to the Nyika Country, either as refugees, or as rebels against their own relatives, on a number of occasions but they could not, from the depth of the Nyika Bush, effectively carry on the government, and two of the family came to grief among the Rabai, as the Author relates, without the Liwali Ahmad b. Muhammad

---

[6] **The Fort**. i.e. Fort Jesus, built originally by the Portuguese.

[7] This seems to be implied by the accounts of Owen and Guillain as well as by that of our Author, as I have tried to show in Note No. 1 to the text of the Chapter concerning the Second Liwali. In the same unpublished MS to which I referred above in this Introduction, it is asserted that the Mazruʿi Liwalis had to be chosen from the Mazruʿi Family, but that the person appointed *had to have the prior approval of the Nabahina of Pate*. Whether this is true or not — and the writer appears to be very biased — it adds a note of probability to the suggestion that rule by agreement was an acceptable method on the Swahili Coast.

being able to do anything about it in the way of penal reprisals. The Mazru'i State was essentially a coastal polity, and as such wide open to domination from across the sea.

Then it must be borne in mind that the rising dominance of 'Uman was not only 'Umani but also British. It was by their favour and support that Mombasa was left to 'Umani conquest; and not so many decades later Britain became the real ruler of the Town, and of those areas which had been its dependencies, and it eventually became Kenya Colony, now Republic.

The tide of international power and influence had ebbed in East Africa, but it returned in a flood which was an all-time high, obliterating the traces of smaller polities. It did however hold back long enough to allow the picture to take form of the interesting, and almost unique, City State and its Rulers, which forms the subject of this History.

The Author's Treatment of his Subject

This Book is a clear and orderly setting forth of the events of the period in which the Mazru'i Dynasty actually ruled, or claimed to rule, first as legitimate representatives of the 'Umani Imam, then as independent rulers of Mombasa. The Author has written it in good Arabic, which only here and there shows signs of a colloquialism, or dialect variation. He writes also with evident family pride; for he is himself a scion of the Mazru'i House. The Mazru'i Liwalis are for him very real and human people, who cannot be cursorily dismissed with a mention of dates of accession and death: still less with negative or derogatory phrases such as "a warlike tribe",[1] or "the turbulent Mazru'i Tribe",[2] nor its individual members in the manner of Captain Owen, when he refers to the Liwali Sulayman b. 'Ali Al-Mazru'i as "an old dotard who has outlived every passion but that of avarice".[3] They were for Shaykh Al-Amin real human beings, men and leaders of no small calibre; and they had reasons for their actions which he seeks to interpret, and in doing so, to clarify the policies which guided them.

This in itself sets the present work in very favourable contrast to the other Arabic histories of East Africa which I have perused, Kitab al-Zunuj and Kawkab al-Dhurriya (the latter so far unpublished), which are bald

---

[1] R. N. Lyne: Zanzibar, p. 30.
[2] Major Pearce: Zanzibar, p. 109.
[3] Owen: Voyages Vol. I, p. 369.

statements of events in none too clear a chronological order, and written in the most slovenly Arabic imaginable.

It seems fitting here to consider three other matters regarding this Book — **(a)** the **cultural nature** of it, **(b)** the **question of bias on the part of the Author** in his presentation of people and events, and **(c) a general evaluation of it** in the literature of East Africa as a whole.

(a) To What Culture does this Work Belong?

The answer to this is that it is primarily a product of Arabic culture. The Author writes good Arabic; his way of looking at folk and at events is Arab. Kubu Mwakikunga, the Chief of the WaDigo, is not described as an African Chief, but as "that Zanji". The battles fought in the War between the Mazari'a and Sayyid Sa'id are, as presented by Shaykh Al-Amin, in the tradition of the Maghazi of Al-Waqidi. The Arab population of the Swahili Coast is usually referred to as a distinct element over against "the others". One gets the impression that the Mazru'i family, whatever they may have become racially in the Author's day, however much they had, by long residence and marital alliance, come to an identity of outlook and interest with those more definitely Swahili, were yet in the days of their glory much more purely Arab, both in language, blood and family pride, so that they could in no sense be called "Afro-Arab" in the sense of the old local Sultans of the Portuguese and pre-Portuguese periods. Perhaps the "Arabness" of the Book, always implicit as a background to the Author's thinking, and more evident in the reading of the original Arabic than in a translation, is nowhere more evident than in the two *Qasidas*, or Odes, from the pen of Shaykh Muhyi al-Din, a contemporary of Salim b. Ahmad, and included by the Author in his account of the latter's reign, and which incidentally must cause revision of Lyndon Harries's remark that there is only one extant poem in Arabic about any event on the Swahili Coast.[4]

(b) Is the Author guilty of unjustifiable bias?

It is part of the merit of this work that the Author seeks to commence from a neutral standpoint in ascertaining and evaluating the actions and policies of the 'Uthmani Mazari'a. His sources, or at least the sources he refers to explicitly, are mainly European, and "Colonialist", so that they express a pro-'Umani, and rather paternalistic and condescending, view of the local leaders which the Author seems definitely out to qualify. Major

---

[4] Lyndon Harries: Swahili Poetry, p. 188.

Pearce, the East African Red Book, Captain Owen and Lieutenant Boteler are all British. He knows apparently nothing of Portuguese sources, nor of Guillain, and he only refers once to an Arabic document in an 'Umani Newspaper, entitled "*Al-Najah*". This is why his more "inside" view of events provides a welcome, and entirely legitimate, counterpoise. There are signs that he misunderstands at times what he disagrees with, as in his criticism of Major Pearce's remarks on Mazru'i Independence, which he calls confused and contradictory, but which are clear to one who obviously takes for granted that the Major has in mind the distinction between *de facto* and *de jure*. We can scarcely blame Shaykh Al-Amin for being unaware of that distinction. On the other hand, his readiness to quote sources at all puts him in a superior position to the more traditional chronicles.

Perhaps we can judge of his impartiality best in relation to one of the most controversial events he deals with, the Battle of Shela and what caused it. This is an event in which accounts conflict, and persons and parties seem to be confused. Is he primarily concerned to arrive at the truth, or simply to put the Mazari'a in a favourable light? His account will be found in Chapter II, Section 6.

Mombasa, Malindi, Lamu, Pate, Siyu and the Banadir all had histories as independent City-states, histories of which they were proud — and resented being regarded as inferior, or subservient to any of their neighbours. As a result of this they exhibited fierce local pride and an independent spirit, and a desire to gain from among their neighbours allies strong enough to co-operate with them, but not to dominate them. Yet the stronger tried to dominate and use the weaker, to maintain their own independence and extend their power and influence, while there was a tendency on the part of the weaker to call in the aid of stronger powers from outside the area — Portugal, 'Uman, or later Great Britain — to fend off the inroads of their neighbours, and by granting them **nominal** sovereignty, to preserve a *de facto* political identity of their own.

The interplay of these motives produced within the states parties who became identified by their policies towards the outside world; and the frequent, almost kaleidoscopic, variations in the alignment of these parties, as they jockeyed for position, acting with or against each other as the political situation changed and developed, gave rise to a confusion in the minds of those who recorded the events, so that it is now exceedingly difficult to unravel the tangle. In Pate the Nabahina were opposed by a party representing a more primitive element in the society which tended to call in Portugal; in Siyu there were the Famao and Somali parties; in Lamu the Zayni and Sa'udi parties; and in Mombasa itself the Thalatha

Taifa, or "Three Tribes", and the Tisa Taifa, or "Nine Tribes", one favouring, and the other hostile to, the Mazari'a.

Shaykh Al-Amin's account of the Battle of Shela shows it as essentially a war by Mombasa against Lamu, and the possible bias lies in the fact that it seems to put the Mazru'i Liwalis in a better light than they deserve, by implying that their "subordinate" allies, the Pate folk, lured them into something that they would not have entered into on their own initiative, corrupted the Amir (afterwards Liwali) 'Abdullah b. Ahmad and then let him down.

There are three pieces of information which may help to shed light on the subject.

Taylor records in his "African Aphorisms"[5] the Proverb: "Mwenda Pate k'auya: liuyacho ni kiriro — He who goes to Pate does not return: all that returns is a cry." He says it originated "when the Mazru'i Liwali of Mombasa, 'Abdullah b. Hamed, insisted on taking his Nyika allies with him to fight the Pate people. . . ." In other words the battle was, according to the tradition he had heard, against Pate not Lamu.

The History of Pate as set out in Freeman-Grenville's "East African Coast"[6] gives a similar account of a great interplay of parties in Pate and Lamu, and indicates in particular that there were pro- and anti-Mazru'i parties in Pate, and that the Lamu people were divided in their views as to the policies that should be adopted in relation to the two more powerful states.

Then Sir Arthur Hardinge has a memorandum[7] in which he goes in some detail into the history of Pate and Siyu and shows that Siyu is reputed to have had a dual system of government, carried on by a Famao and a Somali group of Shaykhs, and that they were opposed to one another over their attitude to Pate. He admits that he has only culled this from oral traditions, but there is no reason to doubt his general accuracy.

These pieces of information may not be evidence in its most proper form, but they seem to be indications of a fairly general situation and are enough to form the basis of a tentative assessment of what really happened.

There were in Pate two factions, one supporting the Nabahina and a second hostile to them. The Mazru'i Government, owing to similarity of origin (both came from 'Uman), and a community of interests, made an alliance with the Nabahina. These two together tried to dominate Lamu to buttress their own independence; but the anti-Nabhani party

[5] Taylor: African Aphorisms, No. 377, pp. 87–8.
[6] Freeman-Grenville: The East African Coast, pp. 241–296, and esp. pp. 272–277.
[7] Parliamentary Papers, Vol. LX (1898) Africa No. 7 (1897) (c8683) p. 14, Report on the Condition and Progress of the East African Protectorate from its Establishment to 20th July 1897, and a paragraph therein relating to Pate (Pattah) and Siyu.

(represented at an earlier period by Mwinyi Hindi b. Kipai) appears to have worked against the Mazru'i/Nabhani plan, and consulted with the Sa'udi party in Lamu to defeat it. When Taylor therefore says that 'Abdullah b. Ahmad went to fight Pate, he was correct in that one party in Pate was opposed to him, and the source from which he drew his information, since it favoured the policy of that party, attributed their views to the people of Pate as a whole. On the other hand, Shaykh Al-Amin, who is more concerned with the Nabhani/Mazru'i Treaty, regards the Nabhani party as representing Pate in general, and therefore speaks of Pate as an ally of the Mazari'a.

If it is thought that this is unjustifiable bias, then it must be said in his favour, that he is not only looking at the problem as any Mazru'i Liwali might view it, but is quite aware of the essential weakness in the situation — the unwisdom of the Amir 'Abdullah, and the resulting swing of the Zayni party to join the Sa'udi party against their former allies, the Mazari'a, which resulted in defeat for the latter; and he criticises the Amir 'Abdullah for his gratuitous folly.

On the whole, it may be said that Shaykh Al-Amin treats the relevant evidence with due respect, making the most of what favours his ancestors in so far as he legitimately can. The only bias I can see which might be terms unjustifiable, is that he keeps silent about certain incidents or details which belittle the Liwalis, or show their position to be more unsure than he would like to believe. These omissions do not however make the picture he draws of the events very inaccurate.

(c) The General Position of this Work in the History of East African Literature as a whole.[8]

This History may be quite distinctive, or even unique of its kind. It was written in the 1940s, when Swahili culture was coming to terms with the European culture which had been dominant during the Colonial Period. At the same time, Arabian culture was beginning to recede, and "Ara-

---

[8] My contention in this section finds recent support in an article issued in April 1993 in which reference is made to Shaykh Al-Amin b. 'Ali Al-Mazru'i as an Islamic leader who saw the necessity for East African Islam to develop in a certain independence from its Arabian Peninsula roots through the use of Swahili rather than Arabic as the medium for the teaching and propagation of Islam, [Justo Lacunza-Balda: Swahili Islam — Continuity and Revival: Encounter (Documents for Muslim-Christian Understanding) Nos. 193–194, published by Pontificio Istituto di Studi Arabi e d'Islamistica].

bian"[9] Islam was becoming less dominant. I do not mean that the Swahili Community was beginning to discard Islam, but that their thinking was becoming less Arabian than formerly, while even their language, Kiswahili, was becoming more independent of Arabic.

Meanwhile modern education in Africa was making known new scientific methods, involving more careful and critical evaluation of evidence; and these methods were beginning to be used, in place of the old, in writing. The old educational and literary methods were being kept to by the people whom we may call Traditionalists, — generally speaking, the older generation, while the younger, who had received what is usually known as a Western Education, inclined to the new.

Shaykh Al-Amin was evidently more progressive than his own generation, for Qadi Muhammad b. Qasim informs us that he was the first to write religious books in Swahili. He also published a newspaper and pressed for the spread of religion in such a manner as to provoke strong criticism and hostility, presumably on the ground that he was guilty of innovation (Arabic: *Bid'a*), a heinous sin in the eyes of the more traditionalist Muslims.

This History partakes of both worlds. In using Arabic, the Author has bowed to the Traditionalist Sentiment. Yet, being well-read in European works on East Africa, which often disagreed with his own family's traditions, as well as those of his own community, in regard to Mombasa, he tried to make his treatment critical in the modern sense. This latter quality is what makes the Book such a remarkable contrast to effusions like the History of Pate and Kitab al-Zunuj, which are disorderly in their chronology, mingle historical event indiscriminately with what appears to be legend, gossip, exaggeration, and false, or very questionable, etymological and linguistic statements; while the latter work above-mentioned is based on an Arabia-centred cosmology and ethnology which has long been outmoded.

It is therefore no wonder that Shaykh Al-Amin hesitated about publishing a work which would have offended the Traditionalists, while the Progressives would most probably have been unable to read it in the original Arabic. The intention to write a version of the History in Kiswahili, mentioned in more than one place in the text,[10] but unfortunately prevented by his demise, shows that he recognised the latter disadvantage.

At the present time, the English language — which even Arabs now

[9] I say "Arabian" deliberately as distinct from "Arabic". Arabic is the language of Islam everywhere, but not all Islam is "Arabian". The Islam of East Africa, and the culture which has resulted from it, has been over the years differentiated more and more from that of Arabia, although in the past it was almost identical with it.
[10] See Chapter II, Section 6, at Note No. 17.

recognise as the "key to the East and the West" — and Western methods, have tended, in a greater or less degree, to be adopted in the production of such books as Shaykh Al-Amin's Mazru'i History throughout the countries of East Africa. Arabic is a language of decreasing significance in the area. The Book therefore would seem to be unique; for it emanates from a point in history at which three cultures were meeting, and it took something from all of them before they began to draw apart again. Its subject must undoubtedly be called Swahili, its language is Arabic, and the methods employed by its Author in the treatment of his subject are a real attempt to be much more critical in the Western and European sense. It may be that no similar book will spring from East African soil in the future.

The Alignment of Parties Among the Swahili Population of Mombasa

It is necessary here to explain a matter which, if not understood at the beginning, will cause much confusion to the reader of this History.

There were, and in fact are to this day, twelve tribal groups among the Swahili population of Mombasa. These "Tribes" fell into two groups known respectively as The "Three Tribes", or *"Thelatha Taifa"*, and The "Nine Tribes", or *"Tisa Taifa"*. The tribes of which these groups were formed are as follows:

(a) The "Three Tribes"

	They are also called:
Mji Kilindini	WaKilindini
Mji Tangana	WaTangana
Mji Changamwe	WaChangamwe

(b) The "Nine Tribes"

Mji Mvita consisting of:	WaMvita
Kabila Mambasi	WaMambasa
Kabila Malindi	WaMalindi
Mji Jomvu	WaJomvu
Mji Mtwapa	WaMtwapa
Mji Kilifi	WaKilifi
Mji Pate	WaPate

Mji Paza	WaPaza
Mji Shaka	WaShaka
Mji Gunya	WaGunya
Mji Katwa	WaKatwa

These two groups are also known as "Miji Tatu" and "Miji Tisa". Group **(b)** gathered round the first two, Mji Mvita and Mji Jomvu, who seem to have been the original, probably Shirazi, inhabitants of Mombasa. Group **(a)** were late-comers to the Island, and there existed a certain antipathy between them and Group **(b)** who seem to have regarded them as interlopers.

It is essential to an understanding of the relationships of the Mazru'i Dynasty with the people of Mombasa to keep in mind that the Liwalis, from very early on, favoured the "Three Tribes", possibly because they themselves were incomers and had a fellow-feeling for them. The people of Group **(b)** were correspondingly disaffected to the Mazari'a, especially when they assumed the status of independent sovereigns.

There is however one exception to this alignment. The section of Mji Mvita known as Kabila Malindi were allies to the Mazari'a. Nasir b. 'Abdullah, the first Mazru'i Liwali, was probably influenced by their connection with the old Kings of Malindi in his choice of a wife from them. The descendants of these kings appear to have had considerable power in guiding the affairs of Mombasa. If Owen's report is to be believed, nothing political could be decided without the Shaykh's presence at the Council Table. The Shaykh was the lineal descendant of the old King of Malindi. The alliance by marriage to this section of the tribe had the effect of detaching the WaMalindi from group **(b)** with which they were naturally aligned, and joining them, as far as concerned their relations with the Mazari'a, with the tribes of Group **(a)**. This is why the WaMalindi are so often mentioned in connection with the WaKilindini, the WaTangana and the WaChangamwe as acting to help the Mazru'i cause.*

---

* A fuller and more detailed account of the Tribes of Mombasa will be found in an article by F. J. Berg, entitled "The Swahili Community of Mombasa 1500–1900", Journal of African History, Vol. No. 1 (1968) p. 35, and also in a paper issued in cyclostyle by the same Author for discussion in University College, Nairobi on 13th October 1966.

CHAPTER I

The Genealogy of the Mazari'a — the Lineages of those who became residents on the Swahili Coast — their Homes in 'Uman — the Date of their Emigration to the Swahili coast — the Extent of their Dominion there — the Number of Inhabitants in their dominion — the Establishment of their Independence — Denial of the Accusation that they were hostile to the British.

The Genealogy and Lineages of the Mazari'a

Before starting on the main subject of this Book, I have thought right to offer readers a glance at the Mazru'i Genealogy, and a brief account of the lineages of those who came to live in the Swahili Country, and the names of some of the famous men in the branches of every lineage from the time that they emigrated to the Swahili Country up to the present day.[1]

The Mazari'a who came to live in East Africa branch out — to put it simply[2] — from 14 lineages, which carry their genealogy back to Zayd b. Kahlan b. 'Adi b. 'Abd Shams b. Wa'il,[3] and go right back to Saba' b. Yashjub b. Ya'rub b. Qahtan,[4] ancestor of the Qahtanian Tribes well-known in history.[5] The 14 lineages above-mentioned are:

---

[1] See the Genealogical Table in Appendix No. 1. All these names have been traced, and assigned to their places in the tables by the efforts of Mr. F. J. Berg, to whom my thanks are due.

[2] **To put it simply** — *'Ala sabili 'l-basat*. This may mean "to put it *in extenso*", i.e. fully.

[3] *Zayd b. Kahlan b. 'Adi b. 'Abd Shams b. Wa'il*. The Arab Tribes traced their ancestry into the Prophet Muhammad's ancestral line if they possibly could.

[4] *Saba' b. Yashjub b. b. Ya'rub b. Qahtan*. These are all proper South Arabian names, and the last, Qahtan, is the supposed Ancestor of all the Southern or Yemeni Tribes, (The A'rab, as opposed to the Musta'rabun, or Northern Tribes). He is thought to be equivalent to Joktan of Genesis chapter 10, vs. 25.

[5] We would rather say "legend" nowadays, for we judge on the basis of modern scientific criticism: but to the Arabs their ancient descent is a matter of great importance.

(1) *Nasir*[6] *b. 'Abdullah b. Muhammad b. 'Abdullah b. Kahlan, the first of the Eleven Liwalis*[7] *of the Mazari'a*

The well-known among his earlier[8] descendants were:

a His Son Mas'ud b. Nasir b. 'Abdullah, the fourth Liwali who held office A. H. 1168–1193.[9]

b His Grandson, Ahmad b. Mas'ud b. Nasir, who was Qadi of Mombasa in the fourth decade of the 13th Century A. H.[10]

and among his later descendants:

a 'Aziz b. 'Abdullah b. Ahmad of Mnarani in Takaungu, famous for his generosity and his frequent entertaining of guests.

b Nasir b. Ahmad b. Muhammad, Qadi of Malindi at present (year A.D. 1945) under the British Government.

(2) *'Uthman b. 'Abdullah b. Muhammad b. 'Abdullah b. Kahlan, the father of the second and third Liwalis, and the ancestor of the Liwalis who succeeded them*

Those famous among his earlier descendants were:

a All the Liwalis from Muhammad b. 'Uthman to Rashid b. Salim.[11]

Each of their names will meet you in the following pages of this book.

and of his later descendants:

a Mbaruk b. Rashid b. Salim, who fought the famous battles with the Sultans of Zanzibar.

b Muhammad b. Sa'ud b. Mbaruk, who was Liwali of Malindi and Takaungu under the British Government.

c Sulayman b. Muhammad, formerly Qadi of Gazi.

---

[6] *Nasir*. This name is locally pronounced Nasur, as are many other names of this vocalic form.

[7] *Al-wali*. On the advice of Shaykh Muhammad Qasim, writer of the Account of the Author in the introduction, and a Chief Qadi of Kenya, I have consistently rendered this Arabic word by its Swahili form "Liwali", rather than by the usual English equivalent "Governor".

[8] *Muta'addami . . . Muta'akhkhari* – **Earlier . . . Later**. Shaykh Al-Amin does not seem to imply anything definite in his distinction between "Earlier" and "Later". It does however seem that he had in mind the end of the Liwaliship of Rashid b. Salim as a kind of period, all before that date being "Earlier" and all after it being "Later".

[9] **A.H. 1168–1193** = A.D. 1754–1779.

[10] i.e. A.D. 1921 and after.

[11] *Rashid b. Salim and Mbaruk b. Rashid*. Shaykh Al-Amin regards Rashid b. Salim as being the last Liwali, but Mbaruk claimed to be the rightful Liwali up to the end of the 19th Century A.D.

(3) *Zahir b. 'Abdullah b. Muhammad b. 'Abdullah b. Kahlan*

Some of the famous of his earlier descendants are:

a Rashid b. Salim b. 'Abdullah, founder of the town of Takaungu and owner of it.

b His two sons Khamis and Sa'id.

c His two grandsons, Rashid b. Khamis and Salim b. Khamis, leaders of the people in Takaungu and holders of office there.

and of his later descendants:

a Rashid b. Salim b. Khamis, famous for his wealth of knowledge in history and genealogies, and

b His Brother Muhammad b. Salim b. Khamis. Each of them was Liwali of Takaungu under the British Government.

c The Historian and Genealogist Khalfan b. 'Abdullah, who held office as Qadi of Takaungu formerly, and

d Khalfan b. Rashid b. 'Abdullah, Mudir[12] of Tiwi formerly under the British Government, and

e His Brother, 'Abdullah b. Rashid, formerly Mudir of Mambrui, and

f Salim b. Rashid b. Muhammad, present Mudir of Takaungu, and

g Sa'ud b. Khalfan, at present Mudir of Gazi, and

h Nabhan b. Rashid, one of the outstanding men of Takaungu.

["All this in the 20th Century" — A Written note by Shaykh Ma'mun]

(4) *Khamis b. 'Amir b. Muhammad b. 'Abdullah b. Kahlan*

One of his famous descendants is Muhammad b. Khalfan b. Kahlan, one of the well-known wealthy men of Takaungu.

(5) *Khamis b. Bashir b. Muhammad b. 'Abdullah b. Kahlan*

Muhammad b. 'Abdullah b. Nasir, the well-known Genealogist, became famous among his descendants.

(6) *Talib b. 'Ali b. Muhammad b. 'Abdullah b. Kahlan*

'Abdullah b. Khalfan was one of his descendants.

(7) *'Abdullah b. Khamis b. 'Ali b. 'Abdullah b. 'Ali*

Among his many descendants were a group in Pemba [to 'Umanis this is

---

[12] **Mudir**. The office of Mudir was an administrative office in rank below that of Liwali.

the Green Island]. Famous among them were the house of Nafi' b. Mazru'
b. 'Abdullah, well-known in Mombasa.

Those notable from this house were:

a The learned scholar 'Abdullah b. Nafi'[13] who was one of the advisers
in the Mazru'i Government in the time of the Liwali Salim b. Ahmad
and his successor. He lived near Mecca for nine years at the end of his
life, and kept company with its most eminent scholars (that was in the
19th Century A.D.) at that period, such as Shaykh 'Uthman Hasan Al-
Dimyati and Shaykh Ahmad b. Muhammad Al-Dimyati and others.

and other well-known members of this house are:

b The learned Ahmad b. 'Abdullah b. Nafi', author of *Al-Tuhfat al-
Murdiya bimuhtasar al-Kalimat al-Wafiya* about Syntax, and a commentary on *Al-Muqaddamat al-Hadramiya* about Jurisprudence, and both
are in Manuscript form.[14]

c Also the Scholar 'Ali b. 'Abdullah b. Nafi'. Among his works composed and in Manuscript form are *Al-Duru' al-Sabigha fi Mas'alat
Ru'yat al-Bari' Subhanuhu wata'ala* and *Al-Subul al-Wadihat*, a commentary on *Dala'il al-Khayrat*, and a synopsis of *Tarajim Asma' Ahl
Badr*, and a short commentary on the good qualities of Al-Tirmidhi,
and other booklets and synopses besides. He was, may God have mercy
on him, Qadi of Mombasa in the time of Sayyid Majid b. Sa'id.

d Also the Scholar Rashid b. 'Ali Nafi', also Qadi of Mombasa at the
end of the reign of Majid b. Sa'id, and after it.

e Also Al–Amir b. 'Ali, and his brother the author of this book.

(8) *'Ali b. Rashid b. Mas'ud*

Among his well-known descendants are:

a Muhammad b. 'Aziz b. Sa'id

b The Scholar Sulayman b. 'Ali, Chief Qadi of Kenya Colony under
the British Government formerly (A.D. 1910–31), and

---

[13] **'Abdullah b. Nafi'.** Mr. F. J. Berg has concluded, as a result of his enquiries, that this man
removed to Mecca because he saw that times had changed, that the days of the Mazru'i
State were numbered, and their position as independent rulers was untenable: and therefore
he removed to avoid getting mixed up in the disturbances which he saw were inevitably
approaching. He was the first of the Mazari'a to adopt the Shafi'i School of Juridical practice.
See the account of the Author by Shaykh Muhammad b. Qasim above.

[14] ***Makhtut . . . Makhtuta.*** This word means that the works are in Manuscript form, neither
printed nor published. It should not be thought however that this is derogatory to the works
concerned. On the contrary, it may indicate that the works are highly regarded, and not for
the use of anyone except scholarly experts. It is to be hoped however that these works may
be made available to a wider public in the future.

c His son, Ma'mun b. Sulayman, present Qadi of Mombasa (A.D. 1932–1937), and

d Sulayman b. 'Ali b. Sa'id in the Island of Pemba.

(9) *Mbaruk b. Ahmad b. Mbaruk b. Gharib (or Ghurayb?)*

Those famous among his earlier descendants were:

a The Scholar 'Abdullah b. 'Ali b. Mbaruk, colleague of the learned 'Ali b. 'Abdullah b. Nafi' in seeking and acquiring knowledge, and

b Jum'a b. Khamis b. Mbaruk, a wealthy man of Takaungu.

and of the later:

a The Scholar Sulayman b. 'Ali b. Khamis, a man of Takaungu and Qadi of it formerly under the British Government, and

b Muhammad b. Jum'a b. Khamis, the Mudir of Roka[15] and Qadi of Malindi formerly, and

c Muhammad b. 'Ali b. Khamis, the former Liwali of Mombasa, and

d Dahlan b. Muhammad b. Jum'a, the present Liwali of Vanga, and

e Muhammad b. Sulayman b. 'Ali, one of the prominent men of Takaungu.

(10) *Muhanna b. Ahmad b. Mbaruk b. Gharib (or Ghurayb?)*

His famous descendants were a group in Pemba among whom were:

a The Writer 'Ali b. Rashid, famous for his fine handwriting and his fine style of writing,[16] and

b Khatir b. Ahmad and Ahmad b. Muhanna and 'Ali b. Sayf and others.

(11) *'Ali b. Ahmad b. Mbaruk b. Gharib (or Ghurayb?)*

His famous descendants were:

a 'Ali b. Muhammad, Captain of the "Kilwa", one of the Zanzibar Government Steamers, and

b Mbaruk b. Muhammad, controller of the Dhow Anchorage at Zanzibar.

---

[15] **Roka**. This is a small town, or rather village, a few miles inland from Takaungu, in the Kenya Coast Province, North of Mombasa.

[16] **His fine style of writing**. This phrase refers to 'Ali b. Rashid's composition and actual written language. The former phrase, i.e. "his fine handwriting", refers to his script. The power of writing a beautiful Arabic hand is one of the virtues of Islamic learning. Certainly, Arabic Script is as high an art as any culture has produced.

(12) *Sa'id b. 'Abdullah b. Muhammad b. Ahmad*, Liwali of Pemba under
his family the Mazari'a.

His famous descendants are: Salim and Muhanna, sons of Ahmad b. Jum'a
b. Salih, prominent men of Pemba.

(13) *Muhammad b. 'Abdullah b. Muhammad b. Ahmad*

Among his descendants are the house of Salim b. Qasim in Mombasa, and
the notable man of this family is: Ahmad b. Salim b. Qasim.

(14) *'Ali b. 'Abdullah b. Muhammad b. Ahmad*

Among his descendants are: Ahmad b. Sulayman in Pemba.

From these fourteen lineages and their branches and descendants are
composed the Mazru'i Family which is spread now through the East African districts of Mombasa, Zanzibar, Pemba, Takaungu, Gazi, Dar Salaam,[17]
Malindi and elsewhere.

Those of these lineages who themselves came as exiles to the Swahili
Coast are:
  a Nasir b. 'Abdullah
  b Mbaruk b. Ahmad and
  c His brother Muhanna b. Ahmad[18]
but only the children and descendants of the rest emigrated to the Swahili
Coast.

The Home of the Mazari'a[19] in 'Uman

The Mazari'a like other Arab Tribes are found singly and in groups in
various districts and villages of 'Uman, but most of them are in Rustaq
and its surrounding villages such as Al-Ghashab and Wabil and Mazahit.
They have in Al– 'Alaya their own town surrounded with walls which have
towers on their sides fortified with artillery and rifles (*Banadiq*)[20] by which

---

[17] **Dar Salam**. This is the form of this name in the Arabic text. Shaykh Al-Amin has written
the name as the people of East Africa pronounce it, and indicates his Swahili provenance.
An Arab from Arabia would write *Daru 'l-Salam*.
[18] That is, the Ancestors of the First, Ninth and Tenth lineages which the author records here.
[19] In connection with this section see Map No. 1 in Appendix No. 2.
[20] **Wal-banadiq**. Literally this words means "rifles" or "muskets". These are rather strange
weapons to fix to a town wall: but perhaps Shaykh Al-Amin implies something like a fixed
battery of light artillery, or perhaps machine-guns.

they are protected in case of need, and ward off the attacks and raids of the enemy, as is the custom with most of the Arab Tribes.

The Mazari'a are ruled in 'Uman at present by their Leader Shaykh Sa'id b. 'Abdullah b. Khamis Al-Mazru'i, may God protect his life.

The tradition handed down from former generations of the Mazari'a of the Swahili Coast is that the majority of those who made their home in East Africa came from that country, and a few of them came from Manah and Suma'il. I have seen in the hand-writing of my father, may God have mercy on him, a form of Attorney (*Wakala*) from Shaykhs Salim b. Khamis and Mas'ud b. Muhammad and 'Aziz b. 'Abdullah, that they made Muslim b. Sulayman b. Muslim Al-Shaqasi their agent to take possession of their property which their ancestors had left in the above-mentioned districts and in Al-Washil; so it appears from this that some of them came from Al-Washil. That is probable because Al-Washil belongs to the Mashaqisa, and there is a relationship by blood and nearness of kin, and a firm connection, between them and the Mazari'a, which has been established by intermarriage over a long period of time.

Their Emigration to the Swahili Coast

The emigration of the Mazari'a to East Africa began after its conquest by the Imam Sayf b. Sultan about the year A.H. 1110, that is, nearly two and a half centuries ago. The first to set foot on Swahili soil were the Liwali Nasir b. 'Abdullah, and the Amir Mbaruk b. Gharib and his children. Then there came at the end of the Ya'rubi rule Muhammad b. 'Uthman, and his brothers 'Ali and Qadib, and their paternal cousins. Then there followed in succession emigrations of the other families until just before Sa'id b. Sultan gained the mastery of Mombasa. Then it stopped, because the Government of 'Uman forbade them to travel there for fear that their people would grow too many on the Swahili Coast. So after that the eyes of their emigrants turned to Zanzibar and Pemba, because their suitability for the 'Umani Arabs was greater than other places on the Swahili Coast, and because of the increasing abundance of the means of sustenance (i.e. ways of getting gain) which were fitting for them there.[21]

But the statement of Major Pearce in his Book "Zanzibar", that the Mazari'a emigrated to East Africa long before the Portuguese occupation

---

[21] ***That were fitting for them***. It is uncertain whether the Author is referring here to what is suitable to their rank, abilities and gifts, or simply to their way of life. He may either be referring to their rank, or it may be simply a way of saying that they could best improve their standard of living there.

is not correct at all, and Sa'id Ruete took it up by his guidance and asserted it in his Book "Sa'id b. Sultan"; but neither of them brought any evidence for what they said, nor traced it back to any of the reliable historians, as if they — and God knows best — said it on their own responsibility as a shot in the dark.[22] But what we have stated is what the great majority of the Mombasa chroniclers and others have transmitted in successive generations from their ancestors. It is also preserved by the Mazari'a themselves, and they are undoubtedly more knowledgeable about the history of their forebears than others, and more careful to preserve the facts concerning those related to them.

The Dominion of the Mazari'a[23]

The Mazari'a ruled all the country in East Africa which lies between Ra's Ngomeni in the North and the River Pangani in the South. There thus came under their rule most of the Swahili Country inhabited by the Arabs and Swahilis, and they stretched out their hands upon the Diwanate of Vumba (the Sultanate of Vumba, whose Sultan was Called *Diwan*),[24] whose location was in the Island of Wasin, and the Sultanate of Buri[25] which was ruled by the original Amirs of Tanga. Their influence[26] reached into the interior of the country to the West from one extremity to the other. All the Nyika Tribes were subject[27] to them, WaGalla, WaGiryama, WaKauma, WaJibana, WaChonyi, WaRibe, WaRabai, WaDuruma, WaDigo, WaBondei, WaSambaa, and some of the Tribe of the WaZigua living North of

---

[22] Major F. Pearce: *Zanzibar, Island Metropolis of East Africa*, pp. 109 and 117 note. I can find no reference in Ruete's Book *Sa'id b. Sultan* to an early emigration of the Mazru'i Tribe to East Africa before the Portuguese. Here I think we must accept the Author's word against the general statement of Pearce. Undoubtedly the Mazari'a would have preserved a memory, either in Mombasa or in 'Uman, of earlier emigrations.

[23] Compare the letter of Sir John Kirk, Appendix No. 4. Shaykh Al-Amin may be painting a very favourable picture of the Mazru'i power. Others tend to show their rule as very dependant on the good will of the Twelve Tribes of Mombasa, nor is it clear how far they could persuade the surrounding populations into Army service on every occasion.

[24] This word is of Persian origin, and may therefore have been brought in by the Shirazi immigrants who came to East Africa before the time of the Portuguese.

[25] *Buri*. Or Bauri. In unvowelled Arabic both these words look alike.

[26] **Their influence** — *Nufudhuhum*. This word has been carefully selected by the Author in contrast to *Hukm* or *Mulk*. It does not imply direct rule. As the Sultan of Zanzibar "piped", and the Tribes by the Lake "danced to his tune", so the Mazari'a "piped" and the people of Pate "danced to their tune", but were not directly ruled by them.

[27] **Were subject to them** — *Khada' lahum*. This is rather strong, and I should say, inaccurate. The word implies a subordination which is too strong for the tribes to break away from. This history shows that they often had to be brought round by skilful diplomacy.

the Pangani River.[28] And they ruled in the Island of Pemba,[29] which became their only source for import of agricultural products, grain, fruit, honey and sugar etc. And they conquered[30] Zanzibar Island, but got no firm footing there owing to the consequences of that ill-omened quarrel which resulted in the assassination of the Liwali 'Ali b. 'Uthman and the murder of his nephew Khalaf b. Qadib, as you shall read in detail when we come to the events which took place in the liwaliship of 'Ali b. 'Uthman.

The Mazari'a almost became rulers[31] of the Island of Lamu, not by the power of the sword, but by the inhabitants giving them the rule of their own free will — if it had not been for the ineptitude of the Amir 'Abdullah b. Ahmad, and the crafty intention which he designed, and which became apparent to the people of Lamu, in his efforts to please his friends the Nabhani Dynasty, whom the people of Lamu regarded as among their bitterest enemies. A detailed account of this event will come at the right place in the Book.

As for the Kingdom of Pate, although it had not come within their dominion in name, it was yet under their domination[32] and their word was listened to there, and their orders obeyed. There was a garrison of the Mazru'i Army on it, commanded by one of the Amirs of the Liwali's family, whose word was not contradicted, nor his opinion disobeyed in Pate, until the Nabahina (Plural of *Nabhani*) conceived a fear in their minds that the Mazari'a would gain complete rule in their country. This was one of the reasons for their asking help from Sayyid Sa'id b. Sultan, to save them from the tyranny of the Mazari'a in their country.

The Mazari'a were determined to extend their dominion, and sent from Tanga an army to conquer the Chagga country, and put in command of this army Qasim b. Gharib Al-Riyami, Liwali of Tanga at that period. This army went out perfectly equipped, and the Liwali Salim b. Ahmad supplied it with soldiers from Mombasa. When they reached a place called Rumbu

---

[28] **WaGalla ... Pangani River**. These names illustrate the difficulty of fitting Bantu names and words into Arabic script. The following points here become clear: (i) Arabic has not enough vowel signs. (ii) Arabic is not adapted for writing two vowels together without a consonant between them. (iii) The Arabs pronounce the words in a different way from the Swahilis. (iv) Certain Bantu consonants can be represented by three, or even four, different Arabic consonants.

[29] See Map No. 5.

[30] **Conquered – *Fatahu***. Again hardly accurate. The Arabic implies "Conquered". The Mazari'a did not conquer Zanzibar, but simply won a battle from which they reaped no final victory. See map No. 6.

[31] **The Mazari'a almost became rulers — *Kada 'l-Mazari'a an yatamalaku***. This is a mistake in Syntax. *Kada* usually takes an imperfect verb with no *an*.

[32] **Under their domination — *tahta saytartihim***. This word is rather strong. The Island of Pate could hardly be reckoned to be "dominated" by Mombasa. Mombasa was at the most an ally of one of the warring factions.

the two armies met, and fought a violent battle. The Mazru'i Army was broken, and was unable to conquer that country.

The area of this dominion is difficult to estimate exactly. But if we look at the tribes which were under the influence of the Mazari'a and the lands they occupied West of the Swahili Coast, and estimate that they reached a distance of only 60 miles[33] from the sea-shore to their utmost boundaries landwards, it is possible for us to say that its area was nearly 12,380 square miles in extent, including the parts of Pemba that were (included) in it.

It is as difficult to estimate the number of inhabitants in it accurately, as it is to estimate the area. Nevertheless, we do not lack means whereby we can deduce the possible number of the inhabitants of this dominion. For Captain Vidal has told us in his "Travels" printed in London in A.D. 1833, that when he arrived in Mombasa he found that the Mazari'a had mustered an army of 25,000[34] to make war against the army of Sa'id b. Sultan. Thus the Kingdom which can gather such an army as this cannot have less than about 1,000,000 inhabitants, if we consider 2.5% of the inhabitants as the maximum number it is possible to enrol in a kingdom which has no compulsory service.

The Independence of the Mazari'a

Here I wish to lift the veil from this matter in answer to the statement of some European writers, that the Mazari'a were rebels who had revolted against their kings. Major Pearce is one of those who said this, for in his Book "Zanzibar" he said what may be translated thus: "In the course of time the Mazari'a cast off their obedience to 'Uman and claimed independence in Mombasa: but the rulers and Imams of 'Uman who succeeded did not recognise that they had this right, and considered them obstinate rebels." But he said in another part of his Book above-mentioned: "The Mazari'a ruled in Mombasa for the period of 139 years sometimes as

---

[33] **60 Miles.** This is probably much too deep into the hinterland: for it would take the area far beyond the boundary of the Nyika tribes into what is now known as Ukambani — the Kamba country.

[34] **An Army of 25,000.** Shaykh Al-Amin really means Captain Owen. See W. F. Owen: Voyages, Vol. I, p. 367. Captain Vidal visited Mombasa in November A.D. 1823. Owen followed on 7th September A.D. 1824. The latter put Lieut. Reitz ashore, and it was he who made the report of 25,000 men. He had had it from "The Shaykh's Son". This estimate was probably exaggerated, either through wishful thinking, or to impress the British Navy whose protection they were seeking. It is doubtful whether the area in question had a population of 1,000,000 at that date. Further, it is unlikely that all the soldiers gathered came from within that area. See Prinz, p. 103 (quoting Guillain, Vol. iii), who would think this grossly exaggerated.

subordinates of the Government of 'Uman, and sometimes as independent Sultans".[35]

As you see, the Major's statements are confused. Perhaps in the first sentence he followed the point of view of the Imams of 'Uman, or was influenced by the environment in which he wrote his history, and so said it without conviction or examination. For it is very improbable that a politician like the Major would believe that a country's independence would await recognition by its original rulers, nor does the independence of kings in countries which they gain by conquest depend on that, as is known of course; for if this were the case, then the Colonial Governments would retain no rights over the countries they had occupied: for their peoples to this day do not recognise their rule, but regard them as oppressors. But the decision in this matter lies with the sword, as Shawqi has said:

> The rule is seized or taken back (and thus)
> One sword falls (keeps falling) heir to another over the land.[36]

But the Major has made the second statement from a firm conviction, in conformity with the heart of the matter. This is not the belief of the Major alone, but of all the earlier Europeans such as Captain Owen and Captain Vidal and others, as you will see in their statements concerning the Mazru'i Liwalis. This is also what the Arabs believe to be true; for in the Newspaper "Al-Najah", No. 12 of 12 Safar A.H. 1330,[37] Abu Muslim Al-Ruwahi said, during his account of those who ruled Mombasa: "Then after that there ruled Muhammad b. 'Uthman, the ancestor of the family who succeeded to the independent Amirate of Mombasa and its dependencies." Abu Muslim is a respected Shaykh of 'Uman, who has spent all his life under the shadow of the children (dynasty) of the Imam Ahmad, and if the Mazari'a had not been independent Amirs he would not have published this statement of his in a newspaper read by the Amirs of the Imam Ahmad and especially by His Majesty the Sultan himself.

Perhaps one might say[38] that the name of "Rebels" was given because they were "Liwalis" on behalf of the Imams of 'Uman, then claimed the rule for themselves. This is correct only of Muhammad b. 'Uthman himself;

---

[35] Pearce: Op. Cit., p. 117 note. Major Pearce was British Resident in Zanzibar.

[36] Al-Shawqiyat, pub. in 4 Vols. by Matba'at al-Istiqama, Cairo 1953 — Al-Andalus Al-Jadida Sect. 7, line 3 at p. 279. But The Author has misquoted: instead of *wahakadha* it should read *walam yazal*.

[37] 12 Safar A.H. 1338 = 31st January A.D. 1911.

[38] Shaykh Al-Amin pleads in this paragraph very ably for his ancestors as legitimate rulers. It can only be said here that they gained power in accordance with a repeated pattern of Islamic History from the 'Abbasid Caliphate onwards. Certainly they had as much right vis-a-vis the family of Ahmad b. Sa'id, as the latter vis-a-vis 'Uman itself. Ahmad b. Sa'id started himself as a rebel.

for he was the one set in authority by the 'Umani Imams, then he made his rule independent of them. But 'Ali b. 'Uthman and his successors took rule by the sword. The independence of the Mazari'a cannot be impugned on the ground that they were Liwalis by authority of the Imams of 'Uman, for many kings whose sovereignty is admitted by Governments have been like the Mazari'a in this, yet they have not been described as revolutionaries or rebels after their independence, and there are many testimonies to this in the History of the Governments of Islam, both in ancient and modern times.

For Sayf al-Dawla and Salah Al-Din Al-Ayyubi and Mahmud Zanki and other Sultans of the period of the 'Abbasid Government were no more than 'Amils.[39] Then they took independent sovereignty, and it became the heritage of their offspring after them. The Imam Ahmad was 'Amil by authority of Sayf b. Sultan over Sohar. Then he conquered it in his (i.e. Sayf b. Sultan's) lifetime, and then conquered the fortresses of Al-Batina after his death.

Al-Salimi mentioned that in (his Book) *Tuhfat al-A'yan*,[40] and the other evidence in support of this is what Muhammad 'Ali Pasha did in seizing the rule of Egypt from the 'Uthmani Government, and making himself independent in it. Then that was not sufficient for him, but he fought with his own Government, and would almost have besieged Constantinople, unless the Great Powers had interfered and stopped him. Nevertheless, he was not called afterwards by the name of "rebel" or "tyrant": and the King of 'Iraq was no more than an 'Amil of the 'Uthmani Government as well, but now here he is called today the King of 'Iraq. If these were like the Mazari'a in what they did without that ugly name being applied to them, then it is a great injustice to apply it to the Liwalis of the Mazari'a.

This is all from the political point of view, but from the point of view of the Shari'a Ahmad b. Sa'id was not the rightful Imam,[41] able to require the Muslims to obey him, because allegiance to him, as said Abu Nabhan and a group of Shaykhs, was without consultation, and was after his gaining possession of the Kingdom by force. Al-Salimi mentioned that in *Tuhfat Al-A'yan*. Therefore rebellion against him is not forbidden in the Ibadi Sect. So if it is not forbidden, the one who revokes his allegiance to him should not be called a rebel or tyrant.

There remains one thing, and that is the calling of the Mazru'i Sultans by the title of Liwali. This title in the modern terminology indicates that

---

[39] *'Amils*. Originally the *'Amil* was a financial Officer under the Caliphate.
[40] This author is Abu Muhammad 'Ali b. Humayd b. Sallum al-Salimi, and the Book is entitled *Tuhfat al-A'yan fi Sirati Ahli 'Uman*, 2 Vols. Cairo, 1332, 1347 H.
[41] Compare the Mombasa Chronicle, Appendix No. 3, at Para. 1.

he was an 'Amil under the Government, and not a Sultan: but this is nothing, because "Governor" and "King" and "Sultan" are names which indicate in language the same thing. And then since the first Liwali Muhammad b. 'Uthman had this title applied to him, it attached also to his successors after him in consideration of what he was. And that is like the Bey of Tunis and Khedive of Egypt; for the meaning of *Bey* is Major of the Army, but is now applied to the Sultans of Tunis, and "Khedive"[42] means *Amir* (i.e. Commander) and this title remained with the Sultans of Egypt until 'Abbas the Second. And just as you cannot criticise the title of Bey and Khedive in respect of the Kings of Tunis and Egypt, so you cannot criticise the title of Liwali in respect of the Mazru'i Sultans.

Were the Mazari'a Enemies of the British?

I would not be mistaken if I said that the Mazari'a were the first of the 'Umani Tribes who sought friendship with the British. The Liwali Muhammad b. 'Uthman had a warm friend among the British named Cook, who was a frequent visitor to Mombasa and was an honoured guest of his. It is he who helped 'Ali b. 'Uthman to scale the Fort, and to shell it with artillery until he gained possession of it. That was before the accession of the Imam Ahmad to the throne of the 'Umani Government by some years. And in the years A.D. 1824 a treaty was established between the Mazari'a and the British, giving them the right of free trade within their dominions. In my opinion, this is the first treaty made between the British and the 'Umani Arabs.

Reference has already been made above to the names of many of the outstanding personalities of the Mazari'a who took important positions under the authority of the British Government. There were among them those in the position of Liwali, and Mudir, and Qadi and Chief Qadi. Some of them still hold these positions to this day — let alone those employed in other posts. All this contradicts those who say that they were noted for adopting an attitude of hostility to the British Government, as Major Pearce alleged.[43] What led the Major to make this allegation was that some of them were in the German Army in East Africa, which used to attack the British on the frontier during the Great War of 1914. But it

---

[42] **Khadawi**. This word is usually spelt Khedive in English. It is a Turkish term and rank.
[43] Pearce: Op. Cit., p. 117 note. "The remnant of the clan who escaped the vengeance of Sayyid Sa'id settled in what is known as German East Africa, and their descendants have, during the war, been generally hostile to the British." One cannot but question whether Shaykh Al-Amin would have thought it necessary to write this paragraph, had he lived in the post-colonial era.

is clear that no one living in German East Africa (now Tanganyika)[44] at that time had any choice but to serve in the ranks of the German Army, whether he wanted or not. For army service was compulsory with them, and whoever held back was liable to death.

Further, just as some of the Mazari'a were found among the German Army, so some were also found in the British Army, and some of them remained in Army Service until the Great War came to an end. Some of those who were in the British Army were Sulayman b. Muhammad and Harb b. 'Abdullah, and among those of most honourable mention is Salim b. Rashid, the present Mudir of Takaungu, and Ma'mun b. Sulayman, the present Qadi of Mombasa.

If it had happened that the two armies in which the Mazari'a were serving had met, then brother would have slain brother in a war for which they had no desire except in showing loyalty and obeying orders.[45]

The position of the Mazari'a in this is like that of other nations such as the Jews;[46] for they were in the British and French Armies, and also in the German and Austrian Armies, yet no one said that the Jews were noted for hostility to the British, nor to France.[47] The like must not be said either concerning the Mazari'a, for there was a common reason for what they both did, and the judgment (i.e. of their actions) changes to fit the motive for them.

When the Government called for volunteers for service in this past War of 1939, the Mazari'a were the first to answer this call, and the people hastened to register their names among the volunteers, and 10% of them were chosen from among all the people. This was a great number in relation to other tribes.[48] Is not this proof enough of their friendship to the British Government?

[44] **Tanganyika** has of course become Tanzania by its union with Zanzibar and Pemba.

[45] **Except in showing loyalty and obeying orders** — *Siwa al-zuhur bimazhari 'l-wila' wa'mti-thali 'l-amr.* I cannot help suspecting that the Author has here written *Wila'* — Loyalty by a slip of the pen for *Liwa'* — Standard or Flag i.e. "In appearing with the Apperance of the Flag". This seems to make better sense.

[46] Shaykh al-Amin wrote a few years before the formation of the State of Israel. Had he been alive now, he might have been unwilling to mention the Jews. Further, the existence of a political state takes them out of the category of races with which the Mazari'a in exile could be compared.

[47] **France.** *Al-Ummu 'l-Hanun*, lit. The Merciful Mother. This epithet for France arose from the protection which France afforded to the Maronites in Lebanon. It may have arisen partly from the portrayal of the figure of Liberte, Egalite et Fraternite on the French coins and generally as a National Symbol. That Shaykh Al-Amin knew of this shows the extent of his knowledge of events in the Middle East.

[48] **Other Tribes.** The Arabic is *Al-Tawa'ifu 'l-Ukhra.* This word is used in Arabic for the Swahili Tribes, but in Swahili the word "Taifa" has come to mean "Nation". Shaykh Al-Amin is not completely consistent in his use of this term. He sometimes uses Taifa and sometimes *Qabila* for the same groups of people.

CHAPTER II
Concerning the Mazru'i Liwalis in the order of their Periods of Office and the Events which took place in the Reign of Each

1. The First Liwali — Nasir b. 'Abdullah b. Muhammad b. 'Abdullah b. Kahlan

The second Portuguese Conquest of Mombasa — The Arrival of the Imam's Army to drive them out of it — The Liwaliship of Nasir b. 'Abdullah — The Battle of Sese Rumbi — The Third Conquest of Mombasa by the Portuguese — The People of Mombasa attack them and drive them out finally — The Children of Sese Rumbi and their Forging of a False Genealogy other than their own.

It is well known that the Imam Sultan b. Sayf b. Malik Al-Ya'rubi,[1] after conquering Mombasa and driving out the Portuguese, was unable to follow them, and finally rout them, since his soldiers had grown weak through the length of the siege. Therefore the Portuguese continued to raid Mombasa time after time, whenever opportunity offered, in their desire to bring it back under their sway as before. Now before the appointment of Nasir b. 'Abdullah as Liwali (he with whom we are concerned now), the Portuguese had attacked Mombasa, which at that time had no strength to withstand it. So they conquered it, and the news reached 'Uman. The Imam at that time was Sayf b. Sultan, entitled Qayd al-Ard (the Bond of

---

[1] **Sultan b. Sayf b. Malik Al-Ya'rubi.** This Imam was the successor of Nasir b. Murshid, the first Ya'rubi ruler, and the conquest referred to was·in A.H. 1060 (A.D. 1650). The Mombasa Chronicle (Appendix No. 3) reports from this period that the People of Mombasa actually sent a request for help to Sultan b. Sayf, and that he appointed as Liwali Muhammad b. Mbaruk. See also Guillain: L'Afrique Orientale, Part I, Book 5, pp. 516–7.

the Earth?).[2] He equipped a great army in A.H. 1110,[3] which he sent to Mombasa to win it back from the Portuguese and drive them out of it.

Here the Shaykhs of the Mazari'a, from whom I have learnt much information concerning their forebears, say that the Imam made Mbaruk b. Gharib Al-Mazru'i[4] Amir of this army, and entrusted its leadership to him, and appointed Nasir b. 'Abdullah Liwali over Mombasa, to take office after the expulsion of the enemy from it. This army arrived and fought the Portuguese fiercely, and caused them to take refuge in flight, and they turned their backs in rout. After that Nasir b. 'Abdullah became Liwali under the Imam, and overseer of his possessions in East Africa.[5] This is what the Shaykhs of the Mazari'a of the Swahili Coast have related to us, and I have not found it in any of the published books, nor of the historical MSS. which are in our possession; but there is support for part of it in what Major Pearce mentioned in his Book "Zanzibar", namely, that the rule of the Mazari'a in Mombasa begins from the day when the Imam Sayf b. Sultan conquered it.[6] That means the Second Conquest after the conquest of his father Sultan b. Sayf, but the Major did not mention the first one of them[7] who ruled there, and perhaps the reason for that is that it was not the subject of his Book. And what supports the other part of this story is what the reliable informants among the people of Wasin relate — that Mbaruk b. Gharib reached Mombasa in the time of the Diwan Abu Bakr b. Shaykh of the Masbala family who were called Ruga.[8]

---

[2] *Qaydu 'l-Ard*. This may either mean "the Bond of the Land" or "The Bond of the Earth". If the former it means simply that he is the one through whom 'Uman is held together. If the latter, the theology of the Ibadis, who were Kharijites, may have led to it. See Appendix No. 6. The Ibadi Sect have very strong views as to the Islamic Community, and the dependence of its leaders on adherence to the Shari'a, or Revealed Law, in order to be valid leaders. This means that, though removable if found to be unworthy, yet while accepted by the Community they would have a very pronounced religious significance. H. E. Lambert's translation "Ruler of the Land" is wrong, since it confuses QAYD = Bond with QA'ID = Ruler, or leader. Both appear the same in Swahili (H. E. Lambert: Chi-Jomvu and Ki-Ngare, p. 87).

[3] **A.H. 1110** = A.D. 1698. The same year is quoted on p. 21 above.

[4] **Mbaruk b. Gharib**. The Author makes no mention of the Muhammad b. Mbaruk of the Mombasa Chronicle, but the occurrence of the name Mbaruk in both suggests that there may have been confusion here as well.

[5] **In East Africa**. Not just in Mombasa. This is probably correct, as Mombasa seems to have been one of the first places occupied by this Imam, and it was certainly the most important.

[6] **When the Imam Sayf b. Sultan conquered it**. I.e. in A.D. 1698. See Pearce: Zanzibar, Island Metropolis of East Africa, p. 109.

[7] **The Major did not mention the first of them**. I.e. the conquest of A.D. 1650. The Taylor/Harries tradition mentioned in Note 1 above indicates from the confusion of names that there seems to be a confusion also as to the course of events in this early 'Umani period.

[8] **Ruga**. Or Runga, or Rungu. The Arabic letter Ghayn is used in KiSwahili to write G, GH, NG, or NG'. This sometimes makes for ambiguity in the pronunciation of words, or the identification of places.

And they said Abu Bakr had reigned, or held the Sultanate of Vumba about the year A.H. 1111,[9] and I have copied from the writing of Shaykh Saʻid b. Salih Al-Miskiri of Pemba, what he had copied from the hand-writing of Shaykh Muhyi al-Din b. Shaykh Al-Qahtani, that the first Mazruʻi Liwali over Mombasa was Mbaruk b. Gharib, but perhaps that was a slip of the pen on the part of the Shaykh, God's mercy upon him.

In the last days of the Liwaliship of Nasir b. ʻAbdullah there happened a very strange occurrence in Mombasa, which Captain Owen mentions in his "Travels" printed in London, and which he copied from Arabic MSS. written in the year A.H. 1239.[10] This was that there were in the Fort a company of the Imam's soldiers who rebelled against him, and seized the Liwali Nasir b. ʻAbdullah,[11] and imprisoned him, and set up an Amir from among themselves whose name was Sese Rumbi;[12] then they sent to the townspeople, informing them that they had made Sese Rumbi their ruler, and requiring them to submit to his jurisdiction. But the people of Mombasa were not satisfied with the rule of this false claimant and they refused to submit to him. So they answered them that they would not obey him, nor would they surrender themselves to him; and more than that, they declared war against them if they would not free the Liwali and come out of the Fort. And the Rebels answered them that they would never come

[9] **A. H. 1111** = A.D. 1699, from 29th June onwards. At this point it may be mentioned that Guillain (Op. Cit., p. 529) mentions a certain Sayf b. Saʻid as having held office during the period commencing with the year A.D. 1650. He may have been a previous appointment made by Sayf b. Sultan, or he may be the same man as the one called Mbaruk b. Gharib here. There seems to be a lot of confusion in the names as recorded in the different sources.

[10] **A.H. 1239** = A.D. 1823. This refers to the Mombasa Chronicle (Appendix No. 3). Shaykh Al-Amin seems to have relied on this source as well as on the oral tradition for the story.

[11] **Seized the Liwali Nasir b. ʻAbdullah**. This may be the occasion from which sprang the proverb; "Mzingile Mwana Mbiji" which may mean "A Maze is the son of (i.e. the result of) the Thornbush", quoted by W. E. Taylor in "African Aphorisms", p. 94, No. 399. There is no talk of Nasir's son being imprisoned with him, but see Note 19 of this section below.

[12] **Sese Rumbi**. This name is variously spelt. Boxer and Azavedo: Fort Jesus and the Portuguese in Mombasa, p. 77, say, from Portuguese sources, that he is a bantu slave, or imply that by their context. Strandes, in his description of this incident, calls the leader of the revolt Alifani (Khalfani) brother of Amade Bunzayde (The Portuguese Period in East Africa, tr. Jean F. Wallwork, pp. 282 ff.). It is possible he was a Baluchi or Central Asian. Taylor (Op. Cit., p. 83, No. 381) quotes the following Swahili Proverb:

Mvunda kwao hakui, illa huwa yeye Mbombwe, OR

Mvunda kwao hakui, illa huwa kama **Sesarumbe**

The destroyer of his native land does not grow,

    But he is an abject person, OR

The destroyer of his native land does not grow,

    But he is **like Sesarumbe**.

If *Kwao* implies "Native Land" in the strict sense, then Sese Rumbi was undoubtedly a Swahili, of whatever stock he may have originally come. But see the tradition of the children of Sese Rumbi mentioned by Shaykh Al-Amin at the end of this Section.

out of the Fort, so the people of Mombasa agreed to fight them, and they fought them. And the heads of the town at that time were Shaykh b. Ahmad Al-Malindi and Mu'allim Ndao b. Mwishafi, and Mwinyi Nguti b. Mwinzagu, and Mwinyi Mwele b. Hajj. And while the war was going on between them at full pitch, lo and behold the Portuguese took them by surprise with a war-fleet consisting of four warships and seventy boats filled with soldiers, ammunition and equipment. This is the last raid by the Portuguese on Mombasa.

The reason for the return of the Portuguese to Mombasa this time, and their raiding of it, was that one of the people of Pate called Mwinyi Hindi b. Kipai[13] had a quarrel with the Sultan of Pate Mwana Tamu Mkuu, who ruled from the year A.H. 1111–1152.[14] This man, then, set out for Moçambique to seek assistance from the Portuguese in making war on the Sultan, and he succeeded in getting it, and came with those soldiers to Pate; and when he reached there he sent to the Sultan, informing him that he had come to make war on him. Then the Sultan did nothing more than to make a settlement with his adversary Mwinyi Hindi, since he saw that he was not able to defend himself against the strength of the Portuguese.

Then the two took counsel together as to some means of keeping the Portuguese away and contenting them. So the Sultan said: "The people of Mombasa are at war with their Liwali Nasir b. 'Abdullah, and have seized him and imprisoned him; so let us send these foreigners[15] to them, and thus we will place Mombasa in their hands, and by this means we shall put them at a distance from our country."

Mwinyi Hindi agreed with him on this happy thought; and they spoke to the Portuguese about it, and made them anxious to get Mombasa, and said how easy it would be to gain the mastery of it. And they were pleased at the idea and set out with the people of Pate until they reached Mombasa. And there, after a few skirmishes, they agreed with the people to fight Sese Rumbi and his supporters and expel them from the Fort. The Portuguese actually sent to the rebels, ordering them to surrender the Fort, and they surrendered it to them straightaway and came out of it, and the

---

[13] **Mwinyi Hindi b. Kipai**. Guillain Vol. I, pp. 530–1, says: "Ahmed ben Koubai" and "Bouana Tamu M'Kouhou". The second name shows that he is talking about the same two people. Boxer and Azavedo (p. 75) call the former "Manni Hanid-bin-Kibai". Shaykh Al-Amin's spelling is undoubtedly the most correct.

[14] A.H. 1111–1152 = A.D. 1699–1739?

[15] **These foreigners** — *Ha'ula'i 'l-Ifranj* Lit. "These Franks". This is the traditional Arabic term for Western Europeans. Most of the Europeans who came into contact with the Arab World were from France — Franks, in fact. The Term *Franji* has continued to this day, and in some areas is still a general word for "Foreigner".

Portuguese let them all go free except their leader Sese Rumbi. They seized him and sent him bound to Moçambique: but the Liwali, after he was brought out of prison, stayed a little while in Mombasa and then travelled to 'Uman.

Immediately the Portuguese had seized the reins of government, they began to treat the people of Mombasa harshly again.[16] They raped their women, and made mockery of religion, and even used to throw stones at the Muslims when they saw them praying. The people of Mombasa could not endure patiently this injustice, and so they awaited the opportunity to attack them, and when it was a Christian Feast Day, and most of the Portuguese had come out of the Fort into the environs of the town for recreation, they attacked them and set about killing them until they were forced to ask for quarter. So they gave them quarter on condition that they would leave the town immediately, and return to Moçambique, and they agreed and escaped with their lives, leaving all they owned in the Fort.[17]

After they had left Mombasa the townspeople were afraid of losing the arms, ammunition and wealth that was in the Fort, so every tribe set one man to guard it until the matter should be reported to 'Uman. And there will follow in the discourse about Muhammad b. 'Uthman what happened after this occurrence, and who ruled as Liwali over Mombasa in the period between him and Nasir b. 'Abdullah.

And concerning Sese Rumbi and his party the rebels, I have this to say:

It has been told me from Rashid b. Sa'ud, one of the well-known leaders of Mombasa — and it comes from the famous genealogist Muhammad b. 'Uthman Al-Matafi[18] — that there were Ya'rubi slaves who came in the

---

[16] **Immediately the Portuguese . . . harshly**. Boxer and Azavedo, pp. 76 ff say this was in A.D. 1728–9. S. B. Miles: The Countries and Tribes of the Persian Gulf, p. 249, says that the Portuguese held the town for about three years from A.D. 1728. Shaykh Al-Amin gives no date or period. For the harsh treatment the Portuguese are alleged to have meted out, Compare Strandes (Op. Cit., pp. 38, 307 and sep. 116) who says: "It was generally considered too at that epoch that any harm which could be inflicted on heathens or Muslims was praiseworthy." Also quoting the Historian Diego do Couto (XII p. 8): ". . . and the Portuguese private citizens were of a type which, according to a contemporary Portuguese historian, provoked offence wherever they chanced to go." See also the Mombasa Chronicle, Appendix No. 3 below. Shaykh Al-Amin omits the story about the distributing of the rice, which is referred to by Guillain and the Mombasa Chronicle.

[17] Boxer and Azavedo (p. 81) state that all but thirty officers elected to remain in Mombasa with their girl-friends, and became Muslims to do so.

[18] **Al-Matafi**. The Arabicised form of the Swahili place-name with the Arabic *Ya* of relationship added, i.e. "of Mtwapa". Mtwapa is a village on the creek of the same name lying about nine miles North of Mombasa. Here the Author gives one of his sources clearly, but I have not succeeded in finding further information about Muhammad b. 'Uthman Al-Matafi.

time of the Imam Sayf b. Sultan, who used to be known in past days as children of Sese Rumbi, and that there has remained till now a group of the descendants of those slaves who have forged for themselves another pedigree to hide their true origin, but it is not the subject of this Book of ours to uncover the true circumstances of these hidden ones, may God grant them pardon and health.

Nasir b. 'Abdullah was accounted a man of determination and bravery, and kindly dealing, and justice by his subjects. His good fortune was to earn the love and respect of the people of the town; and when he wished to marry, the notables of the town offered him their sisters, and he chose the sister of Shaykh b. Ahmad Al-Kabir (i.e. Senior),[19] one of the descendants of the former Kings of Malindi, and he married her, and had by her a daughter who was the mother of Mbaruk b. Ahmad b. Mbaruk b. Gharib Al-Mazru'i.

The date of the return of Nasir to 'Uman[20] is not certainly known. It is said that he returned to Mombasa with Muhammad b. 'Uthman in the time of the Imam Sayf the Second b. Sultan b. Sayf, then returned finally to 'Uman, where he died.

Nasir b. 'Abdullah left of male children Mas'ud and 'Abdullah. This Mas'ud is one of the fourteen lineages who were mentioned at the beginning of this book.

2. The Second Liwali — Muhammad b. 'Uthman b. 'Abdullah b. Muhammad b. 'Abdullah b. Kahlan

The Mombasa Delegation's Journey to 'Uman — The Delegation returns with the Liwali Muhammad b. Sa'id Al-Ma'miri —. The Liwaliship of Salih b. Muhammad Al-Hadrami — His Bad Treatment of its People. — The Seizure of him and his release — He kills Shaykh b. Ahmad Al-Malindi and his son — The Arrival of Muhammad b. 'Uthman in Mombasa as Liwali. — He makes Reconciliation between the People of Mombasa—He sends the *Kharaj* Tax to 'Uman every year — He ceases to send it and declares himself an Independent Ruler — The Imam Ahmad sends someone to kill him by treachery — The Liwaliship of Sayf b. Khalaf Al-Ma'miri.

[19] **Shaykh b. Ahmad Al-Kabir**. He seems to be the same as the one who was murdered with his son 'Ali Kombo by Salih b. Muhammad Al-Hadrami (see the next Section). The descendants of the former Kings of Malindi took up residence in Mombasa after the Portuguese had gained possession of the town, and driven out the original royal family of Mombasa in the person of Don Jeronimo Chinguliwa. See note 12 above. An error may have arisen in the tradition owing to a possible confusion between Nasir's son and 'Ali Kombo.
[20] **The Return of Nasir to 'Uman**. Compare the Taylor/Harries Tradition, p. 82, para. 2, and also the next Section, at Note 11.

After the people of Mombasa had driven out the Portuguese from the town in the Battle[1] of Sese Rumbi and his supporters, as we have already related in the account of the First Liwali Nasir b. 'Abdullah, Shaykh b. Ahmad Al-Malindi and Mwinyi Nguti b. Mwenzagu Al-Kilindini and Mwishahali b. Ndao Al-Tangani set out for 'Uman in company with one person of every Mombasa Tribe[2], and one delegate representing every

[1] *Waqi'a*. This word means "Happening", but it can also mean "Battle". I have translated it here "Battle". Confusion arises from the fact that many of the events recounted in this history are battles, or involve battles.

[2] *Qabila . . . Ta'ifa* — The author uses these words in the opposite way from the usual. *Ta'ifa* usually means one of the Arab/Swahili Groupings of Mombasa, while Qabila usually means a Nyika Bantu Tribe.

These names of individuals are here set out alongside the lists given by Owen and Guillain in their respective versions of the Mombasa Chronicle, Owen's being in English, and Guillain's being in French orthography.

The orthography of these names in Arabic shows the difficulty which is met with in seeking to write these African names in Arabic Script. Confusion is all the greater by reason of the

Al-Amin	Owen	Guillain
Shaykh b. Ahmad Al-Malindi	Sheikh bin Ahmed of Malinda	Cheikh, fils d'Ahmed el Melindi
Mwinyi Nguti b. Mwanzagu Al-Kilindini	Mishhat bin Dace of Tanjan	Maallem Ndao, fils de Mouchafi
Mwishahali b. Ndao Al-Tangani	Mayanij of the People of Muta	Moigni Gouti ben Zago
	Mamak of the People of Tiv	Moingni Mouti ben Hhadji
		Magnagnie de Mtaoue
		Mamako do Tihoui
WaRibe	Riba	Rebabe
WaChonyi	Shunt	Cheboubi
WaKambe	Kamba	Kambe
WaKauma	Gauma	Kouna
WaJibana	Jibana	Djebane
WaRabai	Rabayi	Rabaye
WaGiryama	Jiryamah	Gueriama
WaDuruma	Daruma	Derouma
WaMtwapa	Mutavi	Mtaoue
WaShimba	Shiba	Chimba
WaLungu	Lughu	Lounngo
WaDigo	Diju	Debgou

"Zanji"[3] tribe and appointed by it. And the tribes of the "Zunuj" who sent their men as delegates to 'Uman were the WaRibe, WaChonyi, WaKambe, WaKauma, WaJibana, WaRabai, WaGiryama, WaDuruma, WaMtwapa, WaShimba, WaLungu and WaDigo. This delegation set out to put before the Imam Sayf b. Sultan what had happened in Mombasa concerning the Portuguese. When they arrived there the Imam welcomed them with kindness and liberality and treated them with the utmost honour; and when they returned he equipped them, and transported them in three ships, whose names were *Ka'bras, Malaki* and *Falaki*,[4] with splendid gifts and presents, and sent with them Muhammad b. Sa'id Al-Ma'miri as Liwali of Mombasa. After they reached their country, Muhammad went and lived in the Fort as did the Liwali before him. He permitted the People of Mombasa to take as prize (booty?) all the property that the Portuguese had left behind as a reward for their well-doing and endurance of trouble in driving out the enemy.

The Liwali did not keep any of that property except the ornaments and gunpowder, and brass and tin. After a short time Muhammad b. Sa'id returned to 'Uman, and Salih b. Muhammad Al-Hadrami[5] succeeded him

---

fact that the Arabic speaker tends to write the words as he pronounces them. His pronunciation of Swahili and African names is often a distortion of the original, as indeed are the Swahili pronunciation of Arabic words and names.

F. J. Berg thinks that "WaMtwapa" should be "WaMtawa", a sub-division of the WaDigo. A comparison with the other two lists makes this certain. The WaMtwapa were in any case a Swahili Tribe, not one of the Nyika Tribes. It will be noticed that Shaykh Al-Amin omits the men from Tiwi and Muta (Mvita).

This delegation indicates that to the inhabitants of the Swahili Coast at that time "'Uman meant stabilty". The subsequent course of events at Mombasa seems to indicate that they accepted the Mazari'a basically as representatives of 'Uman, and only as rulers in their own right for as long as 'Uman was incapable of giving them security. When times changed their confidence in the Mazari'a weakened.

[3] *Zanji*, and its plural *Zunuj* are the ordinary Arabic terms for "African" and "Negro". It is peculiar that it should be so similar to the Swahili term *Mzungu* which means "European" or "Foreigner".

[4] *Falaki*. The Mombasa Chronicle says definitely that the name of the third ship was not known. Miles (p. 250) states also that the third ship's name was not known, but he also states that they reached 'Uman (i.e. the Delegation) in A.D. 1731/2, and that Muhammad b. Sa'id al-Ma'miri came and drove the Portuguese out. Badger in *Imams and Sayyids of 'Uman*, p. 93, which is a translation of Salil b. Raziq, gives the fleet of Sayf b. Sultan as consisting of 28 ships, of which he names eight, among them *El Falak, El Malk* and the *Kaa'bras*.

[5] **Salih b. Muhammad Al-Hadrami**. Cf. *The Mombasa Chronicle*. Guillain (p. 535) calls him Salih ben Sa'eed al Hadrami, and puts the date of his assuming office as A.H. 1148 = A.D. 1735, i.e. six years after the Portuguese had been finally driven away, which is plainly too late a date. It must be borne in mind however that "a short time" in view of sailing conditons may have been anything from six months to a year. The following diary is offered as a possible chronological scheme:

as Liwali. But Salih was neither a reformer nor a man of laudable behaviour, for he was unjust to the People of Mombasa and treated them badly. So they complained about him to the Imam, and he sent an order to them to seize and imprison him. They seized him therefore, but had mercy on him and set him free. Then Salih harboured evil intentions in his heart against those who had complained against him to the Imam. He united with the Mombasans[6] and made friends with them, and invited them to make war on Shaykh b. Ahmad and the WaKilindini who were under him. They accepted his invitation and fought them.

When Shaykh b. Ahmad and his people saw what their fellow-countrymen the Mombasans were doing in helping their enemies against them, he went to the Nyika, and brought an army of Zunuj, and ambushed them in Mji wa Kale,[7] and a great number of Mombasans were slain, and a number taken prisoner. Then Shaykh b. Ahmad and those with him made for the country of the WaNyika[8] after this raid, fleeing from the oppression and hostility of Salih.

If Muhammad b. Sa'id Al-Ma'miri failed to return on the S. W. Monsoon A.D. 1729, he would have to wait a year, while Salih b. Muhammad Al-Hadrami could not succeed him before the start of the N. E. Monsoon in the latter part of the same year. This would bring us to A.D. 1730. Salih's injustice is not likely to have appeared before Muhammad B. Sa'id had left at the start of the S. W. Monsoon A.D. 1730. The people's complaint could thus only have reached 'Uman by the S. W. Monsoon of the next year (A.D. 1731), and the Imam's order to seize Salih would have arrived at the beginning of A.D. 1732 Salih's machinations after his release from prison must have lasted at least a year. 'Ali Kombo arrived in A.D. 1733 by the N. E. Monsoon (perhaps after carrying the complaint to 'Uman) at the earliest, so that news of the murder of him and his father cannot have reached the Imam before the middle of that year, but may have been delayed until the S. W. Monsoon of A.D. 1734. Muhammad b. 'Uthman thus probably arrived by the N. E. Monsoon of A.D. 1735. One has to think in terms of years and half-years when considering the dealings which took place between 'Uman and East Africa. An idea of the time lapse involved can be appreciated from the following remark by Boteler (Vol. II. p. 10): "The measure of delivering up the place to the English had long been contemplated, and, when agreed to unanimously, notice to that effect was transmitted in the last Monsoon to Bombay, but no answer had been received. The other Monsoon had set in, and the Imam's forces were daily expected." (See Appendix No. 7, Chronological Table).

[6] *Ahl Mumbasa ... Mumbasiyin.* This terminology is confusing, but not without a certain logic. By *Ahlu Mumbasa* the Author means those living in Mombasa generally. By *Mumbasiyin* he means the two Clans of WaMvita and WaJomvu, who were the original, probably Shirazi, inhabitants. See the Note on the Alignment of Parties in the Introduction above.

[7] *Mji wa Kale.* The Old Town. This lay on the East Coast of Mombasa Island between the Nyali Bridge and the beginning of the present Old Town of Mombasa which was known as Gavana, a relic of the Portuguese occupation.

[8] **Country of the *WaNyika*.** A very sure and convenient hiding-place, beyond the direct reach of the Mombasa authorities. The exact locality is quite indefinite, except that Shaykh b. Ahmad must have been with the Nyika tribe which had a direct Patron/Client relationship with the WaMvita of which he was a member.

It happened after that that 'Ali Kombo[9] b. Shaykh b. Ahmad arrived from 'Uman with money and horses etc. with which the Imam had presented him. 'Ali Kombo did not know about the war which had taken place between the Liwali and his father. Salih received news of his coming, and sent some of the soldiers to him, who seized him and brought him to him. Then he confined him and robbed him of the wealth which he had, and when Shaykh b. Ahmad knew what the Liwali had done to his son, he was overcome with a father's pity, and came out of hiding,[10] and came to the Liwali and asked for his son's release. The Liwali met him with honour and respect, until he thought that he would give him what he asked for. But very soon the Liwali ordered his arrest, and slew both him and his son together.

No sooner had the news of the Liwali's harshness and hostility to the leaders of the town reached the Imam, that he removed him, and proclaimed in place of him Muhammad b. 'Uthman[11] Al-Mazru'i. And the first thing this Liwali set about, after assuming office in the land, was to send to Ahmad b. Shaykh[12] and the WaKilindini who were hiding in the Nyika country, telling them that Salih had been removed, and had left for 'Uman, and asking them to return to the town quickly. And when the Liwali saw what division and quarrelling there was between the two groups, the WaKilindini and the People of Mombasa, he devoted his utmost effort to reconciling[13] their dispute, and God gave him success in this. There resulted friendship and love in their hearts in place of repugnance and grudging. The country became quiet,[14] and the waters returned to their proper courses for quite a long while.

The stories transmitted from the Mazari'a of old time, and others, mention that the Imam continued sending Liwalis to Mombasa from the

[9] **'Ali Kombo**. Note the mixture of Arabic and Swahili/Bantu names here. This seems to indicate an early stage in the process of "Afro-Arabicisation".

[10] **Hiding** — *Makmana*. Lit. A Place of Ambush. It would have been better to use the word *Malja'*, since Shaykh b. Ahmad was "fleeing for refuge" not "Lying in wait".

[11] **Muhammad b. 'Uthman**. Cf. The Mombasa Chronicle, Appendix No. 3. Guillain (p. 534) says that Muhammad b. 'Uthman was appointed in A.H. 1152 = A.D. 1739. This is where the discrepancy first appears in the dating as between the different authorities. See Note 17 below.

[12] **Ahmad b. Shaykh**. This was the son of the murdered Shaykh b. Ahmad, and brother (or Half-brother?) of 'Ali Kombo. He was of the WaMalindi section of the WaMvita. See the prefatory Note on the Mombasa Tribes.

[13] **To reconciling their dispute**. Note the rule by arbitration here. There may be two reasons for this, (a) The Ibadis, represented by Muhammad b. 'Uthman, being Kharijites, may have preserved the old Arab desert tradition of the *Hakam*, or Arbitrator, more strongly than other Muslims, and (b) the Liwalis had not such a power to dominate the local population that they could afford to be dictatorial and autocratic.

[14] **The country became quiet**. So says the Mombasa Chronicle, Para. 6.

time that the Swahili country became part of their dominion, until events happened in 'Uman which weakened the power of the Government, and made him unable to administer the internal affairs of his kingdom, let alone guide the external dominions and their policy. Sayf the Second b. Sultan wished to give the Liwaliship of Mombasa to Nasir b. 'Abdullah[15] again, becaue of his loyalty and good administration, and his perfect knowledge of the conditions of the country and its people, on condition that he would bind himself to pay a certain proportion of the Kharaj Tax every year. But Nasir excused himself on the ground of his old age from accepting the Liwaliship this time, and recommended to the Imam that he should appoint Muhammad b. 'Uthman in his place on those conditions. The Imam acted on this suggestion, and made Muhammad b. 'Uthman Liwali; and the Liwali prepared for his journey to the place of his Liwaliship, and with him were his two brothers 'Ali b. 'Uthman and Qadib b. 'Uthman, and some of their paternal cousins such as 'Abdullah b. Zahir and others.[16]

The traditions differ in regard to the date of the Liwaliship of Muhammad b. 'Uthman, and from the older MSS we have the opinion that he reached Mombasa in the year A.H. 1143,[17] and took the reins of office in that year, and lived as Liwali nearly 14 years. But there is another tradition which differs from this in regard to the period of his Liwaliship. It says that it was nine years. But stories differ from what is in the European (Ifranjiya) sources concerning the history of the Liwaliship. For in the Book "Zanzibar" by Major Pearce, and the Red Book on East Africa, they (i.e. the Authors) say that the Imam Sayf b. Sultan appointed Muhammad b. 'Uthman Liwali of Mombasa in the year A.D. 1739, which corresponds

---

[15] **Wished to give the Liwaliship to Nasir b. 'Abdullah again.** Only Shaykh Al-Amin states that Nasir recommended the appointment of Muhammad b. 'Uthman. The Taylor/Harries tradition (p. 82, para. 2) states that Masudi (sic) said to the garrison: "Miye mnakuwa mzee. Sifai neno tena" = "I have become an old man: I am no good any more".

[16] **'Ali b. 'Uthman ... 'Abdullah b. Zahir.** For these names see the Genealogical Tables in Appendix No. 1.

[17] **A.H. 1143** = A.D. 1730. There is a difference of dating here. The alternatives are as follows:

Al-Amin says that Muhammad B. 'Uthman was appointed in A.H. 1143 = A.D. 1730.

Hardinge said that he was appointed in A.H. 1148 = A.D. 1735.

Guillain, followed by Pearce, the Red Book of East Africa, and Miles at p. 253, says that he was appointed in A.H. 1152 = A.D. 1739. See Appendix No. 7 and the Comparative Chronological Table there. The confusion seems to have arisen on the one hand from allowing too much time for Muhammad b. Sa'id Al-Ma'miri and Salih b. Muhammad Al-Hadrami, and on the other from including their periods of office within the Liwaliship of Muhammad b. 'Uthman as if they had never been there at all. But if Guillain's reading of the date on the Tomb (A.H. 1159 = A.D. 1746) is correct, then the third estimate would be nine years instead of five — not so far off Hardinge's estimate of nine years.

to the year A.H. 1152. My own opinion is that the most accurate account is that which says that he assumed the Liwaliship in the year A.H. 1143 and remained as Liwali for 14 years; because according to this account his death would be in the year A.H. 1157, and that is the year in which he died as written on his tomb (God have mercy on him), whereas according to the European account it would be five years only, and that is an exception to all the other accounts.

After the Liwali had been invested with his office, he used to send to the Imam that amount of money (wealth) which accorded with the agreement previously made between them. And this state of affairs continued for a few years until conditions deteriorated in 'Uman, and the weakness of the Government grew worse, because of the division which occurred in it. Discord spread over 'Uman East and West, and the millstones of war turned between Arabs and Persians at one time, and between the Arabs themselves at another. Imams arose there each claiming the right for himself and calling his fellow a rebel. So Muhammad b. 'Uthman stopped sending what he had been sending,[18] and became an independent ruler and proclaimed his independence.

There were in Mombasa at that time shaykhs of the WaKilifi[19] who had a violent hatred of the Liwali, not because he treated them badly but because he preferred the WaMalindi and the "Three Tribes' — i.e. the WaKilindini, the WaTangana and the WaChangamwe, to them. They were indignant at that for some time, and remained awaiting a favourable opportunity to set upon the Liwali. And when the situation quietened in 'Uman and general loyalty resulted to Ahmad b. Sa'id,[20] they wrote to him[21] concerning him (the Liwali), and informed him of how he had declared himself an independent sovereign of the Coast. The one whose

[18] **Stopped sending what he had been sending**. The Mombasa Chronicle (App. No. 3) gives what must have been Muhammad's true sentiments, for what is said there is in full accord with Ibadi doctrine, except that Muhammad probably thought of himself as *more* legitimate than Ahmad b. Sa'id. See Chapter I above, "The Independence of the Mazari'a".

[19] **The Shaykhs of the WaKilifi**. The Taylor/Harries tradition (p. 83, paras, 3 & 4) indicates that the WaMvita were with the Mazari'a, and the WaKilindini against them. It is possible that Taylor's informant said WaKilindini in error for WaKilifi. In any case, it is wrong since it runs counter to the whole pattern of tribal loyalties. See the Prefatory Note and Note 22 below.

[20] **Ahmad b. Sa'id**. This man helped Sultan b. Murshid, the last Ya'rubi Imam, who was slain in battle before Sohar (Guillain p. 538; Badger p. 150). He was the victorious founder of the Bu Sa'idi Dynasty of 'Uman.

[21] **They wrote to him**. The "Nine Tribes" are here true to their usual policy of inclining to a strong and settled 'Umani Government.

insolence dominated them was one of the WaKilifi leaders at that time (named Sharif Sa'id?)[22].

After this letter had reached the Imam, he sent men to Mombasa[23] to assassinate the Liwali. They were Sayf b. Khalaf Al-Ma'miri and Sayf b. Nasir and Sayf b. Sa'id and Sayf Al-Bitashi and Ma'an b. Kulayb. They arrived in Mombasa without making known what they had come for. The Liwali met them and they told him that they had quarrelled with the Imam, and had left 'Uman intending to stay where he (the Liwali) was staying. Then they made contact with the WaKilifi, and revealed to them the matter, and took from them a promise to help them in performing that errand. So they made a covenant with them and joined forces with them. After they had secured themselves against the People of Mombasa, and those soldiers of the Imam who were in the Fort, they asked the Liwali to equip them for a journey to Kilwa and allow them a sum of money to trade with there. [24] The Liwali granted their request, in complete ignorance of what they were secretly designing.[25] And while he was sitting with them getting ready what they desired, they jumped on him and killed him and seized his brother 'Ali b. 'Uthman[26] and Khalaf b. Qadib and 'Abdullah b. Khamis Al-'Afifi, and threw them into prison. When the soldiers knew that what they had done was simply by command of the Imam, they obeyed at once all their orders. They issued their order for the seizure of all the Mazari'a who were in Mombasa, and some they

---

[22] *(Ismuhu Sharif Sa'id)*. These words were written in brackets and then scored out. Did Shaykh Al-Amin excise this because he was not sure of the name? or was he confusing this occasion with that of the Kilifi leader who stirred up the trouble between the Beni Mas'ud and the Liwali Ahmad b. Muhammad?

[23] **He sent men to Mombasa.** See the Mombasa Chronicle, App. No. 3. The Taylor/Harries Tradition (p. 83, para. 4) refers to these as a class — *Masefu* — The "Sayfs".

[24] **Allow them a sum of money to trade with there.** This was the usual practice in the 19th Century when Swahili Traders went on Safaris up-country; but the source of the money was usually the Banyan, or other Asian Merchants, who issued loans on interest. (Swahili Prose Texts, Von Velten/Harries, p. 178/9). Guillain says they asked Muhammad for money "to raise supporters", i.e. for their supposed fight against the Imam (p. 544). He also gives other details here, in some respects similar to those given in the Taylor/Harries Tradition, pp. 84–87, q.v.

[25] *Wahuwa yajhalu kulla al-jahli lima admaruhu.* There is a slip in the Grammar here. The verb *Jahala* takes a direct object or *bi*, but not according to Wehr the Prepositon *li*.

[26] **Seized his brother 'Ali b. 'Uthman** Guillain mentions at this point an Englishman, whom he takes to be the same as "Mr. Cook" (See the next section of this Chapter). The Taylor/Harries Tradition makes a lot of a "slave" (besari) who kept in touch with 'Ali b. 'Uthman. W. E. Taylor relates in "African Aphorisms" (No. 95, p. 401) a rhyme possibly connected with this event. An old woman is said to have stood outside the window of the house where 'Ali was living, and sung as a warning: "Mzungu migele u Muongo/Mato yako yana tongo Kwani kuata mpango/Kwenda kibango uani?" i.e. "The Foreigner is a cunning deceiver/Your eyes are blinded/Why should you leave your refuge, and go to gaol in the Fort?"

killed, while others were scattered and went up-country (lit. to the Badiya)[27] and hid there.

After that Sayf b. Khalaf was Liwali of Mombasa by agreement of his colleagues, and got all the help they asked for from the WaKilifi[28] and the Mombasans. That was in the year A.H. 1157.[29]

This is what the records are agreed upon, and the late genealogist and historian 'Abd al-Karim b. Talsam (God's mercy on him) confirmed them (or, admitted their truth). It also agrees with what we have seen of Captain Owen's Translation of the Arabic MSS[30] which he copied on this journey.

The male children which Muhammad b. 'Uthman left were 'Abdullah and Ahmad, and all his descendants are from these two sons. We shall mention them therafter (and God knows best).

3. The Third Liwali — 'Ali b. 'Uthman b. 'Abdullah b. Muhammad b. 'Abdullah b. Kahlan

The sorrow of the "Three Tribes" over the murder of Muhammad b. 'Uthman and the Imprisonment of his brother — Mwana Vumbaya bint Shaykh and her effort to save 'Ali b. 'Uthman from prison — The Baluchis help him to escape from prison — The "Three Tribes" await him outside the Fort — He flees to Mrere — The Arrival of Mr. Cook and his help to him — The plot to attack and settle his affairs — The Treaty between him and the "Three Tribes" — The Occupation of the Fort and the Killing of Sayf b. Khalaf — The Elders of the Town congratulate the Liwali and swear Allegiance to him — The Determination of the Liwali to slay the Leaders of the WaKilifi and the Ransoming of them by the "Three Tribes" — The Imam Ahmad b. Sa'id fears that the Mazari'a will gain Mastery of Zanzibar — The Mazari'a attack Zanzibar — Khalaf b. Qadib murders his uncle 'Ali b. 'Uthman, and the reason for his doing so.

We have already said in our account of Muhammad b. 'Uthman that the group of men whom the Imam Ahmad sent to assassinate him seized his

[27] *Al-Badiya*. Ordinarily this would mean "the Desert". In East Africa however it means the "Open Country", that is, the Nyika Bush.
[28] **The WaKilifi**. These were one of the "Nine Tribes" who at this time were actively hostile to the Mazru'i Clan, and always tended to oppose their policy. See the Prefatory Note on the Mombasan Tribes.
[29] **A.H. 1157** = A.D. 1744.
[30] **Captain Owen's Translation of the Arabic MSS**. The translation was really the work of Lieut. Richard Emery, and was included in a footnote at the end of Vol. I of Owen's Voyages, though its translator was unacknowledged by him. The Mombasa Chronicle in Appendix No. 3 is in fact Emery's Translation.

brother 'Ali b. 'Uthman and put him in prison inside the Fort. The murder of Muhammad b. 'Uthman and the imprisonment of his brother stirred up a deep grief in the hearts of the "Three Tribes" and the WaMalindi party, but pleased the WaKilifi and the WaMombasa[1] and their leaders. There was a WaMalindi woman at that time under the WaKilifi leader, whose name was Mwana Vumbaya bint Shaykh.[2] She was angry with her husband because of the marriage relationship and friendship[3] between the WaMalindi and the Mazari'a since the time of Nasir b. 'Abdullah. This woman possssessed the qualities of intelligent men in respect of bravery and craftiness and soundess of judgment. So she encouraged the "Three Tribes"[4] and those among her relatives who were prominent men of the WaMalindi to make an effort to release 'Ali b. 'Uthman by any means they could from prison. On the other hand, she sent presents to the gaolers who were in the Fort until she overwhelmed them with kindness, so that they requited her by giving 'Ali b. 'Uthman relief and lightening the watch and confinement kept upon him. Thus the Liwali was able by this means to meet at times with his near friends, and to speak with them about the manner of escape from this prison which confined his activities. And they agreed that he and those imprisoned with him should scale the wall of the Fort at a certain hour of a certain night, on conditon that they would await them outside it and give them assistance.

'Ali b. 'Uthman had two of the Baluchi soldiers in the Fort who were

---

[1] **WaMombasa**. This name here seems to mean more especially the WaMvita and WaJomvu. The names of the Swahili tribes are given now and hereafter in their Swahili form, though in the Arabic version they are given in the form *Mumbasiyun, Kilifiyun* etc.

[2] *Kana taht za'imi 'l-Kilifiyin ... imra'a ... ismuha Mwana Vumbaya bint Shaykh*. The word here **may** be written with a Qaf, but it is doubtful how many diacritical points there are over it. Chief Qadi Muhammad b. Qasim says that the name should be *Vumbaya*. The Taylor/Harries Tradition gives *Kambaya*. The difference in Arabic is one diacritical point only. Though I have rendered it Vumbaya on the Chief Qadi's advice, it seems on balance more likely to have been Kumbaya since Taylor apparently received the tradition from a Swahili informant orally, and the audible difference between K and V is too great to allow for a mistake. The informant may have himself misread K for V, but as he is earlier he is *prima facie* less likely to be wrong.

She is only referred to in the Taylor/Harries Tradition (p. 88) and here, but her name in the former is Mwana Kambaya wa Shehe. In Shaykh Al-Amin's story Mwana Vumbaya plays the key part in the drama, whereas in the Taylor/Harries Tradition she is little more than an interested onlooker. Shaykh Al-Amin has the much more lifelike and realistic story. He seems to be quoting from an oral tradition, independent of the Taylor/Harries One, which probably preserves a more genuine account of the events.

[3] *walmawlat*. Perhaps this word should rather be *Muwalat* = Nearness, friendship under a contract of clientage.

[4] **The Three Tribes**. The WaKilindini, the WaTangana and the WaChangamwe. See the Prefatory Note on the Mombasa Tribes and F. J. Berg's Article there referred to.

utterly loyal to him; one was named Hamdad and the other Halab.[5] He
let them know what he and the group of the "Three Tribes" had agreed
upon, and they approved this idea and promised to help him; and the
Baluchis had recourse to the skin of an ox from which they made straps
(thongs) so strong as not to break if a man's weight hung on them. And
when the promised night arrived, the gaoler responsible for him feigned
ignorance of it, and he and his companions scaled the wall of the Fort[6] on
the West side opposite to where the High Court is currently located,[7]
since the wall on this side is the lowest of the walls of the Fort, nor was
the ditch that surrounded it dug at that time. Some of his closest friends
were awaiting him outside the Fort, Mwishafi b. Mu'allim Ndao, Hajj b.
Mwinyi Nguta, Khamis b. Mwinyi Jaka (Chaki?) and Ahmad b. Ndao, all
important men of the "Three Tribes".[8] 'Ali b. 'Uthman descended first —
by means of those straps — with his legs fettered with iron, then Khalaf
b. Qadib followed him, and 'Abdullah b. Khamis Al-'Afifi. The company
met them with joy, and took them in haste to their houses under cover of
night, and there took off their fetters. They had already prepared a boat
specially to flee in, and boarded it that night and went to Mrere,[9] which
is a well-known place in the country of the Duruma which belongs to the
Tribe of Changamwe.

Morning came and news spread of the flight of 'Ali b. 'Uthman and his
company from the Fort. The rulers became fearful and sent scouts and
spies to search for them, but were not led to the place they had gone to,
so that all their trouble went for nothing.

---

[5] *Hamdad ... Halab.* Emery's Translation of the Mombasa Chronicle in Owen's Voyages
(Appendix No. 3) calls them *"Halub bin Bashed* and *Hamidaud Abd al-Balusshi.* Perhaps
the Taylor/Harries Tradition means the latter when it refers to "a slave" (Besari).

[6] **Wall of the Fort.** At the time in question the wall had not been built up to its present
height, but was a breastwork over which the cannon could be fired (Kirkman: Men and
Monuments, p. 161)

[7] **Is currently located** i.e. at the time of writing.

[8] The Mombasa Chronicle (Appendix No. 3) says these men were all WaKilindini.

[9] *Mrere.* See Map, Appendix No. 2. The Mombasa Chronicle says *Murairah.* The Taylor/
Harries Tradition gives *Mrerwa.* Harries says in his note that it is a Nyika Coastal Village.
So also say Guillain and the Mombasa Chronicle. Yet a coastal town would not have been
a good refuge. There is only one Mrere known today, and that is on the road from Kwale
to Kinango where the Digo and Duruma countries adjoin. It is inland behind the Shimba
Hills, and is the site of a Mombasa Water Development Scheme. The fugitive probably went
by sea to Tiwi, and then by land over the Shimba Hills.

The statement that it "belongs to Changamwe" is an indication of the "treaty" relationship between the WaNyika and the "Twelve Tribes" of Mombasa, though according to F. J.
Berg [Journal of African History, Vol. IX, No. 1 (1968) p. 35] such relationships were not
clearly defined. Prins: The Swahili-Speaking Peoples, says at p. 83 that Kilindini is a term for
the "Three Tribes" as a whole, of which Changamwe was one member, and at p. 99 that they
stood in alliance with the Digo and Duruma.

While they were in Mrere, Mr. Cook arrived in Mombasa, the Englishman known among the Swahili as "Mzungu King'ung'u (that is, the "Nazal European") in his ship named the "Mumbay".[10] Mr. Cook was a friend of Muhammad b. 'Uthman. He asked about his friend and was told that he had been killed. Then he asked about his brother and the people told him that he had been imprisoned after his brother's murder, then escaped from the prison and fled no one knew where. This European wanted to meet the brother of his friend in case he should be able to help him, even if only with advice. He met with one of the WaMalindi, who pointed out Mwana Vumbaya;[11] so he went to her, but she denied that she knew anything about him, let alone the place where he was. But she only denied it because she suspected that it was a matter of plotting. After the European had left her however, she sent to 'Ali b. 'Uthman telling him about him, describing him and asking if he would like to meet with him. His reply came back that the man really was his brother's friend, and that he wanted to meet him; so she sent him to Mrere with a faithful guide from among her servants. When he met with him the European asked him what he had determined upon, and 'Ali told him he was resolved to take vengeance,[12] and that he was now preparing to attack the Fort. The European agreed

[10] ***Mzunghu kinghunghu... Mumbay*** — or in Swahili *Mzungu king'ung'u* = The Nasal European, or Foreigner. Note again the difficulty of transliteration. Shaykh Al-Amin has used the more modern convention of writing *Nun, Ghayn* for NG'. Older MSS simply use *Ghayn* for G, GH, NG and NG'.

Shaykh Al-Amin is the only one who names the ship — Bombay. No Arabic or Swahili source names the *Mzungu*. "Mr. Cook" is a guess by Guillain. After transliterating his name as M'ZOUNGO KOGOUGOU he adds a note that it might be "Le Blanc Cook" or "Master Coog". The Mombasa Chronicle simply says Mzungu King'ung'u. The Taylor/Harries Tradition says he was a Portuguese sailor aiming to get into Mombasa for his Government. The most that can be said is as follows: (i) The Swahili term does not imply a proper name. (ii) The name Cook seems to be suggested only by Guillain. (iii) The word "king'ung'u" is definitely declared by Shaykh Al-Amin to mean, expressively enough, "Nazal", i.e. one who speaks through his nose. (iv) He is assumed by most European sources to have been English, but the Swahili oral source recorded by Taylor says he was Portuguese. Nazalised vowels are common in Portuguese.

He must have been a freebooter, or merchant, who had been frequenting the Swahili Coast unofficially. The British Authorities seem to have no one called Cook in their list of pirates of the period. Is such a man on record in Portugal or Moçambique? The term "Nazal" *might* suggest American; but there is no one in U.S.A. Records either, so far as has been discovered. But we must bear in mind, that America, as a separate State, had not yet been born at this period. It should be remembered that the infamous Captain Kidd operated in the Indian Ocean about this time.

[11] **Mwana Vumbaya**. In the Taylor/Harries Tradition this lady does nothing about sending messages to 'Ali b. 'Uthman. This author makes her actions correspond much more fully with his description of her character.

[12] ***Bil-tha'r*** =**(resolved to take) vengeance**. This is the usual word employed in connection with the blood-feud of the Bedu in the Arabian Desert.

with him on this idea, and said to him, "Go ahead with what you have resolved upon, and if you are not successful, I will take you and your followers on my ship, and come back with you next year with other ships (furnished) with all you need in the way of weapons of war, that you may continue fighting until God gives you victory." And He recommended him to make ladders[13] as tall as the height of the walls of the Fort, to mount on when they attacked it. And 'Ali B. 'Uthman approved of his advice, and gave orders to build those ladders.

All this happened while the Liwali was in his refuge, but he was in full communication with his friends the leaders of the WaMalindi and the leaders of the "Three Tribes", and letters were continually passing between them, so that nothing escaped him of what was happening in the town; and when the time appointed for the attack drew near, his friends gathered and consulted as to the manner of the raid and its timing. When they had all become of one mind, they swore allegiance to him[14] as their ruler: but the "Three Tribes" laid on him as a condition in this oath of allegiance that he would concede to them the right to receive the customs dues of Pemba as long as the rule of the Mazari'a continued; and he promised them that, and other things which they wrote in their treaty, which I am sorry to say has been lost.

And when the night of the attack arrived, 'Ali b. 'Uthman went out leading at his back an army of his heroic followers,[15] taking with them the ladders which they had made to scale the Fort with, until they reached it and assaulted it. There took place a violent battle between the two parties in which 'Ali b. 'Uthman won against his enemy. When Sayf b. Khalaf saw the difficulty of his position, he took refuge in one of the towers of the Fort, and fortified himself in it; but they brought a cannon from Mr. Cook's

---

[13] **Ladders.** The Taylor/Harries Tradition says that "Mr. Cook" made the ladders for 'Ali in his ship. Here, as in many other details, this account shows 'Ali as being much more isolated and dependant than do the other accounts.

[14] *Baya'uhu* = **They swore allegiance to him.** This is the Islamic term used for swearing allegiance to the Khalifa. The first time it was used in the religious Islamic sense was on the occasion of the "Oath under the Tree" at Hudaybiya in Muhammad's life-time. See Qur'an 48 vs. 19.

Note here that the "Three Tribes" were able to impose conditions. The Mombasa Chronicle, as quoted in Guillain, Vol. I, p. 620, shows that 'Ali b. 'Uthman also depended on the Nyika tribesmen for his army.

[15] *Al-bawasil* = **Heroes.** This is a difficult word to render well in English. *Basil* means basically a bold fighter or champion. The Arabs will more often than not describe fighting men by some laudatory epithet which in English sounds odd and extravagant if rendered literally.

ship, and fired a shell[16] at him from it so that the tower was broken, and they seized Sayf and killed him.

Mwana Vumbaya was aware[17] of all that was happening concerning 'Ali b. 'Uthman. When that night came she got ready the garments worn at the Swahili dances called "Shindwa",[18] and remained awake listening for the sound of the gun which they had agreed should be the sign of victory and conquest; and when she heard the boom of the cannon she immediately hurried to put on her dance-garments, the hood[19] and the long wide gowns, and took in her hand a pipe[20] of thick bamboo, and began to beat the earth with it and dance before her husband's bed while he was in a deep sleep, and to sing a verse of Swahili poetry which means: "Vengeance does not pass the night with us".[21] That WaKilifi leader, the husband of Mwana Vumbaya, awoke terrified, and when he saw his wife in that condition he was scared of her, and asked her what was the news. And she answered him saying: "Only that 'Ali b. 'Uthman has entered the town and conquered the Fort and taken revenge on the murderer of his brother." Then she returned to her dance, and her singing of that stirring verse, with great joy and pleasure, and turned to her husband and said to him in great pride: "Do you see how *men* act?" She meant by them herself and her party; and the man remained silent and knew not what to say.

Morning came and the news spread, and then the Elders of the town and its important men and those with executive authority in it, both

---

[16] *Qunbula* = **A shell**. The word used nowadays in Arabic for a Bomb, or missile with high explosive in it. One wonders whether "Mr. Cook" would have had shells as opposed to ordinary cannon-balls. If so, where did he obtain them?

[17] **Mwana Vumbaya was aware**. The incident recorded in this paragraph is reported rather differently in the Taylor/Harries Tradition (p. 93, para. 16). The Bamboo pipe or Cylinder is there called *Mvungu*.

[18] *Shindwa*. From the root *shinda* = to conquer, but having also developed forms bearing the meaning of Stamping with the feet, plaiting or interweaving, and receiving a shock on hearing of news. Together these imply a Victory Dance in which the feet stamp the ground with intricate steps. (Oxford Standard Swahili/English Dictionary).

[19] *Al-Tartur*. A pointed Cap such as is worn by traditional Court Jesters in Europe.

[20] *Anbubatun mina 'l-khayzarani 'l-ghaliz*. A bamboo pipe or tube used for beating, not for playing tunes on.

[21] *Al-tha'r*. The Swahili word *Dia* is also an Arabic word, but the meaning ahs become distorted in Swahili from the original meaning which in Arabic is "Blood-money".

'indana la yabit. "Does not pass the night with us." The sense of this is either "Vengeance does not delay with us", or "Vengeance is not a passing thing with us." The same saying in Swahili is *Kwetu dia haiyali. Si kombo.* = "Vengeance with us does not sleep. There is no doubt about it." I.e. We do not delay in executing vengeance.

Arabs and others[22], hurried to the Fort to congratulate[23] the Liwali on his victory, and to swear allegiance to him as Liwali. That was in the year A.H. 1158,[24] that is, about a year after the murder of Muhammad b. 'Uthman, and from this date begins the genuine independence of the Mazru'i rule. The Swahili country came under their rule and authority from Ra's Ngomeni to Pangani,[25] and 'Ali b. 'Uthman gained control of Pemba and united it with his dominions; and all the tribes of that country became their subjects from one end to the other, as we have shown before in the section on the dominion of the Mazari'a.

When the Liwaliship had become safe in the hands of 'Ali b. 'Uthman, he desired to pull out the roots of rebellion, and so ordered the arrest of the WaKilifi[26] leaders and their prominent men, and went about to kill them in requital for what they did to him and his brother. But the "Three Tribes" made intercession for them, and offered him the customs dues of Pemba as redemption for them; and the Liwali accepted the ransom and released them. The "Three Tribes" still remind the WaKilifi of their obligation[27] to them in redeeming them up to this day.

The Imam Ahmad b. Sa'id heard of the fall of the Fort of Mombasa into the hands of 'Ali b. 'Uthman, and the return of the Mazru'i rule in it, and was afraid lest the hands of the Mazari'a would be extended to the Island of Zanzibar, and they occupy it as they had occupied the Island of Pemba. So he sent 'Abdullah b. Ja'id al-Bu Sa'idi[28] as Liwali to Zanzibar with a garrison of soldiers to protect it from the Mazari'a.

---

[22] **Arabs and others.** The "others" include the Swahili "Tribes" and the WaNyika. The Mazari'a regard themselves as Arabs, though they have not lived in Arabia for many generations, and are now, though perhaps not in the days of 'Ali b. 'Uthman, of very mixed blood.

[23] **Yuhannun.** This word should be *Yuhanni'un* = congratulate.

[24] **A.H. 1158 = A.D. 1745.** The whole operation seems to have taken the period between the latter part of the N. E. Monsoon in 1745 and the coming of the N. E. Monsoon in January 1746 — say eight months.

[25] **Ra's Ngomeni to Pangani.** See Map in Appendix No. 2.

[26] **WaKilifi.** The Taylor/Harries Tradition mentions the WaMvita here as well (p. 93, para. 17) It also says (p. 94, para. 18) that the WaKilindini tell 'Ali b. 'Uthman that if he thinks he can kill the WaMvita to satisfy his vengeance he had better think again. This is a little stronger than the "intercession" of Shaykh Al-Amin, and indicates rule by consent again, and we are bound to think that in this respect the Taylor/Harries Tradition is nearer the mark, and that the Liwali was limited in his power.

[27] **Yamannun 'ala 'l-Kilifiyin.** This more usually would mean "Generously grant to them without any prior obligation". Here however it seems to mean "Remind them of how much they are obliged to them and demand of them favours on the strength of it." Guillain mentions at this point a raid by the men of Pate in concert with the WaMvita on Kilindini. He says they were persuaded to leave, or were bought off, with presents.

[28] **'Abdullah b. Ja'id Al-Bu Sa'idi** and his occupation of Zanzibar is mentioned by Guillain at p. 547.

The Mazari'a attack Zanzibar

'Ali b. 'Uthman did not determine to occupy Zanzibar until the last days of his life. In the year A.H. 1168[29] he issued an order to the heads of the Tribes under his rule to muster soldiers and prepare for war. All responded to his command, and the tribe of the WaSegeju[30] arrived at Mombasa under their Amir Kadhimbo, and a great company of WaDigo[31] with their Amir Sayyid Ahmad b. Al-Diwan Abu Bakr b. Shaykh of the family of Masbala; and many of the Arabs who were in Mombasa and Tanga and other places on the Swahili Coast enlisted. 'Ali b. 'Uthman sailed for Zanzibar with many ships in his wake full of fighting men.[32] It is said that the number reached 80 ships big and small, carrying soldiers and bearing provisions and ammunition. They reached Zanzibar and attacked it, and fought the Imam's soldiers, and defeated them and occupied the town, and most of the people fled to Unguja Ukuu.[33]

While they were besieging the Fort, and hard-pressing those who were in it, so that they nearly surrendered to them, lo and behold, Khalaf b. Qadib leaped upon his uncle 'Ali b. 'Uthman, and pierced him with a dagger, accomplishing his murder.[34] He himself was killed immediately, and the two of them died at the same time and were buried where (— here the Author has left a blank —), thus (it is) in the MSS which are in our hands, with no mention either of the reason for the murder, nor the manner of punishing the murderer. The oral traditions however mention both the cause and the manner, but differ concerning them. The Chron-

---

[29] **A.H. 1168** = **A.D. 1754/5**. Probably in spring to make use of the N. E. Monsoon. Major Pearce says (Zanzibar, p. 109) "about 1753", and that it was to keep 'Uman out of Zanzibar. See Note 41 below.

[30] **WaSegeju**. A tribe now almost vestigial, inhabiting the Coast near Wasin Island, Tanga, on either side of the Kenya/Tanzania Border.

[31] **WaDigo**. A tribe now wholly Islamic, living between Likoni (South of Mombasa) and Tanga. At this period however they were wholly pagan.

[32] *bil-muqitala*. A quite orthodox, but unusual, collective. The i vowel after the Qaf is not obvious in the unvowelled MS, and at first sight is liable to be read *Muqatala* = Fighting. (Wehr's Arabic English Dictionary).

[33] **Unguja Ukuu**. The old Capital of Zanzibar Island, now a ruin.

[34] **Accomplishing his murder**. 'Ali died in A.D. 1754/5 according to Shaykh Al-Amin. Guillain and Pearce both put his death in A.D. 1753, while Hardinge puts his successor's succession in A.D. 1762. The Mombasa Chronicle says he reigned eight years agreeing with Guillain. There is a discrepancy here which is unsolved. Shaykh Al-Amin quotes Major Pearce (see below at Note 44) as giving the year of the campaign as A.D. 1753, but without commenting on the fact.

The year A.H. 1168 is probably accurate. This corresponds with the period October A.D. 1754 — October A.D. 1755. It seems then that 'Ali's reign was 11 years, reckoning from Muhammad's murder, **not** from his actually taking power a year later. Reckoning from the latter occasion, he reigned 10 years.

iclers of Mombasa[35] say the reason was the strong desire of Khalaf to have the rule, and his hurry to get it, and that 'Ali b. 'Uthman himself, immediately Khalaf struck him, seized him violently and stuck the dagger in his breast, and they both fell. But the Chroniclers of Wasin[36] relate from Sayyid Abu Bakr b. Qasim[37] of the family of Masbala, who was famous for his knowlege in genealogy and his study of the History of the Mazari'a, that Khalaf was smitten by something like madness and drew his dagger and struck his uncle, and then entered a house and locked the door on himself, and Sayyid Ahmad b. Al-Diwan Abu Bakr went to him, and advised him to open it, and so he opened it, and he seized him, and he was killed by an order from Mas'ud b. Nasir. These ascribe the cause of that to the effect of Magic[38] which the people of Dunga from Zanzibar worked for them.

After this sad event Mas'ud b. Nasir grew pessimistic, and stopped prosecuting the battle and returned with the army to Mombasa. It is not known how long they stayed[39] in Zanzibar before leaving it.

We have made most thorough research into the question of the place where his army disembarked, and where the battle took place, and we have asked about it all whom we fancied would be aware of such information among the old men (Shaykhs), but have not become aware of anything which would satisfy the enquirer (lit. on which the heart would be at peace); but Major Pearce mentions in the course of what he says about East Africa certain information concerning the Mazru'i attack on Zanzibar. I set down here an Arabic translation of what he says, as our friend Salih b. 'Ali b. Salih has translated it in the number dated 17th April

---

[35] **The Chroniclers of Mombasa** This does not mean the "Mombasa Chronicle" of Appendix No. 3, but students of Mombasa traditions in general, The Mombasa Chronicle says that Khalaf was instigated by the Devil, while Guillain (p. 550) says Khalaf was urged on by Mas'ud's ambition.

[36] **The Chroniclers of Wasin.** Shaykh Al-Amin gives no indication which would help to identify whom he is referring to, or whether there are any documents supporting his assertion. Perhaps one day these will be identified.

[37] **Sayyid Ahmad b. Al-Diwan Abu Bakr b. Qasim.** Guillain (p. 551) says "A Chief of the WaSegeju". Presumably this is meant to be identical with the man named here. But see above where the Amir of the WaSegeju is called Kadhimbo. Guillain also says that Khalaf committed the murder in secret, and was called to a council after 'Ali's murder and then slain on the spot.

[38] **Magic.** This is widely feared on the Kenya Coast to this day. Dunga is a town near the East Coast of Zanzibar Island. The meaning of the Expression "the people of Dunga from Zanzibar" may mean either "Zanzibaris living in Dunga" or "People from Dunga living in Zanzibar Town", i.e. Unguja Ukuu.

[39] **It is not known how long they stayed.** The doubt as to the length of the campaign would also influence the tradition as to the length of 'Ali b. 'Uthman's Liwaliship.

A.D. 1923 of the Weekly Supplements he used to publish to the Official Gazette of Zanzibar.[40] He said:

> And when the Liwali realised the small inclination[41] that the Imam had in his policy, to interfere in the affairs of Zanzibar and East Africa, he became acquisitive and determined to subdue Zanzibar. So he got ready for it, and prepared a fleet of sailing Dhows,[42] and made Pemba his base. He attacked Zanzibar and occupied the town, but had no power to assault the Fort. Then his commanders quarrelled among themselves and divided into factions, and their arose rebellion among them which resulted in the murder of 'Ali b. 'Uthman Al-Mazru'i who was ruler of Mombasa. When he was killed, they felt they had failed,[43] and took their ships and withdrew to Mombasa.

And he said in another place, when he mentioned the Fort of Zanzibar, as follows:

> The Mazru'i Arabs attacked that Fort in the year A.D. 1753[44] but they drew back from it, and did not attain their purpose.

Then he said:

> Relying on the records of the Portuguese and upon folk tales, I say that the place of the Town of Zanzibar was at Ra's Shangani.

According to what the Major says, the Mazari'a would have attacked Zanzibar from the direction of Shangani in which there was a Fort, and there the Battle took place — but God knows best the truth of the matter.

'Ali b. 'Uthman, may God be merciful to him, was a brave champion of great hopes and far ambitions. It was these qualities that impelled him to attack Zanzibar. After he had conquered Pemba, if God had given him longer life, he would have continued in his conquests to the furthest

---

[40] This is quoted from Pearce: Zanzibar, Ch. 7, p. 109, but it has not been very accurately rendered by the Translator.

[41] **Small inclination**. Ahmad b. Sa'id was so taken up with establishing his position in 'Uman, that he did not find it easy to send help and supplies to Zanzibar, though he had tried to block the Mazari'a by putting the garrison there earlier — with success as it appears from the event.

[42] *Al-Khashabu 'l-Shira'iya*. Lit. "Wood [equipped with] Sails". *Khashab* means "Wood", but this terms is applied rather to the Sailing Dhows of the Indian Ocean than to ships of the type known in English as "Wooden Walls" or "Bulwarks".

[43] **They felt they had failed**. The pessimism of Mas'ud is testified to by all, but this is not very consistent with the kind of ambition which would have led him to instigate murder. The Author is justified in refusing to mention this imputation. It is much more likely that Khalaf b. Qadib was himself the ambitious one, and that any ambition in the situation died with him.

[44] **A.D. 1753 = A.H. 1167**. See Pearce: Op. Cit. p. 109 and also p. 184. This is a year too soon. See Note 25 above.

limits of East Africa. He left Salim and Sulayman, his sons, and we shall speak of Sulayman later, if God will.

4. The Fourth Liwali — Mas'ud b. Nasir b. 'Abdullah b. Muhammad b. 'Abdullah b. Kahlan

He brings back the Mazru'i Army from Zanzibar — Allegiance is sworn to him as Liwali of Mombasa — The Talk of attacking Zanzibar again — The Treaty between the Mazari'a and the Nabahina and the Reason for it — The Command of Khalaf b. Nasir over the Garrison of the Mazari'a in Pate — The WaKilifi encourage the People of Pate to show hostility to the Mazari'a — The Attack of the People of Pate on Mombasa — The Rebellion in Pate and Accusation of Khalaf b. Nasir of responsibility for it — The People of Pate murder Khalaf — The Revenge of the Mazari'a on the Nabahina in Pemba — The Restoration of the Mazru'i/Nabhani Treaty to its Former Status — the Liwali's Death.

This Liwali of ours Mas'ud is the son of Nasir b. 'Abdullah, the first of the Mazru'i Liwalis under the Imam Sayf b. Sultan Al-Ya'rubi about whom we spoke previously in his biography (i.e. Ch. II, Sect. 1 above).[1] Mas'ud was one of the highest officers in the army of 'Ali b. 'Uthman, which he took with him to make war on Zanzibar. After that sad event had taken place, the murder of 'Ali b. 'Uthman and his nephew Khalaf, the people grew pessimistic about this raid, and their hearts weakened and their strength of purpose grew small. When Mas'ud b. Nasir noticed this tendency of theirs he consulted the heads of the Tribes and the Amirs of "The Tribes"[2] (i.e. the Swahili Tribes of Mombasa) as to whether they should remain in occupation, or return to Mombasa; and they all agreed that they should return to Mombasa, but that the battle should be renewed if they were offered the opportunity. Mas'ud had no alternative but to take their advice, so he returned with the Army to Mombasa, and there

---

[1] In regard to Mas'ud's father Nasir being the Liwali of Sayf b. Sultan I (Qayd al-Ard) see the Comparative Chronological Table in Appendix No. VI, there is confusion over the dating of Bal'arab's abdication or death, and Sayf's accession to the Imamate. Badger indicates that the latter part of Bal'arab's reign was virtually civil war, and it may be that Sayf was effective ruler even though not yet elected Imam.

[2] *Ru'asa' al-Qaba'il wa'umara' al-Tawa'if*. The two expressions mean the Heads of the Nyika Tribes and the Leaders of the Swahili "Tawa'if" (i.e. the "Twelve Tribes"). Shaykh Al-Amin uses the terms in a more appropriate way here. The word *Ta'ifa*, of which *Tawa'if* is the Arabic Plural, has come into the Swahili Language and means "Nation". The word *Amir* is a more Islamic word and falls naturally into use in referring to the Swahili Afro-Arab Tribes.

allegiance was sworn to him as Liwali in succession to 'Ali b. 'Uthman. That was in the year A.H. 1168.[3]

The Talk of Making a Second Attack on Zanzibar

It is said that Mas'ud started to prepare equipment to renew the attack on Zanzibar again, and sent information about that to Wasin: and Sayyid Hasan b. Abu Bakr b. Shaykh gathered for him an army of WaDigo "Braves"; then he (i.e. Hasan) sent to Kadhimbo, the head of the Tribe of WaSegeju, calling him to meet him in Wasin with his company, to await the Liwali's passing by them, that they might travel with him to Zanzibar. The Liwali came out of Mombasa with his army and passed by Wasin Island, and Sayyid Hasan and Kadhimbo, chief of the WaSegeju, were waiting with a great host of the people from us (i.e. from our country) to Zanzibar. This is what we have been told by the folk of Takaungu and Wasin, but their stories differ in respect of the place where the army disembarked this time, and in the manner of the fighting. Many deny the occurrence of this second attack. This is what I am inclined to think, because I have never seen anything which gives evidence of it either in the Historical MSS. which are in our hands, or in European Books: and anyone who knows the Liwali's biography, and his great concern over the safety of his country, and his avoidance of anything that would stir up rebellions and wars, will be convinced of the incorrectness of this story.[4]

The Treaty between the Mazari'a and the Nabahina

In the days of Mas'ud b. Nasir a treaty was made between the Mazari'a and the Nabahina, and the two parties agreed on mutual support, help and defence, and to show no hostility to one another, and that the Nabahina should send a garrison under one of their Amirs to Pemba, and the Mazari'a should send a garrison under one of their Amirs to Pate. To show the reason for the Treaty I will set down here what the folk of Pate have recorded in their historical MSS. They said:

---

[3] **A.H. 1168** = A.D. 1754. See the previous section for discussion of the discrepancies in the dating of 'Ali b. 'Uthman's Liwaliship.

[4] There is not any reference elsewhere to a second expedition, but it is obvious that Mas'ud must have been always thinking of it; for he must have known that as long as 'Uman was weak, and unable to attend to its East African base in Zanzibar, he had the best chance of driving out the Bu Sa'idi Liwali there, and making Mombasa dominant on the Coast of East Africa. His thinking, consulting and planning probably became exaggerated into an actual expedition.

"Between the years A.H. 1160 and 1177[5] there ruled over Pate Bwana Tamu the Younger Abu Bakr b. Bwana Mkuu,[6] and in his day the Imam determined to subdue Pate, and sent there an army, and made war on the Sultan and fought him violently, but it did not go in the Imam's favour, so his army returned back after a great part of them had been killed."

From this therefore it appears that the reason for this treaty and the sending by each party of a garrison of soldiers to the country of the other was mutual help in driving off the army of the Imam, who was wanting to gain the mastery of the countries of both parties by force. This state of affairs lasted for some time, and the Mazari'a used to send their garrison to Pate with one of their commanders, and he would stay for a time then return, and another would be sent in the same way in his turn: this also the Nabahina used to do in Pemba.

Khalaf b. Nasir b. Khalaf Al-Mazru'i was among those who were sent to Pate as Amir over the Mazru'i garrison. But Khalaf was not very laudable in his behaviour, and the people of Pate hated him because of his bad relationship with them, and they hated all the Mazari'a because of him.

The WaKilifi who were in Mombasa knew of these circumstances of Khalaf and of his evil behaviour; so they started to encourage the people

---

[5] **Between the years A.H. 1160 and 1177**. That is between A.D. 1747 and 1763.

[6] **Bwana Tamu the Younger Abu Bakr b. Bwana Mkuu**. Cf. Guillain Pt. I pp. 547, 551 and 552. Guillain begins his account with the reign of Fumo Bakari bin Bwana Tamu, and also mentions a certain Bwana "Melani Ngiombe" — i.e. "Cowherd" — who was replaced by Fumo Bakari's sister Mwana Mimi ruling through her wazir, Fumo 'Umar. When he sought marriage however, she sent him to Brava, and he was replaced by Fumo Luti, her young brother. It was this man whose position was established by help of Mombasa under Ahmad b. Muhammad, and then under Khalaf b. Nasir.

Shaykh Al-Amin does not mention Pate's internal quarrels directly, but he is in agreement with the above in three respects: (a) Mombasa was dominant, for whereas the Mazru'i garrison was sent to Pate itself, the garrison of Pate was sent only to Pemba, not Mombasa. This means that Mombasa was able to dictate the terms. (b) The object of the liaison was to keep out the new 'Umani house of Bu Sa'idi as completely as possible. (c) He agrees in making Khalaf b. Nasir one of the Mazru'i Amirs in Pate.

The History of Pate (Freeman-Grenville: The East African Coast, pp. 241–296) gives a version of these stories from the Nabhani point of view, and Mwana Mimi becomes Mwana Khadija, or so it would seem. The unpublished document known as "*Kawkab al-Dhurriya*" (a copy of which is in my possession) gives a rather different impression by averring that while the Nabahina were in treaty with the Mazari'a, yet they had to be consulted at each Mazru'i succession and approve the next candidate before he could be appointed. The Nabhani Tribe were in fact biassed against the Mazru'i Liwalis, and the rancour comes out in "*Kawkab Al-Dhurriya*".

of Pate to show hostility to the Mazari'a.[7] There was a group among the
WaKilifi called Beni Kibanda,[8] who had a blood-relationship between
some of them and the people of Pate: and they sent them letter after letter
calling on them to make war on the Mazari'a in Mombasa, and urging
them to it, and promising to give them help for that purpose, both themselves and the other tribes who were members of their party.

They informed the Sultan of Pate himself of that, but the Sultan paid
no attention to these attempts to stir up hostility. But when the relations
of the Beni Kibanda saw that the Sultan was careless of the opinion of
their relations who were in Mombasa, it made them indignant, and they
made an agreement with the common people of Pate, and the lowest of
them, to make a raid on Mombasa. So their ships arrived and anchored
in the waters of Kilindini, and made havoc in the land, and killed whoever
met them there, and seized the women and boys [subyan] with the intention of taking them prisoners of war: but immediately the news reached
the Liwali he sent a company of soldiers to fight them, and many of the
people of Pate were killed. When those who were in the ships saw what
had come upon their companions they spread the sails and escaped with
their lives, and others fled and took refuge with their relatives the Beni
Kibanda; and the latter took them across the Creek[9] and sent them to
Ribe, and they hid there.

The Liwali sent his order to the people of Ribe[10] to deliver up the
criminals, but since there was friendship and agreement between the
people of Ribe and the people of Kilifi, they refused to deliver them up.[11]

The Liwali decided to send soldiers to them, to seize the criminals and
to punish the people of Ribe if they should continue from day to day in
sheltering the enemy. There was at that time a man of the WaKilifi whose

---

[7] **To show hostility to the Mazari'a**. Guillain gives another reason for this war. He says Fumo
Madi, brother of Fumo Luti, wanted Pate independent of Mombasa as well as of 'Uman,
that he made alliance with the Bajun, or WaGunya of Faza, and met Fumo Luti and Khalaf
b. Nasir in battle as a result of which the two latter were killed (p. 552).

He says nothing of the Wakilifi, nor of a raid at this stage on Mombasa, though we can
well imagine that they may have had a finger in this pie. But see also Note 27 on the previous
section.

[8] **Beni Kibanda**. Or Mbari Kibanda. See the prefatory note on the Mombasa Tribes and F. J.
Berg's Paper referred to therein, p. 19. Also Prins: Op. Cit. p. 99.

[9] *Al-Shatt*. The Creek between Mombasa Island and the Mainland. On the assumption that
they were in the region of Kilindini, they probably crossed to Kipevu or Changamwe, and
so up to Ribe.

[10] *Ribe — Rib(e)*. In Arabic Script this can be written with, or without, a final Ya. Another
instance of the unstable spelling of Swahili words in Arabic Script.

[11] Here is another indication of the powerlessness of the Mazari'a to enforce their orders in
Nyika tribal territory, except indirectly.

name was Mi'raj b. Mira (?)[12] who professed to be[13] very friendly with the Mazari'a. He sent to the Liwali, and asked him for permission to go to Ribe, and promised to bring the criminals on the third day. So the Liwali gave him permission, and he went and spoke to the people on the matter of delivering up the criminals, and cautioned them against the evil consequences: but his words did not strike ears which would listen[14] to him, so he returned to Mombasa disappointed.

The people of Pate seized that opportunity, and travelled by land to their own country, and there they composed a poem in the Swahili language containing abuse of the Liwali, and of Khalaf b. Nasir and some of the prominent men of the "Three Tribes", in which they mentioned them by name; and they boasted in that poem about the raid which they carried out in Kilindini, and we shall record this Poem in the Swahili version of this book, if God will![15]

The Rebellion in Pate and the Accusation that Khalaf shared in it

In the tour of duty of the above-named Khalaf b. Nasir, there happened in Pate a dreadful and painful occurrence which nearly broke the friendship between the Mazari'a and the Nabahina. This was that in the year A.H. 1190[16] there occurred a rebellion against the Sultan Bwana Mkuu b. Shekhe[17] b. Bwana Tamu Mkuu; for he was hated by his subjects, and some of them determined to break in and murder him.[18] But they knew

---

[12] *Mira.* A copy of the MS of this work in my possession seems to show that this should be *Mbira*, but it is by no means clear.

[13] *kana yatazahar.* This word often has the meaning of "pretending" falsely; but here it seems to be used more in the sense of "professed" or "showed", since in his course of action here Mi'raj shows no hint of treachery or desire to deceive.

[14] *Tusghu.* This is in the original MS but in my Photocopy of the MS it has been corrected to *Tusghi*, which is right after *Adhanan*.

[15] These poems have yet to be recorded.

[16] A.H. 1190 = A.D. 1776. This disagrees with Guillain who puts the death of Mas'ud b. Nasir in A.D. 1774 (p. 552), adding simply that the death precluded further hostilities between Pate and Mombasa, which otherwise would have been inevitable because of the coming to power of Fumo Madi.

[17] *Shaykhe.* Another "Arabicised" spelling of a Swahili name. The word is uttered in Swahili with a light H, but the man of Arabic learning cannot forget that it is basically an Arabic term. So he writes and pronounces it SHAY*KH*E.

[18] It seems that this party of assassins must be identified with Guillain's Bajun or WaGunya; but he says the Sultan is Fumo Luti (Foum" Alote), not Bwana Mkuu b. Shehe b. Bwana Tamu Mkuu. The two *may* be the same person. The Nabhani Sultans seem to have had Arabic names and Swahili titles or nicknames, and this is probably the cause of some of the confusion.

that they could not enter because the doors were locked[19] against them. On the other hand, they knew that Khalaf had a time each day when he entered the Sultan's presence, and so they all agreed to lie in wait in a place, awaiting that time, so that, when the door was opened, they might enter with him. One day Khalaf went to the Sultan as usual and sat on a bench awaiting the summons; but when the door was opened for him, here came the mob of Pate emerging from their ambush, racing to attack the Sultan and assassinate him; and they entered together with Khalaf in a crowd. When Khalaf saw what they had come for, he put forth his utmost effort to defend the Sultan. While he was engaged in this, one of the Beni 'Abd al-Salam of the house of the Wazirs of Pate sought him out and slew him, thinking that he had a share with those base men in their hateful doings, or that it was he who had planned this treacherous plot. So after that the Nabahina feared the vengeance of the Mazari'a[20] on those of their number who were on Pemba; so they sent to them telling them what had happened, so that they might take warning and escape with their lives before the news reached the Mazari'a there. But they had no wish to flee and stayed on the Island prepared to defend themselves; and when the news reached the Mazari'a who were on the Island they attacked them and slew them. But after these disasters had happened it became clear to the Nabahina that the accusation they had levelled against Khalaf was not in place, and that he was innocent of it; and they regretted his murder, and sent to the Liwali apologising and he accepted their apology (He excused them!).

Mas'ud b. Nasir was among those well-known for their cleverness (cunning, craft — but here not in a bad sense), and he did not wish to let grudges remain in the hearts of the WaMombasa and the people of Pate through the killings that had come about between them on both sides. So he strove with all his might and cleverness until he did away with rancour in the hearts of all and pulled it out by the roots, and the waters returned to their proper courses (i.e., the situation became normal), and the alliance between the Mazari'a and the Nabahina remained as it was, and indeed firmer than it was. But the Nabahina did not send any more garrison after

---

[19] **Liqafl**. This is grammatically quite correct (see Wehr's Arabic/English Dictionary), but it is more usual to use the fourth form *Iqfal*.

[20] **Feared the vengeance of the Mazari'a**. The fear of vengeance is a controlling factor in Arab society even today, and it certainly has an inhibiting influence upon progress and development of society. As it operates tribally, not individually, the Mazari'a would regard it as quite legitimate to exact satisfaction from the blood of the Nabhani Tribe elsewhere. Guillain says that the Nabhani agent in Pemba was called Badi Sulayman, presumably the Commander of the Nabhani Garrison there.

those who were killed in this trouble, while the Mazari'a continued to send one until Sayyid Sa'id b. Sultan conquered Pate.

Mas'ud b. Nasir died in the Fort of Mombasa in the year A.H. 1193 after remaining in office as Liwali for 25 years[21]. He was buried in the Fort near the place where the mast was set up, but every vestige of his grave has been effaced owing to the successive rule of foreign hands over the Fort. Mas'ud (May God be merciful to him) was of good character, loved by his clan and by all people. He was very far from desiring strife and warfare. For this reason there was never in his long Liwaliship any war of slaying except the punishment of those people of Pate who raided Mombasa; but the talk of his making a second attack on Zanzibar has, in my opinion, no reliability at all. He was (May God be merciful to him) much engaged in trade, and he facilitated it for the people by his measures for security in the country. His days were days of prosperity, ease and peace.

The Liwali was survived by eight sons — Badawi, 'Imran, Ahmad, 'Abdullah, Rashid, Nasir, Khamis and Muhammad. Of these Ahmad b. Mas'ud alone had offspring. Among his descendants are the excellent Qadi of Malindi, the learned Nasir b. Ahmed b. Muhammad, as we have already shown in the first chapter of this book, and God knows best.[22]

5. The Fifth Liwali — 'Abdullah b. Muhammad b. 'Uthman b. 'Abdullah Al-Mazru'i

When Mas'ud b. Nasir died the Mazari'a disagreed as to whom they should make Liwali in succession to him. Every one of the sons of the Liwalis proposed himself, and there was a violent contention between them. Finally they were reconciled and agreed to make 'Abdullah b. Muhammad b. 'Uthman Liwali. This was on the day on which Mas'ud b. Nasir passed on to the next world, in the year A.H. 1193.[1]

This 'Abdullah b. Muhammad is the first of the Mazru'i Liwalis to be born on the Swahili Coast. The four Liwalis who preceded him were

---

[21] **A.H. 1193** = A.D. 1779. But Hardinge says he died in 1787 (= A.H. 1201). This is plainly incorrect as is his genealogical table (see Appendix No. IV). The Mombasa Chronicle says that Mas'ud ruled 24 years, but this may omit the odd part-year. Guillain says 1774, but the weight of evidence makes this five years too early, while Hardinge's date must be one of those which Sir John Kirke declared to be inaccurate (See Kirke's letter in Appendix No. IV).

[22] See the First Lineage in Chapter I above, and also Appendix No. I, Table C1.

[1] **A.H. 1193** = A.D. 1779 (the beginning of the year). Guillain agrees that 'Abdullah b. Muhammad's Liwaliship was uneventful.

all born in 'Uman. The Liwali died in the year A.H. 1195[2] after completing almost two years in his Liwaliship, and he was (May God be merciful to him) of good character like his predecessor and far from (the desire of) making war.

He was survived by two sons, 'Ali and Muhammad, and his line has come to an end.

6. The Sixth Liwali — Ahmad b. Muhammad b. 'Uthman b. 'Abdullah b. Muhammad Al-Mazru'i

His Liwaliship — The rebellion of Mwinyi Simba Sultan of Tanga against the Liwali — Preparations for Rebellion in Tanga — The Liwali sends the Army to subdue it — The Diwan Hasan reconciles the Liwali and the Sultan of Tanga — The Arrival of the Sultan in Mombasa to offer his submission — Trouble in Pate between its people and the People of Lamu and the reason for it — The Liwali Ahmad goes to make reconciliation between them — The Reason for the Attack on Lamu — What the People of Lamu and the People of Mombasa say about it — The Battle of Shela — The Defeat of the Army of the Mazari'a and the Nabahina and the Reason for it — The People of Lamu make Sayyid Sa'id b. Sultan King of their Country — The sons of Mas'ud b. Nasir revoke their Allegiance, and their Reason for doing so — The Civil War between them and the Liwali — They flee to Rabai and Duruma — The Murder of those who fled to Rabai — Mwinyi Hiji b. Faki brings those who fled to Duruma — The Loyalty of the "Three Tribes" to the Mazari'a — The Prohibition of Blood-shedding between them — The Removal of Sharif Sa'id from the Shaykhdom and the Promotion of Ahmad b. Shaykh in his Place — The Bad Administration of the Amir 'Abdullah b. Ahmad — The Death of the Liwali (God's mercy upon him).

The Liwali Ahmad b. Muhammad was the second son of Muhammad b. 'Uthman. He was born in Mombasa and became Liwali after the death

---

[2] **A.H. 1195** = A.D. 1780 (the end of the year). Guillain says he ruled seven years, and that the date on his grave is A.H. 1197 (A.D. 1782). In either case it would be the month of Muharram, and Guillain gives the inscription on his grave, which was presumably in a better state that it is now (Guillain, p. 624)

Shaykh Al-Amin may be credited here for the following reasons: (a) It is possible that Guillain misread 7 for 5 on the tomb, the Arabic form for the figure 5 at that time leaving the door open for confusion. (b) The period of inaction by 'Uman, as related by Guillain, did not end till A.H. 1198 = A.D. 1784. Guillain may not have known so much about the events related in the next section below, and since 'Abdullah b. Muhammad was known to have had an uneventful reign, he may well have assumed that all of this period lay in his Liwaliship. The reading of the gravestone confirmed him in his opinion.

of his brother 'Abdullah b. Muhammad b. 'Uthman in the year A.H. 1195.[1]
All his clan and the People of authority in Mombasa swore allegiance to
him.[2]

You already know from what precedes that the Mazari'a stretched out
their hands upon all that country which lies between Malindi and Pangani.
It was their practice to appoint liwalis under their authority over every
town (or, district) which lay within those limits, yet without removing their
Sultans from their Sultanates, nor their heads from their leadership. It
happened in the time of this Liwali Ahmad b . Muhammad that the Sultan
of Tanga, Mwiny Simba the Great (or, the Elder)[3] revolted, and revoked
his allegiance to the Mazari'a, and got ready for a rebellion. The Liwali
of Tanga sent to Mombasa to inform the Liwali of what Mwinyi Simba
was doing and what he intended. The Liwali got ready an Army to make
war on him and subdue him, and he made his son 'Abdullah b. Ahmad[4]
commander of this Army. The ships which transported this Army arrived
at the Island of Wasin, whose Sultan was the Diwan Hasan b. Nasir[5]
known as the Diwan Shaykh. There was friendship between the Diwan
and Mwinyi Simba, as there was between him and the Mazari'a; so the
Diwan did not think good to see his two friends fighting together within
his own sight and hearing. He went forth therefore to the Amir 'Abdullah
b. Ahmad, and asked him to put off the war until he should have spoken
to Mwinyi Simba and advised him to return to his allegiance. The Amir
granted his request, and the Diwan acted as intercessor to reconcile, and

---

[1] **A.H. 1195** = A.D. 1780/1.

[2] **Swore allegiance to him**. At this point Guillain leaves a period of several years blank; for
he says (p. 567): "Au moment de l'élection de Sa'id ben Soultan" (A.H. 1221 = A.D. 1806)
aucun changement politique n'était survenu à Patta, Mombasa, Zanzibar, Kiloua, depuis
l'expedition faite, par Ahmed be Sa'id peu après l'avènement de son pére à l'Imamat (A.H.
1198 = A.D. 1784)". But Guillain says that Mombasa recognised the sovereignty of Sa'id b.
Sultan. This must refer to the visit of Hamid (Ahmad, Hamad) b. Sa'id "Hubub al-Ghabash"
(see Introduction p. 5 above) who extracted an admission of Bu Sa'idi sovereignty from
Ahmad b. Muhammad Al-Mazru'i in writing. There is some confusion as to the name of the
visitor, but Shaykh Al-Amin is silent on this incident.

[3] *Mwinyi Simba*. This is the man holding the pre-Portuguese office of Sultan, since the
Portuguese mostly left the indigenous rulers. He was probably Shirazi in origin (Prins: Op.
Cit., p. 96).

[4] *'Abdullah b. Ahmad*. He became Liwali of Mombasa after his father and ruled form
A.D. 1814–1823.

[5] *Hasan b. Nasir*. According to Prins (Op. Cit., p. 95) this is part of the Vumba polity. It
arose as a Shirazi State, but its ruler, the Diwan, originated shortly before A.D. 1700, when
a Sharif of the Ba 'Alawi immigrated from the Comoros and changed the ruler's title from
Mwana Kiambi to Diwan. Prins also thinks that the title *Diwan* implies a charismatic
component. This is of significance in the quarrel with Kubu related in the next section (see
note No. 6 in that section).

bring to an end the misunderstanding,[6] which existed between the two parties. He succeeded in doing this, and brought Mwinyi Simba to Mombasa to offer his submission and apologise, and the Liwali accepted his excuses and pardoned him and treated him kindly.[7]

There occurred in the reign of Ahmad great trouble in Pate between the family of Nabhan and the People of Lamu. The reason for this trouble according to the historical MSS of Lamu,[8] was that Bwana Bakari b. Bwana Mkuu, one of the Sultans of Pate, had married a woman in Lamu from the highest of its People, by whom he had two daughters whom he carried off to Pate. One of them married Bayai b. Shehe (?), one of the Sultan's family, and he had by her a son whom he named Fumo Luti, and when Bwana Madi[9] became Sultan of Pate, he bequeathed the Sultanate after him to this Fumo Luti b. Bayai. He simply did that in his desire to put an end to the hatred which dominated (the relationship) between the People of Lamu and the Nabahina. When the above-mentioned Bwana Madi died, his near relatives and his clan disobeyed this will, and swore allegiance to another than the one to whom the bequest was made, (It is most probable that it was the Sultan Muhammad b. Abu Bakr b. Bwana Mkuu),[10] and there took place a great revolt against this Sultan. A party of the Nabahina took sides with the one who was indicated in the will, while others sided with the Sultan to whom allegiance had been sworn. When this information reached the people of Lamu, some of its people travelled to Pate to give support to Fumo Luti, because of the blood- and maternal-uncle-relationship that existed between them. The trouble grew worse, and intelligent men feared there would be unhealthy consequences, for there was no one whose word was acceptable to both parties so that he would be able to quench the brand of insurrection by speaking a word in season, (lit. by the aptness or relevance of his opinion). So a party of

---

[6] *Su' al-tafahum*. This is a rather euphemistic manner of describing the relationship between Ahmad b. Muhammad and Mwinyi Simba. They probably understood one another perfectly. It is however common to describe such situations in a very restrained manner in Arabic.

[7] It is possible that Mwinyi Simba had heard about the visit of Ahmad (Hamid?) b. Sa'id Al-Bu Sa'idi to Mombasa, and of his exacting a confession of 'Umani suzerainty over it. This is the kind of thing which might disturb local loyalties.

[8] **The historical MSS of Lamu**. For "A Chronicle of Lamu" see Bantu Studies, Vol. III No. 1, (March 1938) pp. 8–33, at pp. 18/19.

[9] *Bwana Madi*. This seems to be the same as Sultan Fumo Madi, who according to the "History of Pate" died in, or a little before, A.H. 1224 = A.D. 1809.

[10] *Sultan Muhammad b. Abu Bakr b. Bwana Mkuu*. This is the man, it would seem, whom Guillain calls "Ouizir", and whom he says was made Sultan Ahmad (p. 586). European writers appear to have got confused between the names Ahmad, Hamid, Hammad, Humayd and Muhammad. This is not surprising as names basically Arabic were transformed on entering Swahili. Even Swahili writers seem to have got confused, so it is not to be wondered at that Europeans should also be muddled, since they would hear two forms of those names.

them travelled to Mombasa, and set forth the whole matter to the Liwali, desiring him to journey to Pate to put down that trouble and to resolve the quarrel between the two parties. So he travelled there and made a reconciliation which satisfied everyone; and the People of Lamu returned to their country. The Liwali stayed some days hospitably and honourably received by its people, then he set off back to Mombasa after leaving there a garrison composed of 500 soldiers, and setting over them as commander his son Amir 'Abdullah b. Ahmad.[11] He passed by Lamu, and its people received him with honour and respect. They decided to make him ruler of their country for fear of the violence of the Nabahina and to prevent their oppression of, and hostility to, them. They began to build its (i.e. Lamu's) Fort[12] with the idea of handing it over to him after the building of it was completed. While there the Liwali got acquainted with Rashid b. Dalham Al-Shukayli, the Great-Grandfather of Rashid b. Sa'ud, one of the important men of Mombasa; and the Liwali awakened in him a desire to make Mombasa his home, and he wanted it: so Rashid prepared for a journey and came to Mombasa and adopted it as his home instead of Lamu.

While the Amir 'Abdullah was in Pate, a firm friendship grew between him and its Sultan because of their similarity of temperament; for they were both brave and heroic and fond of war. So the Sultan and the Amir agreed to attack Lamu and gain the mastery of it by force (conquest); but the traditions differ as to the cause of this war. What I have seen in the historical MSS of Lamu[13] is, that the reason for it was that the Liwali

[11] Guillain mentions "Ali b. 'Abdullah as Mazru'i Agent" (p. 586).

[12] **They began to build its Fort**. So says the "History of Pate" (Freeman-Grenville: East African Coast, p. 274), adding "for fear of the violence of the Nabahina".

The confusion apparent in the different accounts of these episodes undoubtedly arose, at least in part, from the complicated clash and interplay of interest and fears in Mombasa, Pate, Lamu and 'Uman, as well as from the fact that different sections of the population in each community favoured different policies and allies.

[13] See "A Chronicle of Lamu", Op. Cit., at pp. 18–20). Guillain may have based his summary of these events on the above Chronicle of Lamu. We quote his account verbatim here from p. 568:

A la suite de sa defaite, Foum' Aloute emmèné a Mombasa et jeté dans un prison, y fut, dit-on, étranglé quelque temps après. Ses partisans s'étaient retiré à Lamou, dont ils avaient décidé la population à ne pas reconnaître l'autorité du nouveau chef de Patta. Lamou devint, à cette occasion, le theâtre d'une lutte à laquelle le cheikh de Mombasa prit personellement une part active. Il marcha contre la ville, et, n'ayant pu s'en emparer dans une première attaque, il en fit le siège. Une second attaque tentée par lui sembla d'abord être plus heureuse. Il était arrivé avec ses troupes au pied des murailles, dont l'une des portes était déjà brisée, lorsque les habitants firent une vigoureuse sortie, forcèrent les assiègeants a s'enfuir, et, les poursuivant jusque sur le rivage, en tuèrent bon nombre et obligèrent le reste à s'embarquer. Ahmed-ben-Muhammad, vaincu, retourna a Mombasas. Ces derniers evènements occupèrent l'intervalle compris entre la fin d 1221 at celle d 1225 (de 1807 à 1811).

Ahmad b. Muhammad reconciled the People of Lamu and the People of Pate, and returned to Mombasa; and then the People of Pate seized Fumo Luti, he who had been bequeathed the Sultanate, and sent him to Mombasa, and there order was given for his execution; and that after the People of Lamu had agreed to unite with the Liwali against the People of Pate, the Liwali broke this agreement and united with the People of Pate, and sent to Lamu a man of the Mazari'a named 'Abdullah b. Zahir to enquire into the circumstances of its people. When this man arrived the People of Lamu got ready a house for him to occupy, but he refused to stay in the town, and passed the night in his ship. Thus the People of Lamu suspected that he was with the Nabahina; and in order to find out what was his real intention, Bwana Zahidi Mngumi,[14] the Head of the People of Lamu, made food which he sent to him at night with a letter by the hand of a sailor, making him imagine that it was from the Sultan of Pate; and in it the Sultan "thinks that his attack on Lamu is too delayed, and shows amazement at him for that, and urges him to hasten it on". 'Abdullah b. Zahir was deceived and thought the food and the letter were from his friend the Sultan of Pate, since no one knew the secret but them; and he wrote an answer with his own hand, saying, "The People of Lamu are building the fort; and the affair will be after the completion of the building of it". He delivered the answer to the sailor, and the latter conveyed it to Bwana Zahidi. When it was clear to him what 'Abdullah b. Zahir intended, he gathered all the Shaykhs of Lamu, and informed them of the letter. Then he sent to 'Abdullah b. Zahir (requesting him) to attend the council, and when he was present he brought out the letter for him, and he admitted that it was from him and was very much ashamed, and left the meeting at once and embarked in his ship and returned to Pate. There the agreement was completed with the Sultan to make war against the People of Lamu. After that 'Abdullah b. Zahir brought a great Army composed of many of the folk of Mombasa and of Pate; but they were broken thoroughly, and defeated, and turned their backs in flight.

This is what is stated by the writer of those historical MSS. But if we

---

The History of Pate (Freeman-Grenville, Op. Cit.) gives a somewhat disorderly account of this same occasion, in which the facts are the same, but its place in the main course of events is quite vague. (pp. 274/5). The man whom Shaykh Al-Amin refers to as 'Abdullah b. Zahir in this text is there simply called "the Governor".

[14] *Mghumi*. This form in Arabic script is the best that Arabic can do for the Swahili MNGUMI. I have transliterated it as a Swahili name in that form on the authority of Shaykh Muhammad b. Qasim Al-Mazru'i, late Chief Qadi of Kenya.

examine it, we cannot see that it is sufficient reason[15] why the Mazari'a and the Nabahina should wage war against the People of Lamu: on the contrary we can see that there is sufficient reason why the People of Lamu should raid Mombasa and Pate. Then it is in the highest degree improbable that 'Abdullah b. Zahir, whom they allege was accompanied only by those in his ship, should attack the People of Lamu, many and brave as they were. And Fumo Luti[16] whom they say was killed in Mombasa, is mentioned in the MSS. of Pate, as having returned from there, and the Mazari'a as having taken part with him in his war against the people of Pate and Sayyid Sa'id b. Sultan until he conquered Siyu.

Further, there is in this story a bare-faced error which is not apparent except to the Mazari'a themselves, and those who, like them have a grasp of their battles (or, of the events of their history). The said error is the connection of this occurrence with 'Abdullah b. Zahir; whereas there are only two who are called by this name, not a third in addition, and one of them had died before this battle by some years, while the other was never made an Amir, nor led an Army. What is well-known among the Mazari'a and all the chroniclers is that the man connected with the Battle of Shela is 'Abdullah b. Ahmad b. Muhammad b. 'Uthman.[17]

There is another version[18] of the reason for this war which is related by the Mombasa Chroniclers and those of Wasin and Takaungu, that the Amir 'Abdullah had made a covenant with Ahmad b. Shaykh, before he became Sultan, that they would help each other, whenever need of help arose; and that after Ahmad b. Shaykh took office, he demanded from the People of Lamu "Kikanda",[19] which means among them duty on produce,

[15] **We cannot see that it is sufficient reason**. In the period in which these events took place, it is a little doubtful whether Shaykh Al-Amin is correct in saying that no sufficient reason appears why Mombasa should attack Lamu. Whatever Mombasa's attitude to Lamu itself, it was still primarily concerned to keep 'Uman out; and on his own showing, there was a section of the People of Lamu who were opposed to the Mazari'a, and presumably wanted to bring 'Uman in. Certainly Lamu was the first of the Coast Towns to ask for 'Umani protection.

[16] **And Fumo Luti . . . is mentioned**. The relevant passage may be found in the "History of Pate" (Op. Cit., at pp. 282–4), also in the Chronicle of Lamu, pp. 18 and 19. *Conquered Siyu.* See "History of Pate" (Op. Cit. p. 286).

[17] **'Abdullah b. Ahmad**. I.e. son of the ruling Liwali of this section. The first 'Abdullah b. Zahir mentioned here by Shaykh Al-Amin is son of the Ancestor of the Third Lineage in Chapter 1 above. See also Appendix I C3. The other is nowhere else mentioned in this book.

[18] **There is another version**. The History of Pate (Freeman-Grenville: Op. Cit., pp. 269–271) has an incident like that here described concerning the Kikanda, but it puts it in the reign of Bwana Madi, or Fumo Madi, whom it calls the last great Sultan of Pate. This is the period described at Note No. 8 above. Here it is possible that Shaykh Al-Amin may be confused, and may have attached the Kikanda tradition to the wrong period.

[19] **Kikanda** means a Little Bag of Plaited Matting (Oxford Standard Swahili/English Dictionary).

but they failed to pay it to him because it was not customary with them in the time of his forebears. So he determined to make war on them, and the Amir 'Abdullah b. Ahmad promised to help him with the garrison which was under his command in Pate. After that the Amir went to Lamu to study its circumstances, and it happened as we have said regarding the People of Lamu becoming aware of his evil intentions. Then he left them and made for Pate. There they prepared for the attack on it (Lamu). He himself sent to the People of Lamu verses of Swahili poetry summoning them to war, and the People of Lamu answered him with poetry also which expressed a great mind and apt intentions. We shall set down these verses in their full text in the Swahili version of this book, if God will.[20] But the Pate MSS. are silent about revealing anything of the causes of this war.

The Battle of Shela

After that,[21] the Sultan Ahmad[22] in partnership with the Amir 'Abdullah got ready a numerous Army in which there was sufficient to conquer the People of Lamu and overcome them and gain the mastery of their Island. They loaded them on to a number of ships with a perfect tally of supplies and munitions of war. There were in Lamu at that time two parties, Zayni and Sa'udi. The Zayni party were friendly with[23] the Mazari'a and liked them, and did not join in this war at first. When the Amir reached Lamu with his Army he disembarked them at Shela.[24] The People of Lamu were ready to fight them to their last breath. So they joined battle, the two parties, and the millstones of war turned, and the battle grew hot, and the People of Lamu were hard pressed, and they withdrew to behind the hill of Hedabu.[25] When the Zayni party saw their compatriots hard-pressed, they feared a defeat which would lead to the humiliation of all of them; so they broke their covenant, and joined with the Sa'udi party in defence of their homeland, and the scales tipped in their favour and lightened on

[20] The verses of 'Abdullah b. Ahmad have been recovered, and are now reproduced in Appendix V by the kindness of the late Mr. John Allen from MS. No. 207 in the Library of the University of Dar-es-Salaam.

[21] **After that**. The "History of Pate" (Freeman-Grenville: Op. Cit. p. 276) gives an account of this Battle substantially in agreement with the course of events as given here. The "Chronicle of Lamu" (pp. 26 and 27) adds extra information.

[22] **The Sultan Ahmad**. This is Ahmad b. Shaykh, not the Mombasa Liwali.

[23] *Kana muwaliyan*. I have rendered this phrase "were friendly with", but it could also mean, "were clients of".

[24] **Shela**. This is a beach on the East Coast of Lamu Island. See Map, Appendix II.

[25] **Hedabu**. Apparently, the Swahili form of an Arabic word *Hadab* = a Hump, or Small Hill. It has also become a Proper Name.

the side of the Mazari'a and the Nabahina, and the attackers were defeated and broken. There were slain in the battle eighty people of the prominent men of Pate alone, and I have seen in the writings of the historian of Lamu Bwana Mshamo(?) b. Kombo (God have mercy on him), that the number of slain on the side of the Mazari'a and Nabahina was 300 people and over. When the Amir 'Abdullah saw the many casualties that had happened to his Army, and how its strength had been weakened, he ordered the remainder to escape with their lives, and they raced to their ships in flight and defeat.[26] In spite of the exaggeration of the chroniclers in regard to the number killed in this battle, I have not found out one name even of the prominent men who were slain, let alone the others; and the Mazari'a do not preserve record (or, memory) of one of them being killed in that battle.[27]

The chroniclers of Lamu ascribe the cause of the defeat of the Mazru'i and Nabhani Army to the influence of magic[28] which Shaykh 'Ali, one of the prominent men of Lamu at that time, worked for them. They say that when Shaykh 'Ali saw the people of Lamu being hard-pressed, he called for a brass bowl, and wrote in it amulets and charms,[29] and took a hen's egg, and wrote the Names upon it (presumably the Names of God), and gave the cup and the egg to a man, and told him to strike with the egg the first of the enemy soldiers he chanced upon, and after that to strike with the bowl and make for the sea until the water reached his navel, and then plunge the bowl in it. The man did as he was told. After only a few minutes the clouds covered the sky, and rained a heavy rain in the direction

[26] **Raced to their ships in flight and defeat.** The Chronicle of Lamu says that the Mombasan Army fled by way of Kipungani at the far end of Lamu Island, not straight to their ships (pp. 26 and 27). See also Taylor: African Aphorisms p. 87, No. 377 — *Mwenda Pate k'auya. Kiuyacho ni kiriro* = He who goes to Pate does not return: all that returns is a sigh.

[27] **And the Mazari'a do not preserve record.** In the circumstances this does not surprise us; but the fact which Shaykh Al-Amin wishes to emphasise is that there does not seem to be any note elsewhere of a leading Mazru'i of the time whose death is not otherwise accounted for.

[28] **The influence of Magic.** The "History of Pate" (Freeman-Grenville, p. 276) has another account of the magic spell cast by Shaykh 'Ali (or, Mwinyi Shehe Ali). This magic appears to be Islamic magic, such as one meets with in Arabia, rather than what is known as "Uchawi" in Africa. The "Hen's Egg" and the "Names of God" are used widely in the Arabic world as means of manipulating the powers of the unseen world. The first is a symbol of life, and is of pre-Islamic pagan origin, being found, for example, on the frieze of the Temple of Jupiter in Baalbek, or the Temples of such places as Beth-shean in Israel. The second is of course Islamic, the Names of God being regarded as endued with power. The egg's breaking against the enemy soldier is obviously a "Fida'", or redemption, for the rest of the Lamu Army. The sinking of the cup, or bowl, is symbolical of the sinking of the enemy into the sea, or possibly a sinking of them in effigy.

[29] *Wafqan watalasim.* The first word seems to have the same meaning as "Hirizi" in Swahili. The second word is the source from which the English word "Talisman" is derived.

where the enemy was, and quenched the fuses of their muskets: but the rain did not encroach in the direction of the People of Lamu, and their muskets were working their work in the Army of the Secondary Agreement(?).[30]

This is not a thing to be relied on in seeking explanation of battles and the deduction of the causes of them; but what led to the defeat, as I see it, was the joining of the Zayni party with the Sa'udi, and that the Amir was deceived before he entered this war in what he knew of the neutrality of the Zayni party in regard to the fighting, and thought that his Army was sufficient to conquer the People of Lamu so long as they were in that state, a state of division and variance: but God wished to help the oppressed; so He inspired them to unite and join together in warding off their attacking enemy. It is obvious what strength there is in unity, and if there is any supernatural cause which it is right to rely on in explaining that defeat, it is the help of God Who has promised it to the oppressed.

The traditional accounts differ as to the date of this battle. The People of Pate say it was the year A.H. 1227, and the People of Lamu say it was in A.H. 1223,[31] but the People of Mombasa have nothing about this. My own opinion is that the account of the People of Pate is the more correct by evidence of the Sayyid's sending his 'Amil to Lamu in the year A.H. 1228; and it is not reasonable to conceive that the Sayyid would delay that step for five years as the People of Lamu go the length of declaring.

Here let me say that the Amir 'Abdullah did not act well in joining with the Sultan Ahmad in making war on the People of Lamu, who had already been content by themselves to make the Mazari'a rulers of their country; for he lost by his stupidity and bad policy that Island by which, had it been united to the districts they already had, their dominion would have stretched to Pate in the North — nay, they could easily have gained

---

[30] **The secondary agreement**. This phrase seems to refer to the Army of the Zayni party that came in during the Battle and turned the tide. The agreement is Secondary because they broke the first agreement which was with the Mazari'a and made another with the Sa'udi party.

[31] **A.H. 1227** = A.D. 1812; **A.H. 1223** = A.D. 1808. Freeman-Grenville adds a foot-note at p. 276 to his text of the "History of Pate", in which he speaks of an informant whom he had interviewed, and who claimed to be 104 years old (100 Christian years?). This old man claimed to have been alive at the time of the Battle. These dates mean that he must have been born about A.D. 1800, and that the interview mentioned in the note cannot have been later than A.D. 1905. The date of the publication of the "East African Coast" suggests that this interview took place much later than 1905. One may therefore be forgiven for doubting the old man's memory. Either he had thought himself back into the stories he heard in his early childhood, until he fancied he had been himself present at the actual events, or the Battle took place much later than A.D. 1812.

possession of the country to the North of it as far as the Banadir.[32] What
the Amir did[33] was what caused the People of Lamu to make Sayyid
Sa'id the ruler of their country, in fear of the encroachment of the Nabahina and the Mazari'a upon them. And it was as well they did.

In the year A.H. 1228[34] Sayyid Sa'id took possession of Lamu and sent
there a liwali under his authority, Muhammad b. Nasir b. Sayf Al-Ma'uli,[35]
with a garrison composed of 500 soldiers, to protect it from the assaults
of the Mazari'a and the Nabahina. This Muhammad b. Nasir was the
first of the Lamu Liwalis appointed by Sayyid Sa'id. After him Ahmad b.
Miftah Al-Hana'i[36] was Liwali, then Sayf b. Ahmad Al-Bu Sa'idi who died
in the year — (the date is not given).[37] When the Government was transferred into the hands of the British, they appointed the liwalis under their
authority, and the first of their liwalis of Lamu was Sayf b. Salim b. Khalfan.

The Civil War between the Liwali and the Sons of Mas'ud[38]
The Liwali had sent the sons of Mas'ud b. Nasir to the Island of Pemba
to take charge of the garrison there, and when they returned to Mombasa to execute their business and visit their relations, it chanced that one
day they passed by a club of the WaKilifi[39] in the quarter of Mji wa Kale

[32] **Banadir**. The Banadir are Barawa, Marka and Mogadishu. The word is the Arabic plural
of the Persian word *Bandar* = Harbour, or Port.
[33] **What the Amir did**. So says the "History of Pate", p. 278.
[34] **A.H.1228** = A.D.1813. This is the first place on the Swahili Coast that Sayyid Sa'id b.
Sultan occupied, apart from Zanzibar.
[35] **Muhammad b. Nasir b. Sayf Al-Ma'uli**. Guillain says (p. 569) that the first 'Umani Governor
was Khalaf b. Nasir followed by "Aross ben Kalabi", then Muhammad b. Nasir Al-Bu Sa'idi. The
"Chronicle of Lamu" (pp. 28, 29) also mentions Khalaf b. Nasir's coming with a garrison
of 500 men. Guillain says that the first two above-mentioned had only short periods of office,
and that they were engaged in building the Fort, which was finished under the latter of the
three. A man of the Ma'uli clan, Muhammad b. Salim Al-Ma'uli, ironically enough, acted
for Sayyid Barghash, Sayyid Sa'id's son, in accepting the carving up of his mainland empire
in favour of Britain and Germany in December A.D. 1886 [Parliamentary Papers, East Africa
(c8274) 1887 Vol. LIX, Letter 118 enclosure No. 2, p. 59]
[36] **Ahmad b. Miftah**. Called in the "History of Pate" (Freeman-Grenville, p. 281) *Hamad
Maftaha*. This is the first mention of an 'Umani Liwali in Lamu in that document.
[37] *Almutawaffa 'am?* This date has not been filled in, but it would be in the latter part of
the 19th Century. The phrase is omitted altogether in the copy MS in my possession.
[38] Cf. Guillain pp. 553–555. He recounts this narrative much earlier in the order of events,
but with no mention of Sharif Sa'id b. 'Umar.
[39] **A club of the WaKilifi**. The Kilifi community as usual cause trouble for the Mazari'a (see
the Prefatory note on the Tribes of Mombasa). The word translated "Club" (Arabic, *Nadi*)
means no more than a gathering place for social intercourse and conversation. It might be
under a baobab tree or on the veranda of a coffee-house. What distinguishes it is that it is
the recognised meeting place of a particular clan or group. It could also be a very suitable
place for the passing of secret information. Guillain says that two families were involved —
the *Banu Mas'ud* and the *Banu 'Abdullah b. Zahir*. He also indicates that 'Abdullah b.

[= The Old Town].⁴⁰ They greeted the folk there who returned their greeting. Al-Sharif Sa'id b. 'Umar, leader of the WaKilifi, was present, and he rose and welcomed them. Then he asked them what was the appointed time for their return to Pemba, and they answered that it would be soon. Then he addressed them, showing amazement and pretending to love them (or, show friendship to them), and said, "You are the sons of the former Liwali and have most right to the Liwaliship. Hasn't he who now sits on the throne (he meant the Liwali Ahmad b. Muhammad) done enough in appropriating the Liwaliship instead of you, that he should have thrown you across to Pemba? Truly we are from God and to Him we shall return!" This talk affected the hearts of the sons of Mas'ud, and they thought it sprang from a heart filled with pity and sympathy for them. Anger stirred their hearts, and they agreed to revolt against the Liwali, so as to make him resort to giving up the Liwaliship to them. So they made for the Fort, and entered his presence and demanded that he should abdicate. The Liwali asked them why he should, and they said: "This Liwaliship is taken by turns. One turn is for the sons of Muhammad b. 'Uthman, and another for the children of Mas'ud b. Nasir, but the turn of the sons of Muhammad b. 'Uthman ended with the office of 'Abdullah b. Ahmad. Now this is our turn, and we are the people (whose turn it is) and have the right to it." The Liwali answered them politely, "It is not as you are saying. The Liwaliship is specially for the sons of Muhammad b. 'Uthman alone. Mas'ud b. Nasir only became Liwali when they were minors, incapable of holding office as Liwali, and unable to carry on its duties."⁴¹ After that they went out from him, and cast off their allegiance. They were helped in this injustice by plotters, and they gathered fighting men and went to Kilindini and camped there. The Liwali sent men to them to advise them to leave fighting and return to their allegiance, but they did not agree.

Mas'ud was sent to Pemba, and Salim b. 'Abdullah b. Zahir to Giryama, by a "Treaty", not by the arbitrary act of Ahmad b. 'Abdullah the Liwali. Shaykh Al-Amin is silent on this point. See the Genealogical Table (Appendix No. I, Table B), which shows that a daughter of Mas'ud had married Salim b. 'Abdullah, thus tying the two families together by marriage bond.

⁴⁰ **Mji wa Kale**. This is not the Present "Old Town" of Mombasa, but the Mediaeval town which lay between the present Old Town and the South end of Nyali Bridge.

⁴¹ The arguments on both sides have some truth. This is an internal dynastic quarrel of a type only too frequent in Islamic History. Guillain says that at this point, they actually attacked and almost gained the citadel, but were repulsed and then fled to Zanzibar. There they prepared their revolt, gathered an Army, and made a feint at Pemba; but Ahmad's Amir Sulayman b. 'Ali met them advancing by land, when he landed at Gazi to get provisions (p. 554). He was thus able to warn the Liwali at Mombasa, before the rebels had time to land at Kilifi. Shaykh Al-Amin has written 'Abdullah b. Ahmad in error for 'Abdullah b. Muhammad in the argument of the sons of Mas'ud.

Then he sent to them a company of soldiers, and the two groups met, and war was carried on between them, and at first the Liwali's troops were defeated. A Number of them were killed, among them Qasim b. Jum'a Al-Ma'miri, and the rest fled. Then the Liwali strengthened his soldiers,[42] and sent them to them, and they fought them; and the rebels were defeated, and some of the heads of the revolt were seized, and the sons of Mas'ud b. Nasir fled. 'Abdullah b. Mas'ud and Salim b. 'Abdullah b. Zahir went to Rabai, and the others betook themselves to Duruma. The Liwali issued orders in all directions to arrest them.

Since Rabai was under the "Nine Tribes"[43] whose chief was Sharif Sa'id, known for his hostility to the Mazari'a, the Sharif found a suitable opportunity to fall upon those who had fled there, and he sent to the chiefs of Rabai, ordering them to kill them, and to take their heads to Mombasa: but the People of Rabai, because they knew of the bravery of those "heroes" respected them,[44] and sent to the Sharif, saying that they would not assassinate them because they were at all times ready to defend themselves. Then the Sharif answered them, "Watch them; and if they enter to pray, then kill them while they are at it." So they waited until it was prayer time and they had entered into prayer,[45] then they attacked them, while they were in the posture of *Ruku'*,[46] and killed them, and they sent to the Sharif telling him of it, and that they were bringing their heads. The Sharif hurried to the Liwali, very pleased, and told him that the People of Rabai[47] had seized the group and were bringing them in the afternoon of that very day. So the Liwali went out with his company,

---

[42] *'Azzaz al-wali 'asakirahu*. Either "increased their number", or "increased their enthusiasm", or "encouraged".

[43] **Since Rabai was under the "Nine Tribes"**. See Prins: Op. Cit., p. 99. The Jomvu and Malindi Shaykhs have dual rights in relation to the Rabai. Here is an added complication for the Mazru'i refugees; for though the Malindi Shaykh was their friend, the Jomvu Shaykh was in the opposite faction, so that treachery was only too possible. The Arabic text here *taht al-Tawa'if al-tisa"* is hardly accurate if it means that the WaRabai were politically subservient to the "Nine Tribes". For the political groups in Mombasa rarely if ever had much power, once they were outside the immediate environs of the Island.

[44] *Habahum*. This word I have translated "respected them", but it really has the idea of awe or fear connected with it as well.

[45] *Ahramu biha*. This expression refers to the uttering of what is known as *Tasmiyat al-ihram*. It is the first utterance of the *Bismillahi*, and puts the worshipper in a state of ritual sanctity.

[46] The posture of *Ruku'* is that of bending forward from the hips, so that the torso is parallel with the ground — a vulnerable position.

[47] **The People of Rabai**. These Rabai were at this time almost certainly pagans, not Muslims; hence they would have no religious fear of falling upon the men while they were at worship. Yet attacking the enemy while at prayer is not unknown even in modern Arabia, where men have been shot at and wounded in the most prominent part of their anatomy, even while they were in the posture of *Sujud*!

to meet them in Makupa,[48] and there were the People of Rabai already arrived, with a basket[49] in their hands, in which were the heads of those who had suffered this wrong, and they set it before the Liwali. He asked them, "What is this?" They said, "The heads of your brethren whom you ordered us to kill." He asked them who had given them this order, and they said, "The Sharif Sa'id". The Liwali said, "No strength nor power but in God the High and Great," and "Truly we belong to God and shall return to Him;"[50] then he said, "If I had wished to kill one of them, I would have killed those who were in our hands." Then the heads were washed and shrouded, and buried where the ruins of Makupa Fort are now.[51]

This is what the People of Mombasa relate concerning the story of the murder of the sons of Mas'ud b. Nasir: but the children of Zahir[52] among the People of Takaungu confirm the issue of an order from the Liwali himself to slay them, but that he denied it for fear of bearing blame and reproof. Perhaps the assertion of the People of Takaungu is correct, and testimony is borne to that in the killing of those who fled to Duruma, as we shall show. The fact that the Liwali did not punish Sharif Sa'id is circumstantial evidence pointing to it.

As for those who fled to Duruma, the leader of the WaChangamwe[53] Mwinyi Hiji b. Faki (Arabic, *Hija b. Faki*) seized them, and sent to the Liwali informing him of that. He ordered him to kill them; but the leader Mwinyi Hiji saw that to slay them would be to break the covenant which the "Three Tribes" had bound themselves with not to shed Mazru'i blood, just as the Mazari'a had bound themselves in the same way in the treaty which 'Ali b. 'Uthman had made. So Mwinyi Hiji gathered his relatives and his clan, and informed them of his view, and they agreed with him.

---

[48] *Makupa*. The village is now covered over with modern development, but the name is preserved in the Causeway which carries the Railway and the Road to Nairobi from the Island of Mombasa to the mainland. See Map. Appendix No. II.

[49] *Zimbil*. "Basket" — but a common South Arabian word, indicating the close connection of the Swahili Coast with South Arabia even in modern times.

[50] *Fahawqal al-Wali wastarja'*. These two words mean respectively to say: "There is no strength nor power but in God", and "Verily we belong to God and to Him we shall return".

[51] **Where the ruins of Makupa Fort are now**. There is no vestige of Makupa Fort now remaining, but it had been built by the Portuguese to protect the Island from the incursions of the Nyika. It probably stood where the Railway Staff Housing Estate, usually called Makande, now stands by the Railway Line as it approaches the Causeway. But Shaykh Al-Amin speaks as though he knew where the Fort stood.

[52] **The children of Zahir**. See note 39 above. It must be remembered that the Banu Zahir were allied by marriage to the Banu Mas'ud.

[53] **The leader of the WaChangamwe**. See F. J. Berg's Article, Note 38, where he deals with the Alliance between the "Three Tribes" (Kilindini, Tangana and Changamwe) and the Digo and Duruma.

They came with the prisoners in a great company of the People of Changamwe and Duruma, singing a "Rajaz" poem in Swahili which means,
"The Sea of Changamwe is calm; no ship is wrecked on its shore."[54] When
they reached the Fort, they presented the prisoners to the Liwali, and said
to him, "These are of your clan. We have brought them alive. If you
pardon them, they are your brothers, but if you kill them, it is you who is
responsible for them. But as for us, the "Three Tribes", our hands cannot
shed the blood of the Mazari'a".[55] So the Liwali interned them, and then
pardoned them.

For the faithfulness of the "Three Tribes" to their covenant with the
Mazari'a, the Liwali Ahmad b. Muhammad used to recommend his clan
to treat them well, and that they should take refuge in the regions under
their influence[56] whenever they should be compelled to take refuge.[57] But
he used to warn them against the "Nine Tribes", particularly the WaKilifi,
and against making for the regions which were under their rule.[58] Now let
me say: The position was thus in the days of the Mazru'i Government: but
after their Government had ceased, the "Nine Tribes" became like the
"Three" in their friendship and nearness to the Mazari'a. The proof of
that is what Khamis Kombo, and his sons and his clan, did to support
Mbaruk b. Rashid, and their companionship to him in his last rebellion.
They put out of their memory all the hostility and hatred that had passed
between their fathers in the days of the Mazru'i Government.

After a time it became clear to the Liwali that all that the sons of
Mas'ud had done was simply through the plots of the Sharif Sa'id and his
company. So he removed him from his Shaykhdom and withdrew it

---

[54] **"The sea of Changamwe is calm; no ship is wrecked on its shore."** This is called a "Rajaz"
Poem, Rajaz being basically an Arabic Meter, as in the two poems recorded in Section 9
below. I have not found the Swahili words of this poem, but it is probably preserved in an
unwritten tradition, even if it has not been written down.

[55] Cf. Note 27 in the Section on 'Ali b. 'Uthman, where the "Three Tribes" intercede for the
WaMvita and WaKilifi. See also the Taylor/Harries Tradition, p. 94, para. 1.

[56] *Nufudhihim* This is a better word to use in describing the nature of the relationship
between the "Three Tribes" and the "Nine Tribes" and the "WaNyika". It was not "rule"
but "influence".

[57] **Whenever they were compelled to take refuge.** This is an extremely suggestive statement.
Shaykh Al-Amin has quite faithfully — though probably quite unintentionally — portrayed
the true situation. The Liwali saw it possible that his clan might have to flee into refuge any
time. They were faced with rival powers on the Coast, and Ahmad b. Sa'id and his successors
were already making 'Umani influence felt there. The Mazari'a had not many resources to
fall back upon. See also the Taylor/Harries Tradition, p. 100, para. 5, where 'Abdullah b.
Ahmad, successor of this Liwali, urged his family to unity on his death-bed by the illustration
of a bundle of Coconut-strands. The last ruling scion of the family, Shaykh Mbaruk b. Rashid,
had his own headquarters in Shimba, which also lies in the Duruma country.

[58] *Taht amrihim.* This word on the other hand is highly unsuitable, as the whole of the
Liwali's extraordinary injunction shows.

(him?)[59] from the "Nine Tribes" and requested them to choose another than themselves to be leader to them (or, to choose someone else from among themselves to be leader to them), and their choice fell upon Ahmad b. Shaykh Al-Malindi (the younger). He was at that stage in Bwaga Moyo or Pangani. So they went to him and brought him, and the Liwali invested him with the Shaykhdom of the People of Mombasa.

The Liwali died (May God have mercy on him) in Rabi' Al-Awwal of the year A.H. 1229,[60] and was survived by eleven sons, Salim, Mbaruk, 'Abdullah, Salih, Sulayman, Khamis, 'Uthman, 'Asim, Muhammad, Rashid and Sa'id. Of his descendants is composed the house of Ahmad of the Mazari'a, among whom is Mbaruk b. Rashid b. Salim, famous for his battles.

7. The Seventh Liwali — 'Abdullah b. Ahmad b. Muhammad b. 'Uthman b. 'Abdullah Al-Mazru'i

His Liwaliship — Kubu the Head of the WaDigo kills Sa'id b. 'Abdullah Al-Buhri — The Liwali mobilises an army to wage war on Kubu — Mediation of the Diwan Sayyid Ahmad b. 'Alawi to reconcile Kubu and the Mazari'a — Kubu pays the blood-price and apologises to the Liwali — The occurrence of Famine in Duruma — The Liwali's help to them — The story of Mr. Hobley with an old man of the Duruma People — The Beginning of the War between Sayyid Sa'id and the Mazari'a — The Appointment of Mbaruk b. Ahmad as Liwali of Pate – Fumo Luti becomes Sultan of Pate — He complains of the Mazari'a to Sayyid Sa'id — The Letter of Sayyid Sa'id to the Liwali to let the People of Pate alone — The Liwali sends him a breastplate and cooking-pot and a wooden spoon (or washing stick) — The Poet Bwana Muyaka and his prophecy of war — The Arrival of Sayyid Sa'id's Army in Pate — The war between him and the Mazari'a — The People of Lamu advise the Amir Hamad to attack the Island (Pemba) — The Island falls into the hands of Sayyid Sa'id — Death of the Liwali.

After the death of the Liwali Ahmad b. Muhammad in the year A.H. 1229,[1]

---

[59] **Wasahabaha**. "And withdrew it", i.e. the Shaykhdom. As it says further on that Ahmad b. Shaykh was chosen and invested with the Shaykhdom, it seems that this should have been *Wasahabahu* = "And withdrew *him*". The Shaykh of the Mombasa Tribes was thereafter from the WaMalindi who were friends of the Mazari'a: yet they were still among the "Nine Tribes". Perhaps Shaykh Al-Amin meant to write "WaKilifi" rather than "Nine Tribes".

[60] **A.H. 1229** = A.D. 1814. Guillain's rendering of the Epitaph on Ahmad's Tomb (p. 624) agrees with this date. Guillain also mentions, among the brothers of Salim, Rashid *and* Nasir. Nasir is either a mistake or a more distant relative — a cousin perhaps.

[1] **A.H. 1229** = A.D. 1814. From this point on the History of the Mazari'a will be found summarised in J. L. Krapf: Travels, Researches and Missionary Labours, pp. 529–37.

his son 'Abdullah b. Ahmad b. Muhammad b. 'Uthman became Liwali.
There was none of his many brothers who opposed him in this Liwaliship,
since they knew him to be a man of experience, and competence.[2] So they
installed him as Liwali, his brothers and the people of authority in his
clan, and the leaders of all the Tribes. Delegations came to him from all
the districts to congratulate him on his Liwaliship and to swear allegiance
to him.

The first thing[3] he embarked on was the strengthening of the Army
by preparing munitions and appointing trained officers. He appointed
competent "liwalis" in all the regions; and among these liwalis he
appointed was Sa'id b. 'Abdullah b. Mas'ud Al-Buhri, the great-grandfather of our friend the learned 'Ali b. Humayd b. 'Abdullah Al-Buhri of
Tanga.[4] The Liwali appointed him liwali of Mtangata. Then this liwali set
out one day from Mombasa en route for the place of his liwaliship in a
small ship. When he came opposite Funzi, something went wrong with the
ship, and he was forced to put in there to repair it. It happened that Kubu
Mwakikunga, the head and Sultan of the WaDigo, was near to the shore.
This Kubu was very enamoured of blood-shedding, and proud of his
strength and the number of his followers. While he was strolling with some
of his followers, there he saw Sa'id b. 'Abdullah at a distance working with
the ship's carpenters to repair it. He shot an arrow at him and wounded
him fatally and he fell to the ground; and the carpenters devoted every
effort to help and treat him, but before long he passed away and died.
Then the sailors worked to repair the ship with all speed, and carried him
upon it to Wasin where he was buried with great solemnity.

The ship returned to Mombasa, and the sailors told the Liwali of the
matter; and he mourned him, and was indignant over the great crime
which that Zanji[5] had committed, and resolved to discipline and punish
him. So he sent soldiers to slay him, and put in command of them his

---

[2] **A man of experience and competence**. Guillain says: "Quoique d'un age déjà assez avancé,
il était encore d'un caractère énergique et d'une grande bravoure" (p. 569).

[3] **The first thing**. The Liwali 'Abdullah must have sized up the situation shrewdly, and deduced
the forthcoming struggle with 'Uman even before the first move in the power-game was
made.

[4] **Liwalis. . . . . . . Tanga**. These were of course of an inferior grade under the orders of the
Mombasa Mazru'i Liwali. It might have been better to call them "Representatives" or
"Commissioners", but since Shaykh Al-Amin uses the same Arabic word *Wulat* as he uses
for the Liwali of Mombasa, I have used the same word but with no capital letter. The late
Mr. J. T. H. Allen formerly of the Colonial Service of Great Britain in East Africa has
informed me that Dr. Joseph Schacht found the Learned 'Ali b. Humayd Al-Buhri one of
the greatest scholars of the Shari'a he had met anywhere in the Islamic world.

[5] ***Dhalika Al-Zanji***. "That African". The *Zunuj* mean in Arabic the pure-blooded Africans,
the Negroes or Bantu, as opposed to the "Arabs". Swahili Tribes would not have called
themselves *Zunuj* nor Swahili, but Arabs, or possibly WaMvita, WaKilifi, etc.

paternal uncle Sulayman b. 'Ali b. 'Uthman,[6] and furnished him with a letter to the Diwan Sayyid Ahmad b. 'Alawi, ordering him to supply the soldiers with ammunition, and to help them with whatever they might need in the way of guides and spies. He instructed his uncle to put in at Wasin first, and give that letter to the Diwan, and to take his opinion on what he advised. When the Amir reached Wasin with his soldiers, he presented the letter to the Diwan. When he had read it and knew what the Liwali's intentions were, he saw the matter in a serious light,[7] and was perplexed and did not know what to do in face of this knotty problem; for he was spiritual head of the WaDigo[8] on the one hand, and on the other a warm friend of the Mazari'a. Therefore, if he helped the Mazru'i Army against the WaDigo, he would lose his leadership of them, and they would probably show him hostility, while he had no power against them: but if he disobeyed the command of the Liwali, the Mazari'a would quarrel with him and accuse him of being friendly with their enemy against them, and the latter course would be more difficult for him than the former. So the Diwan urged the Amir Sulayman b. 'Ali to delay some days until he should see clearly what honest opinion he could give about the hostility between the two sides. But the Amir lost patience through the length of the delay, and determined on going ahead with the attack on the WaDigo. He saw the mistake in his opinion however, since (he realised) that the Diwan would disapprove of his going ahead, and he would then lose the supplies and help he hoped for from him; and over and above that, he would be disobeying the Liwali's orders. Then another idea[9] occurred to him: he gathered all the prominent men of the district in the Diwan's house, and informed them of what he had come for, and that he was

---

[6] **Sulayman b. 'Ali b. 'Uthman.** He became Liwali, though of an advanced age, after 'Abdullah b. Ahmad's death in A.H. 1238 = A.D. 1823. See the next section.

[7] *'Azuma 'alayhi al-amr.* Lit. "The matter was great upon him", meaning either as we have translated it, or "He saw difficulties in the matter".

[8] **The spiritual Head of the WaDigo.** This statement is strange in view of the fact that the WaDigo do not seem to have been Muslims. The Oxford History of East Africa (Chapter IV, p. 130) states that they show no trace of Islam before the end of the 19th Century. Was the Diwan Ahmad b. 'Alawi (or Ba 'Alawi?) regarded by the pagans as a charismatic person even though they were not themselves Muslims? The Diwan was clearly regarded as such by the Coast Muslims, since he was a Sharif or descendant of Muhammad the Prophet. Had this veneration simply "rubbed off" on the WaDigo, or did he have a pagan as well as an Islamic significance which he acquired with the position of Diwan of Wasin? Perhaps the most that can be said is that here is a little light shed on the process whereby Islamic and indigenous Bantu religious practices became mingled in East African Islam.

[9] **Then another idea.** This is the idea that all Arabs would tend to fall back upon; for it is simply the method employed from time immemorial in the Desert when settling disputes or other policy. The Sayyid, or tribal leader, consulted with the *Shura*, or council of elders. The Mazari'a were at this time still very much Arabs as opposed to East Africans.

determined to go ahead with it. Then the Diwan addressed him and said: We know what you have determined on, but let it not be absent from your mind that your attack on this tribe is not assured of success. War has its various fortunes, one day in your favour, another against you; and no man knows what its result will be. If you win, then that is what you sought for: but if not, then the vanity of this African will increase, and that will cause him to despise us all. My own opinion is that we make an effort to reconcile you and him, and bring him back to his allegiance to the Liwali, and then he will be a help to you in the future, not opposed to you. In this way you will reach your object with regard to him without kindling (the torch of) war, the consequence of which no one knows except God." All who were in the council agreed with him in this happy opinion, and the Amir Sulayman b. 'Ali approved of it, and with that the council was adjourned.[10]

The Diwan went out in company with 'Ali b. Ahmad b. Abu Bakr and Sayyid Abu Bakr b. Ahmad, and other chiefs of Wasin Island, and went to Kubu. (Kubu had come to know of the arrival of the soldiers of the Arabs in Wasin to fight him; so he had gathered his people, and they had prepared themselves with arrows and spears to meet the enemy and drive him off.)[11] When the Diwan reached there, Kubu and his people were amazed that this great man should come to them; for it was not the habit of the Diwan to leave his house, let alone his district.[12] Kubu asked him why he had come, and what had led him to undertake the inconvenience of travelling to him: but the Diwan simply threw his turban on the ground and began weeping, and the Sharifs who followed him wept with him. Then he said to Kubu: "You have done a serious thing in murdering that Arab; and now the Arab army has arrived in Wasin and accused us of taking part with you in this crime, and have arrested so-and-so, and so-and-so, and so-and-so" (and he reckoned up for him the heads of the Sharifs who were friendly to him), "and nothing will deliver us from this accusation and save us from the Arabs making war, unless you pay the blood-price of the murdered man, and confess your crime, and apologise

---

[10] **Faftadda**. dispersed. The more orthodox form is *fanfadda*.

[11] This sentence was scored out in the original MS., but it was legible so is included. Its excision may have been to avoid causing some offence, though what offence could be caused is not clear. On the other hand, it may simply have been erased because the Author found it was inaccurate.

[12] **It was not the habit . . . . district**. This is a remarkably genuine detail of everyday life in Islamic society. "The great" in the Islamic World, even at this day, tend to seclude themselves from the public, except at stated times, and would regard it as belittling to their dignity and position to *go out* to others. The lesser always goes to the greater. Here however the Diwan shows a deep knowledge of human nature, as also of the Bantu tribal mentality. His tact and diplomacy are quite remarkable.

to the Liwali for what you have done. If you refrain from doing this then the Arabs will inevitably slay both us and you altogether."

Kubu however did not believe this story at first, and thought there was some deception in the matter; so the Diwan swore an oath which was very solemn among them, and then its truth entered his heart, and he knew that he whom he had killed was not one of the common people. Then he regretted what he had done and ordered 25 slaves to be brought, and twelve tusks,[13] and that these should be sent to the Liwali as blood-price,[14] for the man he had killed without knowing that he was one of the prominent Arabs who are the special concern of the Government itself. But the Diwan was not satisfied with that, but insisted on his coming in person with him to Wasin and going with the Amir Sulayman b. 'Ali to Mombasa to apologise to the Liwali himself. Kubu agreed, and they came to Wasin; and the Diwan gave the blood-price to the Amir. The Amir requested the Diwan to accompany them to Mombasa as this would set Kubu's heart at rest, and he agreed and they went to Mombasa. The Diwan offered the blood-price to the Liwali, and then brought Kubu into his presence and asked him to pardon him; and he forgave him.

In the Liwaliship of this 'Abdullah b. Ahmad, a very bad famine[15] hit the Duruma Country which destroyed many of its people. Crowds of them left their country for Mombasa seeking food to keep body and soul together. Then the Liwali had pity on them and provided them with rations, and sent many Duruma families to Pemba, and instructed the liwali there to look after them. So they remained there in Pemba in a favoured position, enjoying the many good things there until the famine went from their land, and they returned to Mombasa. This benefit which the Liwali gave was not given by any of the Liwalis before him; and it is without doubt a great excellence in his favour, and a clear indication of his kindness to his subjects.

[13] *'ajan*. Lit. "Ivories", i.e. Elephant tusks.

[14] **As blood-price**. Kubu's action was probably dictated as much by policy as by fear. Though the WaNyika were not controlled, or indeed controllable, by the Coast Rulers, yet they were their link with the outside world both in regard to imports and exports; and so the Coast authorities had not only, from the Nyika point of view, to be there, but good relations with them had to be preserved. The Diwan's real diplomatic victory was in persuading Kubu to go with him to Mombasa.

[15] **A very bad famine**. I have not found this famine mentioned elsewhere in the Swahili Traditions, or other literature on East Africa; though famines were periodical disasters which caused migration of tribes and sections of tribes over a wide area and sometimes caused a change in their manner of life. See Oxford History of East Africa, p. 314.

It is related that Mr. Hobley,[16] who was Provincial Commissioner of Mombasa, was itinerating in the Duruma Country; and he met in one of its locations a very aged man, sat down with him, and asked him, "Which is the most just of the two governments, and the most considerate of its subjects? The Arab or the British?" The old man replied, "I do not know which Arab Government you mean; for two Arab Governments have ruled in turn in this land — the Mazru'i Government, and that of the family of Bu Sa'id." Mr. Hobley said, "I mean the two of them together, in comparison with the British Government." He hoped to hear from that old man of the injustice of the Arabs, and their harshness upon their subjects. But it was contrary to what he imagined. For the Old man said to him, "The most considerate of the Governments was the Mazru'i Government." Mr. Hobley asked him, "Why?" So he told him the story of the famine above-mentioned. Mr. Hobley was amazed at what the Liwali 'Abdullah b. Ahmad had done, and he accounted it one of the most strange things, since this sympathy and mercy never came — in his belief — from the hearts of any but Europeans.

The Beginning of the War between Sayyid Sa'id and the Mazari'a

You have got to know from the events which happened in the day of the Liwali Ahmad b. Muhammad, that this 'Abdullah b. Ahmad was Amir of the garrison of the Mazari'a in Pate, and leader of the Army which went to make war on Lamu, and a warm friend of the Sultan Ahmad b. Shaykh Al-Nabhani, so that he was very much respected and honoured by the People of Pate. When he returned to Mombasa and his father died and he succeeded him in the Liwaliship, he sent his brother Mbaruk b. Ahmad to Pate as Amir of the garrison, as was the custom followed by those before him. The Mazari'a remained in Pate, and had the influence which was given to them by the treaty which had been established between them and its People from the time of the Liwali Mas'ud b. Nasir. When the Sultan Ahmad b. Shaykh died, and was succeeded by Fumo Luti b. Bwana

---

[16] **Mr. Hobley**. C. W. Hobley, C.M.G. was a trained engineer and surveyor who became an officer, and latterly a Commissioner, in the Colonial Service in East Africa, first in the Imperial East Africa Co., then in the Kenya Colony and Protectorate, serving in all about thirty years. He wrote books on aspects of tribal culture, which he seems to have studied in some detail, and published in 1929 a Book of Memoirs, in a conversational and at times racey style, entitled "Kenya from Chartered Company to Crown Colony". This incident reflects not only his attitude as shown in that book, but is characteristic of the attitude of most Europeans in the Nineteenth and early Twentieth Centuries. So far as I can see, this incident is unrecorded, and so must have been told orally to Shaykh Al-Amin.

Madi,[17] he found the influence of the Mazari'a in his kingdom objection-
able, and wished to get rid of it. There were among the Nabahina two
factions, a faction of the Sultan's opinion, and another friendly to the
Mazari'a and desirous of no substitute. So the Sultan, and those who were
of his opinion, agreed to make Sayyid Sa'id ruler of their country (or, put
Sayyid Sa'id in possession of their country), since he was the only man
capable of opposing the Mazari'a. So he sent to him conceding to him the
sovereignty of Pate, and complaining to him of the hostility of the Mazari'a
towards them. The Sayyid sent a letter to the Liwali 'Abdullah b. Ahmad
in which he cautioned him against any encroachment on the People of
Pate. This cautioning of Sayyid Sa'id's and his interference between him
and the People of Pate, the allies of the Mazari'a, stirred the Liwali's
wrath. He answered by sending to the Sayyid by the hand of Husayn
b. 'Ali b. 'A'ish Al-Junaybi a breastplate (coat of mail?), cooking-pot and
washing-stick (*Miqaf*, a stick for quelling ebullition).[18] He meant that as a
symbol, (implying that) if he was a man of war, then he (the Sayyid)
should arm himself and come down into the arena of war. It is also said
that he sent him some gunpowder and an empty bushel-measure.

When the People of Mombasa got to know what he had done they
were indignant at him, and were certain that war would come soon. This
incident became the talk of the people in the "clubs". There was in

---

[17] **Sultan Ahmad b. Shaykh .... Fumo Luti b. Bwana Madi**. There is some
vagueness or error in these Nabhani names. The "History of Pate" (Freeman-Grenville: East
African Coast, pp. 282–3) calls the former "Fumoluti Kipunga" and the latter "Bwana Sheikh
son of Bwana Fumomadi". The Mazari'a are said to have supported a Fumo Luti b. Shaykh,
but it is not clear whether he is the Fumo Luti b. Bayai referred to in the "History of Pate"
(Op. Cit., p. 280) and by Shaykh Al-Amin in Section 6, of this Chapter (above in the text
between Notes 9 and 10) or another. Guillain (p. 571) says Bwana Shaykh was called Foum"
Alote As-Serir (i.e. Al-Saghir = The Little, or the Younger) to distinguish him from his
elder brother of the same name. This then seems to be the man whom Shaykh Al-Amin
calls Fumo Luti b. Bwana Madi, and who was first supported by 'Uman, and then by
Mombasa. Guillain also says however that this Fumo Luti only lived a little time, and that
it was his son Bwana Kombo b. Shaykh who was alive when the Mazari'a were driven out
of Pate (pp. 572 ff.).

Neither Shaykh Al-Amin nor the "History of Pate" mentions that 'Uman had already
been concerned in supporting one of the parties on Pate, but that they changed sides when
they found Mombasa supporting their first nominee.

[18] **He answered by sending**. Lyne: Zanzibar, p. 30 ff., following Owen, says he sent "powder
and shot, a shirt of mail and a kebaba". The Taylor/Harries Tradition (Op. Cit., p. 97) says:
"Kanzu ya Chuma na sifuria na mwiko" = A coat of mail, a cooking-pot and a large spoon.
Lyne says that this happened on the accession of Sayyid Sa'id in A.D. 1814. Badger gives
the Sayyid's accession as 1804, so that the date in Lyne is probably a misprint. Such an action
is much more likely to be provoked by a direct warning challenge such as the letter, than by
a general public event such as an investiture which does not of itself indicate political or
hostile intentions. But see the slight ambiguity in Hardinge's memorandum (Appendix No. 4).

Mombasa at that time Bwana Muyaka b. Hajj Al-Ghassani, the noble
Swahili Poet, and a man of great shrewdness and insight; and the people
sent to his "club", and asked him what would be the possible result of
that action of the Liwali's. He remained silent a moment with eyes cast
down. Then he raised his head and recited two stanzas of poetry, the literal
translation of which is as follows:

> Al-Junaybi has dived, setting a trap in the sea,
> And if he comes out of it something serious will happen in Mombasa.
> So tell the folk of the villages[19] not to remain arrogant
> For at the beginning of the summer[20] there will be shelling at the
>   investment (i.e. siege).
> For at the beginning of the summer when its blasts blow,
> You will see the falcons, the Lions of Ra's al-Khayma.[21]

The summer of the year A.H. 1238[22] had hardly begun when Sayyid
Sa'id's fleet cast anchor in the waters of Mtanga Wanda,[23] composed of 30
ships filled with 4,000 soldiers, and Hammad b. Ahmad Al-Bu Sa'idi[24] in

[19] *Ahl al-qura.* "The people of the villages" are the Swahili Tribes. (See F. J. Berg's Article)
[20] *Fafiy Awwal Al-Sayf.* "At the beginning of the Summer". The word *Sayf* in Arabic is
Shaykh Al-Amin's rendering of *KASIKAZI* = The Swahili word for the N.E. Monsoon,
which commences in January at the beginning of the hot season.
[21] **Two Stanzas.** What Shaykh Al-Amin means here by "two" is not clear: there are three
couplets in Swahili which in the original are as follows:
> Jenebi mtaga tambo hapo yulizile mbizi
>   Atakapozuka ni mambo gongwa itenda kazi
> Wambieni wa ziambo wasikae kwa makuzi
>   Awali ya kasikazi pembe siwe viunoni
> Awali ya kasikazi pepo zichanza kuvuma
>   Mtawaona makosi, simba wa Ras al Khaima

I am indebted to Mr. F. J. Berg for the discovery of the third stanza in H. E. Lambert:
Chi-Jomvu and Ki-Ngaro, Sub-dialects of the Mombasa Area — Kampala 1958. For the first
two I am indebted to Mr. J. T. H. Allen. Shaykh Al-Amin uses the Arabic word for Summer
to correspond with the hot season of the N.E. Monsoon. He does this consistently throughout
the Book. Ra's Al-Khayma is one feature on the Coast of the Trucial Promontory, but means
'Uman as a whole. The word "Lions" has a very ancient usage. The word *Asad*, which
means "Lion" in Modern Arabic, means in Ancient South Arabian "Man" or "Soldier". I
have heard the Expression "Ya Asad" addressed to a small boy in Aden as a term of praise
and encouragement. *"Qarn al Asad"* near Rada' in Yemen is so named because it is backed
by a steep conical hill which carried the same name — "The Man's Peak", or "The Soldier's
Peak" (for only the young and active can climb it). One is reminded of the Gaelic "Sgurr
nan Gillean" — "The Peak of the Youths". There are no lions in Yemen, only leopards.
[22] **A.H. 1238** = January A.D. 1823.
[23] **Mtanga Wanda.** This is a small place on the West Coast of Pate Island facing the mainland,
providing an ideal anchorage.
[24] *Hammad bin Ahmad Al-Bu Sa'idi.* The original MS had what appeared to be *Jim* so that
the name read Jummad. My own photocopy of a handwritten copy of the original has
Hammad bin Muhammad. As the difference between *Hammad* and *Jummad* is only a
diacritical point, I have assumed that it is a slip of the pen on the part of Shaykh Al-Amin.
In the other traditions it is clearly Hammad.

command of them; and they camped there. The leader of this Army sent to the Amir Mbaruk b. Ahmad a letter commanding him to surrender, and declaring war if he desisted from it. When this letter was delivered to the Amir Mbaruk he mustered his soldiers, and prepared for war: but he had not at his disposal even a tenth of the forces that the Amir Hammad[25] had brought, and over and above that, most of the people had gone over to the side of the Sayyid, because they were over-awed by his (strength of) numbers and equipment, and he had nothing remaining to rely on except his Mombasan soldiers. The Amir Mbaruk knew that he was inevitably defeated. Yet he did not think he should surrender to the enemy, and submit to them without the arbitrament of the sword between him and them. So the two armies met, and the flood of that war distinguished Mbaruk with his well-known heroism, and the Sayyid's Army retreated; then they "returned the ball" upon him again (i.e. they made a second attack), and he defeated them a second time, very severely. When the Amir Hammad saw what had happened to his army, he requested the People of Pate to use deceit on the Amir Mbaruk so that he would leave Pate; and they did so. And he set out on his return to Mombasa with a number of his soldiers not exceeding 60. Thus by the trick which they played, the Amir Hammad was able to gain possession of Pate, after his army had been defeated twice by Mbaruk b. Ahmad. Captain Vidal[26] mentions that in his "Travels", as a tradition transmitted by those who had seen these battles with their own eyes.

The Amir Hammad only remained a little while in Pate, then got ready to travel to Mombasa; but when he passed by Lamu[27] and met with the leaders of the people there, they advised him to attack Pemba first, and

---

[25] **Hammad b. Ahmad**. The "History of Pate" (Freeman-Grenville, p. 82) calls this man the Liwali Hamad confusing him with the identity of the Mazru'i Amir. Neither Hammad nor Mbaruk was a Liwali; they were both Amirs, or Commanders of forces. Hammad was nicknamed Al-Sammar = The Nailer, or Walad Sammar in the unpublished MS Kawkab al-Dhurriya.

There is no mention of battles in the "History of Pate". Fumo Luti and the Amir Mbaruk just retreat to Mombasa. In view of this it is a pity that Shaykh Al-Amin is not more explicit as to the guile that was used to make them withdraw; for without such an explanation his account cannot but appear biassed. On the other hand, Mbaruk only took 60 men with him back to Mombasa. He must have had at least two hundred but certainly not more than four hundred if, as Shaykh Al-Amin says, he had "less than a tenth" of the 4,000 soldiers of Hammad's army, so that he does appear to have suffered a good number of casualties. But here again, were they dead or wounded? Or were they deserters? Cf. also Boteler's Account (Voyages, Vol. I, p. 374).

[26] **Captain Vidal**. Here again I think Shaykh Al-Amin means Owen's "Travels", which included information supplied by Vidal, Boteler, Emery and many others.

[27] The other accounts make no mention of Lamu at this stage: but this account is fully consistent with the course of events.

told him it was the one store-house for the Mazari'a supplies, and the source of their wealth; and that if he gained possession of it he would weaken them, and it would be easy to attack Mombasa. He took their good advice, and travelled on until, on coming opposite Mombasa, he fired a cannon. The Mazari'a knew beforehand what he was about, and had made every preparation to defend themselves; but, lo and behold, the ships changed course and made towards the Island (Pemba).

The War in Pemba

The Sayyid's fleet reached the Island unawares, and the Mazari'a who were there were not aware of the matter so as to be prepared for it. The Amirs who were there were Salim b. Ahmad, 'Abdullah b. Sa'id b. Khamis[28] and Sa'id b. 'Ali Al-Hinawi. The Amir Hammad landed his soldiers in Birikao,[29] and the Mazru'i soldiers met them; and the fighting between them lasted days, and the blood of the two sides flowed like rivers; and at last the Amir Hammad conquered and gained possession of the Island. This news reached the Liwali 'Abdullah, and he mobilized another army over which he set his brother Mbaruk b. Ahmad as Amir, formerly liwali of Pate; and he set out with his army in company with Sayyid Ahmad b. Abu Bakr Al-Ba'Alawi,[30] one of the brave Sayyids of Wasin, in the hope of recovering the Island, and taking it out of the hand of Amir Hammad. They met the Sayyid's (Sayyid Sa'id's) soldiers in Chwaka,[31] and the fire of war was kindled between them, and both sides lost no small number of dead and wounded. The Amir Mbaruk showed great gallantry, and displayed a bravery which confirmed his right to the praise and adulation of this country.[32] Odes were composed in his praise which continued to

[28] **Salim b. Ahmad, 'Abdullah b. Sa'id b. Khamis.** The former became the Ninth Liwali of Mombasa, the last whose story is here related. The latter is probably grandson of the Ancestor of Lineage 4 or 5 set out in Chapter I above. See also Appendix I, Tables C4 and 5.
[29] **Birikao.** This is a place on Pemba Island, not to be confused with Burkao, the better-known place near to Port Durnford in Somalia, and now known to be the site of the ancient Shungwaya, the legendary dispersal point of many of the Bantu Tribes of East Africa.
[30] *Al-Ba 'Alawi.* To judge by its form this is a name from the Hadramawt, and indicates that the Hadrami influence, now dominant among the Arab/Swahili population of the East African Coast, had already started by the end of the Eighteenth Century.
[31] **Chwaka.** This is on the N.E. Coast of Pemba Island.
[32] See Owen's "Voyages", Vol. I, p. 426; Boteler's Narrative, Vol II, p. 24; R. N. Lyne: "Zanzibar in Contemporary Times", p. 22. Lyne says that the Mazru'i hero of the Pemba war, celebrated in song by the inhabitants of Pemba even in his day, was Mbaruk b. Rashid b. 'Uthman, who died in A.D. 1806 (I think A.D. 1806 is an error for A.D. 1826), and that these songs show that the People of Pemba preferred the rule of the Mazari'a to that of 'Uman. In another book (Apostle of Empire, p. 48) he mentions that the final resistance of the Mazari'a in Pemba was only crushed by L. W. Mathews in A.D. 1877.

circulate among the folk up to no very distant period. It was that which consoled this hero, and cooled the thirst of his sorrowful heart. In spite of the gallantry shown by the Mazru'i Army in defending their Island, those tremendous forces which Sayyid Sa'id brought against them overcame them, and his army won a second signal victory; and it took possession of the Island in spite of its people's preference for the government of the Mazari'a rather than the Bu Sa'idi Government. The Amir Mbaruk returned to Mombasa in a black frame of mind, and told his brother what had happened in the Island, and the Liwali sorrowed deeply so that he heart was affected (i.e. he was cut to the heart with sorrow), and he died in dejection.[33]

The passing of the Island out of Mazru'i hands was one of the main reasons which contributed to Sayyid Sa'id's taking the rule from their hands, and the Amir Hammad saw the correctness of the advice of the People of Lamu.

The Liwali died (May God have mercy on him) on the 13th Ramadan in the year A.H. 1238[34] and was survived by one son, Khamis b. 'Abdullah.

8. The Eighth Liwali — Sulayman b. 'Ali b. 'Uthman b. 'Abdullah b. Muhammad Al-Mazru'i

His Liwaliship — A Deputation is sent to Bombay to seek Protection of the British Government — Arrival of Capt. Vidal in Mombasa — Lieut. Boteler and his meeting with the Liwali — the Discussion on the Request for Protection — The Liwali's Hospitality to Captain Vidal — The Arrival of Capt. Owen — The Treaty for a Protectorate — The Appointment of Third Lieutenant Mr Reitz as Commissioner for his Government in Bombay — 'Abdullah b. Sulaym, leader of Sayyid Sa'id's Army, and his Disembarkation in Mombasa — The Amir Mbaruk b. Ahmad goes with Capt. Owen to Pemba — The Removal of the Liwali from the Liwaliship.

After the death of the Liwali 'Abdullah b. Ahmad, his brothers differed as to who should succeed him as Liwali. Each one wanted the Liwaliship for himself, and they almost fought one another over it.[1] Then finally they

---

[33] **He died in dejection**. Or "of dejection". For a Swahili Account of the taking of Pemba, and 'Abdullah's re-action on meeting Mbaruk and hearing the news, see the Taylor/Harries Tradition, pp. 99–100.

[34] **A.H. 1238** = A.D. 1823.

[1] **And almost fought one another over it**. Sir A. Hardinge says in his memorandum (Appendix No. 4) concerning Sulayman b. 'Ali: "The latter, an aged and feeble prince, who had been chosen in order to avert a civil conflict between two kinsmen with better hereditary claims than himself ..."

agreed to make their paternal uncle, Sulayman b. 'Ali b. 'Uthman, who was formerly liwali of Pemba, Liwali, and they put him in office on 12 Shawwal A.H. 1238.[2] Sulayman b. 'Ali was an intelligent man, decisive and a lover of peace: and when he saw the fall of Pemba into the hands of Sayyid Sa'id, and the blocking of the outflow of provisions which the Mazari'a used to rely on in their wars, and felt himself too weak to resist their enemy as they should, he determined to seek the Protection of the British Government in the interest of sparing lives and stopping war, and quelling the trouble between them (i.e. the Mazari'a) and Sayyid Sa'id b. Sultan. The Liwali consulted the prudent men among his relatives, and the leaders of the "Tribes", about this matter, and they agreed with him about it and thought his judgment sound. In execution of it he chose Khamis b. Nasir and Muhammad b. 'Abdullah b. Muhammad BaShaykh, ancestor of the family of BaShaykh who are in Mombasa, and others with them, and sent them as a delegation to Bombay (written by the Author, Mumbay) to discuss with the Indian Government the setting of their country under the protection of the British Government. They met responsible people there, and set the question before them, and they promised to inform the departments concerned with such matters[3], and to send them the answer later.

A few months after the delegation had been sent, Capt. Vidal[4] arrived in Mombasa waters in the evening of 27 Rabi' al-Awwal in the year A.H. 1239.[5] Since it was night-time the Captain did not manage to contact the people of the town. Next morning the Amir Mbaruk b. Ahmad went with twenty-six men to meet the Captain and give him greeting in the name of his uncle Sulayman b. 'Ali. In this meeting he informed him of the conditions of the country, and the determination of its people to put it under the protection of His Majesty the King of England: then he asked permission, in the name of his uncle, to raise the British Flag on the Fort.

---

[2] **12 Shawwal A.H. 1238** = About the middle of A.D. 1823. He was appointed a month after 'Abdullah's death.

[3] **They promised to inform the Departments concerned.** Had the Liwali realised that such a matter had to travel not only to Bombay, but possibly right on to London, to the Colonial Department or Foreign Office, before a definite reply could be given, he might have despaired. It is important to remember the effect of travel time on the course of events.

[4] Captain Vidal and the others mentioned here were part of an Admiralty Expedition under the Command of Captain Owen, sent to survey the Coast of Africa. Captain Owen himself however seems to have used the occasion as much for the furtherance of his anti-slavery enthusiasm as for the charting of the Coastal Waters, which was the primary object of the Expedition.

[5] **27 Rabi' al-Awwal in the year A.H. 1239** = 31st December 1823. But Boteler in his narrative (Vol. II, p. 2) definitely says 3rd December. It seems clear that Shaykh Al-Amin has inadvertently read 3 as 31, and then converted it into Islamic dating.

Since this matter required some consideration, they agreed to postpone it till the following day: but the Captain then awoke ill, and sent as his representative Lieutenant Boteler.[6] Here I leave space for this lieutenant to tell us what happened between him and the Liwali, and what he was eye-witness of, as it is mentioned in Captain Owen's "Voyages". The Lieutenant says:[7]

"After I had disembarked I remained a little waiting for the Shaykh's nephew. When he had arrived in company with a crowd of Arabs, they took me into the Fort. There the Shaykh and the members of his Council awaited us. We noticed the appearance of those Arabs, and they definitely showed weariness and misery, even though their weapons were bedecked with ornaments. These are they who, while they were in the fulness of their strength were able to stop the miseries caused by the Portuguese when they attempted to gain possession of the Swahili Country; and these are they who today are resisting the forces of the Imam of Masqat. They are

---

[6] **Lieutenant Boteler**. It is necessary to bear in mind that Captain Owen, Commander of the whole expedition, was sailing in, and personally commanding, H.M.S. Leven, while Captain Vidal was under his command, and in command of H.M.S. Barracouta. The latter reached Mombasa first, and the former a month later. Lieutenant Boteler was First Lieutenant on the Barracouta under Vidal, and assistant Surveyor. Owen and Boteler each wrote an account of the voyage, each account being in two volumes. Owen seems to draw on Boteler since he reports some of Boteler's experiences and uses very similar language about the same events. [7] Cf. Owen Vol. I, pp. 367–371 and 403–412, and Boteler Vol. II, pp. 2–12. The version translated, and re-translated here, is that part of Boteler's account written into Owen's Book. It is very clear and detailed, and Guillain and Lyne both use it in their Books. Here however the wording and sense is varied from the original, and the following more important differences may be noticed: (a) Lieutenant Boteler was obviously more sympathetic to the Mazari'a and the Mombasans than was Owen. Owen for example, refers to Sulayman b. 'Ali as "the then chief of Mombas . . . an old dotard who had outlived every passion but that of avarice." One should remember however that he was faced with a "Protectorate" for which no sanction had been given, and the responsibility of decision must have irritated him. Yet both write without the least personal feeling for the Mazru'i family. Shaykh Al-Amin however has paraphrased their account to give as favourable impression as possible. (b) Shaykh Al-Amin omits mention of the curiosity of the Arabs who observed the landing of Boteler's party. (c) The weariness and misery apply in Boteler's own account not to the Liwali and his company, but to the curious onlookers. (d) The "Miseries caused by the Portuguese" of Shaykh Al-Amin 's rendering are in the original "seeking boundless dominion". (e) Shaykh Al-Amin gives the names correctly, while Boteler and Owen both show the typically English bad ear for unfamiliar names in a foreign language. The Swahilis are Sowhylese for Owen, while for Boteler they are Soallese. (f) Boteler says, "Soon after we arrived the Shaykh entered". This becomes here "We entered the Shaykh's presence and saw him to be . . ." (g) Shaykh Al-Amin renders in Arabic; "we were compelled to await the Shaykh of the Swahilis the Amir of Malindi" what in the original text is: "It was necessary to await the arrival of the Sowhylese (Soallese) Chief, without whose sanction nothing could be finally adjusted." (h) Shaykh Al-Amin also omits Boteler's statement that the Shaykh of Malindi was Portuguese Consul, and he makes no mention of his African features.

There will follow further particular points in the succeeding text.

a people not incapable of defending their honour: but the power of the enemy has increased against them, and their own power has begun to decrease until they are almost tasting the humiliation of slavery. And here I may say that the People of Mombasa (he means by them the Mazari'a), even though they have lost their power, and their country has been violated, yet they are respected by everyone in the Swahili Country.

"We entered the Shaykh's presence and saw him to be a man of tall stature, spare of body, prematurely aged by the weight of worries he had to bear: yet his appearance indicated gentleness. Before we withdrew to a private place, we were compelled to await the Shaykh of the Swahilis, the Amir of Malindi (perhaps it was Ahmad b. Shaykh al-Malindi, leader of the People of Mombasa). After a short time this Shaykh entered and those present greeted him and he shook hands with me cheerfully,[8] and greeted me in broken Portuguese: then he sat down with an air of gravity. His appearance showed his quick-wittedness and intelligence. He was in his sixty-fifth year, short of stature, thin, of good figure.[9] He was wearing a green cloak with a Turban on his head.

"After that we moved into another room with some of the important men, and the door was locked, and the request for a Protectorate was tabled for discussion.[10] The Shaykh[11] began to explain to me the dislike of the Mombasa people of having their country possessed by foreigners, they being people of pride and honour (nobility).[12] He said that what pained the heart was to become oppressed and to have one's rights trodden under foot, and that their lives (spirits) should be destroyed in defending them: for not one piece of land had the Imam of Masqat become possessed of without their defending it with all the bravery and heroism[13] they had been endowed with. 'And now since the strength of the enemy has got the better of us, the hope of saving ourselves is weak. This is the reason which has prompted us all to place this country of ours under the power of the British. For though they differ from us in custom and belief, yet they

---

[8] *bibashasha*. The original word in Owen's account is "heartily". The Arabic word means basically "with a smiling expression".

[9] *Hasan al-khalq*. This could be also *Hasan al-khuluq*. The first means "of good figure, well set-up"; the second means "polite, of good manners". As the original expression in Owen is "well-made" it must have the former meaning here. But it does not go very well with *Nahif* = Thin, spare.

[10] *'Ala basat al-bahth*. Literally "on the carpet, or rug, of enquiry". The Bedu traditionally had no tables, but conducted their business sitting on the ground with a mat between them.

[11] **The Shaykh**. Shaykh Al-Amin does not make clear that the leader in the discussion is not the Liwali but the Shaykh of Malindi. This is explicit in Owen.

[12] **People of pride and honour**. At this point Owen's version mentions "the Imam's resentment". Shaykh Al-Amin is silent on this.

[13] **Bravery and heroism**. This is Shaykh Al-Amin's rendering of "defend to the last".

are not incapable of helping the oppressed and assisting the cause of freedom' ".[14]

The Lieutenant further says: "Their reasons were worthy of notice, because their request for freedom came from the depth of their hearts, so that I could not restrain myself from sympathising with them." And again: "After the Shaykh had finished speaking, he requested me to raise the British Flag on the flag-staff of the Fort. I was prevented however from doing that by the orders I had received from Captain Vidal, but I promised them that I would send their petitions speedily to Bombay. On the following day we disembarked with Captain Vidal, and went to the Fort to visit the Liwali, and met with the important men of the town there; and after the meeting had dispersed, he (the Liwali) invited us to his house to partake of food, and we were four — Captain Vidal, the Shaykh's nephew, the Leader of the Swahilis and myself. We then said good-bye and went."[15]

After Captain Vidal had set off the Mazari'a were afraid that Sayyid Sa'id's ships, which were soon expected[16] to arrive, would take them by surprise while they were still unprepared to resist them: for Sayyid Sa'id, as they had already been informed, had mobilised those tremendous forces to crush them, and the taking of Pemba out of their hands had weakened them. So they raised on the Fort the British Flag,[17] even though they had no permission to do so, seeking the safety of many of their subjects. After a time the Sayyid's Army arrived under the command of 'Abdullah b. Sulaym.[18] He was puzzled when he saw the British Flag on the Fort, and desisted from his attack and contented himself with an investment from the sea.

On 6 Jumada al-Akhira A.H. 1239[19], Captain Owen came and saw the

---

[14] **Assisting the cause of freedom.** This is the rendering of "respected the shrine of liberty" in Owen's version.

[15] These last quotations are rather paraphrases than translations, and very much shorter than the original. In quoting this account Shaykh Al-Amin shows that he is not any more exempt than others from the difficulties inherent in translation from one language to another. He is however prone to omit matter which would seem to belittle the standing and general "image" of the Mazari'a, or to modify it so as to make a more favourable impression. He seems to have no local source for the events he recounts in this section.

[16] *Allati kanat yurja wusuluha.* Rather an awkward sentence. One would have expected *Kana* rather than *Kanat*. The word *yurja* = Hoped for. This expressed the sentiment of Sayyid Sa'id. The Mazru'i attitude would have been better expressed by such a word as *yutawaqqa'* = Expected (regardless of any emotion) or *yukhsha* = Feared.

[17] **So they raised on the Fort the British Flag.** See Owen, Vol. I, p. 367.

[18] **'Abdullah b. Sulaym.** His name is mentioned in Owen in connection with Mogadishu. Owen states that he called at that place en route for Mombasa in A.D. 1823. He preceded Owen's arrival, but arrived after Vidal had left (Owen Vol. I, pp. 359, 370).

[19] **6 Jumada Al-Akhira A.H. 1239** = 8th February A.D. 1824. This date agrees with Owen, who is followed by Guillain and Lyne.

British Flag fluttering on the Flagstaff of the Fort, and saw around
the Island of Mombasa Sayyid Sa'id's ships investing it. When he had
entered Mombasa Third Lieutenant[20] Mr Reitz landed with an interpreter,
and was greeted with a salvo of five guns. He went to the Fort to greet
the Liwali: then he returned to his warship accompanied by the Amir
Mbaruk b. Ahmad.[21] The Lieutenant knew[22] in regard to Mombasa that
the Mazari'a had mustered about 25,000 soldiers[23] to regain the Island
(Pemba), but that there were no ships at that time to transport these men
to it, since most of their vessels had been sunk in the two battles for the
Island, and the remainder had been captured by the enemy.

The Treaty of Protection

The next day in the morning Captain Owen disembarked, and the heads
and prominent men of the town received him and took him to the Fort.
The members of the Council were awaiting him, and after exchanging
greetings, the Liwali admitted to him that he had raised the British Flag
without permission, and told him the reasons which had impelled him to
do it; and the Captain excused him. Then the Liwali requested him
to accept the placing of Mombasa, and all the countries lying between Ra's
Ngomeni and Pangani,[24] under the Protection of the British Government.
Captain Owen agreed to that, on condition that he bind himself to stop
the Slave-Trade in all those countries. The Liwali undertook to perform
this condition, and Captain Owen undertook on behalf of His Government

[20] **Third Lieutenant Mr Reitz**. This refers not to his official rank but to his position in the
ship's crew. There is no substantive rank of Third Lieutenant in the British Navy, — unless
the Author means "Midshipman", the rank which Lyne records as having also been held by
Mr Phillips.
[21] **Mbaruk b. Ahmad**. He is referred to by Owen (vol. I, p. 403) as "Mombarrok". We have
preserved the Swahili form of the name in which the Arabic participial Mu- has been
converted into the Bantu "Hummed M" prefix. This is so common on the Swahili Coast that
we have preferred that to the orthodox Arabic *Mubarak*.
[22] *Wa'alam al-mulazim min akhbar mumbasa*. The first word might also be *Wa'ullim*.
The sentence might therefore mean either "The lieutenant *knew* in regard to . . .", or "The
lieutenant had been informed or made aware . . ." The former reading is the most probable.
[23] **25.000 soldiers**. See Note 15 in Chap. I above; also Owen Vol. I, p. 367. Compare this with
Prins: The Swahili-speaking Peoples, p. 103. The examples Prins quotes are gatherings of not
more than 4,000 men. Lieutenant Reitz "was told" that they had 25,000 men in readiness. It
may have been an exaggeration to encourage British support and interest, and generally to
impress on them that a Protectorate would be worthwhile. If Lieutenant Boteler actually
saw men mustered, he may have committed the common fault which eye-witnesses make of
overestimating a crowd. If however it is from a record of recruitment, it may be quite correct.
The Mazru'i Government was making a special effort at the time.
[24] **Between Ra's Ngomeni and the River Pangani**. See the Map in Appendix II. Compare
Shaykh Al-Amin's remarks in Chap. I above about the extent of the Mazru'i territory.

to return to the Liwali's rule all the countries which the enemy had taken by force. The Treaty of Protection[25] was immediately made binding[26] between the two parties. It contained six clauses as follows:

(1) That Great Britain should cause to return to (the Jurisdiction of) the Liwali of Mombasa all the countries he ruled formerly.

(2) That the Chief of the Mazari'a should administer the "Sultanate" and that it should be hereditary in his descendants.

(3) That the Commissioner of the Protecting Power should reside with the Liwali.

(4) That the duties (Arab — *'Ushur* = Tithes) should be divided[27] between the contracting Powers equally.

(5) That British subjects should have permission to trade in the "inland" regions, or "possessions". (Arab. — *Al-Mamalik al-Dakhiliya*).

(6) That an end should be put to the Slave-Trade in Mombasa.

To carry out the Clauses of this Treaty the Third Lieutenant[28] of the warship "Leven", Mr John James Reitz, was appointed Commissioner for Great Britain in Mombasa, and Mr George Phillips[29] was appointed Commander (Arab. *Qa'id*) of the soldiers with the assistance of three British men.

After this Treaty had been completed, and 'Abdullah b. Sulaym,[30] the Commander of Sayyid Sa'id's Army, had been informed, he ordered his ships to be brought into the harbour, and he himself disembarked, and was received with warmth by his brethren the Mazari'a; and he was

[25] **The Treaty of Protection**. The conditions of the Treaty are set out in Guillain (p. 578) and are identical with the list here. Lyne's list also corresponds exactly, but neither Owen nor Boteler do more than refer to the terms *ob iter*.

[26] **Was immediately made binding**. The Arabic word is *Ubrimat*, which means "was made binding", when applied to a covenant or treaty. It must however be remembered that Owen's action was only provisional until it had been ratified by the British Government. This had to come at least from Bombay, but more probably from London, since the Mazru'i State was being treated as an independent sovereign power. That ratification never appears to have been given. Therefore Mr Emery's withdrawal later on was not a breaking of an agreement, but simply the natural result of a refusal to ratify.

[27] **Yuqsam Al-'Ushur**. This should be *Tuqsam al-'Ushur*. It is possible that this and other grammatical errors were in the original Arabic Text of the Treaty. *'Ushur* literally means "Tithes", but it has come to mean Taxes generally.

[28] **The Third Lieutenant**. See Note 20 above.

[29] **Mr George Phillips**. Mr Phillips seems to have had a civilian post, rather than a military command as here stated; but his duties were probably not clearly defined nor strictly limited.

[30] **Sulaym**. Ruete: "Sa'id b. Sultan", p. 50, calls this man 'Abdullah b. Suleyyim. In unvowelled Arabic, however, that would be written in the same way as Sulaym.

delighted at the Treaty concluded between them and the British, which had taken off his back the burden and responsibilities of this war.

On the eleventh of the month before-mentioned[31] Captain Owen set out in the direction of Pemba in company with the Amir Mbaruk b. Ahmad and fifty of his men with him.[32]

This is all I am aware of of the events of the time of Sulayman b. 'Ali, that gentle Liwali, lover of peace. In the third year of his rule the sons of Ahmad b. Muhammad b. 'Uthman agreed upon his removal; and so they removed him, and he travelled to Pemba, and lived and died there (May God's mercy be on him). The preceding generations did not mention the reason for the removal of the Liwali, but what is quite clear is his strong inclination to peace, and his easy readiness[33] to obtain it, so that the Sons of Ahmad b. Muhammad were afraid that he would surrender to the enemy if he remained as Liwali. God knows best the true position.

The Liwali was survived by his only son Ahmad, but he had no issue so the line came to an end.

9. The Ninth Liwali — Salim b. Ahmad b. Muhammad b. 'Uthman b. 'Abdullah Al-Mazru'i

His installation as Liwali — The "Mimiya" of the learned Scholar Muhyi al-Din congratulating him — The arrival of Commodore Christian, and his Meeting with the People of the Town in the house of Merry (Emery) the

---

[31] **The month before-mentioned**. I.e. Jumada al-Akhira, equivalent to 13th February 1824.

[32] Guillain states at this point (p. 580) that Owen actually attempted to get "Sa'eed Muhammad Al Akhabiri", as he calls the 'Umani Governor of Pemba, to evacuate it in favour of Mombasa; but the Governor refusing, he had no power to force him to do so.

Mbaruk tried to get the Governor of Mauritius, Mr Cole, to ratify the Protectorate Treaty, but did not succeed (Owen Vol. II, pp. 25–26; Boteler Bol. II, p. 194). Guillain further reports (p. 581), on authority of Owen and Boteler, that the Treaty was infringed in respect of Slave-trading. Some freed slaves who had been settled at English Point by Lieutenant Emery (Lyne says, Midshipman Phillips) had nearly been lifted again by the Arab owner, who was judged on board H.M.S. Leven when Owen returned to Mombasa, and sentenced to be deported to Seychelles.

It is probable that the Mazru'i Shaykh had not much power to control this trading anyway, seeing that he depended very much on the Swahili "Tribes" for the holding of his position. Cases would have happened in spite of his prohibition, and in all likelihood without his knowledge. The Liwali was however not only Arab but also a Muslim; thus the idea of a society without slaves would at that period have seemed quite unrealistic to him, and the condition in the Treaty something to be accepted as a form but expected to remain a dead letter.

[33] *Tahawunuhu*. I have rendered this "Easy readiness". The word actually means "slackness" or "laziness" or "Easy-goingness". But none of these expressions seems to fit the meaning which is intended by Shaykh Al-Amin.

Englishman — The End of the British Protection of the Mazari'a — Mr Lyne shows the True Reason for the British Withdrawal from this Protectorate — The First Attack of Sayyid Sa'id upon Mombasa — Babu Kafi b. Mwishafi and his Stirring up of Enthusiasm in (people's) Hearts — The War between the two Parties — The Secret Conference between the Sayyid and 'Abdullah b. Zahir regarding a Settlement — 'Abdullah b. Zahir sways the Liwali's Heart in Favour of Accepting a Settlement — The Treaty of Settlement — Sayyid Sa'id dishonours the Treaty — Nasir b. Sulayman and his Bad Treatment of the Mazari'a — The Fighting between him and them — The Mazari'a besiege the Fort — The Sayyid Hilal sends provisions to help those in the Fort — The Bravery of Kiyati b. Mwinyi Uvi and his Conquest of the Provision Ship — Nasir b. Sulayman asks for Safe-Conduct — He is seized and killed — "Lamiya" of the learned scholar Muhyi Al-Din on the Battle of the Siege of the Fort — The Sayyid attacks Mombasa a Second time — The Defeat of his Army and its Loss — The Building of the Town Wall and Makupa Fort — The Civil War in Siyu and the Help which the Liwali gave its People against the Sayyid — The Sayyid attacks Mombasa for the Third Time — the Battle of Chagga — The Mazari'a try to regain Pemba but fail — Mwinyi Simba, the Sultan of Tanga, is seized — Rashid b. Salim founds the Town of Takaungu — the Death of the Liwali (God's Mercy upon him).

After the removal of the Liwali Sulayman b. 'Ali, the sons of Ahmad b. Muhammad b. 'Uthman chose their brother Salim, and made him Liwali and swore allegiance to him in the middle of the year A.H. 1241,[1] and the rest of the Arabs and the leaders of the "Twelve Tribes" swore allegiance to him, and the chiefs of the Africans came swearing allegiance to him and promising obedience. The learned scholar Muhyi Al-Din b. Shaykh Al-Qahtani heard that they had made him Liwali while he was in Mtangata,[2] one of the towns of Tanga; so he sent to him a "Qasida Mimiya",[3]

[1] **The middle of the year A.H. 1241** = The beginning of A.D. 1826, or the end of A.D. 1825. Guillain (p. 584) makes it A.H. 1242, or A.D. 1826. This section is longer because there is more information recorded about East Africa from the beginning of the 19th Century onwards, and because the Author's own family's memories would be fresher.

[2] *Mtanghata*. The Author uses *Ghayn* in writing this word. In the introduction to the Poem below the same word is written with a *Jim* (*Gim* in South Arabia).

[3] *Qasida Mimiya*. An Ode in which the last syllable in every line begins with the Arabic letter *Mim*. I have translated this as literally as possible. It will be seen to be highly conventional, and with an elaboration of metaphor which appears in English forced, e.g. "As though the flash of lightning smiles". By English standards the adulation is rather overdone, but it must be remembered that the poet is modelling his work on the Traditional Ode Form, which had its origin in the Desert in Pre-Islamic times.

The measure of the line is not in every case perfectly worked out, but it is the Arabic meter known as "Rajaz", which consists of a line of six, or less commonly four, feet, three (or two) in each half, with variations on its basic form, which may be represented thus:

$$- - \smile - / - - - \smile - / - - - \smile - // - - - \smile - / - - - \smile - / - - - \smile - //$$

See Wright: Arabic Grammar Vol. II, p. 362.

congratulating him in it concerning the Liwaliship. We set it down here in its full text, which we have copied without change or amendment. It is as follows:

Muhyi Al-Din b. Al-Shaykh b. 'Abd al-Shaykh Al-Qahtani Al-Barawi composed these verses in the Port of Mtangata when the news reached him of the accession of the excellent Liwali Salim b. Ahmad b. Muhammad b. 'Uthman Al-Mazru'i (God be merciful to him, Amen) —

> In the Name of God the Merciful the Compassionate[4]
>
> O messenger, reveal the wonderful, and make clear to the under-
> standing
> > News which even without speaking, slakes the thirst.
> Go quickly as far as Mombasa
> > Where are the Full-moons brightening that heaven:
> Where are the Shaykhs of Kahlan,
> > They, the Sayyids of Kahlan, of good lineage,
> Noble lions, sons of Ahmad, among men
> > As generous as the sea, or as torrents of rain.
> When[5] you come hurrying to its Fort,
> > Stand at its door, and ask for entrance that you may
> > understand.
> When you enter by their leave, go in haste
> > Eastwards[6] advancing, and giving salutations.
> When you take your seat, remain facing them respectfully;
> > Greet them from me in a manner which does them honour.
> Ask them clearly and humbly,
> > What caused estrangement after friendship
> As though the marks of friendship were effaced from between us
> > And had become objectionable after being as clear as a
> > banner?
>
> Time passed, but we found none who brought news
> > Of their state, or of their dwellings — most delightful of
> > retreats!
> All news of Mombasa was cut off from us.
> > What happened there, I wonder? Ask that we may understand.
> Has she been divorced before the legal period (has expired)?

[4] The main point of the poem is that the Mazari'a are the rightful "spouses" of the Town and Fort of Mombasa, and the fittest to defend her. This idea occurs again in the Second Ode in this section concerning the Battle with Sayyid Sa'id's forces.

[5] *Bikutiha*. The word *Kut* is a word used in the Gulf and Iraq and appears to have originated in India, but is not used in S. W. Arabia.

[6] *Nahwa al-sabah*. Towards the morning, i.e. Eastwards. The direction here indicated is from the entrance of the Fort, and so may refer to the room of the Arabic Inscriptions, which the Mazari'a may have used as their *Baraza*, or Audience Chamber. The late Mr. James Kirkman, formerly Warden of Fort Jesus, had that room restored some years ago.

Or has not one of suitable rank been found for her?
That she has held back, and delayed her engagement
        Until she finds one suited to her who will give her protection?
Ask her, and obtain from her a healing answer,
        Which will quench the thirst and end the heart's blindness.

The messenger returned with happy news,
        His brow marked with brightness.
He urged his pace quickly in his hurry,
        While light shines in the sky as though
The full moon in the darkness filled the horizon with its light,
        And as though the flash of lightning smiled.

So I remained staring at that brilliance,
        Wondering what had taken place in the sky.
"Are you telling us what had happened in the Kingdom there,
        Or of 'Laylat al-Qadr',[7] than which there is no greater?"

And see, the messenger gives as his answer good news,
        Rejoicing, and saying with singing:
"Hurrah, Hurrah! That good news concerns him
        Whose stars of good fortune have risen and who has become
                great.
He it is whom Mombasa has been pleased to take as husband,
        and has rejoiced in, and taken to herself,
And boasts of, and has pride in as Ruler,
        So that she glitters at his exaltation, and is herself exalted in
                fame.
I mean by him Salim the Liwali of the Land.
        His descent is exalted by relationship to Ahmad,
The Full Moon of the sons of Kahlan most noble, and their truest son,
        How good a Khalifa, the palm of whose hand is like an over-
                flowing sea!
Just, honouring to his subjects, dealing fairly,
        The help of the weak, whose good will never be lacking,
A cave (of refuge) for widows and orphans, and whoever
        Depends for favour on his generosity will never be in want.
    The Imams of our time are made jealous by his justice,
        And the wrongdoer, because of his justice, refuses to do evil."

I answered him, when he had so well described his character,

---

[7] *Laylat al-Qadri*. This is a reference to Sura 97 of the Qur'an. It is understood by Muslims to mean the Night in which the First Section of the Qur'an (the first verses of Sura 96) were revealed to Muhammad. This expression means "The Night of Power" or "The Night of Destiny"; but it is so technicalised in Islamic Theology that I prefer to transliterate it rather than to render it into English. *Laylat al-Qadr* is thought to fall within the last ten days of Ramadan, some say on the 26th or 27th of that month.

And enlarged on his description, in fear of the envious and
    spiteful,
"Slowly, may God guide you, O best of messengers,
    You have brought us news of a fact which slakes the thirst,
and gives us certain and clear information
    Which heals the breast and lifts the blindness of the heart."

How generous a guest to come in our direction!
    How good a visitor to come to our door!
O, brethren of the beloved Liwali, and you his supporters,
    Be, all of you, stars like the Pleiades:
Beware of being foreigners to one another like the Stars of the Great
    Bear (i.e. scattered).
    Humiliation simply consists of antagonism; for how often
Have the many been humiliated through quarrelling, and how often
        Have the few become glorious through agreement, by God's
        Mercy![8]
Be all of you his helpers against the enemy,
    In spite of the scorn of the envious, that they may be grieved.
May God help you, — and how good a helper is He to you!
    He gives bountifully, but is pleased (to receive) less than that.

I give you my greeting of peace as a salutation,
    From Shaykh Muhyi Al-Din, who here completes his poem.

We have seen in the historical MSS which are in our hands copied "from
the handwriting of"[9] the learned scholar Muhyi Al-Din b. Shaykh (God's
Mercy upon Him) that there was in Mombasa and Englishman named
"Merry".[10] On 5 Dhu Al-Hijja A.H. 1241[11] this Englishman invited all the
Shaykhs of the Town and the Leaders of the Swahili to his house. When

---

[8] **For how often. . . . .mercy of God**. For a repetition of this sentiment on another
occasion, see the Taylor/Harries Tradition, (p. 100, para. 5), where the Liwali 'Abdullah on
his death-bed warned his relatives of the danger of disunity, by means of a bunch of coconut
fibres.

[9] *Manqula min*. "Copied from", or it may mean "Transmitted from" using the word in its
technical sense. It is possible also that the Author may mean "copied in the handwriting of".
It is a pity that these MSS. are not more clearly specified by the Author. The root *NAQALA*
can also mean "translate", but I do not think it can have that meaning here.

[10] **Merry** (Arabic: Mariy). Arabs often leave off the first syllable of foreign names beginning
with a vowel, especially if the second syllable is weak, or the first syllable is closed so that
two consonants follow it. This should in fact be "Emery". Guillain p. 581; Owen Vol. II
p. 148; Boteler Vol. II p. 186–7 all agree that he had been appointed in place of Lt. Reitz by
Commodore Nourse of H.M.S. Andromache, who called at Mombasa in July A.D. 1826: but
the two latter say that a Lt. Wilson was appointed at the same time. When Shaykh Al-Amin
questions the authority of this Englishman, it seems clear that he confuses him either with
Phillips, a sort of acting Commissioner, or with Captain Acland (see below) — more probably
the former, as Captain Acland had not yet arrived.

[11] **5 Dhu Al-Hijja A.H. 1241** = 16th July A.D. 1826.

they had all assembled, he asked them, "Who has the Liwaliship of Mombasa, I or the Liwali Salim b. Ahmad?" They all replied, "It belongs to the Liwali, and you are nothing but a pledge in his hand." Then they went away. The chroniclers have not related to us the business of this man, nor what authority he had to ask people this extraordinary question. It seems to me that this Englishman was the Agent for Great Britain in the place of Mr Reitz, whom Captain Owen had appointed after the conclusion of the Treaty of Protection; for it is not fitting for an ordinary man, or such a man as a merchant, to come forward with such a question as this. But what, do you think, was the motive for this question? The answer will be clear to you from what follows.

On 16 Dhu al-Hijja A.H. 1241,[12], Captain Christian, whom the historians of Mombasa call Captain Aklan,[13] held a public meeting in the house of the afore-mentioned Merry, and sent to the Liwali requesting him to attend this meeting: so he sent as his deputies his brothers the Amir Mbaruk b. Ahmad and Rashid b. Ahmad. There went with them the Leaders of the Swahilis, and the important men of the town, among them the learned Muhyi Al-Din. After they had sat down at the meeting he (i.e. Aklan) said to them, "This Town and the other areas under its rule belong to His Majesty the King of Britain so long as the British Flag flies over it: that is in accordance with the Treaty which you concluded with Captain Owen. Is this not the case?" Mbaruk b. Ahmad answered him, "That was not the case. What we agreed upon with Captain Owen was that the British Government should have half the customs revenue ('Ushur), and that it should return to us our lands in Pemba and elsewhere which were taken from us by force: but the country, its rule and its administration belong by right to the Liwali." The captain said, "If the position is thus[14] then there is no place for us here; for we do not remain in a country in which we have no power to command nor to forbid. I am

---

[12] **16 Dhu Al-Hijja A.H. 1241** = 27th July A.D. 1826.

[13] **Captain Christian, whom the historians call Captain Aklan.** Shaykh Al-Amin here confuses two people. Christian was really a Commodore, but was stationed either at Mauritius or at the Cape of Good Hope. "Aklan" is really Captain Acland, who was commanding the ship which actually called at Mombasa (Boteler Vol. II, p. 187).

[14] **If the position is thus. . . .** . There is no mention of the infringement of the Anti-slavery conditions, recounted by Boteler and Owen, and repeated by Guillain, Pearce, Lyne and others in their accounts. Of course, the Europeans all regard the continued acts of slave-trading as heinous crimes. But the true evaluation of this situation is rather that the Mazari'a could not hope to stop a traffic for the restraint of which neither they nor the British had enough means available. For accounts of the acts in question, see Lyne. p. 27 (bottom), Guillain p. 581, Owen Vol. II p. 148–153, and Boteler Vol. II p. 187 and 201–3. It may be noted that Boteler has a more friendly estimate of the Swahilis than Owen. In his account of the illicit slavery he takes occasion to commend the Swahilis for bravery. This may have been because his contact with them had been much closer than Owen's.

going away from you with Merry." Then the Amir said, "If you choose to go from us of your own free will we do not hinder you; but you should know that we did not drive you out of our country." The Captain answered, "No blame attaches to you, Amir, but I am sorry that you did not understand what Captain Owen said.[15] Or perhaps he did not understand what you said; and it may be that the interpreter who was interpreting for the two parties let you down in his translation, and thus caused the Treaty to be written contrary to what you wished, and what was hidden before has only today been made clear." Then they went to the Fort, and lowered the British Flag, and took it away, and entered their ship on the evening of that day, and weighed anchor in the morning of 17 Dhu al-Hijja.

From that day the British Protection ended over this country, after lasting for two and a half years. Mr Lyne says in his book "Zanzibar"[16] printed in London in the year 1905 that the interference of the British in the politics of Mombasa grieved Sayyid Sa'id, who was obedient to Great Britain and friendly to the British People, and so objected to the Bombay Government over what happened in Mombasa. The Government replied to him that they were determined to cast aside all that had to do with Mombasa in the future, and to rescind what Captain Owen had brought about.[17] Mr Lyne says as well that Great Britain had been saddled with the blame for withdrawing from Mombasa: but that the advantage of that withdrawal was great in the Persian Gulf, and the pursuit of that advantage necessitated keeping friendly relations with Sayyid Sa'id. All honour to Mr Lyne;[18] for he has shown us the true reason which caused Britain

[15] **That you did not understand**. This is a patent dodge of diplomacy. Shaykh Al-Amin is justified also in blaming the British for not returning Pemba to Mombasa's possession, as they had undertaken to do.

[16] **Lyne: Zanzibar in Contemporary Times pp. 26–7**. Here a difference of attitude is apparent. The rising Imperial power of Britain was primarily interested in pleasing the power with the widest influence. Lyne, writing from this stand-point, thus thinks Sayyid Sa'id a fine person, and his friendliness to Britain only appears to him to be frank and open-hearted for its own sake, with no ulterior motive. But Shaykh Al-Amin simply sees the withdrawal of the Protectorate from Mombasa as an act of faithlessness by "Perfidious Albion". From our point in history it is clear that East Africa would have developed in the same way, whichever course Britain had adopted, since Mombasa eventually came under British Rule and influence anyway. British friendship was motivated by commercial interest, but it is doubtful whether the Mazru'i leaders were really deceived as to the true motive for Commodore Christian's action.

[17] *Wa'ibtal ma ata bihi al-Qabtan Uwin*. "And cancelling, or rescinding, what Capt. Owen had done". It must be remembered that Owen's and Vidal's compacts were never more than provisional. It would perhaps have been more appropriate to say: *"Wa'adam ibram (ithbat) ma ata bihi."*

[18] *walillahi durr almistar Layn*. An idiomatic expression meaning: "Well done, Mr. Lyne!". The same expression occurs in Line 32 of the Poem on p. 92 above.

to remove her Protectorate from the Mazari'a, and to tear up the Treaty concluded between her and them. Captain Christian however concealed this reason from them.

The First Attack of Sayyid Sa'id on Mombasa

We know that the Sayyid was grieved by the interference of the British in the affairs of Mombasa, and without doubt he was exceedingly glad at their withdrawal from it. He started to prepare equipment for an attack upon the Mazari'a, to take away their possessions from out of their hands. When he had completed his preparations, he set sail from Masqat in nine ships full of heavy artillery, and many armaments and thousands of soldiers. He himself commanded this army, and he was in the flagship "Liverpool".[19] He reached Mombasa with these forces on 17 Jumada Al-Akhira A.H. 1243[20] with the purpose of subduing the Mazari'a and reducing them to his obedience, or of destroying them to the last man. As soon as the "Liverpool", and the ships which followed it had anchored in the waters of Kilindini, the Sayyid sent two letters,[21] one to the Liwali and the other to Ahmad b. Shaykh, leader of the Swahilis. The messenger went with the two letters to the Fort. At that time the chiefs of the "Tribes" and the prominent men of the Town, and the Amirs and Commanders (*Quwwad*), had gathered to take counsel concerning this war. The Liwali received the two letters, and took that which was for himself, and gave the other to the one for whom it was meant; then he turned to those who were present and told them the contents of the message, namely that "Sayyid Sa'id wishes us to submit to him and resign from (the rule of) our country in his favour, otherwise he will make war on us, and overcome us by force." Then he requested the Council members to advise him as to what appeared to them to be right. There was in the Council Babu Kafi b. Mwishafi, the orator of the WaKilindini and their learned man, and one

---

[19] **The Flagship "Liverpool"**. This was a British-built ship and had been presented to Sayyid Sa'id by the British Government. According to Capt. Hart, quoted by Lyne (Op. Cit. p. 16), it carried 74 guns.

[20] **17 Jumada al-Akhira A.H. 1243** = 6th January A.D. 1828. The beginning of the N.E. Monsoon. Guillain here speaks of a locality named Sera-Koupa. I can find it on no plan, but it apparently lies on the West side of the Island of Mombasa next to Kilindini.

[21] **Sent two letters.** It is apparant from this that Sayyid Sa'id, from the start, aimed at driving a wedge between the Mazari'a and the Swahili "Tribes". His move also shows that he was well aware of the effectiveness of the Swahili check on the Mazru'i power, or that he had been well advised by those who knew. Ahmad b. Shaykh was probably the WaMalindi leader referred to by Shaykh Al-Amin in the previous section in his note in bracketed parenthesis to Boteler's account of his meeting with the Mombasan Leaders. See Also the Introduction p. 6.

of those noted for his bravery. He rose and addressed the messenger thus: "O Arab, this country is Salim's, and if he wishes of his own choice to cede it to Sa'id, there is nothing to hinder him. But we have no power against you as long as you are in the ships; so disembark and come on shore." His people approved his words, and all cried out, "Let them disembark, let them disembark!" They sang songs of war and danced with their spears, bows and muskets, and thus aroused enthusiasm in the hearts of those present. The Liwali turned to 'Abdullah b. Nafi' and ordered him to write to Sayyid Sa'id an answer to his letter to the effect that he would not yield, and that he was ready to defend his country. After the messenger had gone with the answer, the Liwali divided his army into detachments, and appointed a commander over every detachment; and he sent some to Kilindini[22] to face the enemy, and others to Makupa, and others again to Shimanzi. The Sayyid also disembarked his soldiers and the battle was joined.

Sayyid Sa'id was an Arab of exceptional cunning. He did not simply rely on strength and bravery only in his wars, but used to prefer to these "diplomacy" with all that that word implies; for war, as it is said, is deception. The Sayyid knew that the sons of Zahir b. 'Abdullah[23] carried in their hearts[24] a grudge against the sons of 'Uthman b. 'Abdullah because of the way they treated them; so he thought he would seek their help against their own side — "Nothing notches iron but (other) iron".[25] So he sent to 'Abdullah b. Zahir to meet him with all speed in Kilindini.

While the war was in progress, here was Sayyid Sa'id sitting on the deck of his warshp in private session with 'Abdullah b. Zahir,[26] conferring with him in secret concerning a reconciliation, and displaying to him his

---

[22] **Kilindini. . . . . . Makupa. . . . . . . Shimanzi**. These places are all on the South and West sides of the Island of Mombasa, where it was easier to land than at the Old Town.

[23] **The Sons of Zahir b. 'Abdullah**. See the Section on the Sixth Liwali Ahmad b. Muhammad b. 'Uthman above, at heading "The Civil War between the Liwali and the Sons of Mas'ud", and Appendix I, Tables B and C3 for the connection between the Sons of Mas'ud and the Sons of Zahir.

[24] **Bayna Junubihim**. Literally "Between their flanks", i.e. in their hearts.

[25] **"Nothing notches iron but (other) Iron"**. i.e. Nothing will break the power of the Mazari'a so well as other members of their own clan. This was not however the policy which finally won Sayyid Sa'id Mombasa.

[26] **In private session with 'Abdullah b. Zahir**. Guillain (p. 586) says that he and Rashid b. Ahmad (which may be an error for Rashid b. Salim) had been sent the previous year to Masqat; and that Sayyid Sa'id had himself brought them back with him, keeping Rashid, the least favourably disposed towards himself, on board, and sending 'Abdullah with a gift of 300 piastres. Shaykh Al-Amin's statement that the gift was 3,000 Riyals seems more realistic. The smaller sum was perhaps reported by those who wished to belittle the Mazari'a, or 'Abdullah b. Zahir, by showing how ready he was to betray the cause of his brethren for quite a petty sum.

strong desire for it. 'Abdullah b. Zahir agreed with him on that, and promised him to make every effort to bring about a reconciliation between him and the Liwali in a way which would please him. The Sayyid was delighted at this good news, and agreed with his friend to reward him with 3,000 Riyals if the reconciliation was completed by his agency. When he was on the point of disembarking from the warship, the Sayyid offered him 1,000 riyals as an advance, on the understanding that he would pay him the remainder after his work was completed. 'Abdullah accepted this with thanks, and went on shore and hurried to the Liwali, and set before him the matter of a reconciliation, and made it as desirable as he could to him, and sought to turn his heart towards it with all the shrewdness he had been endowed with, until he regarded it favourably, and summoned his advisers and informed them of the proposal 'Abdullah had brought. They agreed to stop the war, until they should meet with the Sayyid and look at the conditions of this reconciliation.

The fighting stopped, and the Sayyid invited the Liwali, and met him and his brother Mbaruk b. Ahmad and a few of his company, and a group of the leaders of the Town. After discussion and debate, and exchange of views, they reached a reconciliation and concluded a Treaty of reconciliation together as follows:[27]

(a) The Fort should be surrendered to Sayyid Sa'id, and a garrison should be left in it consisting of 50 soldiers, on condition that they should be of a tribe compatible with the Mazari'a.

(b) The Liwali should live in the fort as he did before.

(c) The sovereignty should belong to Sayyid Sa'id, but the Government should belong to Salim during his life, and to his descendants after his death.[28]

(d) The customs revenue ('Ushur) should be divided equally between the contracting parties, and Salim the Liwali should have the right of choosing whom he wished to administer the Customs posts.

after concluding (the Treaty) in this form, each one bound himself to be

---

[27] For the clauses of this Treaty, compare Guillain p. 387. According to him the Tribe compatible with the Mazari'a were the Hinawi Tribe: yet he adds in a footnote that the Hinawis were rivals of the Ghafiris. Hardinge (See Appendix IV) on the other hand asserts that the Mazari'a were Ghafiris. It looks as if either he or Shaykh Al-Amin has misunderstood the implications of this condition. Guillain wrote so near the event that it is difficult to see how he could have been mistaken as to the Tribes; Yet Al-Amin has probably got the actual terms of the Treaty more accurately. Perhaps Guillain's "assure-t-on" tips the scales against him.

[28] **To his descendants after his death**. It is interesting to see in this third condition, and in the Nineteenth Century, a concept of hereditary Governorship which appeared in Islam as far back as the 'Abbasid Caliphate in the early 9th Century with the Tahirids of Iran, and probably goes back further.

loyal to what he had undertaken to his partner, and they swore to each other upon it with every hard oath. In actual fact the Liwali surrendered the Fort to the Sayyid,[29] and he put his soldiers in it, and set out for Zanzibar accompanied by the chief of the Mazari'a to see him off.

If we consider this Treaty we shall see that it was in the interests of the Mazari'a, because it deprived them of nothing of their rule except the name only; and if it had continued as it was, the relationship of Sayyid Sa'id with them would have been like the relationship of the rulers of the East today with the Colonial Governments. This shows that the Sayyid felt the awkwardness of his position in face of the strength of the Mazari'a. Otherwise, he would not have accepted these conditions which weakend the very rule he was fighting for — unless[30] he was concealing in himself an intention to be disloyal to it (the Treaty), as in fact happened. That is partly what is meant by "diplomacy", and there will appear in the circumstances which follow the proof of what we state.

After nearly two months from the date of this Treaty, the Sayyid supplied the garrison which he had left in the Fort with Arab and Baluchi soldiers, and put Jama'dar Shahu Al-Jundigali[31] in command of them. The ship which carried them arrived at Mtwapa, and they came on foot to Mombasa and entered the Fort. The Liwali no longer lived in the Fort from the day of the conclusion of the Treaty, because he disdained to live in it with the Sayyid's soldiers; but he took a house for himself in Ndia Kuu and began to build a mosque behind it. [This mosque was not finished because of the wars with which Salim's Liwaliship was interspersed, but the ruins of it remain to this day. It is South-East of the house of Isma'ilji Jiwanji.][32] Then the Sayyid sent after those soldiers Nasir b. Sulayman Al-

---

[29] Sayyid Sa'id entered the Fort on 11 Jumada al-Akhira A.H. 1243 = 11th January A.H. 1828. Compare Guillain p. 588. Rudolph Sa'id Ruete in his Book "Sa'id b. Sultan" p. 52 gives a letter dated 17 Jumada al-Akhira A.H. 1243 = 17th January 1828 from Sayyid Sa'id, reporting this Treaty as a great victory. Lyne however calls it, probably rightly, the "Shadow of a Treaty", which he accepted from policy in place of the "substance of victory" (p. 54).

[30] *Allahumma illa idha*. Lit. "O God, unless if . . ." The meaning is that there is no avoiding the conclusion that Sayyid Sa'id was acting in bad faith, though the writer has no delight in drawing that conclusion.

[31] *Al-Zandigali*. It seems that the Letter *Jim* is here also meant to be pronounced as G, for it usually appears, when written in European letters, as we have written it. Guillain says that some of the soldiers were Zeudgali (p. 589). Shaykh Al-Amin here uses the letter as it is pronounced in South-West Arabia, but he usually uses *Ghayn* for hard G. Guillain also says that the Arabs had a commander of their own named Sa'id b. Muhammad b. Walid.

[32] **Isma'ilji Jiwanji**. This man died as recently as in the week 11–18 December 1966.

Isma'ili,[33] who was liwali under his authority in Pemba. Though this matter was contrary to the first and third terms of the Mazru'i/Sa'id Treaty, the Mazari'a respected this liwali of theirs completely, for fear they should do something which would bring the charge of having broken the covenants they had imposed upon themselves.

The Event of the Siege of the Fort[34]

After the Sayyid had spent nearly three months in Zanzibar, he returned to 'Uman, and Nasir b. Sulayman began to treat the people badly[35] and act toward them harshly, and to insult the foremost among them, until they were disgusted at him and hated him. At last, he began to abuse the Mazari'a and to insult them. They sent to him to stop showing hostility to them, but Nasir gave them no consideration at all. When the Shaykhs of the Town, and the leaders of the "Tribes", saw the quarrel intensifying between him and Mazari'a, fearing that evil would result they tried to mediate a reconciliation between them. The Mazari'a accepted the reconciliation on the understanding that each of them should desist from displaying hostility to the other, and that they should send their complaint to 'Uman, and await the orders of the Sayyid in regard to this matter.

Nasir b. Sulayman did not accept this settlement,[36] and after a short time he sent to the Liwali ordering him to surrender the rule of the Town to him, and declaring war upon him if he did not do so: but the Liwali refused to do it, and considered it a shocking insult against his rights in view of its breaking the Treaty made between him and the Sayyid. The people were also amazed at this action of Nasir's, and tried to get him to postpone this matter until the Sayyid's reply should be brought back from

---

[33] **Nasir b. Sulayman Al-Isma'ili**. Guillain gives two versions of the appointment of this man: (a) That he persuaded Sayyid Sa'id that the Mazari'a would not honour their agreements, which agrees with the unpublished "*Kawkab al-Dhurriya*", and (b) That the Sayyid took the initiative in sending him. He finds that (b) cannot be discounted in view of the Sayyid's subsequent treachery.

[34] **The Event of the Siege of the Fort**. For Guillain's account of this siege see pp. 591–4.

[35] **To treat the people badly**. Guillain says he tried to curry flavour with the Swahilis by giving them gifts. For Shaykh Al-Amin "The People" sometimes tends to mean "The Mazari'a", or the Arab section of the population.

[36] **Did not accept this settlement**. Guillain says that Nasir claimed that his "figure", i.e. his mere presence, was sufficient proof of the fact that he had Sayyid Sa'id's authority; whereupon Mbaruk answered that his person was not even good enough to represent the Sayyid's Sandal-sole! — a shocking insult among Arabs, but one feels in the circumstances that it was made by Mbaruk under extreme provocation.

'Uman, but the liwali persisted[37] in requesting it, and told the Shaykhs that what he (Nasir) was doing was exactly what the Sayyid had told him to do, and that it was not possible for him to go against his orders.

On 5 Dhu al-Qa'da in the year A.H. 1243[38] the banner of war was unfurled[39], and an order was given to shell the Town, and to open fire with muskets upon its populace; and a large part of it was burnt by artillery-fire, and Nasir went out with his soldiers and made for the dwelling of the Liwali Salim and his clan, that they might arrest them and fetter them with iron fetters. Others spread out through the Town creating havoc in it, and they shed the blood of many innocent people. The Mazari'a immediately met this evil course of action with the like.[40] They took the field against the soldiers of Nasir and set about killing them, slaying them with musket-fire, sword and dagger-thrust, and the survivors took refuge in the Fort and locked the gates upon themselves and fortified themselves in it. The Liwali Salim ordered a siege of the Fort and a beleaguerment of it.[41] There were a few houses in front of the entrance of the Fort on the North side, which he ordered to be destroyed, and he used the place where they were as a military camp. The West wall of the Fort was low, and he was afraid one of them might escape from that direction; so he issued an order to dig a trench[42] outside that wall, which was done.

The siege continued very close until all the food which those inside the Fort had, was used up, and they were so starving that they ate rats and creeping animals. It is said that the price of a measure of millet was ten riyals, and the price of one rat a whole riyal.

The Liwali was afraid of the occurrence of treachery during the siege which would upset his plans; so he gathered the Arabs and the "Twelve

---

[37] *Al-Wali*. This word causes confusion. Here it refers to Nasir b. Sulayman, the would-be "Governor", appointed or self-appointed in breach of the Treaty. But Shaykh Al-Amin also uses it in referring to the Mazru'i Liwali Salim. I have given it a small letter in its Swahili form when it refers to Nasir.

[38] **5 Dhu al-Oa'da in the year A.H. 1243** = 19th May A.D. 1828. That means that the quarrel had lasted over four months before open war was declared.

[39] *Nashar or Nushir*. Either, "He unfurled the banner of warfare", or "The Banner of warfare was unfurled". The context suggests the latter, but if so the word should really be "*Nushirat*".

[40] Shaykh Al-Amin is here more detailed than Guillain and has probably received his account from oral family traditions.

[41] *Wal-tashdid 'alayhi*. This should be *Wal-tashdid 'alayha*, if it refers to the Fort. If it refers to Nasir the last occurrence of his name is too remote for clarity.

[42] **To dig a trench**. This trench exists today, and has been cleared out under the direction of the former Warden of Fort Jesus, the late Mr. James Kirkman.

Tribes" and made them promise obedience and loyalty,[43] and they swore it to him, and agreed that if there appeared any treachery whatever from anyone, he should be handed over to his party to be slain at their hands as a recompense for the treason they had committed against their land. Not long after taking this oath it became evident that Kombo b. Khamis[44] and his brother Muhammad and some of his people had adopted full plans to help those in the Fort by sending food to them; and among those plans they threw to them at night millet cobs which they hung upon featherless arrows, and shot by means of their bows. Folk thought that they were shooting at them with arrows to kill them, whereas they were shooting food to them to keep them alive. The Liwali received this news and told the Leaders of the "Tribes" what treachery Kombo b. Khamis was about; and they condemned him to death. But the Liwali postponed the carrying out of the sentence for fear of division while they were in a state of war.

The news of the siege reached Zanzibar, over which Sayyid Hilal b. Sa'id was deputy for his father. He sent a ship loaded with provisions to help the beleaguered. The Mazari'a got to know that this ship had set out. They waited for it, and no sooner had it entered the harbour than Kiyati b. Mwinyi Uvi b. Hunzi,[45] one of the champions of the "Three Tribes", made for it; for he girded on his Swahili Sword (*Sime*) and went in a small skiff. He took a coconut palm branch for an oar, and rowed quickly towards it until he had tied it on to it, then he assaulted it and hurled himself upon those in it, and no one escaped except those who threw themselves into the sea. Then he took the ship and anchored it in the harbour, while the people all shouted and were amazed[46] at his strength and courage. When he had disembarked from the boat, he called those present to witness that all its contents were spoil of his own which no one should share with him; and the Liwali granted him that, and bought it from him for 2,000 Riyals. But this valiant man was as exceptional in his generosity as in his bravery, and gave the 2,000 Riyals to the Mazru'i Army to help them to buy arms and munitions. The Liwali accepted them with thanks, giving due estimation to his great work.

[43] **Made them promise obedience and loyalty.** Salim follows the example of the Prophet Muhammad himself, who, when at Hudaybiya and under similar fear of his followers defecting, made them take what is known as "The Oath under the Tree". Qur'an Sura 48 vs.18 is a reference to that event. Salim's action on this occasion was quite statesmanlike, as indeed was Muhammad's, whose example he followed.

[44] **Kombo b. Khamis.** His rather amusing act of treachery indicates that a party of the Swahilis were swinging away from the Mazari'a, and favouring the direct rule of 'Uman.

[45] **Hunzi.** This is the Swahili for "Blacksmith".

[46] *Ya'jabun.* This is grammatically correct, though the more usual form would have been *yata'ajjabun.*

When Nasir b. Sulayman felt the pressure of the siege, and nearly died of hunger, he and those with him in the Fort, he called for a safe-conduct and the raising of the siege from it. Salim responded to this and gave him and his soldiers safe-conduct for themselves and their property; and they came out of the Fort on 22 Jumada al-Akhira in the year A.H. 1244,[47] like dead people who had come out of their graves. Nasir surrendered the Fort to the Liwali with all the arms in it, and he (the Liwali) put his own soldiers in it. The next day he permitted Jama'dar Shahu to travel, and he and the soldiers that remained set out for Zanzibar: but Nasir remained a few days in Mombasa then asked permission to travel to Pemba, and he was permitted (to go). On 17 Rajab in this year the Liwali transferred his dwelling to the Fort.[48] The length of the siege was eight months and seventeen days.

While the Liwali was examining the arms which the enemy had left, he discovered in a corner of one of the store-rooms of the Fort fetters of iron, on each of which was the name of one of the chiefs of the Mazari'a, and of course he himself was among the number; so the Liwali was even more certain that what Nasir did was without doubt by command of the Sayyid Sa'id. He therefore sent his soldiers after him to follow him, until they overtook him at Funzi and seized him, and he was brought to Mombasa, thrown into prison, and then slain.

It is clear from what we have related that Major Pearce's Statement[49] in his book "Zanzibar", that the Mazari'a seized the chance of besieging the Fort during the absence of the Sayyid, and the rest of it, is not reliable. If the Major had read of what Nasir b. Sulayman did, it would have been clear to him that the Mazari'a did not begin this war but were compelled to enter it; and he would have known who was to blame, and to whom it was more fitting to ascribe responsibility for it. There is no doubt that he would have made excuse for the Mazari'a for what they did to defend themselves and their honour. In the statement of Nasir b. Sulayman that he obeyed the orders of the Sayyid in what he did, we have a circumstance which proves that the Sayyid had no intention, while the Treaty ran, of being loyal to what he had undertaken, nor of adhering to the oath which

---

[47] **22 Jumada al-Akhira in the year A.H. 1244** = 30th December 1828.

[48] **17 Rajab A.H. 1244** = 23rd January 1829. That was twenty-four days later. Guillain's account of Nasir's fate is different (p. 594). He says he was treated as a prisoner on parole, but imprisoned after two attempts to escape. He was strangled there when Sayyid Sa'id's fleet appeared, to avoid Sa'id demanding his return.

[49] **Major's Pearce's statement**. See "Zanzibar" pp. 116–7. Pearce is of course quite clearly biassed as an admirer of Sayyid Sa'id, and a servant of the British Colonial Office, which always tended to love and admire Arab rulers. Guillain's account is in essential agreement with Shaykh Al-Amin. The unemotional way of interpreting what happened is probably nearest the truth. The bravery of the Mazari'a it is hardly necessary to doubt.

he had sworn. It was as if he had made that Treaty as a subterfuge by which to dupe the Mazari'a so that when he felt safe from them, and they had put away their arms and relied upon their humble attitude, he could attack them and fetter them with iron.[50]

I have recorded from the late Historian and Genealogist, 'Abd Al-Karim b. Talsam, that the secret in sending Nasir b. Sulayman, and making him "liwali" in contravention of the text of the Treaty, was that he might spy upon the condition of the Mazari'a for the Sayyid, and observe them at close quarters, so that if the opportunity offered, he might fetter them and send them to Zanzibar. But Nasir was not a diplomatic person like his master, and would not wait patiently in the matter, but acted hurriedly in it, and was punished by ill-luck and the exposure of his plans. I here bring as testimony in support of what I have related concerning the event of the siege of the Fort from first to last, and set down (in writing) an Ode (Qasida) of the learned Historian Muhyi al-Din b. Shaykh Al-Qahtani (God's Mercy upon him) in which he includes a narration of this event as he witnessed it with his own eyes. The reader will read the clear truth from the tongue of that just (reliable?) witness; so we set it down here as we have transcribed it, after comparing it with a number of copies;[51]

---

[50] **And fetter them with iron.** It becomes more evident from this account that the Mazru'i dynasty were formidable opponents, that their power was real, and that it was stabilising to the Coast. But this history also makes clear that it was a rule based on agreement, and on co-operation between them and the "Twelve Tribes". In the end, the Tribes saw that the 'Umani Sultan offered the greatest stability, and allowed themselves to be turned against the Mazari'a; and from that time the latter had no viable place as rulers in Mombasa. Shaykh Al-Amin stresses, and justifies, the Mazru'i point of view here. There may have been thorns in the side of Sayyid Sa'id, but he certain broke faith very blatantly, — and for no very lasting sovereignty, as it turned out.

It is appropriate here to quote what Guillain says about the attitude of the Swahili population as a whole towards the Mazari'a:

"Chez beaucoup de Souhheli, d'ailleurs, le mécontentement s'appliquait à la famille entière des M'zara, dont les luttes incessantes contre le sultan de Mascate n'offraient au pays que la perspective de guerres et de misères sans fin. Les désirs de vengeance du vieux sheikh avaient donc été facilement accueillis par les chefs de cette population, et ceux-ci, apres s'être concertes sur les moyens d'en finir avec une domination qui leur etait antipathetique, decidèrent que quelques-uns de leurs se rendraient immediatement a Mascate pour engager le Sultan à entreprendre une nouvelle attaque contre Mombase, lui promettant le concours de tous les Souahheli (p. 602)". (Cf. also H. E. Lambert: ChiJomvu & Ki-Ngare, pp. 13,14)

[51] This is a Didactic Poem also in the Rajaz Meter. It is called a "Lamiya" because the last syllable of every line beings with the Arabic letter *Lam*, or L (see note 2 above). The moralising in it is all based on the stories and sentiments found in the Qur'an. The laudatory epithets applied to Sayyid Sa'id must not be thought of as reflecting the poet's true mind. They are conventions of Arabic poetry, and may also have been used either sarcastically, or for reasons of policy.

O you who seek evil by crafty guile, —
    Its sweetness is the honey-taste of fatal poison,
Even though it is only as much as a gnat's wing,
    And one did not taste of it as much as a child's draught.[52]
How many an influential man has it struck down,
    And destroyed speedily and without delay!
Or have you not heard what it has done to nations in the past?
    To 'Ad and Thamud?[53] — So consider (i.e. draw a lesson.)
They were kings victorious over mankind;
    The nations of the first age were under their rule.
They hewed out houses from the rocky mountains.
    They fancied they would remain in them without change.
The Apostles of Death came to dwell with them, and they became
    Overthrown like long branches fallen from palm-trees,
Pharaoh (leader) of powerful men and the worst of unbelievers,
    Since he said, the accursed one, "I am the exalted Lord".
But the might of God came upon him to remove him:
    His saying benefitted him not at the time of testing.
(He said), "I believe there is no God but he whom
    I believe in" — and he rebelled against the apostle.
O you who have been lured away (from the truth), give attention!
    Where are the leaders and the just kings?
Where are the Judges, where the Lords of piety?
    Where is he with whom to take refuge against the time of
    terror
Where is the friend who, if you earn (the guilt of) sin
    Will requite you with good as if you had never committed it?
Their allotted periods have carried them off, and they have been
    changed
    And it is as if they had never dwelt in the house.
But there remain those who, if you slip into sin,
    Cut you off on one side in a place of isolation.
This is sufficient for you, if you will take my advice
    As an exhortation, and look not at the deeds of men of vice,
And remember the circumstance of former centuries, that you may
    consider
    The condition of the Evildoer. Do not be like the neglectful.

So I will tell you what happened in our land
    Of Mombasa among the noble and excellent,
When they came to it, by (God's) most generous guidance,

---

[52] **liljahili**. The work *Jahil* (plur, *Juhal*) is used in Colloquial South Arabian for "Child" or "Infant".

[53] **'Adiha wathamudiha**. To 'Ad and Thamud. Two ancient Arabian Tribes which were destroyed after rejecting the message of a prophet calling them to monotheistic worship. The feminine possessives attached to them are quite untranslateable, being inserted to help the meter rather than to add anything to the sense.

The Sun among Kings, one of genuine perfection,
I mean our Lord Sayyid Sa'id,
Son of Sultan the noble and most bold.
He desired from his servants the Fort,
(His servants) the sons of Ahmad, and they were led to comply
by his courteous protestations.
They gave up to him the illustrious Fort willingly,[54]
And he gave them the Liwaliship in it under his Government.
He established in it as Liwali for the people
Salim, son of Ahmad, because of his suitability
As long as he lived, and to his descendants as long as they lasted,
God testifying between them as Guarantor.
Prosperity lasted on the signing of those covenants
As long as what was agreed between them was approved.
He dwelt in the illustrious Fort as representative
of the descendant of Al-Walid, Sa'id the Protector of the
Stronghold.
Who provided him with soldiers of a Tribe suitable to him
And with their Shahu[55] and other functionaries (lit. those with
long sleeves)
They were all respected in the land
and (treated) as if they were the sons of our High Lord.

So with the aid of the Merciful our Lord journeyed
Towards the Land of the Zanj, a land most excellent to
dwell in.
But when he was concerned about his (country) 'Uman, and set out
for it,
He appointed for us Nasir an empty person.
When he came, he changed the land by what he did,
And took action the like of which had never been taken.
The people of the land all hated him,
(The impatient man does not attain what he hopes for),
He stirred up the dying embers of rebellion.
O the Impatience of those of weak intelligence!
And a command from the Sayyid called him to that!
Shame upon him! Nay, but it must have been falsely said of
him
Talk passed between him and our Shaykhs,
The sons of Ahmad, what men they were!
When we saw his fire kindled
Into flame, as though its sparks were a lofty castle,

---

[54] **Fort**. The word used here in Arabic is *Kut*. It seems that it is used in 'Uman and it occurs in Turkish and Persian. It seems it is the Indian word KOT adopted into Arabic. The classical Arabic word is *Qal'a*. Cf note 5 above.

[55] ***Min ahlihi wabishahuhum***. This seems to refer to the Hinawi soldiers and their Officer Shahu Al-Jundigali

We rose patching up (sc. our quarrels) to quench its flame
    (Which burned) as though (fit) garments for the bribes of that
        empty one

They agreed to suspend their action until
    The matter of the infringement of the Protectorate should be
        concluded
And that whatever decision came to them from the Sayyid
    They would accept with humble compliance.
This covenant was concluded between them by mutual oaths,
    — But God is the Best One to rely on!

After that we saw a great number of letters,[56]
    From Nasir,[57] saying, "Hand the country over to me,
"Or else a holy war (lit. The War of God) will fall upon you."
    But they preferred to answer, "No, except with a letter."[58]
When he received their answer to his letters,
    He ran up the flags on high over the Fort,
And the muskets and cannon boomed
    With the sound of thunder, rumbling fearfully.
The country was burned up by its kindled fire,
    And the citizens were killed without any reasonable cause.[59]
The Sons of Ahmad bared their arms for the battle
    Like neighing, prancing, high-bred steeds.
The wealthy among the Arabs built the fortified[60] strong-point
    And protected the Tribes of all the Swahili Coast.
The war continued between them at full pitch,[61]
    Until the news of the grievous battle reached
Our illustrious Sayyid, Hilal of Hilals,[62]
    Son of our most just Lord, Sa'id.
There came to them letters bearing advice from him,

---

[56] *Shufna Khututan Jumlatan.* "We saw letters in quantity." Muhyi al-Din becomes very colloquial here. Both the verb and its object are pure South Arabian colloquial.

[57] Nasir is of course Nasir b. Sulayman.

[58] *la illa bikhattin mufaddalu.* "No, unless with a letter" was preferred. That is, the Council of the Mazari'a debated the matter and preferred to return answer "No", unless written authority came from Sayyid Sa'id as proof.

[59] *bighayri mawjibi maqtali.* "Without the need of being killed", or perhaps "in an unseemly manner". The first is the better rendering.

[60] *Al-siba al-Hamya.* "The well-defended, or well-protecting strong-point." The word "Sib" is also a very colloquial word in South Arabia. The phrase probably refers to the blockhouse Salim built opposite Fort Jesus after destroying a few houses there (See p. 102 above)

[61] *ma zala baynahum al-hurubu mushammara.* The word should rather be spelt with an Arabic *Ta marbuta* or an *Alif Tawila*. *Hurub* is plural and the word *Mushammar* either agrees with it, or it is an adverb which should be in the accusative (without nunation as it is the end of the half-line).

[62] *Lilbadri sayyidina hilali al-Ahillati.* A pun on the name of Sayyid Hilal b. Sa'id. His name means "New Moon" or "Crescent". Badr is the "Full Moon".

Sent accompanied by diamonds from him (perhaps meaning
    funds or a bribe)
Then he came himself and added his own orders to his letters —
    But Satan the great deceiver did not accept.
He waged open war with all his might,
    And everyone rose up girded for battle.
God destroyed the people by His decree,
    A destruction which was not expected by the people.
The battle still continued between them fiercely,
    While the men in the Fort were in a wasting siege.
There passed for them a long period in which nothing
    Came to them to revive their starving souls.
They endured, and completed a lengthy period in siege,
    In which they made food out of the skins of their shields
Until, when all means of sustenance had vanished from among them,
    Not even rats were left which they did not eat.
They requested safe-conduct, to come out of their (sic) Fort,
    With life and property, safe from slaughter.
They all came out safe, and travelled away,
    Except he who was to weak from hunger.[63]

Certainly craftiness surrounds none with its plague
    Except the one who conceives it, as (it is written) in the
        revealed Word.[64]
God causes whom He will to inherit the earth;
    Glory be to Him Who is not liable to subordination to another.
Does the Fort remain, returning to her husband
    After divorce? Is it allowable to ask?
I reply, "If it is thrice, or if redemption has been made,[65] then
    It is not lawful; otherwise the return is permitted."

I have spoken what I intended; take it as an exhortation.
    Think about it, consider it and meditate upon it.
Then (finally) blessings on the Prophet and his Family,
    The best of mankind, our Intercessor with the Most High.

The statement of the Poet (May God's Mercy be upon him): "The Fort
remains, returning to her husband, etc.", has a Metaphor in it likening the
Mazari'a to the husband of a woman, and the Fort to the wife of that
husband, and their going out of it to divorce. Then it is as if a questioner
asks him, "Will the rule of the Mazari'a return to what it was, after their

---

[63] *Alladhi hafara al-tawa fiy masbali.* This is hard to translate. It seems to refer to those of
the besieged who were either too weak to travel or had died of hunger.
[64] *Fiy al-munazzali.* In that which was sent down, i.e. in the Revealed Word, roughly
equivalent in English to "According to the Scriptures".
[65] **Or if redemption has been made.** That is, for the wife to gain her release from the marriage
contract. See Qur'an Sura 2 vss. 29–38 for legislation concerning divorce.

exit from the Fort this time?", and he answers, "Yes. That rule will return
to them until their exit is repeated three times. Then their rule will not
return, — like a husband when he divorces his wife three times." It
happened as the Poet said. The Mazari'a went out from the Fort the first
time after the murder of Muhammad b. 'Uthman; Then they returned
during the Liwaliship of his brother 'Ali. They also went out after the
Mazru'i/Sa'id Treaty, and returned after the occurrence of this siege. The
Third time was fulfilled by the exit of Rashid b. Salim,[66] as we shall see,
and they returned to it no more. I do not know[67] whether it happened
as the Poet said by chance, or whether he learned it by the skill he
acquired in fortune-telling (Raml) and Astrology (Tanjim).[68] God knows
the truth of the matter, but *what* he prophesied came to pass *as* he
prophesied.

After gaining the victory, and the removal of the Liwali back to the
Fort, and his setting it in order again, he determined to execute sentence
upon Kombo b. Khamis. When the latter got to know about it however,
he fled in the direction of Jibana.[69] So the Liwali sent after him a few of
the Government slaves, and they overtook him at a place called Mwanzai,[70]
and seized him and brought him to Mombasa. His object — so it is said —
was to muster an army and take it to Lamu, and then take it by sea to
Zanzibar and bring Sayyid Hilal with this army to make war on the
Mazari'a.

The news of this arrest reached his clan, and they determined to bar
the way by which he would pass and attack those who had seized him,
and take off his fetters: but they shrank from this venture since it was
very dangerous for them. Kombo was brought before the Liwali, and he
rebuked him for his action: but many of the Arabs and others interceded
for him, among whom were the Qadi Ahmad b. Mas'ud b. Nasir Al-

---

[66] **As we shall see**. Shaykh Al-Amin never managed to complete this history as he stopped
short at the reign of the Liwali Salim, father of Rashid. It was Rashid's son Mbaruk who
caused trouble to the British Administration in the later 19th Century. See the Epilogue
below.

[67] **I do not know whether . . .** The author here touches unwittingly on the whole question of
inspiration, and it is a wonder that, being a man of the world, he did not add that this
prophecy may have been uttered out of a very shrewd judgment of the events of his time by
the Poet.

[68] *Al-ramlu wal-tanjim*. These words are derived from the use of Sand(*raml*) and the
observation of the movements of stars and planets(najm) in the process of casting horoscopes.

[69] **Jibana**. The WaJibana are a Nyika Tribe adjacent to, and associated with, the WaGiryama
and WaRabai. Their treaty relationship appears to have been with the Shaykhs of the
WaMvita and WaJomvu (Prins p. 99), which indicates that Kombo b. Khamis and his friends
were somehow connected with them.

[70] **Mwanzai**. This place is North of Mombasa, near Ribe and between the Ribe escarpment
and Mombasa Island.

Mazru'i, who was persistent in interceding for him and influencing the Liwali in his favour. But the Liwali did not think it right to accept anyone's intercession on his behalf since there was danger, if he accepted it, of encouraging the audacity of others to do the same thing in the future, relying on people's intercession on their behalf. What the Liwali did was what the laws of war required. No blame can be placed upon him: rather, he should be commended and thanked for commuting the sentence of death to imprisonment, contrary to the sentence of the "Umma"[71] when they took the oath of loyalty during the siege.

This opposition of Kombo to the Mazari'a is to be wondered at, seeing that they were friends of his father. For his father Khamis b. Tani[72] had come to Mombasa seeking protection from the Nabahina who wished to kill him, and he sought out the Liwali Ahmad b. Muhammad b. 'Uthman, who gave him protection and sheltered him in his own place, and helped him against his enemies. So his children ought to have estimated their obligation to him at its true value, and showed friendship to the Mazari'a, not hostility. But Satan, may God curse him, whispered in their ears so that they did what was not seemly for them to do, may God pardon them.

The Second Attack of Sayyid Sa'id on Mombasa

Sayyid Hilal b. Sa'id sent to his father in 'Uman, informing him of the occurrence of the siege of the Fort. Then the Sayyid mustered soldiers, and gathered them from different tribes in 'Uman, and their number amounted to 2,000 and more. He himself went out on board his steamer "Liverpool", with four warships and six sailing ships carrying stores and supplies; and he reached Mombasa at the beginning of summer in the year A.H. 1245.[73]

Instead of clearing himself of blame for what his 'Amil Nasir b. Sulayman had done, and the commander of his army Jama'dar Shahu, in the way of monkey-business,[74] in contravention of the Treaty he had himself

[71] **Umma.** I have left the Arabic word here in the text of the translation, because it is difficult to render exactly into English. It might mean either "public", or "the Community", or "his own Tribe". It probably means the second.

[72] **Khamis b. Tani.** I have not found any reference to this man elsewhere.

[73] **A.H. 1245** = the end of A.D. 1829. Compare Guillain p. 594, for his version of the story. He says the six ships other than the warships were: Three corvettes — The "Sultan", the "Rhamani" and the "Mentes". Three Beurrhela (Arab. *Baghla*), which are troop and supply transports.

[74] *Min al-afa'il.* I have translated this very expressive extended plural form with "monkey business", which seems to catch the shade of meaning better than any other English phrase. It means acts which cause damage or trouble and are out of order.

concluded with the Mazari'a, and making an effort to restore friendship
and renew the Treaty between them, he sent a warning to the Liwali
Salim, and a very strong threat, and declaration of war against him. This
is another indication that Sayyid Sa'id was not intending to be loyal to
those promises, — and also an indication that the actions of Nasir b.
Sulayman were by his orders, not, as Sa'id Ruete says[75] in excuse for him,
that Nasir claimed the Liwaliship without having been appointed, and
acted without orders. It is very peculiar[76] that a man should come to a
country and claim that he is liwali under the authority of the Sultan, and
that people should believe him and commit their business to him without
either proof or objection. But Ruete usually says such things as this. He
said that Muhammad b. 'Uthman was not appointed Liwali by the Imam,
but that he took the Liwaliship by force. He says that though the weight
of all opinions are against him. If what he had said had been true, then
Sayyid Hilal b Sa'id[77] would have started by drawing attention to it, and
cautioned the People of Mombasa against that man and against believing
what he claimed. There is no doubt — for he was in Zanzibar — that he
was aware of all that Nasir b. Sulayman caused in his time (sc. in
Mombasa). Further, Sayyid Sa'id would have cleared himself of blame
in the matter when he arrived in Mombasa this time.

The Mazari'a did not worry about that threat which the Sayyid sent to
them, but prepared to resist with all the strength they were able; and the
Sayyid disembarked his soldiers in Kilindini, while others (disembarked)
in Shimanzi. The Liwali divided his army and made Mbaruk b. Ahmad
Amir of the Arabs, and Kiyati b. Mwinyi Uvi Amir of the Swahilis.[78] The
battle was joined between the two sides, and it lasted six days, one day in
favour of one side, and another in favour of the other. On the seventh

---

[75] **Not as Sa'id Ruete says**. "Said bin Sultan", p. 58. See also p. 47, where he says that
Muhammad b. 'Uthman arrogated to himself the office of Wali. What impugns Sayyid Sa'id's
good faith is for Ruete illegal.
[76] **It is very peculiar**. Shaykh Al-Amin argues very soundly here. There must have been
certainty in relation to Sayyid Sa'id. The Swahili population were at first satisfied; the
Mazari'a had committed themselves whether they liked it or not. In the end it was probably
the shelling of the Town that finally turned the Swahilis against Nasir to side with the
Mazari'a. Both Arabs and Swahilis only resorted to active opposition as a last resort.
[77] *Sayyid Hilal b. Sa'id*. The second son of Sayyid Sa'id, whom he left in Zanzibar as viceroy when he returned to attend to the critical state of affairs in 'Uman. He is said to have
been a very weak and characterless person, and the hint of bribery conveyed in the foregoing
poem by the term "Diamonds" is evidence of his character. He pre-deceased his father.
[78] **Kiyati b. Mwinyi Uvi**. This man was hero of the Siege, and had earned his rank as
commander. See above where he captures a provision ship single-handed, p. 103.

day the Sayyid's soldiers attacked the Mazru'i army in a true assault, and they retreated; and the others advanced until they had entered the village of Kilindini and gained possession of it. The ships helped them by firing off their cannon against the enemy. At this point the Amir Mbaruk b. Ahmad rose and addressed his army, and breathed a new spirit into them which made them despise death in the way of fighting for honour and freedom. They returned upon the Sayyid's soldiers with the utmost bravery and defeated them, and they ran in flight to the shore seeking an escape. Owing to their great panic they embarked thirty and forty at a time on boats which carried no more than ten to twenty; and the Mazari'a opened fire upon them with bullets, and the boats upset upon them owing to their struggling in them, so that they drowned. The Sayyid lost in this thrust 400 dead besides those wounded and drowned. It is said that the total number amounted to about 900 men, and the corpses of the drowned were floating about on the surface of the water and passing the Sayyid's ship, and he was looking at them with expressions of sorrow and amazement. Two of the Sayyid's Baghlas[79] were swept by the water to Makupa, after their anchors had been cut, and fell into the hands of Khamis b. Ahmad who was on garrison duty there with a company of soldiers. They took them as spoil, and all the supplies that were in them, and killed all their crews. The Mazari'a took as spoil in this battle many things such as armaments and the like.

The Amir Mbaruk b. Ahmad and Sa'id b. 'Ali Al-Hinawi and Kiyati b. Mwinyi Uvi showed in this war such bravery and heroism as became the talk of people after them.[80] It is related that some twenty odd men of the Sayyid's soldiers saw Mbaruk b. Ahmad, and opened fire on him with their muskets (rifles), but luckily they all missed: but before the smoke had cleared away, he had left them all slaughtered, wallowing in their own blood. As for Sa'id b. 'Ali, he saw the enemy racing to get into the Mosque of Kilindini to fortify themselves in it; so he waited until the Mosque was full of them, then attacked them; and none escaped except those who threw themselves out of the window and fled.

There was in the army of the Sayyid a champion of the BuSa'idi family known for his bravery, and famous among the people of Mombasa by the

---

[79] **Baghlas**. The Baghla, or Baghala, was a type of sailing ship. It has been described thus: Baghla: High, curved, galleon stern, high free-board, straight sloping bow. Capacity up to 200 tons (now obsolete). (Donald Hawley: The Trucial States, Appendix A12, p. 302.)

[80] These anecdotes of the Battle are in a very long Arabic and Arabian tradition. This indicates how deeply the East African Arabs where imbued with the spirit and outlook of their Arabian Ancestors. See e.g. W. M. Watt: Muhammad at Mecca.

name of "Walad Sa'id Muqaddar".[81] This daring man[82] did not wish to
stain his sword in the blood of one inferior to himself in bravery (heroism);
so he started to walk through the ranks calling the name of Mbaruk b.
Ahmad, seeking to challenge him. Now Mbaruk had a sign by which he
was distinguished from others in war. It was an ostrich feather on the
front of his turban. When "Walad Sa'id Muqaddar" saw him, he confronted
him and challenged him; then they circled one another like two race-
horses, and Mbaruk knew that today he was before his match, and that if
he did not kill him quickly, he himself would be killed. So he played a
trick upon him, and cried out, "Don't strike him from behind", as if he
were stopping a person who wished to strike Walad Sa'id from behind.
Then the man turned round and Mbaruk stabbed him in the side with the
point of his sword, threw him on the ground and finished him off.

The losses of the Mazari'a were not light. Many of them were killed,
and also many of the "Three Tribes". In this war were killed Muhammad
b. 'Ali Al-Busami and Kiyati b. Mwinyi Uvi and the 'Aqid Bwangi, all of
them well-known for their bravery, and the pride of the people of Mombasa. The Amir Mbaruk b. Ahmad was struck in the leg by a bullet which
later caused his death; and Sa'id b. 'Ali was wounded many times, but the
wounds were not serious.

When the Sayyid saw what a sound defeat had befallen his army, he
weighed anchor and made for Zanzibar, and left the corpses of his dead
soldiers behind him; and the people of Mombasa worked for four days
burying them and their own dead. The distinguished Rashid b. Sa'ud[83] told
me, on information received from his long-lived uncle Matar b. Salim Al-
Shukayli, that among the Sayyid's soldiers who were killed, were about
seventy men of Beni Shukayl, and a great number of Beni BaHasan.

The People of Mombasa were delighted at the clear victory they had
gained in this battle. The Liwali grasped thereafter the danger that

---

[81] **Walad Sa'id Muqaddar.** Such nicknames as this are difficult, or impossible, to translate,
since the often have a significance which is lost on all but those who are familiar with the
circumstances of their origin. This name might mean:
The estimable, or power-endowed, or fateful son, or slave, of Sa'id, or
The son, or slave of the estimable Sa'id.
It seems fairly evident that Sa'id refers to Sayyid Sa'id b. Sultan.

[82] **Falam yasha" hadha al-mighwar. This *daring man* did not wish.** The word *Mighwar* is
another poetic word. Shaykh Al-Amin tends to use words like these when he is recounting
warlike exploits.

[83] **The Distinguished Rashid b. Sa'ud.** This is one of the few places where Shaykh Al-Amin
states the authority for his oral sources. It is regrettable that he did not do so more often,
as one feels much other information might also have been preserved in similar places, or in
the memory of folk who outlived him. Matar b. Salim must have been an eye-witness of this
Battle.

threatened him. If the Sayyid's Army had succeeded in advancing as far as Mombasa Town, it would have been easy for him to enter it without trouble, because it was unwalled. So he gathered the Arabs and the "Tribes", and put before them the plan of building the Wall[84] round the town; and they agreed to it. They immediately began to build it, and all the "Tribes" shared in the work with determination and energy, so that they completed it in quite a short time. Rashid b. Salim,[85] the founder of Takaungu, has a large share of the credit in the building of this Wall; for he undertook himself to build a large section of it, and completed with his money what some of the "Twelve Tribes" were incapable of doing. May God reward him on behalf of his country with good. This wall was three cubits (ca. 4½– 5 feet) thick, and on some parts of it there were built raised towers. This wall was destroyed when the Town was extended, but there remain small ruins of it on the Eastern shore of the Town North of the house of Tarya Tubin, which has recently[86] been taken as a hospital for sick women and children.[87]

Some historians say that the Wall was built after the siege, not after the second attack on Mombasa. But anyway, it is among the relics of the Liwali Salim.[88]

---

[84] **The plan of building the Wall**. The "staticness" of the Islamic world, particularly of the Arabian Islamic world, is apparent here. For in the 19th Century, thirty years after Napoleon had irrupted into the Middle East, we still find them thinking in terms of sieges in the old style, while in Arabia itself towns in remote areas are still walled, with gates which are closed at night.

[85] **Rashid b. Salim**. This is not the son of the Liwali, but a second cousin once removed to him, a member of the Zahiri branch, whose father had been killed in the revolt of the sons of Mas'ud. See Section 6 above.

[86] *Qariban*. "Recently", but it is more usual to say *Mu'akhkharan*. This word here means more often "shortly" or "soon", referring to the future.

[87] The hospital here referred to is the Lady Grigg Maternity Home, not far from the Nyali Bridge.

[88] Guillain (pp. 595–6) adds at this point that further negotiations followed this battle, and that Sayyid Sa'id suggested forgetting the past and returning to the terms of the Treaty; and that Salim agreed to recognise his sovereignty, to pay tribute and customs dues, but not again to allow Sayyid Sa'id possession of the Fort. His two brothers Rashid and Nasir (See note 60 on Section 6 above) accompanied Sayyid Sa'id to Zanzibar. Shaykh Al-Amin is silent about anyone called Nasir b. Salim.

For the building of the Town Wall, compare Boteler Vol. II, p. 207, where he refers to "the present Shaykh's inability to pay for the lime for the erection of the Town Wall". This must have been Sulayman b. 'Ali; for H.M.S. Barracouta last visited Mombasa early in A.D. 1825, and left on 5th February of that year. Compare Owen Vol. II, p. 182. Boteler may of course be referring to the state of affairs at the time of his writing a year or two later: but this is to assume that he kept in touch with Mombasa from afar, which is highly unlikely.

The Attempt to regain Pemba

When the Liwali saw the great measure of success he had in opposing
Sayyid Sa'id in his first and second attacks,[89] he grew desirous of regaining
Pemba, and seizing it from his hand. He equipped an army, and made his
nephew 'Abdullah b. Mbaruk b. Ahmad Amir over it. This 'Abdullah was
like his father in bravery and stoutness of heart. He sent him to the Island
in the year A.H. 1248.[90] The army arrived there, and took the field against
the Sayyid's soldiers in Wesha,[91] and fought a fierce battle: but the Mazru'i
forces were not sufficient to defeat the fortifications which the Sayyid had
constructed, nor to break that powerful army which the Sayyid had sent
to the Island, to protect it from the assaults of the Mazari'a upon it. So
they were defeated there, and turned back disappointed.

The Civil War in Siyu and Pate

In the year A.H. 1249[92] occurred a civil war[93] in Siyu and Pate between
the Sultan Bwana Wazir b. Bwana Tamu and Sayyid Sa'id on the one part,
and the Amir Fumo Luti b.Shaykh and the Chief Bwana Mataka b. Shaykh
on the other. The Sultan was friendly to Sayyid Sa'id and under obedience
to him: but Fumo Luti was friendly to the Mazari'a and an ally of Bwana
Mataka. The two sides joined battle, and it went in favour of the Sultan
Bwana Wazir and against Fumo Luti. The latter fled with Bwana Mataka
and reached the open country (*Badiya*), and there they sent to the Liwali
Salim, to ask his help against their enemies Bwana Wazir and Sayyid Sa'id.
The Liwali set out to bring them help with a company of soldiers. The
Sultan and Sayyid Sa'id failed, and their army retreated and was defeated;

[89] Sayyid Sa'id, it must be remembered, was during this time fighting Hamud b. 'Azran b.
Qays in 'Uman. Hence the Liwali Salim hoped to take him at a disadvantage. See Guillain
pp. 596–7.
[90] **A.H. 1248** = A.D. 1833–4.
[91] **Wesha**. This place is on the North shore of the Creek of Chake-Chake on the West Coast
of the Island. It appears to be just the kind of landing-place for an invading army to assault
Chake-Chake from.
[92] **A.H. 1249** = 1833–4.
[93] **A civil war**. This quarrel is reported by all the extant authorities, but there is disagreement
over the grounds and details of the dispute.

Guillain pp. 599–601 says that Bwana Wazir revolted against Sayyid Sa'id, and that it was
he who called in the Mazari'a. After having established himself in Pate, he had then gone
to seek recognition in Masqat. Sa'id had recognized him and sent Muhammad b. Sulayman
Al-Marzuqi to Pate as his agent. This Muhammad had then had Bwana Wazir assassinated,
and put in his place Fumo Bakari.

The confusion of names among the Nabhani Sultans of Pate makes it difficult to know
the truth; but it is more probable that Shaykh Al-Amin was less confused than Guillain, a
foreigner with an imperfect ear for the relevant names.

and the Liwali advanced to Siyu with his army, and took possession of it and gave it to Fumo Luti and Bwana Mataka. They thanked him warmly for the assistance he had brought them.

This Fumo Luti had become Sultan of Pate in the year A.H. 1236[94] and its people had removed him and set in his place Bwana Shaykh b. Madi, and his life had been in danger from the hostility shown to him by those revolting against him. So the Mazari'a had given him protection, and brought him to Mombasa; and he had dwelt there until the year A.H. 1249.[95] Then he returned to his country and there united with Bwana Mataka, and what happened to him is what we have just related.

Sayyid Sa'id was angry at the help given by the Liwali to Bwana Mataka and Fumo Luti, as, but for that, he would not have suffered that great defeat in this battle. He wanted to use cunning against the Liwali; so he sent a company of soldiers to lie in wait for him on his route, when he was returning to Mombasa, and kill him by surprise. But God guarded him, and he returned in safety to his country, victorious while at the same time having done his duty to his friend and his friend's ally.[96]

Among the events which happened after the Sayyid's second attack on Mombasa, is a story related by Mr. Lyne in his book "Zanzibar". When the army of the Sayyid was overtaken by that speedy slaughter in that attack, and many of his Baluchi soldiers were smitten with fever, and he was no longer strong enough to continue fighting the Mazari'a, it occurred to him to ally himself by marriage to Madagascar in the hope of getting soldiers to help him in his wars. So he asked the hand of its Queen[97] and sent to her an advance on her dowry. After that he sent requesting her to give him the assistance of 2,000 men. The messenger brought the answer and overtook him in Lamu, when he was departing from the war in Siyu: and he presented to him the Queen's message, in which (she said) "that her ministers could not marry her to him, for the law of the country did not allow the queen to marry anyone. But there was a young princess in the Royal Court. If he chose to marry her, he could do so. As for the men he could have any number he might wish."

---

[94] **A.H. 1236** = A.D. 1820–1.
[95] **A.H. 1249** = A.D. 1833–4.
[96] According to Guillain (p. 600) This incident took place in A.H. 1251 = A.D. 1835. The Liwali Salim escaped by night and reached Kilifi Creek in safety, landed at Takaungu, and got back to Mombasa where he died in March or April.
[97] Lyne: Zanzibar in Contemporary Times, pp. 28–30, puts the year of this wooing as A.D. 1823. He relates the story more fully with some humorous details.

The Third Attack of Sayyid Sa'id on Mombasa[98]

When the Sayyid returned from the war in Siyu, he passed by Mombasa; but he could not think of passing it without[99] causing any loss he could to it and its people; so he anchored his ship in the direction of Nyali and landed artillery which he pulled to Mkomani[100] and aimed at the Fort; and he fired shells[101] at the Fort and the town, and the artillery in the Fort replied with the like. A few brave men of the "Three Tribes" determined to get possession of the artillery of the Sayyid's army; so they crossed the Creek to Kisauni and climbed up to Mkomani. Before they reached the gun position however, the soldiers saw them, fired shells at them, and killed them to the last man. Rashid B. Muhammad b. Rashid Al-Shukayli was the most skilful artilleryman in the Mazru'i Army. While he was firing his gun on the bastion opposite Mkomani, Al-'Ajami, the Sayyid's Artilleryman aimed his gun at him, and fired a shell at him which made his head fly off. This is all the chroniclers have related to us about this attack.[102] The Sayyid had no success except the enjoyment of seeing Mombasa burning with his artillery fire. When he knew he could do nothing, he weighed anchor and set out for Zanzibar.

The Battle of Chagga

One of the events in the Liwaliship of Salim was that a group of the WaChagga[103] were raiding the villages situated near Tanga, causing havoc in them, killing and plundering. The liwali of Tanga under the authority of the Mazari'a was Qasim b. Gharib Al-Riyami. He asked the Liwali's permission to make war on this tribe, and he allowed him and sent supplies

[98] Compare Guillain pp. 597–9. He says this attack was made direct on Mombasa in A.H. 1246–7, that is, presumably, between November A.D. 1831 and April A.D. 1832. He puts his account of it before the war between Pate and Siyu. There is a difference in dating here also since Guillain says Salim's death was in A.H. 1251 = A.D. 1835, whereas Shaykh Al-Amin puts it in A.H. 1250 = A.D. 1834–5. The date is not a difficulty however if it is understood that A.H. 1250 ran from 10th May A.D. 1834 to 29th April A.D. 1835. Since Salim's death was in April, about two days" difference could alter the year.

[99] ***Dun (An)***. I have taken the liberty of adding the word *An* in the Arabic text as I think it had been omitted in error.

[100] **Mkomani**. This is the place now called English Point, opposite the Old Town and Fort Jesus.

[101] ***Bil-Qanabir***. This is the same word as *Qanabil* which appears a few lines further on. There are some words in Arabic which in colloquial speech can use *Lam, Nun* or *Ra* interchangeably, e.g. *Finjan, Finjal* or *Finjar* are all possible.

[102] **This is all the chroniclers have related to us about this attack**. But Guillain relates that Muhammad b. Ahmad, brother of the Liwali Salim, was mortally wounded in the battle.

[103] The WaChagga are a Bantu Tribe living inland from Tanga in the Kilimanjaro area and to the South West of the WaTaita.

to him from Mombasa, and made him Amir of that Army. Qasim went out with his army until he reached Rumbu in the territory of Chagga, and declared war upon them, and the fighting continued between them some days. But he could not conquer that country because of the difficulty of bringing supplies to it through the length of the journey and the roughness of the road.[104]

The Arrest of Mwinyi Simba Sultan of Tanga

This Mwinyi Simba revoked[105] his allegiance in the time of the Liwali Ahmad b. Muhammad b. 'Uthman, and the Diwan Hasan b. Nasir had striven to bring him back, as we have mentioned in our account of the Liwali Ahmad. In these days he rebelled again, and stirred up rebellion in Tanga. So the Liwali sent an army against him which fought him, and captured him and brought him to Mombasa. Many of the honourable men interceded for Mwinyi Simba, among whom were Rashid b. Salim, the founder of Takaungu, and the Diwan Ahmad b. Abu Bakr, known as the Diwan Punda.[106] But the Liwali's policy was not to accept any intercession on behalf of rebels, or those who tried to make people disobey the orders of the Government; so he ordered him to be imprisoned. It angered Rashid b. Salim that his pleading should not be accepted, and he determined to leave Mombasa. That was what led to the founding of the Town of Takaungu.[107] Some chroniclers state that what angered Rashid b. Salim was that the Liwali did not accept his intercession on behalf of Kombo b. Khamis. This statement is worthy of credit, and indicates the sympathy of the Mazru'i leaders for Kombo and his clan in spite of the sins they committed.

---

[104] **The roughness of the road**. The Nyika Wilderness is an effective barrier which was only pierced in the second half of the 19th century. It is thorny savannah with a rainfall, but lacking any effective natural water-supply.

[105] **This Mwinyi Simba**. The Sultan probably saw the Mazru'i power declining, and wished to get on the right side of 'Uman. See Section 6 where an account is given of his father, Mwinyi Simba the Elder, who revolted against the Liwali Ahmad, Salim's father.

[106] **Punda**. This is a Swahili name but it is not clear in the unvowelled script whether the first vowel should be U, A or I. All are possible roots in Swahili. The form we have given means "Donkey".

[107] See the 7th Genealogy in Chapter I together with Note 6 in that Chapter.

The Death of the Liwali

The Liwali died (May God have mercy upon him) in Dhu al-Qa'da in the year A.H. 1250,[108] leaving a great grief in the hearts of the People of Mombasa. He was the most decisive of the Liwalis of the Mazari'a, the soundest in judgment, and the strongest of them in might. His like did not appear among the Liwalis. He was good company, of fine character, and had a great soul, with a liking for high things, preferring advice in all his public business. He never embarked upon any course of action until he had consulted with the prominent men and leaders of the country. Therefore the people loved him, and the leaders of the "Twelve Tribes" began to reckon that they shared with him in the government — especially the leaders of the "Three Tribes", who were regarded by him as sympathetic brothers. He did not like it if anyone set about corrupting his government, or causing rebellion and resorting to disobeying orders in his country (May God have mercy upon him). For this reason he never used to excuse the disobedient and rebellious, nor accept intercession for them. How sensible was this policy!

The Liwali was survived by nine male offspring; Rashid, 'Abdullah, Sulayman, Durgham, Saba', Ahmad, Zaman, Sa'id and Ka'b. The first three were among the twenty-five who were seized by the Sayyid and exiled to Bandar 'Abbas, and those who had children were Ahmad, Rashid and Zaman.

But God knows best.

---

[108] **A.H. 1250** = A.D. 1834. The conclusion of the History of the Mazru'i dynasty is summarised in the Editor's Epilogue hereto.

EPILOGUE
The Last Chapter of the Saga of the Mazari'a

We take up the story where Shaykh Al-Amin left it, and apparently had no time to complete it. After the death of the Liwali Salim b. Ahmad in A.D. 1835 his brother, not mentioned in the Genealogy of Chapter I, Khamis by name (See Appendix No.1, Table B), became Liwali for about a year. In A.D. 1836 he was replaced by Salim's son, Rashid, who was Liwali until in the following year (A.D. 1837) he and twenty-four others of the Mazru'i family were lured on board one of Sayyid Sa'id's ships by Sayyid Sulayman al-BuSa'idi[1] and carried away for good, — some say, to be thrown overboard in the Indian Ocean; others, that they were incarcerated in Bandar 'Abbas until they died; others again, that they were deliberately starved to death there.

Mbaruk b. Rashid b. Salim, son of the last Mazru'i Liwali, had been warned of the treachery and did not go on board with the rest, but fled to the interior with his older relatives who had brought him up. The Oxford History of East Africa says he retired to Gazi, and was allowed to remain there by Sayyid Sa'id.[2] The fact is however that Sayyid Sa'id, once he had fled, had no alternative. Whenever he might have approached Gazi, Mbaruk had only to disappear into the Nyika which was at that time impenetrable to an army such as the Sayyid had at his disposal.

European writers of the late 19th and early 20th Centuries regarded him — paternalistically in the flush of Empire — as a brigand and rebel of a Gilbertian type. Mr. Hobley graced him with the epithet "a fine figure of a man".[3] Yet he was to be put out of action simply because, like Prince Charles Edward and his Highlanders, he did not fit in.

But looked at in the perspective of Shaykh Al-Amin's rather more sympathetic account of the History of the Dynasty, we can appreciate his

---

[1] See R. Coupland: East Africa and its Invaders, from the Earliest Times to the Death of Sayyid Sa'id in 1856 pp. 217–94.
[2] Oxford History of East Africa Vol. I, p. 246.
[3] C. W. Hobley: Kenya from Chartered Company to Crown Colony.

motives for his behaviour much better. He was a lineal representative and heir of a line of independent Liwalis, and felt that in the effort to uphold their past glory his honour *as an Arab* was at stake. He actually came back fighting. He would never personally accept a subsidy from the Zanzibar Ruler, but always sent an agent; nor did he present himself personally at Zanzibar to profess his allegiance. He rebelled to enforce recognition of his independence in A.D. 1850 and 1872. The remnants of Mazru'i power in Pemba, which had, it seems, remained active even after its occupation by Sayyid Sa'id in A.D. 1823, had been finally ended there by Captain Matthews and his anti-slavery militia in 1877. There were thus only the two centres of Gazi and Takaungu left to give Mbaruk either material or moral support, yet he still rebelled in A.D. 1882 and 1895. It was the campaigns of Matthews and Commissioner Sir Arthur Hardinge which resulted in the final destruction of his fortress in Mwele, broke his resistance and caused him to flee for asylum to German East Africa. When he fled it could truly be said that the last spark of Mazru'i political significance had been quenched.

Unlike Prince Charles he came back fighting four times at those who had ousted his dynasty. Unlike him again he had not fled across the sea, but simply moved into another district of the same East Africa which had given him birth into a noble family of a remarkable resilience in the face of many vicissitudes. Rather like Rob Roy McGregor he could say at the last, "My foot is on my native heath. My name is Mbaruk Al-Mazru'i. Here I have lived and here I will die." It is true to say that he never truly surrendered.

APPENDIX 1
Genealogical Tables of the Mazru'i Family

(a) A Table of the Origins of the Fourteen Mazru'i Lineages set out in Chapter One

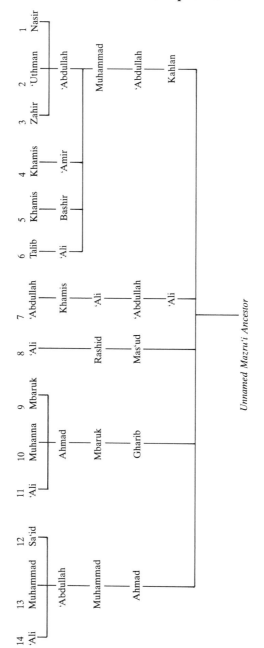

Note: Only the Ancestors of Lineages 1, 2 and 10 actually emigrated to the Swahili Coast. Shaykh Al-Amin mentions no date for the emigration of Mbaruk b. Ahmad and Muhanna b. Ahmad. Their descendants were scholarly but they may have antedated the emigration of Nasir b. 'Abdullah, though Shaykh Al-Amin asserts that no Mazru'i arrived on the Swahili Coast before A.D. 1698

(b) The Descendants of Kahlan indicating the Relationship and Descent of all the Liwalis from Nasir b. 'Abdullah to Mbaruk b. Rashid

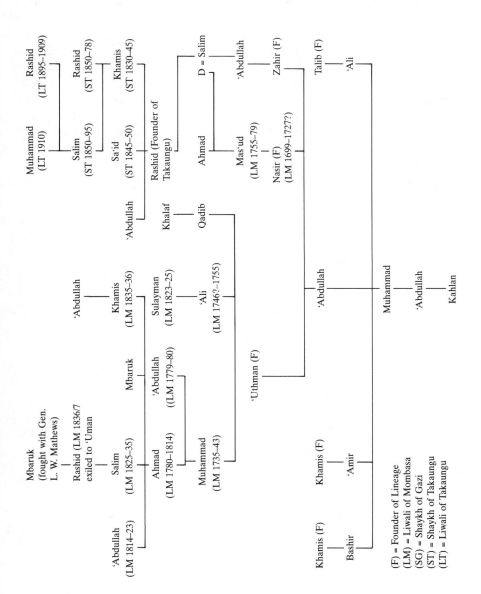

(F) = Founder of Lineage
(LM) = Liwali of Mombasa
(SG) = Shaykh of Gazi
(ST) = Shaykh of Takaungu
(LT) = Liwali of Takaungu

(c) The Fourteen Mazru'i Lineages according to Shaykh Al-Amin b. 'Ali Al-Mazru'i

I am indebted to Mr. F. J. Berg for the following Tables to which he has prefixed the following note:

All the names contained in Shaykh Al-Amin's First Chapter have been traced. Six of the fourteen lineages are broken; the others are uninterrupted. In the genealogical tables which follow, the names which Shaykh Al-Amin mentions are italicised and identified in the manner he indicated, when there was such an indication. (Some are merely mentioned without regard to having held any position or been in any way distinguished). Those names which are necessary only to maintain genealogical continuity are not underlined, and there is no indication of their owners' rank or notable qualities, if any. I have been able to keep all the members of a given generation on a line parallel to each other, which should help in reading the genealogies.

(Signed F. J. Berg)

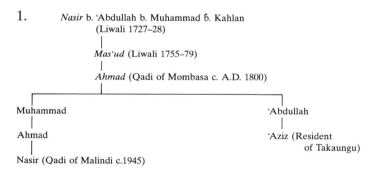

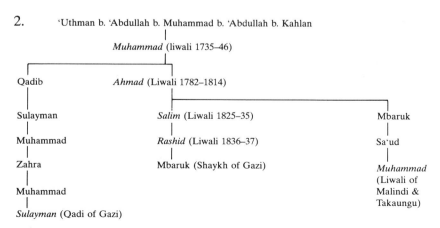

Note: The 'Uthmani Liwalis not included in this sectional Genealogy will be found on the Main Liwali Chart eg. 'Abdullah b. Muhammad b. 'Uthman the fifth Liwali

3.

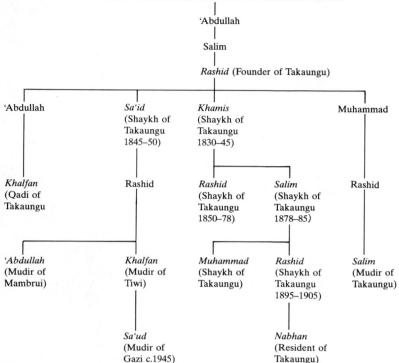

Zahir b. 'Abdullah b. Muhammad b. 'Abdullah b. Kahlan

'Abdullah

Salim

Rashid (Founder of Takaungu)

'Abdullah	*Sa'id* (Shaykh of Takaungu 1845–50)	*Khamis* (Shaykh of Takaungu 1830–45)	Muhammad

| *Khalfan* (Qadi of Takaungu | Rashid | *Rashid* (Shaykh of Takaungu 1850–78) | *Salim* (Shaykh of Takaungu 1878–85) | Rashid |

| *'Abdullah* (Mudir of Mambrui) | *Khalfan* (Mudir of Tiwi) | *Muhammad* (Shaykh of Takaungu) | *Rashid* (Shaykh of Takaungu 1895–1905) | *Salim* (Mudir of Takaungu) |

Sa'ud (Mudir of Gazi c.1945)

Nabhan (Resident of Takaungu)

4.

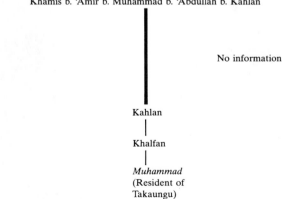

Khamis b. 'Amir b. Muhammad b. 'Abdullah b. Kahlan

No information

Kahlan

Khalfan

Muhammad (Resident of Takaungu)

5.   Khamis b. Bashir b. Muhammad b. 'Abdullah b. Kahlan

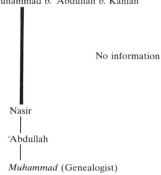

No information

Nasir

'Abdullah

Muhammad (Genealogist)

6.   Talib b. 'Ali b. Muhammad b. 'Abdullah b. Kahlan

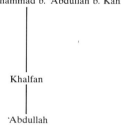

Khalfan

'Abdullah

7.

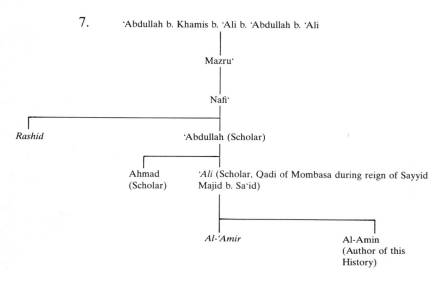

'Abdullah b. Khamis b. 'Ali b. 'Abdullah b. 'Ali

Mazru'

Nafi'

Rashid   'Abdullah (Scholar)

Ahmad (Scholar)   'Ali (Scholar, Qadi of Mombasa during reign of Sayyid Majid b. Sa'id)

Al-'Amir   Al-Amin (Author of this History)

8.

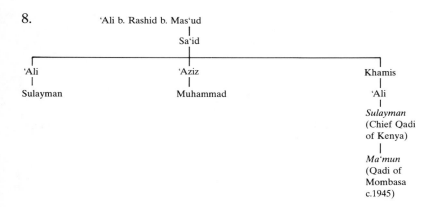

'Ali b. Rashid b. Mas'ud

Sa'id

'Ali — 'Aziz — Khamis

Sulayman   Muhammad   'Ali

Sulayman (Chief Qadi of Kenya)

Ma'mun (Qadi of Mombasa c.1945)

9.

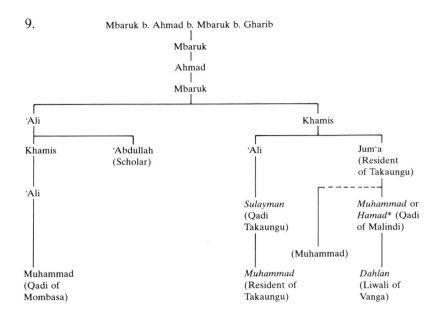

Note: Most of my sources call this man HEMED (Arabice — *Hamad*). There was also a different Muhammad b. Jum'a b. Khamis, as indicated above. The former Qadi, Shaykh Muhammad b. Qasim was very insistent on this point, which I took care to raise myself.

10.

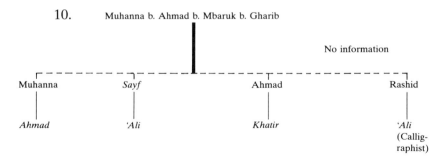

11.   'Ali b. Ahmad b. Mbaruk b. Gharib

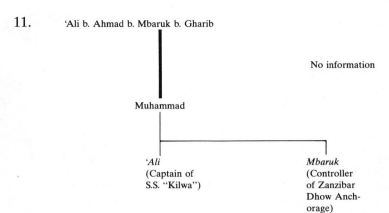

No information

Muhammad

'Ali
(Captain of
S.S. "Kilwa")

Mbaruk
(Controller
of Zanzibar
Dhow Anch-
orage)

12.   Sa'íd b. 'Abdullah b. Muhammad b. Ahmad

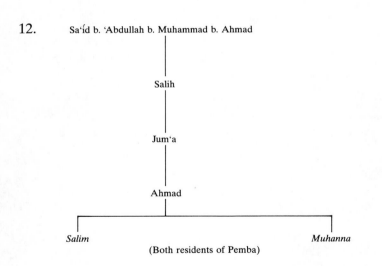

Salih

Jum'a

Ahmad

Salim   *Muhanna*
(Both residents of Pemba)

13.

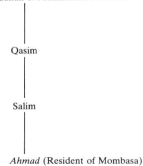

Muhammad b. ʿAbdullah b. Muhammad b. Ahmad

Qasim

Salim

Ahmad (Resident of Mombasa)

14.

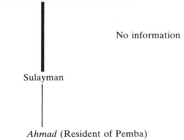

ʿAli b. ʿAbdullah b. Muhammad b. Ahmad

No information

Sulayman

Ahmad (Resident of Pemba)

APPENDIX 2
Maps

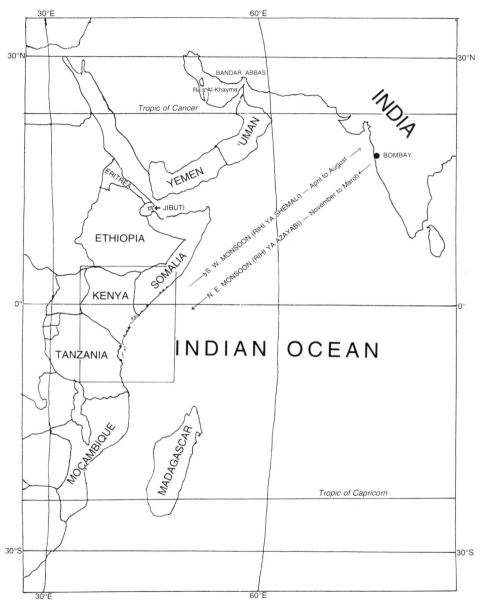

Map 1. General map of the whole area within which the events recorded by Shaykh Al-Amin took place, with inset on facing page.

Enlarged Inset from Map 1.

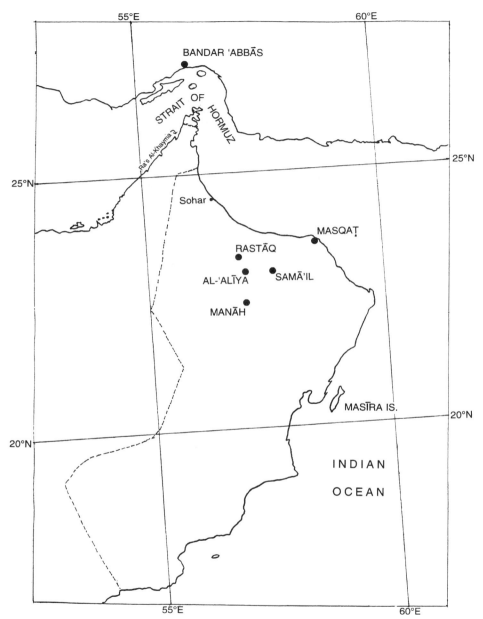

Map 2. Masqat and 'Uman showing the places of origin of the Mazari'a according to Shaykh Al-Amin. *Note*: Al-Ghashab, Wabil and Al-Mazahit are all in the neighbourhood of Rastaq. Washil is in the neighbourhood of Sama'il.

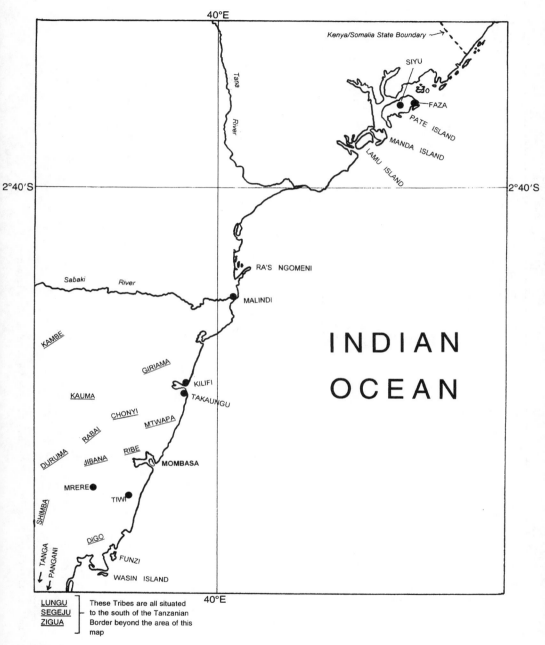

Map 3. The East African coast over which the Mazru'i Dynasty held sway during their period of independence. *Note*: All names of tribes are underscored.

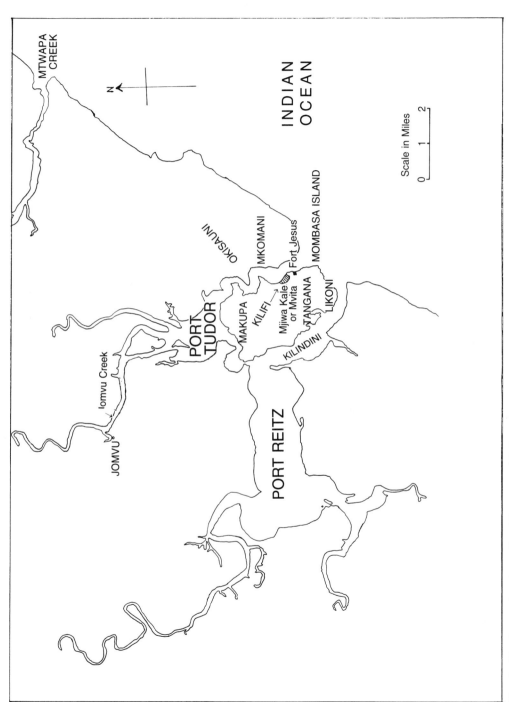

Map 4. Mombasa and environs. *Note*: The course of Salim's town wall is not certainly known.

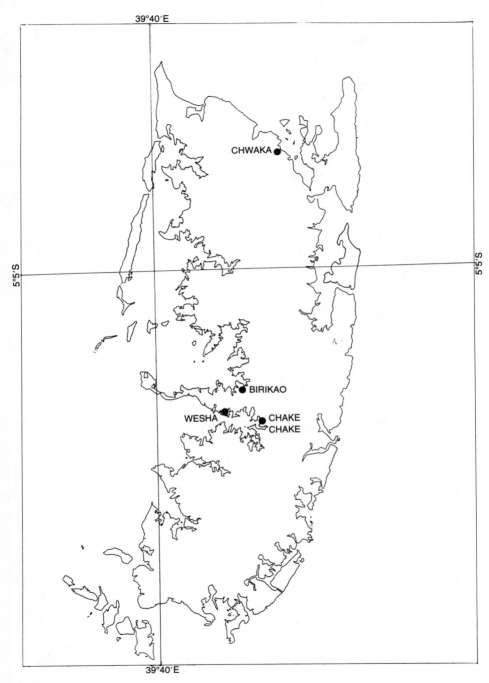

Map 5. Pemba Island.

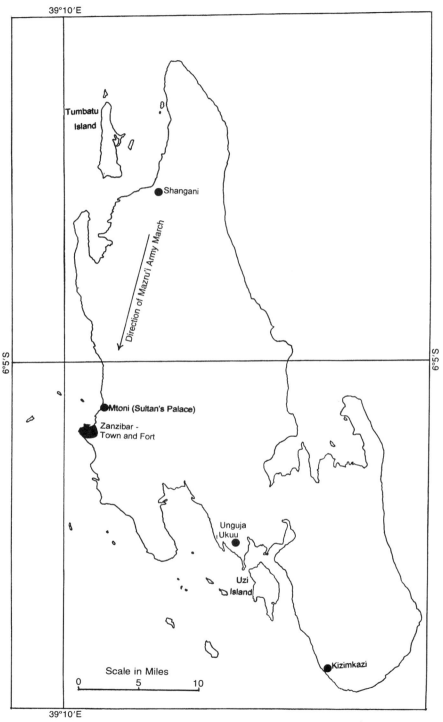

39°10'E

Tumbatu
Island

● Shangani

Direction of Mazru'i Army March

6°5'S   6°5'S

●Mtoni (Sultan's Palace)

Zanzibar -
Town and Fort

Unguja
Ukuu ●

Uzi
Island

Scale in Miles

0   5   10

● Kizimkazi

39°10'E

Map 6. Zanzibar Island.

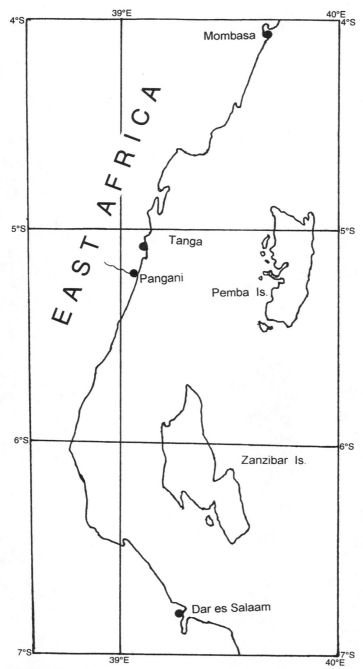

Map 7. Mombasa to Dar es Salaam including Pemba and Zanzibar Islands. *Note*: Pangani, shown on this sketch-map on the coast south of Tanga, is the southernmost limit, according to Shaykh Al-Amin, of the jurisdiction of the Mazari'a.

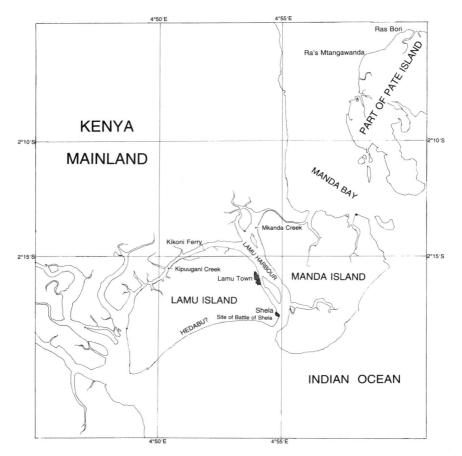

Map 8. Showing Lamu and Manda Islands in relation to Pate.

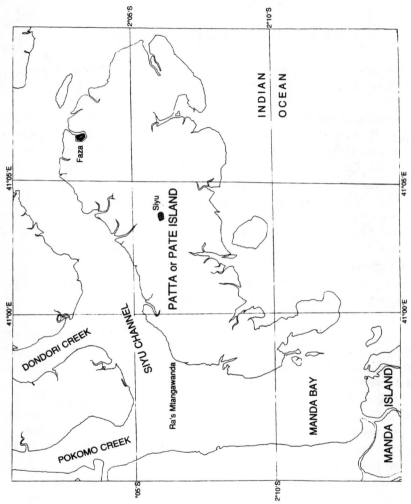

Map 9. Pate Island and part of Manda.

APPENDIX 3
The Mombasa Chronicle

As translated from the Arabic (now lost), and printed in Owen's Voyages, 1833, Vol. I, pp. 414–422 as a footnote, this being the earliest version extant.

This translation was printed in Owen's Voyages without any acknowledgment to Richard Emery who did the actual work of translation. Guillain has included a French rendering of Emery's Version in the Appendices to "L'Afrique Orientale: Première Partie". The translation is so exact that the Arabic expressions can almost be guessed at from the English expressions. The distortion of the names is because Emery has transliterated from the Arabic Manuscript exactly as he saw the letters. He is so accurate that it would be possible to re-write the names in Arabic characters, and they would be found to correspond very closely to Shaykh Al-Amin's spelling.

As to the possibility of a Swahili version of this document behind the Arabic which Emery used, I can only quote what Sir John Gray has to say:

"... It is to him (Emery) that we owe the English translation of the *Mombasa Chronicle* which Owen subsequently printed without any acknowledgement in the Narrative of his voyage. Curiously enough, although 'Swahili is generally used at Mombasa', Emery informed Cooley that, 'having always accustomed myself to speak Arabic', he never became fluent in Swahili as in Arabic. Consequently, when the *Mombasa Chronicle* was presented to him 'in the Swahili language and Arabic character', he had it translated into Arabic". (The British in Mombasa 1824–1826, p.70).

That the Arabic is lost is understandable if it was an *ad hoc* rendering for Emery's benefit. What is more of a mystery is that the Swahili document should not have survived. Either it will sooner or later be forthcoming as a result of scholarly researches, or we shall be left wondering whether Cooley really took Emery up wrong, or whether the document as originally presented to Emery was itself a Swahili rendering of the Arabic, the original Arabic being substituted when it was found that Emery could not use the Swahili. The whole question of when and how far Swahili had come to replace Arabic as the common written language by the third decade of the Nineteenth Century is posed by this strange absence of Emery's original. We can but hope it will be solved in the end.

The following account of the early history of Mombasa is translated from an Arabic Manuscript which we obtained there, and is perhaps the only one in existence.

IN THE NAME OF GOD THE MERCIFUL, THE CLEMENT
Praise to the Lord of all worlds, and blessings and peace on our Lord, Muhammad the seal of the Prophets. And then. This is the antient tale about Mumbasat, and what passed there between the Arabs of Oman and the Portuguese, and those inhabitants of the Coast who were then at Mumbasat.

It hath been reported to us by those who are worthy of credit that the last of the Chiefs of Shiraz, who were sovereigns of Mumbasat, was Shahat son of Masham, and they used to call him Shahat, or Mifta, and after him the chiefs came from Malinda.

Now, the Portuguese came to Mumbasat in the reign of Shahat, and sent stones ready cut from Rainu to Mumbasat, and built the citadel which stands to this day, and garrisoned it, and subdued the people of Mumbasat; and the inhabitants of the coast were weak.

And they exercised oppression and tyranny there, and went beyond all bounds. The inhabitants of the coast could not bear their oppression, and deliberated about going to Uman, to the Imam Sultan b. Sayf, the prince of that country and tribe. So they went and complained to him of the violence of the Portuguese and their tyranny in Mumbasat. So he went with his army to Mumbasat to fight the Portuguese, and fought with them five years, till he drove them out of the fort. So the fort fell into his hands, and he made Muhammad Ibni Mubarak the Governor.

Then the Portuguese returned with troops to give battle to the Arabs, and fought against them till they expelled them from the fort; and they became supreme, and exercised violence, and vehemently oppressed those coast people who dwelt at Mumbasat, and put them to death, because they had gone to Uman and complained to the Imam. Thus, the coast people were unable to dwell at Mumbasat by reason of this tyranny, and took counsel together, and their opinion was, that they should flee to the Imam at Uman, and they went there accordingly. And the Imam, at that time was, Sayf-ibnu-Sultan, to whom they made their complaint. Then he marched and fought with the Portuguese, and God helped him, and he drove them out of the fort, and gave the command to Nasir-bin-Abdullah of Mazrua. And there were in the fort some retainers of the Imam, who rebelled; and they meditated seizing the Governor, and giving the command to their own chief, Saysah Rumbah, which they accomplished. Then they sent to the people of Mumbasat, saying, that they had made Saysah their Governor, and calling upon them to obey him; but they replied, they would not submit to incompetent authority, and that they should leave the fort. The rebels replied, "If the sun and the moon should descend from the sky, we will depart from the citadel." So they and the coast people went to war. The chiefs of the coast-people, at that time, were:

1 Shaikh-ibn-Ahmad of Melinda
2 The Muallim Dav-ibn-Mashaf
3 Mighut-bin Zag
4 Mi-Mul-bin Hal

And while this was going on, God brought in the Portuguese which was thus:

A man, of the nation of Battah, by name Manni Hanid-bin-Kibai, had a quarrel with the Prince of Battah, who was called Banah Tam Maku. So Manni Hanid set off for Mozambique, and invited the Portuguese to attack Battah, and they went there with four ships. And when he arrived, he sent to the Sultan, and said, "We are come to give you battle;" — but the Sultan said, "Come, let us agree; there is no use in devastating our country." So Manni accepted the terms of the Sultan, and they made peace.

Then Manni Hanid said to the Sultan, "What shall we do with the Portuguese; for I brought them out of their country in expectation of war." The Sultan said, "The people of Mumbasat are at war with their Governor; let us send the Portuguese to them, and give them the possession of Mumbasat, and get rid of them from our land." Manni Hanid approved of the scheme, and the Sultan set the army in order, and they departed for Mumbasat in four ships, and seventy Mutaifiyah (supposed to be small craft).

And when they reached Mumbasat, they entered in by the gate (or straits) of Kilindin, and they agreed with the people of Mumbasat about attacking Saisah Rumbah, and driving him out of the fort: so they sent a messenger to him that he should leave the fort, and give it up to the Portuguese. He left it, therefore, without resistance, and the Portuguese obtained the dominion over the people of Mumbasat, and settled in the fort. Then the Sultan of Battah took leave of the Portuguese, and said he would return to Battah; adding, "I advise you to punish these people, and to work them like slaves." And he returned.

The Portuguese acted upon his words, punishing the people and treating them cruelly; and made their chief people serve them, among whom was Shaikh-ibn-Ahmad of Melinda: and they flung stones at the people while they were at prayers; and they used to turn the people out of their houses, and take possession of them; and take their wives to themselves: till the people of Mumbasat were driven to despair, and could bear it no longer. So they consulted together about resisting them, and went to the Portuguese and said to them, "We have heard that the Imam of Uman is coming with an army against Mumbasat; what is your opinion?" And they answered, "What do you say to it?" They replied, "We think you should distribute the paddy (rice in the husk) among the people, that they may beat it out for you; and do not keep any of it back, but lay up rice in store." They approved of this and sent out all the paddy which was in the fort, and divided it among the people that they might beat it out; and there was but very little paddy left in the fort. Then the people of Mumbasat did not give back the rice to the Portuguese; but every one who had received any paddy to beat out kept the rice. So when the great festival of the Portuguese came, they all went out of the fort to the feast; except a few who remained in it: and the coast-people surrounded them and slew them, and seized the son of their Governor. And they fought, and the Portuguese were defeated. Then the son of the Governor, who had been made prisoner, sent to his father, saying, "Make peace with the people, and leave the fort: or else I shall be slain; for I have no means of escaping from them." So the Portuguese made peace with the people of Mumbasat, and asked quarter, and they gave them quarter, and sent them to Mozambique, with their ships and their mariners. And then Mumbasat was left without a sovereign. But those retainers of the Imam who had seized upon Nasir-ibn-Abdullah, and had made their own leader, Saisah Rumbah, Governor, when the Portuguese arrived, had been put in confinement with handcuffs of iron. But afterwards the Portuguese released them, that they might go where they pleased: they sent the Chief, Saisah Rumbah, however, to Mozambique, where he remained till his death; and Nasir they set at liberty, and he went to Uman.

Then the people of Mumbasat seized the keys of the fort, and every tribe placed a man of their own in it, that nothing of what was in it should be lost. Then they went to Uman to the Imam, and there went among them

1 Shaikh-ibn-Ahmad of Melinda,

2 Mi-Ghut-bin-Zag of Kilindin,

3 Mishhat-bin-Dace of Tanjan:

And of the people of Mifta there went one man of each Tribe: and of Vanikat, one man from each city; among who were

1 Mayanij, of the people of Muta, and

2 Mamak, of the people of Tiv.

And the cities of Vanikat, are Ribah, Shuni, Kambah, Gaume, Jibanah, Rabayi, Jiryamah, Darumah, Mutavi, Shibah, Lughah, Diju. These people went to Uman to the Imam Sayf-ibn-Sultan, and told him their situation with regard to the Portuguese, and the wars that had been between them. So the Imam set out with three ships: one called Kab-ras; the second, Malik: and the name of the third is not known: and he sent Muhammad-ibn-Saeed of Maamar as Governor of Mumbasat; and he granted to the people of Mumbasat all that was in the fort, except the gunpowder, the lead (or tin), and the copper. After that, Salih-bin-Muhammad of Hazram went as Governor to Mumbasat, and Muhammad-ibn-Saaid returned to Uman. Then Salih-bin-Muhammad began to exercise violence in Mumbasat, and was tyrannical over the people. So they complained to the Imam, and he commanded them to seize him, and they kept him in confinement for some time, and then released him by general consent. And when they set him free, he made war with Shaikh-ibn-Ahmad of Malinda and the people went to Vanikat from fear of the Governor Salih, and the people of Mifta were joined with Salih in battle against Ibn Ahmad and the people of Kelindin.

Now it happened that Shaikh-bin-Ahmad had sent his son Ali-Kumbu to the Imam before the war, and the Imam gave him money and a horse, and when he came to Mumbasat he knew nothing of the war, so Salih seized him with all his property. And when Shaikh-bin-Ahmad heard of the arrival of his son, and how he had fallen into the hands of Salih, he lost all his patience, and could not bear the loss of his son, and went to Salih. And when he arrived Salih treated him with great respect and honour, and gave him supreme command in the fort, but treacherously. Then Salih had no provisions in the fort, so he went to the Island for provisions, and he commanded his lieutenants that Shaikh-bin-Ahmad and his son should not leave the fort till he returned from the island, and as soon as he came back he killed them both.

Now it happened that, before this, Shaikh-bin-Ahmad and his son Ahmad-bin-Shaikh, and the Kilindinies with him, sent the army of Vanikat to fight against the people of Mifta, who were in the old town: so they killed them and plundered them, because of their alliance with the Governor Salih in his war against them.

Then a report reached the Imam of the wickedness of Salih in the land, and his tyranny over the people; so the Imam sent Muhammad-ibn-Othman to be Governor of Mumbasat, and Salih returned to Uman. Then Muhammad-ibn-Othman sent to Ahmad-ibn-Shaikh, and the men of Kilindin, who had gone to Vanikat, that they should come to Mumbasat, that he and they might make peace, and the land have rest. So Ahmad and the men came and made peace with the Governor, and he brought about a peace between them and the people of Mifta, and the land had rest.

Then the Imam died at Uman, and Ahmad-ibn-Saaid of the tribe of

Bu Saaid, took the chief authority there. So when the Governor heard of the usurpation of Ahmad-ibn-Saaid in Uman, who was not of the family of the Imams, he also assumed independent authority over Mumbasat, and would not give up the place to the Imam, and said, "The Imam is a common man like myself, he has usurped Uman, I have usurped Mumbasat."

And when the Imam heard the words of the Governor, he sent Saif-bin-Khalaf, Saif-bin-Nasir, Saif-bin Saaid, and Saif-ul-Battah, and Maana-bin Kulaib to Mumbasat, that they might use some artifice with the Governor and kill him. When they arrived they used deceit, and said to him: "We have quarrelled with the Imam, and are come to thee, swearing, that we desire to be with thee, to halt where thou does halt, to depart whence thou doest depart, and we wish that thou wouldest give us some money that we may travel to Kilvah and other places to be seen." And the Governor answered them according to their desires, and whilst he was making preparations for their journey, behold they used treachery and killed him, and they put his brother Ali-bin-Othman in prison, with Khalaf-bin-Kazib, Abdullah-ibn-Khamis of Aafif, and they usurped the authority in Mumbasat, and made Saif-bin-Khalaf governor.

And there were in the fort Halab-bin-Bahed and Hamidaud-Abdal-Balusshi, who were attached to Ali-bin-Othman, and they lived in the fort; so they used a stratagem to send him and his companions down, and they tied long pieces of raw leather together from the top of the fort to the bottom, and let them all down without the knowledge of the people of the fort. And when Ali-bin-Othman and his companions were come down they were received by the principal men of the town, among whom were Mishaf-bin-Dav, Haj-ibn-Maul Mughlut, Khamis-bin-Mizakal, and Ahmad-bin-Dav, all of Kilindin, and who accompanied them to Vanikat to the sea-port of Murairah. And the people of Mifta were at that time with Saif-bin-Khalaf, the Governor.

And there was in the harbour of Kilindin an English ship, and the people of Mumbasat used to call the Captain of her Muzugh-Kighugh (query Mr. Cook?) and he was intimate with Ali-bin-Othman; so the Englishman went to Murairah to Ali, and advised them to make war against Saif-bin-Khalaf, for, if they subdued him, it was finished, and if not he would take Ali-bin-Othman and his adherents aboard his ship Mambai (Bombay) and next year would send them to Mumbasat with some ships, and then fight against Saif and drive him out of the fort. They liked his plan. Then he told them to. make a ladder as high as the fort, which they did. And they marched from Vanikat and entered Mumbasat by night, and fixed the ladder and all entered unawares, and fought with the people of the fort, and subdued them. And the governor, Khalaf, mounted a large bastion which was in the fort, and they could not get at him, and he fought with them three days. Then the Englishman landed a gun from his ship, and mounted it against the bastion and fired at it, and made a breach in it, and the Governor Saif cried out for quarter and threw down his arms, so they took him and put him to death. And they made Ali-bin-Othman Governor, and gave up to the people of Mumbasat all that was in the fort of any worth, except the arms and ammunition, and the lead. And the Governor Alib-bin-Othman made an engagement with the people of Mumbasat for many privileges that he would grant them — and the same with the people of Vanikat. Then Ali-bin-Othman prepared for war with Zanguibar, and he marched and entered it, and besieged the people, till they were distressed by what had come upon them. Then the Devil instigated Khalaf-bin-Kazibe to kill the Governor: so he fell upon him in an unguarded moment, and stabbed him with his dagger, and he died. And Masaud-bin-Nasir succeeded him, and the army returned to Mumbasat, and they made Masaud Governor in Mumbasat, and he lived till God put an end to his days.

And the reign of Ali-bin-Othman was eight years, (8) and the reign of Masaud-bin-Nasir was twenty-four, (24) years. Then, after him, they gave the authority to Abdullah-bin-Muhammad-bin-Othman of Mazrua, and he enjoyed it for eight (8) years, and died. Then they chose Ahmad-bin-Muhammad-bin-Othman of Mazrua, who lived in the possession of his power thirty-four (34) years. Then they appointed Abdullah-bin-Ahmad-bin-Muhammad-bin-Othman of Mazrua, who lived in the exercise of authority eight (8) years, and died. And then they chose as Governor Sulayman-bin-Ali-bin-Othman of Mazrua, and he is Governor at the present day. And God knows the truth. And we have abridged this story, and have left out what was long and full. And we pray to God for a happy end in death, Amen. And this copy was made the 28th Shaaban, in the year 1239.

N.B. When Shasah-bin-Mish-ham died, there was sent after him a chief from Shiraz — but after him the Chiefs (Shaikhs) came from Malinda; then Sultan Yusuf; and he had been brought up among the Portuguese, and used to eat pork and all their other food; and his government began on Saturday, the 7th Muharram, at the tenth hour, in the year 1040 after the Hegira: and when he was in power, he was very tyrannical, and made people eat hog's flesh, and he was wicked and disobedient. And he was dependent on the Sultan of Rainu; but he opposed his authority, and rebelled against him; so the Sultan of Rainu marched against him, and drove him out of the fort, and he fled to Yaman, and died in the seaport of Jeddah. And there was not after him any sultan but chiefs (Shaikhs) only — But God knows best.

APPENDIX 4
Official Letters and Memoranda in British Government Records

(1) Parliamentary Papers, Vol. LIX (1896) Africa No. 6 (C 8247) — Enclosure No. 1 to Letter No. 26 (pp. 30–35)

Memorandum from Mr. A. Hardinge respecting the Mazru'i Chiefs, their History, etc. up to the recent Disturbances at Takaungu in 1895.

The Mazruis, or, to use the correct Arabic plural, Mazaria, originally came from Muscat when the present Zanzibar dominions were wrested from the Portuguese by the Muscat Arabs under the Imam Sef-bin-Sultan al-Yorabi at the end of the seventeenth Century.

They all claim descent from a Muscat Arab named Abdullah, of the Ghafiri clan in the Oman, whose two sons, Othman and Zaher, were the respective founders of the Gazi, or elder, and Takaungu, or younger branch, between whom the chieftainship was divided in the present century. The first Mazrui of any importance was Mahomed bin Othman, the grandson, of Abdullah, who was Wali or viceroy of Mombasa for the Imam of Muscat in 1730, and who in that capacity ruled the old coast from Malindi in the North to Pangani (in German East Africa) to the south, as well as the Island of Pemba, Zanzibar, which was not then, comparatively speaking, of any importance, being administered by one of the Imam's Akidas. The tie which connected Mombasa with the distant court of Muscat was very weak; the supremacy of the Imam, as its name implied, was mainly spiritual; preoccupied by their troubles with Persia, which, under Nadir Shah, ended in the overthrow of their power, the Yorabi princes could give little attention to their remote African dependancies, and Mohamed-bin-Othman had accordingly no difficulty in throwing off his allegiance to his Sovereign, and transforming himself from a Viceroy into an independent Sultan. His brothers, sons, and nephews succeeded him, according to the Mahomedan rule of hereditary descent, and exercised unquestioned sovereignity at Mombasa, although Seyyid Ahmed-bin-Said, the second Prince and real founder of the Albusaidi dynasty (which, having shaken off the Persian yoke, had succeeded the Yorabis on the Throne of Oman, but which, being of the Hinawi clan, the Mazruis refused to recognise), once compelled from them, in 1785, a temporary recognition of his overlordship. It was not however till after the accession, in 1806 of Sayyid Said-bin-Sultan, the fourth Albusaidi Imam, that the Court of Muscat conceived the design of actually re-annexing its old African possessions. Taking advantage of an appeal on the part of the people of Patta for assistance, Sayyid Said first expelled from Patta and Pemba (in 1822) the then ruling Mazrui chief, Abdullah-bin-Hamid (who on his accession, in 1814, had scorned to send the usual gifts to Muscat, dispatching merely, as an insolent hint, a mail shirt and a small quantity of powder), and then threatened at Mombasa itself his successor Suleiman-bin-Ali. The latter, an aged and feeble prince, who had been chosen in order to avert a civil conflict between two kinsmen with better hereditary claims than himself, now invoked (1823) the protection of the British Government, and it was granted to him, subject to the approval of the British Government, by Captain Vidal, of Her Majesty's ship "Barracouta", who was at that time cruising on the East African Coast, Lieutenant Reitz, R.N., being left with him as British Resident, to assist in the Government of Mombasa, with a right to retain half its revenue. The British Government, however, refused to ratify this arrangement, and withdrew its protection from Mombasa. Salim-bin-Ahmed, who had deposed Suleiman-bin-Ali in 1826, accordingly submitted to Seyyid Said, and agreed to surrender the fort on condition of being allowed to remain as hereditary Governor of the town, and to retain one half of the Mombasa revenue. The peace thus concluded was, however, only a truce. Successive Mazrui insurrections against the rule of the Muscat Arabs were followed in each case by a temporary reconquest, till, in 1837, Seyyid Said took Mombasa for the third and last time, placed a governor of his own over the fort, supported by a strong Muscat garrison, and sent the reigning Mazrui, Rashid-bin-Salim, whom he had persuaded to remain in the town by the most solemn oaths that his personal freedom would be respected, and then treacherously arrested, to perish, with some twenty of his principal adherents, in the dungeons of Bunder Abbas. Three years later he himself moved his capital from Muscat to Zanzibar, and thus secured his hold on the opposite coast.

The effect of the final capture of Mombasa was to break up the unity of the Mazrui state, which, deprived of its capital and center, split into two divisions, the one to the southwest, and the other to the northeast of Mombasa. In the southern district Abdullah-bin-Hamis, the first cousin, and by Sheria, rightful heir of Rashid-bin-Salim, was permitted by Seyyid Said to govern as a petty chief at Gazi, whilst the Mazrui Arabs to the north of Mombasa formed a separate centre at Takaungu under the rule of Hamis-bin-Rashid, the head of the younger or Zaherite branch of the race.

It was now that Mubarak-bin-Rashid, the present Chief of Gazi, first began to appear upon the scene. The son of Rashid-bin-Salim (the last independent ruler of Mombasa, who had died as related above in the dungeons of Seyyid Said), he had grown up at Gazi under the care of Abdullah-bin-Hamis, the eldest male, and therefore chief of the branch of Othman, and of his own elder brother, Mahomed-bin-Rashid. No sooner, however, had he reached man's estate than he formed the design of wrestling Takaungu from the Zaherites, and accordingly, raising a force of his own, but supported by Abdullah, he attacked and expelled its ruler, Rashid-bin-Hamis, who had just succeeded his father, Hamis-bin-Rashid. The latter was supported by Seyyid Said, and the two between them drove Mubarak back to Gazi. They permitted him, however, to reside there unmolested, and on Abdullah's death he was recognised by Seyyid Majid, who had succeeded Seyyid Said on the Throne of Zanzibar, as Sheikh or Chief of the district around Gazi, and was granted, as had been the case with his predecessor before him, an annual subsidy from Zanzibar, in return for which he was supposed to administer his little vassal state, and furnish solders, if requisite, to the Sultan. He was not, however, quiet for long. Seyyid Majid having attempted to restrain his too high-handed exercise of his authority, he broke out into rebellion, and it became necessary to stop his subsidy and send a force from Mombasa to attack him. Majid, however, dying shortly afterwards, his brother and successor, Barghash, made peace with Mubarak, and restored his subsidy, until a few years later, on account of some domestic dispute, (one story being that the Sultan had imprisoned one of his relations, and another that the people of Wanga had refused to send him a wife), he suddenly rebelled for a third time, and at the head of a strong force burnt and plundered Wanga. Again his pay was stopped, and an army, this time under General Matthews, was sent against him from Zanzibar. Matthews drove him first from Gazi, and then after a three weeks' siege from his hill stronghold at Mwele; and though, during his temporary absence at Zanzibar, Mubarak recovered sufficient strength to sack Mombasa and other coast towns, Matthews eventually compelled him, on his return to the coast, to come to terms, and to make his submission at Zanzibar to Seyyid Barghash. He was then permitted to return to Gazi, but received no pay until Barghash was succeeded by Seyyid Khalifa, who, as a gracious act on his accession, both restored Mubarak's subsidy and released several of his relations and followers who had been taken prisoners during the last rebellion. The Imperial British East Africa Company, on taking over the mainland concession from Seyyid Khalifa in the following year, continued the subsidy, Mubarak supplying them with mercenaries from the ranks of his fighting slaves. Notwithstanding, perhaps in consequence of this arrangement, their relations with him were never entirely satisfactory, and though professing for the sake of the subsidy, to be their servant, habitually disregarded their orders, and allowed their resident at Wanga, of which one of his sons was governor, no real power. It should, however, be said in his favour that he actively assisted them on two occasions, once to establish their authority in the face of an incipient rebellion at Mombasa, and once to suppress a somewhat serious disturbance in Teita, and that promises of increased wealth and power were made to him, when they first took charge, by their agents, the non-fulfilment of which he regarded as a bitter grievance.

Meanwhile, the younger or Zaherite branch of the Mazruis were ruling somewhat more quietly over Takaungu and the adjacent district. Rashid-bin-Hamis, the Chief against whom Mubarak of Gazi had waged his first war, was succeeded by his younger brother, Salim, who, though once arrested and imprisoned for six months by Seyyid Barghash, was, on the whole, a good deal more loyal than his kinsman of Gazi to Zanzibar. Salim-bin-Hamis received no regular pay from the Sultan, but he paid an annual visit to Zanzibar till after the accession of Seyyid Khalifa, and was given on every occasion a present in money, which practically amounted to a subsidy, and enabled him to keep up his state and dignity as a Chief, and to maintain a certain force of fighting slaves. His last visit was paid on the accession of Khalifa; after that he always sent as his Representative his eldest nephew and heir apparent, Mubarak-bin-Rashid, who received and took back the Sultan's gifts. He never would accept a salary from the Company or recognise their right to interfere in the affairs of Takaungu, nor did they seriously attempt to do so till his death in February last. They then sent there Mr. McDougall, their district Officer at Malindi. He was at first badly received both by the Sheikhs and the people, but his resolute attitude soon overcame the opposition which was simmering on his arrival, and enabled him to assert his authority.

His first duty was to see to the appointment of a successor to Sheikh Salim. Mubarak-bin-Salim, the legal heir according to Moslem law, and his younger brother, Aziz, were both believed to be turbulent and ill-disposed to Europeans, and the Company therefore resolved to pass them over, and to appoint Rashid-bin-Salim, the late Chief's eldest son, who was known to be of a docile disposition, and so friendly to the English that he had always been employed by his father whenever the latter required to transact any business with Mombasa. In order, however, to minimise the chances of a conflict, and secure, if possible, a semblance of popular acquiescence in his nomination, Mr. McDougall called the Arabs and Elders together in Baraza, and asked them whom they would wish appointed. They all, including Mubarak, Aziz, and Rashid, replied that they recognised the Company's authority, and would accept whomever it selected; and on Mr. McDougall then announcing that the choice had fallen on Rashid-bin-Salim, who would rule the district with the title (a new one for the district) of Wali, Mubarak and Aziz both promised him obedience, the former offering to go to Gonjoro and administer it as his subordinate. Rashid on his side to conciliate his cousin, made over to him all Sheikh Salim's personal property, including (so little are the Sultan's laws obeyed) his slaves, whom Mubarak at once armed and marched away with to Gonjoro. A personal dispute a few weeks later between the two cousins served as a pretext for Mubarak's permanent withdrawal from Takaungu; taking up his own quarters at Gonjoro, he placed, without reference to the Wali or the Company, his brother Aziz in charge of Tanganyiko, and prepared to all appearance to attack Rashid. It was then that Mr. Piggott's application for a gun-boat at Kilifi brought about intervention from Zanzibar.

It is open, of course, to question whether the setting aside of Mubarak and Aziz in favour of a younger kinsman was altogether a politic act. It might, perhaps, have been wiser to have made Mubarak Wali on his promising compliance with certain conditions, and to have kept him at Takaungu under the supervision of a European officer, supported by a military, and, if necessary, a naval force, Gonjoro and the inland districts being simultaneously intrusted to the more peaceful and loyal Rashid, who could have ruled them as his cousin's deputy. The Company, however, did not consult me as Her Majesty's acting Commissioner (I was absent indeed at the time on the Tana), and so responsibility for the origin of the trouble can therefore be imputed to Her Majesty's Government. But whether their appointment was well or ill advised — and I am certainly not prepared to say that it was the wrong one — it was clear that, once made, it must be supported. A hereditary claim, respectfully submitted, might have deserved consideration; to recognise an indefeasible hereditary right, asserted in a tone of menace, would have been to constitute an *imperium in imperio*, which would have been fatal to the authority of the Government. I accordingly recommended that if Mubarak could not be brought to reason by peaceful means, he should be coerced, and my recommendation was approved by Her Majesty's Government. The subsequent development of events, the expedition to Gonjoro and Sokoke, the attack by Aziz on Takaungu, the flight of the rebel chiefs to their kinsmen at Gazi were all reported to me as they occurred. I have merely sought in this memorandum to connect them with the earlier history of the two ruling Mazrui families, so as to present as clear a picture as possible of the true character of the Mazrui power in its relation to the other elements in the East African political situation. Your Lordships will thus have all the facts before you on which to base such instructions as you may decide to give me with respect to my eventual dealings with the three Mazrui Chiefs should they, as they probably will in the end, sue for peace, as also with respect to the future maintenance under European control or non-maintenance, as the case may be, of a new Mazrui native Ruler at Gazi, Pongwe or Wanga.

(signed) ARTHUR H. HARDING
Zanzibar, August 26, 1895.

(2) Letter dated 16th July, 1898 from Sir Arthur Hardinge to Lord Salisbury, Foreign Secretary.

The following excerpt was given to me by Mr. F. J. Berg but without full reference. It appears to be from one of the series of Parliamentary Papers but not the same series as the previous report report is found in. I include it here however since it throws light on the cause of the migration of the Beni Zahir to Takaungu. The quarrel referred to in the excerpt was of a nature similar to that which caused 'Abdullah b. Nafi' to migrate to Mecca (See note 6 to Chapter 1).

"The Great-grandfather of Rashid bin Salim had a difference about a century ago, with the then Mazrui ruler of Mombasa, which was at that time *de facto* independent of Muzcat, and withdrew with a certain number of Mazrui Arabs belonging to this branch of the ruling clan to the present site of Takaungu, where he founded the town, and was recognised as the Arab Chief of the adjacent coast, for a distance of from 20–30 miles, by the neighbouring Galla, Wasania, and Giriama tribes, and also, though this is less clear, by his Mazrui kinsmen at Mombasa. When in 1837 the Sultan Said-bin-Sultan of Mascat and Zanzibar finally wrested Mombasa from the Mazrui Arabs, a large number of them went to Takaungu, the successive chiefs of which, unlike Mubarak of Gazi, remained generally loyal to the Court of Zanzibar, and were permitted by that Court to collect certain sources of revenue, on the assumption, which both they and the Sultan found convenient, that they were the unpaid hereditary governors on behalf of His Highness of that part of his mainland dominions. No formal document recognising or confirming this right to administer and levy dues or taxes in the district was ever granted them, but the Wali of Takaungu contends that "Usage and suffrance" extending over a period of nearly sixty years from 1837 to 1895 since the conquest by the Sultan of Zanzibar, and for half a century previous to that conquest by the *De facto* rulers of the country, has given his claim a legal validity entitling him to a pecuniary commutation. The Imperial British East Africa Company always acquiesced in it, and recognised Salim-bin-Hamis, the present Wali's father, as their administrator, but paid him no salary (I believe, indeed, that he himself declined to receive one), and in practice made little attempt, beyond placing a Customs Officer at Takaungu in order to collect the export and import duties allowed to the Sultan by the treaties, to interfere in its internal affairs.

The sources of revenue which Sheikh Salim and his predecessors appropriated were various. He claimed all the flotsam and jetsam, all ambergris found on the shores of the district, one tusk of every two brought by the Galla or Wasania hunters to his town, and he also levied a fee for licence to trade and keep shops in Takaungu, Tanganyiko, Gonjoro, and other villages in the neighbourhood on the Indian and native merchants. It seems probable that the total revenue derived by him from these sources never exceeded £200 a year, for largely owing to his excessive liberality to his retainers, and to the military force which he maintained, he died not only poor but in debt."

(3) Foreign Office Confidential Print, Africa, F.O. 403/210, 300–1.

A letter from Sir John Kirke to Sir Percy Anderson (F.O.)

Sevenoaks, Kent, September 28, 1895.

The history of the Mazrui (called collectively Mazara) was this. When Seif-bin-Sultan took Mombasa from the Portuguese in 1670 he left one of the Mazara as his lieutenant; no less that three times the Portuguese retook the place before being finally expelled in 1730, and each time the Arabs returned some one of the Mazrui family was left in charge (only on two occasions, and then for a short time, were members of other families made Governors of this place). Thus the Mazrui came to regard the office of Governor of Mombasa as theirs by right. They were, however, only Governors and keepers of the strong fort and agents for the Imam of Muscat.

The people of Mombasa and the surrounding country were ruled through elders of the several tribes; thus the powerful Shiraz or Persian element, the old lords of the land, had over them the elders of their own group. The Kilindini people had their Headman, and so also the oldest

settlers of all, descended from the men of the Khawarij who fled to East
Africa after persecutions in Oman in the 65th year of the Hejra. These
old colonists are still one of the Mombasa clans, and live under Khamis
Kembe (Khamis b. Komb?) as their elder.

To the elders the Muscat Imams paid a yearly subsidy which in my
time amounted to 1,000 dollars each, unless in the case of one, whose
subsidy was cut down because he would not, or could not, give up the
murderer of a Banyan, a British subject.

When the Ya'rubi dynasty lost the Government in Oman, in the year
1741, and power passed to Ahmed, the first Imam of the Al Bu Said
dynasty, the same rules both Muscat and Zanzibar, the Mazrui Governors
refused to follow the new rulers, and declared for independence.

They placed the district under the protection of Great Britain as a last
resort when pressed by Seyyid Said, the grandfather of the present ruler
of Zanzibar.

The matter was referred here, and Seyyid Said was able to satisfy the
British Government that the Mazrui were rebels, who from being only
Governors had taken advantage of a change of dynasty to declare for
independence. We therefore withdrew our flag, and gave the place over
to Seyyid Said, who by treachery seized the Mazrui headmen and had
them starved to death at Bunder Abbas. I knew well old Seyyid Suleiman,
the man who decoyed them from Mazrui (SIC — Mombasa Fort), at a
feast, and had them seized and shipped off. . . .

I can give (Sir Arthur) Hardinge the correct dates that appear on the
tombs of the Mazrui Chiefs.

The succession he gives in his genealogical table is quite correct, but
his dates are often inexact. (Hardinge's own history of the Mazrui appears
on Command Paper 8274, British Parliamentary Papers). . . .

Since writing about Mubarak (bin Rashid Al-Mazrui) I have referred
to notes; I find I gave Colonel Kitchener information which he embodied
in his despatch from Zanzibar of the 15th March 1886, relative to this
man's history. You will find this in Kitchener's No. 10 of the 15th March
1886. This shows that Mubarak's connection with Gazi in that district was
quite a thing of recent date, and that to keep the family out of the district
south of Mombasa would be no injustice. He has been in that country
only for about twenty-five years, having previously lived at Takaungu, to
which district the Mazrui Chiefs, after being expelled from Mombasa, were
restricted by Seyyid Said, who took Mombasa. . . .

I mention this to show that Mubarak has no old rights near Gazi, and
I know that he has treated the poor WaDigo as his slaves; it will therefore
be a good matter to put an end to all government of that district by any
of the family, who will never be loyal to us.

The Shimba Hills, from which Mubarak has just been expelled, is one of the best places we have for coffee, etc., near the Coast, but the Mazrui were always opposed to improvement.

APPENDIX 5
Two Poems relating to the War between Lamu and the Allied Forces of Pate and the Mazari'a

The following two poems were brought to my notice by the late Mr. J. T. H. Allen, who supplied me with a copy labelled MS. No. 207, presumably from the Library in the University of Dar-es-Salaam, where he was working at the time. I have however acquired another copy of the text, thanks to Dr. Jan Knappert of the School of Oriental and African Studies in London, who drew my attention to it. It is in an article by Professor Ernst Damann in "Zeitschrift fur Eingeborenen Sprachen", Band xxi Heft 3 (April 1941) at p. 172, and this appears more accurate. I reproduce the text here together with an English rendering, and in the Swahili I have approximated some of the spelling to Standard KiSwahili for the sake of clarity, though the dialect is Kiamu. Verse No. 1 in the first poem is not present in Mr. Allen's text, while Verses No. 8 and No. 9 in the second poem are Nos. 3 & 4 in Mr. Allen's version.

Mashairi ya Zita za Watu wa Lamu na Pate

Imetungwa na

Abdullah bin Hameidi Mazru'i

In shalla Rabi, mujahani, khawatambiwa Kiwandeo
Muyashikapo mawani, mtafidi, mtakao.
Msitiwe chafukani nakuwafisha, khawa fuu!
Ni yeo siku, ni yeo, maisha ni kaburini!

Mimi niko Pate Yunga, nifuete Ahamadi.
Kati si mwenye kuzinga, ulimi wangu sirudi.
Pinga zenu Mungapinga, hazitanguwi ahadi.
Siku ya thuluthi l-hadi tutaonana fundoni.

Wachumba (or Watumwa?) msiwe mbale, mkikaa kandokando,
Jivuteni, muje mbele, tuonyeshane zitendo.

Mtaona wateule, nguo wafungene pindo
Siku ya kuchinja (Kiamu — kutinda) fundo tutaonana fundoni.

TRANSLATION

Poems of the War between the People of Lamu and of Pate

Composed by

'Abdullah b. Ahmad al-Mazru'i

If God my Lord will, you prosperous people, those who live in Lamu[1]
will not escape misfortune.
If you insist on the struggle,[2] you will obtain what you desire.
Do not be afraid and cause them (i.e. folk) to die without any
advantage.
Today is the day, today! Life is in the grave.

I am here in Pate Yunga,[3] I follow Ahmad.[4]
I am not one to change; I do not go back on my word.
Even if you were to put your obstacles in my path, they do not nullify
my vow.
On Tuesday (or, on the third day) we will see one another on the
battle-field.

Dear friends,[5] do not keep at a distance, while you sit on one side.
Bestir yourselves and come forward, that we may show one another
what we can do.
You will see champions, who have clothed one another (i.e. for battle)
to the last detail.
On the day of slaughter in battle, we will see each other on the field.

Jawabu Ahali Lamu[6]

Muhibi wangu, mugwana, nione wako waraka
Khafahamia ma'ana, kicheko kikanitoka.

---

[1] **Kiwandeo** is another name for Lamu.
[2] **Mawani** really means "In the graveyard", i.e. "If you (insist on) holding to the graveyard, you will end up there finally".
[3] **Yunga** is an old name for Pate.
[4] **Ahmad**. Damann takes this to refer to Ahmad b.Shaykh, Sultan of Pate, who made a treaty with the Liwali Ahmad of Mombasa in A.D. 1814. If Allen's suggestion of authorship is correct however, it is equally possible — or more probable — that it refers to the Liwali Ahmad himself. Damann only gives the author of the first poem as "Ein Pateman".
[5] **Dear Friends**. This is the rendering of Damann's version, Watumba, or Wachumba in Standard Swahili, being "One who is wooed" or "A suitor". The address is of course sarcastic. Allen's version, Watumwa, means "Slaves". If that is the correct word, then it is contemptuous.
[6] Note that this Phrase is in the Arabic form. The proper Swahili form would be *Jawabu ya Ahali ya Lamu*.

Nguo muyapofungana, zitawakusa mashaka.
Mtotea zisikwakwa, masiri kuwa kazini.

Kwamba uko Pate Unga, nami niko Kiwandeo
Sikae, ukijipinga! Hutofidi muradio.
Mume huja akasonga, hasemi: "Leo ni leo",
Waole phaa walio, watureo msituni.

Hatuchi. Situtusheni! Hatuituki zishindo
Tangu kale na zamani tuwa zoevu wa nondo.
Ivu la moto wa kuni twawalitenda kitendo
Siku ya kuchinja fundo tutaonana fundoni.

Wallahi, twawapa kwa Mungu na mtume Muhamadi
Ndooni (Njooni), muwe machungu, mudhalilike jisadi!
Muwe karamu ya tungu na tai kuwafisidi!
Na tama'a ya kurudi kwenu sifikirini.

Mkiwa mu wenye kuja — na pasiwe mshawasha —
Kwanda (Kwanza) watani wasia wa wana kuwarithisha!
Wake muwape zifaya maeda yao kweusha.
Mukija tutawashusha mashukio ya zamani.

Na kwamba muiliwee bandari yenu la kale,
Wauzeni wasaliee, wazele wenu, wazele!
Muuzeni usaliee, bwana bin Salale!
Hat ya leo walele, kamwe hawazundukani!

Wa kwamba mna kiu, njoo, tupo nasi kuwalinda!
Nguo zenu sifungeni, wenye nahudha bora!
Tuketie milangoni, huwalinda kuwatenda.
Mwisapo pata Mkanda, nasi twashukia pwani.

Sifikile kandokando! Nina huja sharia
Ule mtamani kondo ndiye wa kukurubia.
Maneno, yaso zitendo, mwisowe hujinamia,
Jaribu kutegemea, tukutanie fundoni.

Simba kiwa maindoni, hafunuwi zakwe ndole
Huzivika mtangani, mwindwa asiziole.
Uliza, utasakani! Ujuwe uzingatile.
Nyoka za nongo umbile hatuchi, situtusheni!

TRANSLATION

Answer of the People of Lamu

My dear and noble sir, I have seen your letter.
I understand your meaning, but it only wrung a laugh from me.
If you clothe one another, it will bring you only discomfort.
Whoever pokes about in the firewood before it is kindled, labours
  without benefit.

If you are there in Pate Yunga, I also am here in Lamu.
Do not stay there, bragging about yourself. You will not gain your desire
A true man comes forward and approaches, and does not say withal, "Today is Today!"[7]
Look at the dwarf antelopes, how they jump about in the bush.

We are not worried. Do not just try to scare us! We are not frightened by the din.
We have been used to warfare from of old.
We made you by our own action like ash out of a wood-fire;
On the right day for waging battle, we will see one another on the battle-field.

By God, we swear to you by God and the Apostle Muhammad,
Come, drink bitter pain, and be physically humiliated!
You will be a feast for the ants, and vultures will destroy you,
And as for the longing to return home, do not think on it.

If you folk are determined to come — have no misunderstanding about it —
First leave behind a will making your children your heirs.
Give the womenfolk ample sustenance, to provide for them during their widow's waiting time.[8]
If you come, we will send you down on the same descent as of yore.

And if you have forgotten your former haven,
Then ask those who have survived, your aged and experienced ones.
Ask also Bwana b. Salale about who escaped there.
To this day they sleep there, and waken not to the slightest degree.

If you are thirsty, come here where we are awaiting you.
Gird on your raiment, you who have such admirable leaders!
We are sitting at the door, awaiting you, to work our deeds upon you.
If you reach Mkanda, we also will go down to the shore.

Do not arrive before the time! I have demands in accordance with custom.
He who desires battle is the one who must come for it.
The end of words without deeds is humiliation.
Try to establish yourself here, and we shall meet one another on the battle-field.

When a lion is on the hunt, it does not uncover its claws;
It covers them with the sand, so that its quarry does not see them.
Ask now, and you will be assured beyond doubt; know it, and ponder it well!

---

[7] **Today is Today**. This saying seems to imply the covering up of delay by bragging words.
[8] This refers to the *'Idda*. That is, the time provided by the Shari'a to allow a possible pregnancy.

Serpents made out of strips of leaves of the Dom-Palm[9] we do not
fear: do not then try to scare us.

The most important question to answer about these two poems is
whether the challenge and the taunting response which they respectively
hold were made before the Battle of Shela and in view of its imminence,
or after it by a few years, and referring to that Battle as a thing of the
past. I attempt below to marshal the evidence in support of each view.

(a) Supporting a date after the Battle of Shela
Professor Damann takes Line 4 of Verse 5, and all of Verse 6, in the
second Poem as referring to the Battle of Shela which he places about
A.D. 1810. The former haven referred to he takes to be the sandy shore
where the dead of Pate and the Mazari'a lay, their bones scattered, "never
to waken". He takes the Poem as having been written about the year 1814
just prior to the deaths of both Ahmad b. Muhammad Al-Mazru'i and of
the Pate Sultan, Ahmad b.Shaykh. The references are remarkably vivid
and apposite and give vivid point and meaning to the whole poem.

(b) Supporting a date before the Battle of Shela
The date of the Battle of Shela is in dispute. Shaykh Al-Amin states that
besides A.D. 1810 there are traditions that it took place in A.D. 1808 or
1812. The latter date would leave even less chance for the poem to be
composed and the answer returned before the deaths of the two Ahmads,
Sultan and Liwali.

The tone of "Challenge" and "Response" would require at least
another plan of attack by Pate and the Mazari'a on Lamu: but this, so far
as I can find, was never contemplated, and is unlikely in view of the
Mombasa proverb current after the Battle: "He who goes to Pate returns
not: all that returns is a wail".

It is not clear who Bwana b. Salale was. I can find no reference to him,
and Damann only says he is "ein mann aus Pate". Shaykh Al-Amin
says nothing of such a man, and yet his account is more connected and
circumstantial than the others. Damann refers, in comments on another
poem in the same article, to Mwinyi Shehe Ali as a supporter of the Lamu
leader Zahidi b.Mngumi who sent the false letter to the Amir 'Abdullah.
But though he knows about Mwinyi Shehe Ali's magic, he does not connect
it with the Battle of Shela, but simply says he practised it "bei einem

---

[9] The Dom-palm is a common tree in Egypt, the Sudan and the South of Arabia. It has fan-
like sprays of leaves and its fruit consists of large rather hard nuts which can be scraped
with the teeth and give out a very astringent juice.

einfall der Mazru'i". Shaykh Al-Amin on the other hand identifies the
"einfall" with the campaign which ended in the Battle of Shela.

As for Line 4 of Verse 5, and Verse 6, they may be taken in either of
two ways:

(i) They may be a general reference to former campaigning in the
past, and to the defeated and their fate in any battle. "Mashukio ya
zamani" could mean "on the old descent" in the sense of "the inevitable end of all who are defeated". But the reference to Bwana b.Salale
militates a little against that interpretation.

(ii) They may be — and I think they most probably are — a reference
to a former campaign between Pate and Lamu which is described in
the "History of Pate" (Freeman-Grenville: The East African Coast,
p. 262) as having taken place in the reign of Sultan Bwana Tamu the
Younger of Pate. Pate at that time attacked Lamu to gain possession
of some Portuguese guns which the people of Lamu had unearthed
from Hedabu Hill. They invaded Lamu and succeeded in getting the
guns aboard their ships, but the people of Lamu attacked and defeated
them, and the guns sunk the ships by their weight in Lamu Harbour.
The people of Lamu seem to have been more confident and successful
when fighting on their own ground. This would support the tone of
taunting confidence in their answer to the Amir 'Abdullah. The references in the Poem are very relevant and appropriate to that occasion.

It seems that the weight of evidence is in favour of the Poems having
been written at a date before, rather than after, the Battle of Shela, and
the challenge and response in them as referring to the Shela Campaign.
This means that they are most probably the verses referred to by Shaykh
Al-Amin in Chapter II Section 6 at Note 17.

APPENDIX 6
The Title of Imam in the Ibadi Sect of Islam

It is not necessary here to go in detail into the history either of the usage of the word itself, or of the Ibadi Sect which came to employ it, since this has already been very ably done by Badger in his Book "The Imams and Sayyids of 'Uman". Let it suffice here to say that the Ibadi Sect formed as a development of the Kharijite group who separated themselves from 'Ali b. Abi Talib after the Battle of Siffin. On the theory which I think to be the most probable, and which is clearly set forth by Dr. W. M. Watt in "Islam and the Integration of Society" (pp. 101–103) the Kharijites were a kind of "harking back", by the desert Arabs of the Muslim Armies, to the pre-Islamic social set-up of the tribe in the desert, to which they were accustomed, albeit based not on blood-relationship, but on the solidarity of religious belief; and on this theory it is not surprising to find that the old nomadic term for a tribal leader is used by them to describe the religious leaders they recognised and accepted.

Among the Kharijites the solidarity of the Community and its "Sunna" or Law, by which of course they meant the Islamic Community and the Qur'an, were elements of paramount importance; so the leader must be fitted by personal manliness and bravery, and also by his knowledge of the Law of the Qur'an and Islamic belief, before he is elected to be Imam. Candidates were judged on that basis before election, and on that basis they could (in theory) be removed from office if for any cause they began to fall short. A short passage from Badger will make clear the manner in which this was worked out in respect of the Imams of 'Uman by the Ibadi Sect which has been dominant there for centuries:

"It is evident from these dates that the Imamate of 'Uman owes its origin to the peculiar religious tenets of the Khawarij (i.e. Kharijites), as adopted by the Ibadiya. They disallowed the claims of the Baghdad Khalifas as well in civil as in religious matters, and set up one of their own, whom they invested with the corresponding powers in both capacities. They acted upon the same principles by uniformly electing Imams for their personal merits or popularity, irrespective of family descent, for the space of nearly 900 years, reckoning from Julanda (A.D. 751) to the accession of Nasir b. Murshid of the el-Ya'arubu (A.D. 1624), and if the nominees during that period were mainly confined to the El-Azd, it was because that was the predominant tribe and possessed greater influence in the elections.

"After the supremacy had fallen into the hands of the El-Ya'arubu, and throughout the century during which they held it, these principles underwent a modification. Like their predecessors – and not unlike what took place in the Kingdoms of the Western and Eastern Franks – the 'Umanis started from the same point. The Imam was elected, but with a strong preference for the ruling family over strangers, and with a strong preference for the son, not necessarily the eldest, of the last Imam, over the other members of the family." (Badger: Imams and Sayyids of 'Uman: Appendix A "On the Title of Imam" at p. 376).

The last ruler to bear the title of Imam was Sa'id b. Ahmad al-BuSa'idi, son of the Founder of the BuSa'idi dynasty. Badger discusses very fully the possible reasons for its discontinuance (Op. Cit. pp. 378–81), and the strongest reason for its suppression appears to be the avoidance of friction and offence with the powerful Wahhabis of the Nejd, who at the time were developing in political strength and showing active hostility to 'Uman. Sir Arthur Hardinge's statement in his book "A Diplomatist in the East" that Sayyid Sa'id b. Sultan was denied the title after allowing himself to be photographed, and not only so, but to be photographed in company with unveiled European ladies, is probably culled from popular gossip in Zanzibar, but can have nothing to do with the matter since the title had been dropped prior to A.D. 1804 when Sayyid Sa'id b. Sultan acceded to the Throne of 'Uman.

The appended Chronological Table only covers the period during which there is conflict or uncertainty as to the dating.

APPENDIX 7
Comparative Chronological Table of the Imams and Sayyids of 'Uman and the Liwalis of Mombasa

YEAR A.D.	'UMAN	MOMBASA	COMMENT
1624	Nāṣir b. Murshid Al-Ya'rabī		
1649	Sulṭān b. Sayf I Al-Ya'rabī		
1650		First Occupation of Mombasa by 'Umān	Only imperfectly & intermittently effective
1688		Second occupation of Mombasa *Nāṣir b. 'Abdullāh al-Mazrū'ī* was appointed Liwali	
1711	Sayf b. Sulṭān I "Qayd al-Arḍ" Sulṭān b. Sayf II (same year)		
1718	Sayf b. Sulṭān II Muhannā b. Sulṭān		This Imam seems to have been deposed and restored on two occasions
1721	Ya'rab b. Bal'arab		
1722	Sayf b. Sulṭān II (First restoration)		
1724	Muḥammad b. Nāṣir al-Ghāfirī		
		Sese Rumbi's rebellion leading to intervention of Portuguese occurred	Shaykh al-Amīn makes only a passing reference to the unsettled condition of

YEAR A.D.	'UMAN	MOMBASA	COMMENT
		about this time	'Umān during these years
1728	Sayf b. Sulṭān II (Second restoration	Portuguese finally driven out of Mombasa *Muḥammad b. Saʿīd Al-Maʿmirī Ṣāliḥ b. Muḥammad Al-Haḍramī Muḥammad b. ʿUthmān Al-Mazrūʿī acc. to Al-Amīn* Appointed 1730: *Hardinge*	The most probable date is Hardinge's. Guillain's date leaves
1735		Appointed 1735: *Guillain* Appointed 1739:	no time for the probable length of Muḥammad b. ʿUthmān's Liwaliship, and Sulṭān b. Murshid would not by
1738	Sulṭān b. Murshid, the last Yaʿrabī Imam		1739 have been in a position to concern
1739			himself with E. Africa. On the other hand, Shaykh
1741	Aḥmad b. Saʿīd Al-Būsaʿīdī, Founder of the Būsaʿīdī dynasty		Al-Amīn leaves no time for Muhammad's immediate predecessors and all the monsoon
1743		Muḥammad b. ʿUthmān murdered	travelling which would have been
1744		*Sayf b. Khalaf Liwali for ʿUmān*	necessary in connection with their removal and appointment. (See Note 4 in
1745		*ʿAlī b. ʿUthmān effectively Liwali*	Ch II sect 2). The tombstone is the only evidence for the end of the reign, and rather weakens

YEAR A.D.	'UMAN	MOMBASA	COMMENT
			than strengthens the period of 14 years for the reign of Muhammad which Shaykh Al-Amīn states to be traditional in his family
1754–5		'Alī b. 'Uthmān murdered in Zanzibar by Khalaf b. Qaḍib *Mas'ūd b. Nāṣir Liwali*	
1779 1780–1	Ḥamad b. Sa'īd	*'Abdullāh b. Muhammad Liwali* *Aḥmad b. Muḥammad Liwali*	Appointed after the death of Mas'ūd
1783	Sa'īd b. Aḥmad, the last Imām		
1785			Recognition of 'Umānī Sovereignty extracted in writing from the Liwali Aḥmad by "Hubūb al-Ghabash"
1787		Mas'ūd b. Nāṣir died, acc. to Hardinge	
1792	Sulṭān b. Aḥmad		
1804	Sālim b. Sulṭān Sa'īd b. Sulṭān		
1814		*'Abdullāh b. Ahmad Liwali*	
1823		'Abdullāh b. Aḥmad died (13 Ramaḍān) *Sulaymān b. 'Alī Liwali (12 Shawwāl)*	*— After loss of Pemba to* 'Umān — After family disagreement
1823–5			Owen's Protectorate of Mombasa
1825 or 6		*Sālim b. Aḥmad Liwali*	

YEAR A.D.	'UMAN	MOMBASA	COMMENT
1834–5		*Khāmis b. Aḥmad Liwali*	
1836		*Rāshid b. Sālim Liwali*	
1837		Rāshid and 24 other Mazāri'a lured on board one of Sayyid Sa'īd's Ships and carried off to Bandar Abbas	Mbāruk b. Rāshid b. Sālim flees and remains in Gazi
1850			Mbaruk takes Takaungu but is expelled
1854	Khālid b. Sa'īd, then Mājid b. Sa'īd governor of Zanzibar		
1856	Mājid b. Sa'īd ruler of Zanzibar		Sayyid Sa'īd b. Sulṭān dies at sea
1870	Barghash b. Sa'īd ruler of Zanzibar		
1872			Mbaruk rebels again and then flees to the Bush
1877			Mazarū'ī power in Pemba finally crushed by L. W. Matthews, appointed that year
1882		Mbāruk b. Rāshid b. Sālim returns to Mwele	Rāshid raids Vanga with 2,000 men. Matthews captures Mwele with 400 troops. Mbāruk swears allegiance.
1886			Kirk leaves Zanzibar. Haggard visits Simba at Witu and surmises that he will join forces with Mbāruk b. Rāshid

YEAR A.D.	'UMAN	MOMBASA	COMMENT
1895		*The last Chapter of the Saga* Mbāruk b. Rāshid b. Khāmis of Takaungu is disaffected by being passed over in the succession to the Shaykhdom there. Sir Arthur Hardinge becomes Commissioner for the East African Protectorate this year. Mbāruk b. Rāshid b. Khāmis rebels. His cousin Mbāruk b. Rāshid b. Sālim temporises then sides with his cousin and joins the rebellion, taking his cousin to Mwele. Matthews and Hardinge make a campaign that year and Mwele fortress is destroyed. Mbāruk b. Rāshid b. Sālim escapes and flees to German East Africa where he remains in exile till his death.	

Index

DATE DUE

HIGHSMITH #45230

Printed
in USA

تأريخ المزارعة

ترجمة المؤلف

هو الاستاذ الامام العلامة الشيخ الامين بن علي بن عبدالله بن نافع بن مزروع بن عبدالله بن خميس بن علي بن عبدالله بن علي المزروعي ، وعبدالله بن خميس هذا هو الاصل السابع من اصول المزارعة الذين نزحوا الى بلاد السواحل كما هو مذكور في الفصل الاول من هذا الكتاب ، وجدُه العلامة الشيخ عبدالله بن نافع هو اول من انتحل المذهب الشافعي من جماعة المزارعة ،

ولد الشيخ الامين رحمه الله ببلدة مباسة في الخامس عشر من جمادى آخرة عام ١٣٠٨ﻫ الموافق ٢٧ يناير عام ١٨٩١ م وتوفي والده وهو في الرابعة من عمره ، فنشأ يتيما في احضان قرينه العلامة الشيخ سليمان بن علي بن خميس المزروعي رئيس قضاة كينيا الاسبق ، ومنه تلقى معظم فنون العلوم الدينية ، وكثيرا ما كان يتردد الى زنجبار ليتعلم عند العلامة السيد احمد بن ابي بكر بن سميط والعلامة الشيخ عبدالله بن محمد باكثير ، فتبحر في العلوم حتى فاق اقرانه وصار العلماء من زنجبار و تانغة ولامو وغيرها من اقطار شرق افريقية يقصدونه ليغترفوا من بحر علمه الفياض ، ومن تلاميذه فضيلة العلامة الشيخ مأمون بن سليمان بن علي المزروعي قاضي مباسة السابق ، وفضيلة العلامة الشيخ عبدالله بن صالح الفارسي قاضي زنجبار الحالي ، وفضيلة الاستاذ العلامة الشيخ محمد بن احمد البريكي ، والاستاذ الحاج الشيخ احمد بن ابرهيم بن احمد الكوكني والاستاذ الحاج الشيخ سعيد بن احمد سعيد القمري ، والاستاذ المرحوم الشيخ محمد عبدالله غزالي ، والاستاذ المرحوم الشيخ راشد بن قاسم المزروعي ، والحقير كاتب هذه الترجمة ، وكان المرحوم العلامة الشيخ علي بن حميد البحري قاضي تانغة السابق يتبجح بانه من تلاميذ المرحوم ،

كان رحمه الله محبا للمسلمين عامة ولشعبه خاصة ، ففتح لهم مكاتب ومدارس دينية وانفق نفائس اوقاته في التعليم والتدريس وتأليف الكتب الدينية كان لها اثر عظيم في انتشار الاسلام في البر ، وكان اول من ألف الكتب الدينية باللغة السواحلية ،

ولو لم يكن له الا كتابه المسمّى **بهداية الاطفال** الذي يقرأ في جميع المساجد والمدارس في شرق افريقية وغيرها لكفاه مأثرة في الدنيا وذخرا في العقبى ،

ولما رأى ما للجرائد من المنافع العظيمة تاقها لشعبه ، فاصدر في ٤ جمادى الآخرة عام ١٣٤٩ ه (٢٠-١٠-٢٥ م) صحيفة باللغة السواحلة اعتنت بالمسائل السياسية والاجتماعية والدينية خصوصا نشر السنّة ورفض البدع ،

فعاداه قومه عداوة شديدة وصبر على اذاهم متوكلا على الله مصداق قوله تعالى (ردوا صبرا على اذاهم وتوكل على الله ان الله يحب المتوكلين) وقد انتشر بحمد الله كثير من الحق وزهق كثير من الباطل ، وكان يكتبها بيده وينسخها بالآلة الناسخة ويوزعها مجانا ، ثم في ٢٢ شوال ١٣٥٠ ه (٢٩-٢-٢٢ م) اصدر جريدة اسبوعية باللغتين العربية والسواحلية سمّاها < **الاصلاح** > مصدرة بالآية الكريمة (**ان اريد الا الاصلاح ما استطعت وما توفيقي الا بالله عليه توكلت واليه انيب**) فذاع صيتها في جميع آفاق افريقية الشرقية ،

ثم تولى قضاء مباسة في رمضان عام ١٣٥١ ه (ديسمبر ١٩٣٢ م) ، فقام بهذه الوظيفة خير قيام وكان مثالا للعدل والانصاف ، ثم في ربيع الاول ١٣٥٢ ه (يونيو ١٩٢٧ م) تولى رئاسة القضاء فشغل هذا المنصب العالي بجدارة واستحقاق ، وكان قدوة حسنة لمن بعده ، ولم تمنعه اعماله القضائية والافتائية عن التأليف والتدريس والسفر الى كثير من بلاد افريقية الشرقية للدعوة والارشاد ،

ثم انتقل الى جوار الله و رحمته عصر الثلاثاء ٨ جمادى الاولى عام ١٣٦٦ ه (حادي ابريل ١٩٤٧ م) تاركا في قلوب المسلمين اسفا شديدا وحزنا عميقا ، تغمده الله برحمته ورضوانه واسكنه فسيح جناته مع الذين انعم الله عليهم من النبيين والصديقين والشهداء والصالحين وحسن اولائك رفيقا ،

خلف المرحوم من الاولاد الذكور الشيخ حارث بن الامين المزروعي الذي كان واليا على لامو ، والدكتور علي بن الامين المزروعي استاذ السياسة في جامعة مكيريرى ،

محمد قاسم المزروعي

الفصل الاول

نسب المزارعة ـ اصول من استوطن السواحل منهم ـ مساكنهم بعمان ـ تأريخ هجرتهم الى السواحل ـ سعة مملكتهم بها ـ عدد سكان مملكتهم ـ اثبات استقلالهم ـ نفي تهمة عداوتهم للانكليز ،

نسب المزارعة واصولهم

قبل المشروع في الموضوع الرئيسي لهذا الكتاب رأيت ان اقدم للقراء طرفا من نسب المزارعة ، وبيانا مختصرا عن اصول من استوطن ارض السواحل منهم ، وأسماء افراد من مشاهير فروع كل اصل من اصولهم منذ هاجروا الى البلاد السواحلية الى يومنا هذا ،

فالمزارعة الذين استوطنوا افريقية الشرقية متفرعون ـ على سبيل البسط ـ من اربعة عشر اصلا ينتهي نسبهم الى زيد بن كهلان بن عدي بن عبد شمس بن وائل ، ويرتفع الى سبأ بن يشجب بن يعرب بن قحطان جد القبائل القحطانية المعروفة في التأريخ ، والاصول الاربعة عشر المذكورون هم ـ

الاول ـ ناصر بن عبدالله بن محمد بن عبدالله بن كهلان ، الوالي الاول من ولاة المزارعة الاحد عشر ، واشتهر من متقدمي ذريّته ابنه مسعود بن ناصر بن عبدالله الوالي الرابع الذي تولى من سنة ١١٦٨ ـ ١١٩٣ هـ وحفيده احمد بن مسعود بن ناصر الذي كان قاضيا على ممباسة في العقد الرابع من القرن الثالث عشر الهجري ، ومن ذريته المتأخرين عزيز بن عبدالله بن احمد صاحب مَنَران بتَكوُنغُ المعروف بسخايه وكثرة قراه للضعيف ، ومِنهم ناصر بن احمد قاضي ملندي الحالي من قبل الحكومة الانكليزية ،

والثاني عثمان بن عبدالله بن محمد بن عبدالله بن كهلان ، والد الوالي الثاني والثالث وجد الولاة المتعاقبين بعدهما ، والمشاهير من ذريته المتقدمين جميع ولاة

٢

المزارعة من محمد بن عثمان الى راشد بن سالم ، وسيمر بك اسم كل واحد منهم فيما يلي من صفحات هذا الكتاب ، ومن المتأخرين مبارك بن راشد بن سالم صاحب الوقايع المشهورة مع سلاطين زنجبار ومنهم محمد بن سعود بن مبارك الذي كان واليا على مَلِنْدي وتَكَوُنْغُ من قبل الحكومة الانكليزية وسليمان بن محمد قاضي غاسي سابقا ،

والثالث زاهر بن عبدالله بن محمد بن عبدالله بن كهلان ، من مشاهير ذريته المتقدمين راشد بن سالم بن عبدالله مؤسس بلدة تَكَوُنْغُ وصاحبها ، وولداه خميس وسعيد واحفاده راشد بن خميس وسالم بن خميس زعماء القوم في تَكَوُنْغُ واصحاب الامر فيها ، ومن المتأخرين راشد بن سالم بن خميس المشهور بغزارة علمه في التأريخ والانساب ، وأخوه محمد بن سالم بن خميس وكل واحد منهما كان واليا على تَكَوُنْغُ من قبل الحكومة الانكليزية ، ومنهم المؤرخ النسابة خلف بن عبدالله الذي تولى قضاء تَكَوُنْغُ سابقا وخلف بن راشد بن عبدالله مدير تِيوِي سابقا من قبل الحكومة الانكليزية ، واخوه عبدالله بن راشد مدير مَمْبْرُوِي سابقا ، وسالم بن راشد بن محمد مدير تَكَوُنْغُ الحالي ، وسعود بن خلفان مدير غاسي حالا ، ونبهان بن راشد احد اعيان تكونغ المعروف ،

والرابع خميس بن عامر بن محمد بن عبدالله بن كهلان ، من مشاهير ذريته محمد بن خلفان بن كهلان احد اغنياء تَكَوُنْغُ المعروفين ،

الخامس خميس بن بشير بن محمد بن عبدالله بن كهلان ، واشتهر من ذريته محمد بن عبدالله بن ناصر النسابة المشهور ،

السادس طالب بن علي بن محمد بن عبدالله بن كهلان ، ومن ذريته عبدالله بن خلفان ،

السابع عبدالله بن خميس بن علي بن عبدالله بن علي ، ومن ذريته جماعة في الجزيرة الخضراء والمشهور منهم – – – – – – – – – – ومنهم بيت نافع بن مزروع بن عبدالله المعروف في مُبْياسة والمشهور من هذا البيت العلامة عبدالله بن نافع الذي كان احد المستشارين في دولة المزارعة في عصر الوالي سالم بن احمد ومن بعده ،

٤

جاور مكة في آخر عمره مدة تسعة سنين ولازم اجلة علمائها في ذلك الزمان كالشيخ عثمان بن حسن الدمياطي والشيخ احمد بن محمد الدمياطي وغيرهما ، ومن مشاهير هذا البيت العلامة احمد بن عبدالله بن نافع صاحب كتاب < **التحفة المرضية بمختصر الكلمات الوفية** > في النحو ، < **وشرح المقدمة الحضرمية** > في الفقه وكلاهما مخطوط ، ومنهم العلامة علي بن عبدالله بن نافع ، ومن آثاره مؤلفاته المخطوطة منها < **الدروع السابغة في مسألة رؤية البارئ سبحانه وتعالى** > ، و < **السبل الواضحات** > شرح < **دلائل الخيرات** > ، ومختصر في تراجم اسماء اهل بدر ، وشرح لطيف على شمائل الترمذي وغير ذلك من الرسائل والمختصرات ، وكان رحمه الله قاضيا على مُمْباسَة في زمان السيد ماجد بن سعيد ، ومنهم العالم راشد بن علي بن نافع قاضي مُمْباسَة ايضا في اواخر ايام السيد ماجد بن سعيد ومن بعده ، ومنهم الامير بن علي واخوه مؤلف هذا الكتاب ،

الثامن علي بن راشد بن مسعود ، ومن ذريته المعروفين محمد بن عزيز بن سعيد ، والعلامة سليمان بن علي قاضي قضاة مستعمرة كينيا من قبل الحكومة الانكليزية سابقا وولده مأمون بن سليمان قاضي مُمْباسَة الحالي ، ومنهم سليمان بن علي بن سعيد بالجزيرة الخضراء ،

التاسع مبارك بن احمد بن مبارك بن غريب ، والمشهورون من ذريته المتقدمين العالم عبدالله بن علي بن مبارك زميل العلامة علي بن عبدالله بن نافع في طلب العلم وتحصيله ، وجمعة بن خميس بن مبارك مشري تَكَوُنْغُ ، ومن المتأخرين العالم سليمان بن علي بن خميس صاحب تَكَوُنْغُ وقاضيها سابقا من قبل الحكومة الانكليزيه ، ومحمد بن جمعة بن خميس مدير رَوكَة وقاضي مَلِنْدِي سابقا ، ومحمد بن علي بن خميس والي مُمْباسَة السابق ، ودحلان بن محمد بن جمعة والي فَاَنْغَة الحالي ، ومحمد بن سليمان بن علي بن احمد اعيان تَكَوُنْغُ ،

العاشر مهنَا بن احمد بن مبارك بن غريب ، والمشهورون من ذريته جماعة في الجزيرة الخضراء ، منهم الكاتب الاديب علي بن راشد المعروف بجميل خطه وبراعته في الكتابة ، وخاطر بن احمد واحمد بن نهنَا وعلي بن سيف وغيرهم ،

٥

الحادي عشر علي بن احمد بن مبارك بن غريب ، والمشهور من ذريته علي بن احمد قبطان الباخرة < كِلْوَة > من بواخر حكومة زِنْجِبار ، ومبارك بن محمد الذي كان مراقبا لمرسى السفن الشراعية بزِنْجِبار ،

الثاني عشر سعيد بن عبدالله بن محمد بن احمد والي الجزيرة الخضراء من قبل عشيرته المزارعة والمشهورون من ذريته سالم ومهنًا ابنا احمد بن جمعة بن صالح من اعيان الجزيرة الخضراء ،

الثالث عشر محمد بن عبدالله بن محمد بن احمد ، ومن ذريته بيت سالم بن قاسم بمُمْبَاسة والمشهور من هذا البيت احمد بن سالم بن قاسم ،

الرابع عشر علي بن عبدالله بن محمد بن احمد ، ومن ذريته احمد بن سليمان بالجزيرة الخضراء ،

فمن هؤلاء الاصول الاربعة عشر وفروعهم وانسالهم تكوّنت جماعة المزارعة المنتشرون الان في بلدان افريقية الشرقية من مُمْبَاسة وزِنْجِبار والجزيرة الخضراء وتَكَوُنغ وغاسي ودارسلام ومَلِنْدي وغيرها ،

والذين نزحوا الى السواحل من هؤلاء الاصول هم ناصر بن عبدالله ومبارك بن احمد وأخوه مهنًا بن احمد ، واما الباقون فانما هاجر الى السواحل اولادهم وذرياتهم ،

مساكن المزارعة بعمان

المزارعة كغيرهم من قبائل العرب يوجد منهم افراد او جماعات في شتى بلاد عمان وقراها ، غير ان اكثرهم في رستاق وما حولها من القرى كالغشب ووبل ومزاحيط ، ولهم بالعلاية بلدة خاصّة بهم محاطة بسور في جوانبها ابراج محصنة بالمدافع والبنادق يحتمون بها اذا دعت الحاجة ويدافعون منها هجمات العدو وغاراتها كعادة اكثر قبائل العرب ، ويتولى المزارعة الان في عمان زعيمهم الشيخ سعيد بن عبدالله بن خميس المزروعي فسح الله في عمره ،

والمنقول من اسلاف مزارعة السواحل ان اكثر الذين استوطنوا افريقية الشرقية منهم جاءوا من تلك البلاد وقليلا منهم اتوا من منح وسمائل ، ورأيت بحط والدي

رحمه الله صورة وكالة من المشايخ سالم بن خميس ومسعود بن محمد وعزيز بن عبدالله انهم وكلوا مسلم بن سليمان بن مسلم الشقصي في قبض اموالهم التي خلفها اجدادهم في البلدان المذكورة وفي الوشيل ، فيظهر من هذا ان بعضا منهم جاء من الوشيل ، ولا يبعد ذلك لان الوشيل للمشاقصة وبينهم وبين المزارعة قرابة ورحم وصلة متينة اوثقها رباط المصاهرة من قديم الزمان ،

هجرتهم الى السواحل

ابتدأت هجرة المزارعة الى افريقية الشرقية بعد فتح الامام سيف بن سلطان لها حوالي عام ١١١٠ ه اي منذ قرنين ونصف قرن تقريبا ، واول من وطنت قدمه ارض السواحل هم الوالي ناصر بن عبدالله والامير مبارك بن غريب واولاده ، ثم جاء في اواخر دولة اليعاربة محمد بن عثمان واخواه علي وقضيب وابنا عمومتهم ، ثم توالت الهجرات من البيوتات الاخرى الى قبيل استيلاء سعيد بن سلطان على مُمْباسة فانقطعت بسبب منع حكومة عمان لهم من السفر اليها حذرا من تكثير سوادهم في السواحل ، ثم بعد ذلك توجهت انظار مهاجريهم المتأخرين الى زِنْجِبَار والجزيرة الخضراء دون غيرهما من البلاد السواحلية ولتوفر اسباب الرزق التي تليق بهم هناك ،

واما قول الميجر بيرس في كتابه < زِنْجِبَار > ان المزارعة هاجروا الى افريقية الشرقية من ازمان بعيدة قبل احتلال البُرْتُغَال فهو قول لا صحة له بالكلية ، وقد اخذ به على علاته سعيد رُوِيت فأثبته في كتابه < سعيد بن سلطان > وكلاهما لم يأت لما قاله بدليل ولا عزاه الى احد من رواة الاخبار المحققين كانهما ــ والله اعلم ــ قالاه من عند انفسهما رميا بالغيب ، والذي ذكرناه هو ما عليه جمهور الاخباريين من اهل مُمْباسة وغيرهم تناقلوه خلفا من السلف ، وهو المحفوظ عند المزارعة انفسهم ، وهم بلا شك اعلم باخبار اسلافهم من غيرهم واحفظ لوقائع من ينتمون اليهم ،

مملكة المزارعة

تملك المزارعة في افريقية الشرقية جميع البلاد الواقعة بين رأس نَغُمِين شمالا

ونهر بَنْغان جنوبا ، فدخلت تحت ولايتهم اكثر البلاد السواحلية الآهلة بالعرب والسواحليين وبسطوا ايديهم على ديوانية فُومْبَ (سلطنة فُومْبُ التي كان يقال لسلطانها ديوان) التي كان مقرُها بجزيرة وَاسِين وسلطانة بَورى التي كان يحكمها امراء تَانْغَة الاصليون ، ووصل نفوذهم الى داخل هذه البلاد وغربا من اقصاها الى اقصاها ، فخضع لهم جميع الطوائف الساكنة في باديتها من وَغَالة ووَغريامة ووَكُومة ووَجبانة ووَشُوني ووَرِيبي ووَرَباني ووَدُرُومة ووَدِيغُو ووُبُنْدَي ووَشَمْبَاءَ وبعض من طائفة وَزِغُوَ الساكنة شمالي نهر بَنْغان ، وتملكوا الجزيرة الخضراء (جزيرة بِمْبَا) فكانت مستوردهم الوحيد للحاصلات الزراعية من الحبوب والثمار والعسل والسكر وغيرها ، وفتحوا جزيرة زِنْجِبَار غير انه لم تستقر بها قدمهم لما طرأ من ذلك الخلاف المشؤوم الذي ادى الى اغتيال الوالي علي بن عثمان وقتل ابن اخيه خلف بن قضيب كما ستقف على تفصيل ذلك عند ذكر الوقائع التي حدثت في ولاية علي بن عثمان ، وكاد المزارعة ان يتملكوا جزيرة لَأَمُوه (لامو؟) ـ لا بقوة السيف بل ـ بتمليك اهلها لهم عن طيبة نفس لولا سوء تدبير الامير عبدالله بن احمد وما ظهر لاهل لاموه مما اضمره لهم من المكيدة سعيا في مرضاة اصدقائه النباهنة الذين كان اهل لاموه يعدُّونهم من اعدائهم الالِدّاء وسيأتي تفصيل هذه الواقعة في محله من هذا الكتاب ،

اما مملكة بَتَّة فانها وان لم تكن دخلت في مملكتهم اسمًا الا انها كانت تحت سيطرتهم ولهم فيها الكلمة المسموعة والامر المطاع ، وكان بها حامية من جند المزارعة عليها امير من امراء بيت الوالي لا يرد قوله في بَتَّة ولا يخالف رأيه حتى اوجس النباهنة في انفسهم خيفة من تملك المزارعة لبلادهم فكان ذلك سببا للاستنجاد بالسيد سعيد بن سلطان في تخليصهم من استبداد المزارعة بالامر في بلادهم ،

وعزم المزارعة على توسيع مملكتهم فارسلوا جيشا لفتح شَاغَة وأمَّروا على هذا الجيش قاسم بن غريب الريامي والي تَانْغَة في ذلك الزمان ، فخرج هذا الجيش بكامل عدته وأمده الوالي سالم بن احمد بعسكر من مُمْبَاسَة حتى اذا وصل الى محل يقال له رُمْبُو التقى الجمعان فاقتتلا قتالا شديدا فانكسر جيش المزارعة ولم يقدر على فتح تلك البلاد ،

اما مساحة هذه المملكة فيصعب تقديرها بالضبط ولكن اذا نظرنا الى الطوائف

الذين كانوا تحت نفوذ المزارعة وما شغلوه من الاراضي غربي السواحل ، وقررنا انهم وصلوا الى بعد ستين ميلا فقط من ساحل البحر الى آخر حدودهم في البر امكن لنا ان نقول ان مساحتها تبلغ تقريبا ١٢٢٨٠ ميلا مربعًا مع ما فيها من الجزيرة الخضراء ،

واما سكانها فهم كالمساحة في صعوبة تقديرهم بالضبط ، ومع ذلك فلا نعدم وسيلة بها نستطيع على استنباط عدد ممكن لسكان هذه المملكة ، فقد ذكر لنا القبطان فيدال في رحلته المطبوعة بلندن عام ١٨٣٢ م انه لما وصل مُمْبَاسَة وجد المزارعة قد جمعوا ٢٥٠٠٠ جنديا لمحاربة جيش السيد سعيد بن سلطان ، فالمملكة التي تقدر على حشد هذا الجيش لا يقل سكانها عن مليون نفس تقريبا باعتبار ٢ ١/٢ في كل مائة من السكان ، وهذا اقصى عدد يمكن تجنيده في مملكة لا إجبار على التجنيد فيها ،

استقلال المزارعة

هنا اريد ان اكشف الغطاء عن هذه الحقيقة ردًا على قول بعض كتّاب الافرنج المتأخرين ان المزارعة كانوا عصاة خارجين عن طاعة ملوكهم ، وممن قال بهذا القول الميجر بيرس فانه قال في كتابه ‹ زِنْجِبَار › ما ترجمته ـ « وعلى ممر الايام نبذ المزارعة طاعة عمان وادّعوا الاستقلال بمُمْبَاسَة ، ولكن حكام عمان وائمّتها المتعاقبون لم يعترفوا لهم بهذا الحق ، وكانوا يعتبرونهم عصاة متمردين › ولكن قال في موضع آخر من كتابه المذكور ‹ تولى المزارعة في مُمْبَاسَة مدّة مائة وتسع وثلاثين سنة تارة بصفة التابعين لحكومة عمان ، وتارة بصفة سلاطين مستقلّين › ،

فكلام الميجر كما تراه مضطرب ويحتمل انه في الجملة الاولى جارى ائمّة عمان ، او انه تأثر بالمحيط الذي كتب فيه تأريخه ، فقاله من غير اعتقاد ، او من غير رؤية ، اذ من البعيد جدا ان يعتقد سياسي مثل الميجر بتوقف استقلال البلاد على اعتراف ملّاكها الاصليين ، فاستقلال الملوك بالبلاد التي ملكوها قهرا لا يتوقف على هذا كما هو معلوم ضرورة ، ولو كان الامر كذلك لما بقي لدول الاستعمار حق على

البلاد التي احتلوها الى اصحابها الى هذا اليوم لان لا يعترفون لهم بالملك بل يعدُّونهم غاصبين ، لكن الحكم في هذه القضية راجع الى السيف كما قال شوقي –

< الملك يؤخذ او يردُ وهكذا   يرث الحسام على البلاد حسام >

واما الجملة الاخيرة فقد قالها الميجر عن اعتقاد جازم موافق لما في نفس الامر ، وليس هذا باعتقاد الميجر وحده بل هو اعتقاد جميع متقدمي الافرنج مثل القبطان اوين والقبطان فيدال وغيرهما كما سيظهر لك من عباراتهم اثناء الكلام على ولاة المزارعة ، وهو الحق الذي يعتقده العرب جميعهم ، ففي جريدة < **النجاح** > عدد ١٢ الصادرة في ١٢ صفر ١٣٢٠ قال ابو مسلم الرواحي اثناء الكلام على من تولى مُبَّاسَة – < ثم تولى بعد ذلك محمد بن عثمان جد العائلة الذين تعاقبوا على الامارة الاستقلالية على مُبَّاسَة ومتعلقاتها > ، فابو مسلم شيخ جليل من العرب العمانيين شب وشاب تحت ظل دولة اولاد الامام احمد ، ولو لم يكن المزارعة امراء مستقلين لما جاهر بقوله هذا في جريدة يقرأها امراء بيت الامام احمد على رأسهم عظمة السلطان نفسه ،

وربما يقول قائل ان اسم العصاة انما أطلق عليهم لانهم كانوا ولاة من قبل ائمّة عمان ثم ادّعوا الملك لانفسهم ، فهذا انما يصح على محمد بن عثمان وحده فهو الذي أقيم من قبل ائمّة عمان ثم استقل بالملك دونهم ، واما علي بن عثمان ومن عاقبه من الولاة فانهم اخذوا الملك بسيوفهم ، ثم لا يقدح في استقلال المزارعة ان كانوا ولاة من قبل حكومة عمان لان كثيرين من الملوك الذين تعترف لهم الدول بحق الملك كانوا مثل المزارعة في هذا ثم لم يستصحبهم اسم الثوار او العصاة بعد ان استقلُّوا ، ولهذا شواهد كثيرة في تأريخ دول الاسلام قديما وحديثا ، فسيف الدولة وصلاح الدين الايوبي ومحمد زنكي وامثالهم من سلاطين عصر الدولة العباسية ما كانوا الا عمالا ثم استقلوا بالملك وصار بعدهم وراثيا في اعقابهم والامام احمد كان عاملا من قبل الامام سيف بن سلطان على صحار فتغلب عليها في حياته ثم تغلب على حصون الباطنة بعد موته ، ذكر ذلك السالمي في < **تحفة الاعيان** > والشاهد الآخر على هذا ما فعله محمد علي باشا ملك مصر من انتزاع ملك مصر من الدولة العثمانية

والاستقلال به ، ثم ما كفاه ذلك حتى حارب دولته وكاد يحاصر القسطنطينية لولا تدخُل الدول الكبرى وايقافها له ، ومع ذلك لم يطلق عليه فيما بعد اسم العاصي او الباغي ، وملك العراق لم يكن الا عاملا من عمال الدولة العثمانية ايضا ، وهوذا يقال له اليوم ملك العراق ، واذا كان هؤلاء مثل المزارعة في اعمالهم ولم يطلق عليهم ذلك الاسم البشع ، فمن الظلم اطلاقه على ولاة المزارعة ،

هذا من الوجهة السياسية ، واما من الوجهة الشرعية فان احمد بن سعيد لم يكن بالامام الحق الواجبة طاعته على المسلمين لان بيعته ــ كما قال ابو نبهان وغيره من المشايخ ــ كانت على غير مشورة وبعد استيلانه على الملك قهرا ، ذكر ذلك السالمي في < **تحفة الاعيان** > ، واذاً فالخروج عليه ليس بمحظور في المذهب الاباضي ، واذا لم يكن محظورا فلا يسمى الخارج عليه عاصيا ولا باغيا ،

بقي شيء واحد ، وهو تلقيب سلاطين المزارعة بلقب الوالي ، وهذا اللقب في الاصلاح الحديث يدل على انه عامل من عمال الدولة لا سلطان من السلاطين ، وهذا ليس بشيء لان الوالي والملك والسلطان اسماء تدل في اللغة على معنى واحد ، ثم انه لما كان الوالي الاسبق محمد بن عثمان اطلق عليه هذا اللقب استصحب المتعاقبين بعده اعتبارا لما كان ، وذلك مثل باي تونس و خديوي مصر ، فباي معناه قائد الجيش ويطلق الان على سلاطين تونس وخديوي بمعنى الامير ودام هذا اللقب على سلاطين مصر الى عباس الثاني ، وكما لم يقدح اسم الباي والجديوي في ملوك تونس ومصر كذلك لا يقدح لقب الوالي في سلاطين المزارعة ،

هل المزارعة اعداء للانكليز؟

لا اكون مخطئا اذا قلت ان المزارعة اول قبيلة من قبائل عمان خطبت ودَّ الانكليز قبل غيرهم ، فالوالي محمد بن عثمان كان له صديق حميم من الانكليز اسمه كوك كان يتردد الى ممباسة وينزل ضيفا كريما عليه ، وهو الذي ساعد علي بن عثمان على تسلق القلعة ورميها بالمدافع حتى استولى عليها ، وكان ذلك قبل تبوُّءِ الامام احمد على عرش حكومة عمان بسنين ، وفي عام ١٨٢٤ م ؟ ه ابرمت بين

المزارعة والانكليز معاهدة تخولهم حرية التجارة داخل مملكتهم ، وفي ظني ان هذه اول معاهدة عقدت بين الانكليز والعرب العمانيين ،

وقد مر بك فيما تقدم اسماء كثيرين من رجالات المزارعة تولوا مناصب عُليا من قبل الحكومة الانكليزية ، وكان منهم الوالي والمدير والقاضي وقاضي القضاة ، وما زالت هذه المناصب مشغولة بافراد منهم الى الان ، دع عنك الموظفين في الوظائف الاخرى ، وكل ذلك ينفى ما يقال فيهم انهم اشتهروا بنصب العداء للحكومة الانكليزية كما زعم ذلك الميجر بيرس ، والذي دعا هذا الميجر الى هذا الزعم ان وجد نفر في الجيش الالماني في افريقية الشرقية الذي كان يهاجم الانكليز على الحدود اثناء الحرب العظمى لعام ١٩١٤ (- ١٩١٨) ولا يخفى انه لم يكن لاحد من سكان افريقية الشرقية الالمانية (تَنْغَنْيِكَا الان) في ذلك الوقت مندوحة عن الانخراط في سلك الجيش الالماني رعية او رهبة ، لان التجنيد عندهم كان إلزاميا فمن امتنع منه فقد عرض بنفسه للهلاك ،

ثم كما وجد في الجيش الالماني نفر من المزارعة فقد وجد مثل ذلك في الجيش الانكليزي ودام بعضهم في الجندية الى ان وضعت الحرب العظمى اوزارها (١١/١١/١٨) والذي كان في الجيش الانكليزي منهم سليمان بن محمد وحرب بن عبدالله ، واشيد بالذكر منهم سالم بن راشد مدير تَكَوْنْغُ الحالي ومأمون بن سليمان قاضي مباسة الحالي ، ولو قدر ان التقى الجيشان اللذان فيهما المزارعة لقتل الاخ اخاه في حرب لا مطمع لهم وراءها سوى الظهور بمظهر الولاء وامتثال الامر ،

وشأن المزارعة في ذلك كشأن غيرهم من الطوائف الاخرى مثل اليهود ، فانهم كانوا في الجيش الانكليزي والفرنساوي كما كانوا في الجيش الالماني والنساوي ، ومع ذلك لم يقل احد ان اليهود اشتهروا بنصب العداء للاسد البريطانى ولا للام الحنون ، وكذلك ينبغي ان لا يقال مثله في المزارعة لان العلة الجامعة بينهم واحدة والحكم يدور مع العلة حيث دارت ،

ولما نادت الحكومة الى التجنيد في هذه الحرب الحاضرة لعام ١٩٢٩ ، كان المزارعة اول من لبّى هذا النداء واسرع الناس الى تسجيل اسمائهم في سجل المتطوعين وانتخب منهم للجندية عشرة في المائة من بين سائر الناس ، وهذا عدد

عظيم بالنسبة الى غيرهم من الطوائف الاخرى ، افلا يكون هذا دليلا على موالاتهم للحكومة الانكليزية ؟

****

الفصل الثاني

في ذكر ولاة المزارعة على ترتيب ولايتهم ، وما حدث
في ايام كل واحد من الوقائع

الوالي الاول

ناصر بن عبدالله بن محمد بن عبدالله بن كهلان

استيلاء البرتغال ثانيا على ممباسة ـ وصول جيش الامام لاخراجهم منها ـ ولاية ناصر
بن عبدالله عليها ـ واقعة سِيس رُمْبي ـ استيلاء البرتغال ثالثا على مُمْباسَة ـ هجوم
اهل ممباسة عليهم واجلاؤهم نهائيا منها ـ اولاد سيس رمبي وانتحالهم نسبا غير نسبهم

من المعلوم ان الامام سلطان بن سيف بن مالك اليعربي بعد فتح ممباسة
واجلاء البرتغال منها ، لم يتمكن من متابعتهم وقطع دابرهم لما اضعف العساكر من
طول الحصار ، ولذلك ما زال البرتغال يغيرون على ممباسة مرة بعد اخرى كلما
سنحت لهم الفرصة طمعا في اعادتها الى ملكهم كما كانت سابقا ، وقبل تولية الوالي
ناصر بن عبدالله الذي نحن بصدده ، كان البرتغال قد هجموا على ممباسة ولم يكن
بها من القوة ما تدافع بها عن هذا الهجوم ، فاستولوا عليها ، وبلغ هذا الخبر الى
عمان والامام يومئذٍ سيف بن سلطان الملقب بقيد الارض ، فجهز في عام ١١١٠ هـ
جيشا عظيما انفذه الى ممباسة لاستردادها (استرادها) من البرتغال واخراجهم منها ،
وهنا يقول شيوخ المزارعة الذين نقلنا منهم كثيرا من اخبار اسلافهم الماضين ان
الامام امّر على هذا الجيش مبارك بن غريب المزروعي واسند قيادته اليه وعيّن ناصر
بن عبدالله واليا على ممباسة يتولاها بعد اجلاء العدو منها ، وصل هذا الجيش
فقاتل البرتغال قتالا شديدا حتى الجوءهم الى الفرار فولوا هاربين ، ثم قام بعد
ذلك ناصر بن عبدالله واليا من قبل الامام ومشرفا على املاكه بافريقية الشرقية ، هذا

ما رواه لنا شيوخ مزارعة السواحل ولم أجده في شيء من الكتب المدونة ولا المخطوطات التاريخية التي بايدينا ولكن يؤيّد بعضه ما ذكره الميجر بيرس في كتابه < زنجبار > ان حكم المزارعة في ممباسة يبتدئ من يوم افتتحها الامام سيف بن سلطان يعني الفتح الثاني بعد فتح والده سلطان بن سيف ، ولم يذكر الميجر اول من حكم فيها منهم ، ولعل السبب في ذلك انه ليس من موضوع كتابه ، ويؤيّد البعض الآخر من هذه الرواية ما حكاه رواة الاخبار من ثقات اهل واسين من ان مبارك بن غريب وصل ممباسة في زمان الديوان ابي بكر بن شيخ من آل المسبلة الملقب بروغة ، وقد تولى السيد ابو بكر المذكور سلطنة فُومبا حوالي عام ١١١١ ه ونقلنا من خط الشيخ سعيد بن صالح المسكري صاحب الجزيرة نقلا عن خط الشيخ محيي الدين بن شيخ القحطاني ان اول وال على ممباسة من المزارعة هو مبارك بن غريب ولعل ذلك سبق قلم من الشيخ رحمة الله عليه ،

وفي اواخر ايام ولاية ناصر بن عبدالله وقعت في ممباسة حادثة غريبة ذكرها القبطان اوين في رحلته المطبوعة بلندن نقلا عن مخطوطات عربية مكتوبة في عام ١٢٣٩ ، وذلك انه كان في القلعة طائفة من عساكر الامام فخرجوا عن الطاعة وقبضوا على الوالي ناصر بن عبدالله وحبسوه وولُّوا اميرا من انفسهم اسمه سِيسْ رُومْبِي ، وبعد ذلك ارسلوا الى اهل البلد يُنبِّنُونهم انهم قد ولوا سيس رومبي عليهم حاكما وطالبوهم بالدخول تحت طاعته ، فلم يرض اهل ممباسة بحكم هذا الدعي وأبت نفوسهم ان ترضخ له ، فردوا عليهم بانهم لا يطيعونه ولا يستسلمون له ، وفضلا عن ذلك آذنوهم بالحرب إن لم يطلقوا سراح الوالي ويخرجوا من القلعة ، فرد عليهم البغاة قائلين انهم لا يخرجون من القلعة ابدا واتفق اهل ممباسة على قتالهم فقاتلوهم ، وكان رؤساء البلد في ذلك وقت شيخ بن احمد الملندي ومعلم نْداو بن مُوشافي ومُوني غُوتِ بن مُونْزَاغُو ومُونِي مَوْلِي بن حاج وبينما الحرب قائمة بينهم على قدم وساق ، اذِ فاجأهم البرتغال في عمارة بحرية محتوية على اربع سفن حربية وسبعين مطافية ملأى بالجنود والذخيرة والعتاد ، وهذه هي الغارة الاخيرة للبرتغال على ممباسة ،

وكان السبب في عودة البرتغال الى ممباسة هذه المرة واغارتهم عليها ، ان واحدا من اهل بتة اسمه مْوِنْي هِنْدِي بن كِباي خاصم سلطان بتة مْوَانَة تَامُو مْكُو الذي تولى عام ١١١١ ــ ١١٥٢ ه فسافر هذا الرجل قاصدا الى مُوزَنْبِيق لطلب النجدة من البرتغال على محاربة السلطان ، فتمَّ له حصولها منهم فجاء باولائك العساكر الى بتة ، ولما وصلوا الى السلطان ارسل يخبره بانه جاء لمحاربته فلم يكن من السلطان الا ان صالح خصمه موني هندي لما رأى من قوة البرتغال التي لا طاقة له بمدافعتها ، ثم تشاور الاثنان في وسيلة تبعد البرتغال وترضيهم عنهم ، فقال السلطان ان اهل ممباسة في حرب مع واليهم ناصر بن عبدالله وقد قبضوا عليه وحبسوه فلنرسل هؤلاء الافرنج اليهم ونضع لهم ممباسة في أيديهم ، وبهذه الوسيلة نكون قد ابعدناهم عن بلادنا فوافقه مْوِنْي هِنْدِي على هذا الرأي الصائب وشافهوا البرتغال بذلك وأطمعوهم في ممباسة وهوَّنوا عليهم امر الاستيلاء عليها ، فرضوا بذلك وسافروا مع اهل بتة حتى وصلوا ممباسة ، وهناك بعد مناوشات قليلة اتَّفقوا مع اهلها على محاربة سيس رومبي وجماعته واخراجهم من القلعة ، فلم يكن منهم الا ان سلموها لهم وخرجوا منها ، وخلا البرتغال سبيلهم غير رئيسهم سيس رومبي فقبضوا عليه وارسلوه مقيدا الى مُوزَنْبِيق واما الوالي فبعدما أُخرِج من السجن مكث قليلا في ممباسة ثم سافر الى عمان ،

وحالما قبض البرتغال على زمام الحكم ، عادوا الى معاملة اهل ممباسة بالشدة والفظاعة كعادتهم في الايام السابقة ، فاستخدموهم في الاعمال الشاقة وهتكوا اعراض نسائهم واستهزئوا بالدين حتى كانوا يرمون المسلمين بالحجارة اذا رأوهم يصلون ، فلم تطق اهل ممباسة الصبر على هذا الضيم فانتظروا الفرصة للهجوم عليهم ولما كان يوم عيد من اعياد النصارى وخرج اكثر البرتغال من القلعة الى ضواحي البلد للنزهة ، هاجموهم وامعنوا فيهم القتل حتى اضطروا الى طلب الامان فأمَّنوهم على شرط مغادرة البلد حالا والرجوع الى موزنبيق فقبلوا ونجوا بانفسهم تاركين كل ما يملكونه في القلعة ، وبعد خروجهم من ممباسة خشي اهل البلد من ضياع ما في القلعة من الاسلحة والذخائر والاموال ، فاقام كل قبيلة منهم رجلا للحراسة الى ان يبلغوا الامر الى عمان ، وسيأتي في ترجمة محمد بن عثمان ما حدث بعد هذه الواقعة ومن تولى على

ممباسة من الولاة في المدة التي بينه وبين ناصر بن عبدالله ،

وعلى ذكر سيس رومبي وجماعته البغاة ، ا قول ــ رُويت من راشد بن سعود احد اعيان ممباسة ووجهائها ، وهو عن النسابة الشهير محمد بن عثمان المطافي ، انه كان في ممباسة عبيد لليعاربة جاؤوا في زمان الامام سيف بن سلطان كانوا يعرفون في الايام السالفة باسم اولاد سيس رومبي ، وانه بقي من ذرية اولئك العبيد للآن جماعة انتحلوا لانفسهم نسبا آخر إخفاءً لاصلهم ، وليس من موضوع كتابنا هذا انكشاف عن حال هؤلاء المستورين عافاهم الله ،

وكان ناصر بن عبدالله من الرجال المعدودين بالحزم والشجاعة وحسن المعاملة والانصاف بين الرعية ، فحظي بمحبة اهل البلد واكرامهم ، ولما اراد ان يتزوج عرض عليه اعيان ممباسة كرانمهم فاختار كريمة شيخ بن احمد الكبير احد سلالة ملوك ملندي الاقدمين فتزوجها ورزق له منها بنت هي والدة مبارك بن احمد بن مبارك بن غريب المزروعي ،

لا يعرَف بالتحقيق تأريخ رجوع ناصر الى عمان ، ويقال انه رجع الى ممباسة مع محمد بن عثمان في زمان الامام سيف الثاني بن سلطان بن سيف ، ثم رجع نهائيا الى عمان وتوفي فيها ،

خلف ناصر بن عبدالله من الاولاد الذكور مسعود وعبدالله ، ومسعود هذا هو احد اصول المزارعة الاربعة عشر الذين تقدم ذكرهم اول الكتاب ،

****

الوالي الثاني

محمد بن عثمان بن عبدالله بن محمد بن عبدالله بن كهلان

سفر وفد مباسة الى عمان ـ رجوع الوفد مع الوالي محمد بن سعيد المعمري ـ ولاية صالح بن محمد الحضرمي ـ معاملته السيئة مع اهلها ـ القبض عليه والافراج عنه ـ اتحاده مع المباسيين ومحاربة الطوائف الثلاث ـ قتله شيخ بن احمد الملندي وابنه ـ وصول محمد بن عثمان الى مباسة واليا ـ اصلاحه بين اهل مباسة ـ ارساله الخراج الى عمان كل عام ـ انقطاعه عنه واستقلاله بالملك ـ ارسال الامام احمد من يقتله غيلة ـ ولاية سيف بن جلف المعمري ،

بعد ان طرد اهل مباسة البرتغال منها في واقعة سيس رومبي وجماعته كما تقدم الكلام في ترجمة الوالي الاول ناصر بن عبدالله ، سافر الى عمان شيخ بن احمد الملندي ومْونْي غُوتِ بن مَونْزَاغُو الكلنديني ومْوشَهالِ بن ثَداو التنجاني ومعهم من كل قبيلة من قبائل مباسة شخص ، ومن كل طائفة من طوائف الزنوج مندوب من قبلها ، وطوائف الزنوج التي ندبت رجالها الى عمان هي وَرِيبِي ووشُونِي ووكَامْبَة ووكُومَا ووجْبانة ووِرَيِبانِي ووغِرْيَامَة ودُرُومَة ومَطَابة ووشَبْا ولُنْغُو ووِديغُو سافر هذا الوفد لعرض ما جرى في مباسة من امر البرتغال على الامام سيف بن سلطان ، ولما وصلوا هناك انزلهم الامام على الرحب والسعة واكرمهم غاية الاكرام ، وعند رجوعهم جهّزهم ونقلهم في ثلاث مراكب وهي كعبراس والملكي والفلكي مع الهدايا الفاخرة والجوائز ، وارسل معهم محمد بن سعيد المعمري واليا على مباسة ، وبعد وصولها لوطنهم نزل محمد بن سعيد في القلعة كعادة الولاة قبله ، واباح لاهل مباسة جميع ما فيها من الاموال التي خلّفها البرتغال غنيمة لهم جزاء على جميل صنيعهم وبلائهم الحسن في طرد العدو ، ولم يمسك الوالي من تلك الاموال سوى الاسلحة والبارود والنحاس والقصدير وبعد مدة وجيزة رجع محمد بن سعيد الى عمان وخلفه على

١٨

الولاية صالح بن محمد الحضرمي ، ولم يكن صالح مصلحا ولا محمود السيرة فجار على اهل مباسة وأساء معاملتهم فشكوه الى الامام فأرسل اليهم الامر بالقبض عليه وحبسه ، فالقوا عليه القبض ولكنهم اشفقوا عليه واطلقوه ، واضمر صالح في نفسه شرا لمن شكوه الى الامام ، فاتحد مع المباسيين وصادقهم ودعاهم الى محاربة شيخ بن احمد ومن كان تحته من الكلندينيين فأجابوا دعوته وحاربوهم ، ولما رأى شيخ بن احمد وقومه ما فعله مواطنوهم المباسيون من مساعدة عدوهم عليهم ذهب الى نْبِيكَا وجاء بجيش من الزنوج وباغتهم في مْجوكال ، وقتل من المباسيين عدد عظيم واسر منهم جماعة ، ثم قصد شيخ بن احمد ومن معه بعد هذه الغارة الى بلاد نْبِيكَا فرارا من جور صالح وعداوته ،

وحدث بعد ذلك ان وصل علي كُومبُو بن شيخ بن احمد من عمان ومعه اموال من النقود والخيل وغير ذلك مما اهداها اليه الامام ، ولم يكن علي كُومبُو عالما بما جرى في مباسة من الحرب بين الوالي وبين والده ، وبلغ صالح خبر قدومه فبعث اليه نفرا من جنوده وجاؤا به اليه فاعتقله ونهب الاموال التي كانت معه ، ولما علم شيخ بن احمد ما فعله الوالي بابنه غلب عليه شفقة الابوة فبرز من مكمنه وجاء الى الوالي وساله الافراج عن ابنه فقابله بالتعظيم والاجلال حتى ظن انه سيعطيه سوله ، ولم يكن الا هنيهة حتى امر الوالي بالقبض عليه وقتله هو وابنه معا ،

وما كاد يصل الى الامام اخبار الوالي وقساوته واعتدانه العظيم على عظماء البلد حتى عزله واشتهر بدلا منه محمد بن عثمان المزروعي ، وكان اول ما باشره هذا الوالي بعد تقلده امر البلاد ان ارسل الى احمد بن شيخ والكلندينيين الذين اختفوا في اراضي نْبِيكَا يخبرهم بعزل صالح وتسفيره الى عمان ويطلب منهم الرجوع الى البلاد سريعا ، ولما رأى الوالي ما حل بين الطائفتين الكلندينية والمباسية من الشقاق والخصام ، بذل غاية جهده في اصلاح ذات بينهم فوفقه الله لذلك ، فحدث الالفة والمحبة من قلوبهم محل النفور والضغينة ، فسكنت البلاد ورجعت المياه الى مجاريها مدة غير قليلة ،

تذكر الروايات المنقولة عن قدماء المزارعة وغيرهم ان الامام ما زال يرسل الولاة

الى ممباسة منذ دخلت بلاد السواحل في ملكه ، الى ان حدث في عمان حوادث
اضعفت قوة الدولة وصيّرها غير قادرة على ادارة شؤون داخل مملكته فضلا عن
ادارة الممالك الخارجية وسياستها ، فاراد الامام سيف الثاني بن سلطان ان يعيد
لناصر بن عبدالله ولاية ممباسة ثانيا لاجل اخلاصه وحسن ادارته ، ومعرفته التامّة
باحوال البلاد واهلها ، على ان يلتزم على نفسه دفع قدر معلوم من الخراج كل سنة
ولكن ناصر اعتذر عن قبول الولاية هذه المرة لشيخوخته واشار على الامام ان ينصب
مكانه محمد بن عثمان على تلك الشروط ، ففعل الامام برأيه وولى محمد بن عثمان ،
وجهز الوالي للسفر الى مقر ولايته ومعه اخواه علي بن عثمان وقضيب بن عثمان
ونفر من ابناء عمومتهم كعبدالله بن زاهر وغيره ،

وتختلف الروايات في تأريخ ولاية محمد بن عثمان ، فالذي رأيناه من
مخطوطات المتقدمين انه وصل ممباسة سنة ١١٤٣ وتقلد زمام ولايته في تلك السنة ،
وانه عاش في الولاية اربع عشرة سنة تقريبا ، وهناك رواية اخرى تختلف عن هذه
في مدة الولاية فهي تقول انها تسع سنين ، وكلتا الروايتين تختلف عما في المصادر
الافرنجية في تأريخ الولاية ، ففي كتاب ‹ زنجبار › لميجر بيرس ، **والكتاب**
الاحمر لافريقية الشرقية يقولان ان الامام سيف بن سلطان ولى على ممباسة
محمد بن عثمان في سنة ١٧٢٩ ميلادية ، وهي توافق سنة ١١٥٢ هجرية ، وعندي
ان الرواية التي تقول انه تولى سنة ١١٤٣ ومكث في الولاية مدة اربع عشرة سنة
هي اصح من غيرها ، لٔانه على هذه الرواية تكون وفاته في عام ١١٥٢ ، وهي السنة
التي توفي فيها كما هو مكتوب على ضريحه رحمه الله ، واما على الرواية الافرنجية
فتكون مدة ولايته خمس سنين فقط فتشذ عن الروايات الاخرى كلها ،

وبعد تقلد الوالي وظيفته كان يرسل الى الامام ذلك القدر من المال على موجب
الاتفاق المتقدم فيما بينهما ، ودام على هذا الحال مدة بضع سنين حتى ساءت
الاحوال في عمان واشتد ضعف الدولة بما حدث فيها من الانقسام ، وعمت الفتن
شرقي عمان وغربيها ودارت رحى الحرب بين العرب والعجم تارة وبين العرب بعضهم
بعضا تارة اخرى ، وقامت هناك ائمة كل يدعي الحق لنفسه وينسب البغي لصاحبه ،

فانقطع محمد بن عثمان عما كان يرسله واستقل بالملك واعلن استقلاله ، وكان بممباسة في ذلك الوقت مشانخ من الكليفيين يبغضون الوالي بغضا شديدا ، لا لسوء معاملته معهم ، بل لتقديمه الملنديين والطوائف الثلاث التي هي الكلندينية والتنجانية والشنغامية عليهم ، اغاظهم ذلك مدة من الزمان فقعدوا يتحينون الفرصة للايقاع بالوالي ، ولما سكنت الاحوال بعمان وخلصت الامامة لاحمد بن سعيد ، كاتبوه في شأنه واعلموه بما فعله من اعلان الاستقلال بملك السواحل ، والذي تولى كبره منهم رجل من زعماء الكليفيين في ذلك الوقت (اسمه شريف سعيد ـ ممحو في المخطوطة) ،

وبعد ورود هذا الكتاب الى الامام ، ارسل الى ممباسة نفرا للاغتيال بالوالي وهم سيف بن خلف المعمري وسيف بن ناصر وسيف بن سعيد البطاشي ومعن بن كليب ، وصلوا ممباسة غير متظاهرين بالذي جاءوا من اجله ، وقابلوا الوالي واخبروه بانهم تخاصموا مع الامام وهاجروا من عمان قاصدين الاقامة حيث هو مقيم ، ثم اتصلوا بالكايفيين وكاشفوهم بالامر واخذوا منهم العهد على ان يكونوا عونا لهم على تأدية تلك المهمة ، فعاهدوهم واتحدوا معهم ، وبعد ان استوثقوا من اهل ممباسة وممن في القلعة من جنود الامام ، طلبوا من الوالي ان يجهز لهم السفر الى كلوة ويمنحهم مبلغا من المال للاتجار به هناك ، فاجاب الوالي طلبهم وهو يجهل كل الجهل لما اضمروه في نفوسهم ، وبينما هو قاعد معهم يجهز لهم ما ارادوه اذ وثبوا عليه وقتلوه وقبضوا على اخيه علي بن عثمان وعلى خلف بن قضيب وعبدالله بن خميس العفيفي وزجوهم في السجن ولما علم الجند بان الذي فعلوه انما هو بامر الامام لم يكن منهم الا ان يطيعوهم في كل ما يأمرونهم ، فأصدروا امرهم بالقبض على من في ممباسة من المزارعة فقُتل بعضهم وتشتت آخرون فذهبوا الى البادية واختفوا هناك ، وقام بعد ذلك سيف بن خلف واليا على ممباسة باتفاق زملانه وحصل لهم من الكليفيين والمباسيين كل ما يطلبونه من المعونة ، وكان ذلك في عام ١١٥٢ هـ ، هذا ما اتفق عليه الروايات واقرها المرحوم النسابة المؤرخ عبدالكريم بن طلسم رحمة الله عليه ، وهو مطابق لما رأيناه من ترجمة المخطوطات العربية التي نقلها القبطان اوين في رحلته ،

خلف محمد بن عثمان من الاولاد الذكور عبدالله واحمد وجميع ذريته من

ولديه المذكورَين ، وسيأتي ذكرهما فيما بعد والله اعلم ،

****

الوالي الثالث

علي بن عثمان بن عبدالله بن محمد بن عبدالله بن كهلان

حزن الطوائف الثلاث على قتل محمد بن عثمان وحبس اخيه ـ مَوَانَة فُبَنَاية وسعيها في تخليص علي بن عثمان من السجن ـ البلوشيون يساعدونه على الفرار من السجن ـ انتظار الطوائف الثلاث له خارج القلعة ـ هروبه الى مَريرة ـ وصول المستر كوك ومساعدته له ـ المؤامرة على الهجوم وتدبير امره ـ المعاهدة بينه وبين الطوائف الثلاث ـ الاستيلاء على القلعة وقتل سيف بن خلف ـ مشانخ البلد يهنئون الوالي ويبايعونه ـ هُمُ الوالي على قتل زعماء الكليفيين وافتداء الطوائف الثلاث لهم ـ خوف الامام احمد بن سعيد من استيلاء المزارعة على زنجبار ـ هجوم المزارعة على زنجبار ـ قتل خلف بن قضيب لعمّه علي بن عثمان وسببه ـ رجوع الجيش الى مباسة ،

قد سبق لنا القول في الكلام عن محمد بن عثمان ، ان الجماعة الذين ارسلهم الامام احمد للاغتيال به قبضوا على اخيه علي بن عثمان وحبسوه في سجن داخل القلعة ، فاورث قتل محمد بن عثمان وحبس اخيه حزنا عميقا في صدور الطوائف الثلاث وجماعة الملنديين كما سُرّ بذلك الكليفيون والمباسيون وزعماؤهم وكان تحت زعيم الكليفيين في ذلك الوقت امرأة من الملنديين اسمها مَوَانَة فُبَنَاية فحنقت على زوجها لما بين الملنديين وبين المزارعة من المصاهرة والموالاة من زمان ناصر بن عبدالله ، وكانت هذه المرأة حائزة لصفات الرجال العقلاء ومن الشجاعة والدهاء وسداد الرأي ، فشجعت الطوائف الثلاث واهل قرابتها من اعيان الملنديين على السعي في تخليص علي بن عثمان من السجن بكل وسيلة يستطيعونها ، ومن جهة اخرى كانت ترسل الهدايا الى من في القلعة من السجانين حتى غمرتهم بالجميل فكافؤوها برفع الحجر عن علي بن عثمان وبتخفيف المراقبة والتشديد عنه ، فاستطاع الوالي بهذه الوسيلة ان يجتمع في بعد الاحايين باهل ولانه ويتحدث معهم في طريقة النجاة من هذا السجن الذي ضاق به ذرعا ، فاتفقوا على ان يتسلق هو والمسجونين معه جدار

القلعة في ساعة معلومة من ليلة معينة على ان ينتظروهم خارجها ليسعفوهم ،

وكان لعلي بن عثمان في القلعة رجلان من العساكر البلوشيين مخلصان له كل الاخلاص ، اسم احدهما همداد واسم الآخر هلب ، فاطلعهما على ما اتفق هو وجماعة الطوائف الثلاث فاستحسنا هذا الرأي وعاهداه على مساعدته ، وعمد البلوشيان الى جلد بقر فاتخذا منه سيورا متينة بحيث لا تتقطع اذا تعلق بها الانسان ، ولما وافت الليلة الموعودة ، تغافل عنه السجان الموكل به وتسلق هو وجماعته جدار القلعة من الجهة الغربية المقابلة لبناية المحكمة العليا الآن ، لان جدار هذه الجهة اقصر جدران القلعة ولم يكن الخندق الذي احاط بها محفورا في ذلك الوقت ، وكان في انتظاره خارج القلعة نفر من اخص اهل ولانه وهم مَوشَافِ بن معلم نْداو ، وحاج بن مَوْنِي نَغْوتِ ، وخميس بن مَوْنِي جَاكِ واحمد بن نْداو ، وكلهم من عظماء الطوائف الثلاث ، ونزل اولا علي بن عثمان – بواسطة تلك السيور – ورجلاه مقيدتان في الحديد ثم تبعه خلف بن قضيب وعبدالله بن خميس العفيفي ، فتلقاهم الجماعة وهم مسرورون ، وذهبوا بهم مسرعين الى منازلهم تحت ظلام الليل ، وهناك حلوا قيودهم ، وكانوا قد اعدوا قاربا خصيصا للفرار به ، فطلعوا فيه تلك الليلة ، وذهبوا الى مْريرة ، وهو موضع معروف من ارض درومة التابعة للطائفة الشنجامية ،

اصبح الصباح وشاع في البلد خبر هروب علي بن عثمان وجماعته من القلعة ، فاوجس الحكام في انفسهم خيفة وارسلوا الطلائع والعيون للبحث عنهم ولكنهم لم يهتدوا الى المكان الذي ذهبوا اليه ، فذهب اتعابهم ادراج الرياح ،

في اثناء وجودهم في مْريرة ، وصل مبماسة المستر كوك الانكايزي المعروف عند السواحليين باسم ‹ مْزْنْغُو كِنْغُنْغُو › (اي الافرنجي الاغنُ) في مركبه المسمى

‹ مُمْبَيْ › وكان المستر كوك صديقا لمحمد بن عثمان ، وسأل عن صديقه فقيل انه قُتل ، وسأل عن اخيه فاخبره الناس بانه كان مسجونا بعد قتل اخيه ثم فر من السجن الى حيث لا يُعلم ، فود هذا الافرنجي لو يلتقي باخي صديقه لعله يستطيع ان يساعده ولو برأي ، واجتمع باحد الملنديين فدله على مَوَانَة فُبَيَاية فذهب اليها وانكرت انها تعلم شيئا من اخباره فضلا عن المكان الذي هو فيه ، وما كان

٢٤

انكارها الا لظنها ان في الامر دسيسة ، ولكنها بعد قيام الافرنجي من عندها بعث الى علي بن عثمان تخبره بما كان من امر كوك الافرنجي وبأوصافه وتسأله عما اذا كان يريد الاجتماع به ، فوصل اليها جوابه بان الرجل صديق اخيه حقا وانه يود ملاقاته ، فأرسلته الى مُريرَة مع دليل امين من خدامها ، ولما اجتمع به سأله الافرنجي عما عزم عليه فقال له علي انه عازم على الاخذ بالثأر وانه الآن في استعداد للهجوم على القلعة ، فوافقه الافرنجي على هذا الرأي وقال له امض فيما عزمت عليه وان لم تفلح آخذك مع اتباعك على ظهر مركبي وارجع بكم في العام القابل مع مراكب اخرى بكل ما تحتاجون اليه من آلات الحرب لتواصلوا على قتالهم الى ان يفتح الله عليكم ، وأشار عليه بصنع سلالم طوال على ارتفاع جدران القلعة ليرتفعوا بها عند اقتحامهم عليها ، فاستحسن علي بن عثمان رأيه وامر بصنع تلك السلالم ،

جرى كل ذلك والوالي في مفره وهو متصل كل الاتصال باصدقائه عظماء الملنديين وزعماء الطولئف الثلاث ، والرسائل بينهم غير منقطعة لا يفوت شيء مما يجري في البلد ، ولما قرب اوان الهجوم اجتمع اصدقاؤه وتشاوروا في كيفية الاغارة ووقتها ، وبعد ان تمَّ بينهم الاتفاق على رأي واحد بايعوه حاكما عليهم ، واشترط عليه الطوائف الثلاث في هذه البيعة ان ينازل لهم عن عشور الجزيرة الخضراء مدة بقاء حكم المزارعة ، فعاهدهم على ذلك وعلى امور اخرى كتبوها في معاهدتهم المأسوف على ضياعها ،

لما وافت ليلة الهجوم خرج علي بن عثمان يقود وراءه جيشا من اتباعه البواسل ومعهم سلالمهم التي صنعوها لتسلق القلعة بها ، الى ان وصلوا اليها فاقتحموها ، ووقع بين الفريقين قتال شديد فاز فيه علي بن عثمان على عدوّه ، ولما رأى سيف بن خلف شدة ما هو فيه لجأ الى احد ابراج القلعة وتحصن به ، فجاؤا بمدفع من مركب المستر كوك ورموه بقنبلة منه فانكسر البرج وقبضوا على سيف وقتلوه ،

وكانت مَوَانَة فُمْبَايَة مطّلعة على كل ما يجري في شأن علي بن عثمان ، ولما كانت تلك الليلة اعدت ثياب الرقص السواحلي المسمى ‹ شِنْدْوَا › وباتت ساهرة تتسمع الى صوت المدفع الذي اتفقوا ان يكون علامة على الظفر والاستيلاء ، فما

٢٥

سمعت دوي المدفع الا واسرعت الى لبس ثياب رقصها من الطرطور والاردية الطويلة العريضة ، واخذت بيدها انبوبة من الخيزران الغليظ وصارت تضرب بها الارض وترقص قدام سرير زوجها وهو غارق في النوم ، وتنشد بيتا من الشعر الساحلي مفاده

‹ الثأر عندنا لا يبيت › ، استيقظ ذلك الزعيم الكليفي زوج مْوَانَة فُمْبَايَة من نومه مذعورا ، ولما رأت (رأى؟) زوجته على تلك الحالة ارتاع منها وسألها ما الخبر ؟ فأجابته قائلة لا شيء سوى ان علي بن عثمان قد دخل البلد واستولى على القلعة واقتص من قاتل اخيه ، ثم عادت الى رقصها وانشاد ذلك البيت الحماسي فرحة مسرورة ، والتفتت الى زوجها وقالت له مفتخرة أرأيت كيف يفعل الرجال؟ تعني بهم نفسها مع جماعتها فوجم الرجل ولم يدر ماذا يقول ،

اصبح الصباح وشاع الخبر فهرع مشائخ البلدة واعيانها وأولو الحل والعقد فيها من العرب وغيرهم الى القلعة يهنُّون الوالي بالظفر ويبايعونه على الولاية ، وكان ذلك في سنة ١١٥٨ اي بعد قتل محمد بن عثمان بسنة تقريبا ، ومن هذا التأريخ يبتدئ استقلال حكم المزارعة استقلالا حقيقيا فدخلت تحت سلطانهم بلاد السواحل من رأش نْغُمين الى بنْغَانِ واستولى علي بن عثمان على الجزيرة الخضراء وضمها الى مملكتهم ودانت لهم جميع القبائل من اقصى هذه البلاد الى اقصاها كما تقدم بيان ذلك في الفصل الاول عند ذكر مملكة المزارعة ،

وبعد ان خلصت الولاية لعلي بن عثمان ، اراد ان يجتث جذور الفتنة فأمر بالقبض على زعماء الكليفيين واعيانهم وهمَّ بقتلهم جزاء ما فعلوه به وبأخيه ، فتوسط الطوائف الثلاث بالشفاعة لهم وعرضوا عليه عشور الجزيرة الخضراء فداء لهم فقبل الوالي الفداء واطلق سراحهم ، وما زال الطوائف الثلاث يمنون على الكليفيين بافتدائهم الى هذا اليوم ،

بلغ الامام احمد بن سعيد خبر سقوط قلعة ممباسة في يد علي بن عثمان وعودة حكم المزارعة فيها ، فخاف من ان تمتد ايدي المزارعة الى جزيرة زنجبار فيحتلوها كما احتلوا جزيرة بِمْبَ شسا ، فبعث عبدالله بن جاعد البوسعيدي واليا على زنجبار مع حامية من العساكر يحميها من المزارعة ،

٢٦

هجوم المزارعة على زنجبار

لم يعزم علي بن عثمان على الاستيلاء على زنجبار الا في آخر ايام حياته ، ففي سنة ١١٦٨ اصدر امره الى رؤساء القبائل الذين تحت حكمه بجمع العساكر والاستعداد للحرب ، فامتثل امره الجميع ووصل الى ممباسة طائفة من وَسِغيجُو وعليهم اميرهم كَذِمْبُو وجماعة كبيرة من وَدِيغُو مع اميرهم السيد احمد بن الديوان ابي بكر بن شيخ آل المسبلة ، وتجند كثيرون من العرب الذين كانوا في ممباسة وتانغة وغيرهما من البلاد السواحلية ، فأبحر علي بن عثمان الى زنجبار يجر وراءه سفنا كثيرة ملآى بالمقاتلة ، قيل انها بلغت ثمانين سفينة مما بين كبيرة وصغيرة ومقلَّة للجنود وحاملة للمؤن والذخائر ، وصلوا زنجبار وهاجموها وقاتلوا عساكر الامام فهزموهم واحتلوا البلد وفر اكثر الناس الى أنْغُوجَ أكُو ،

وبينما هم في حصار القلعة وقد ضيقوا على من فيها وكادوا يستسلمون لهم ، اذ وثب خلف بن قضيب على عمه علي بن عثمان وطعنه بخنجر اصاب منه المقتل ، وحالا قتل هو ايضا ومات الاثنان في وقت واحد وُدفنا حيث ــ ــ ــ ــ ــ ــ ــ ــ ــ ــ هكذا في المخطوطات التي بايدينا بلا ذكر سبب القتل ولا كيفية الاقتصاص من القاتل ، واما الروايات اللسانية فتذكر السبب وكيفيته ولكنها مختلفة فيها ، فرواة الاخبار من اهل ممباسة يقولون ان السبب هو طمع خلف في السلطة واستعجاله بها ، وان علي بن عثمان نفسه حالما طعنه خلف امسكه بقوة وأغرز في صدره الخنجر وسقط الاثنان كلاهما ، والاخباريون من اهل واسِين يُرْوُون عن السيد ابي بكر بن قاسم آل مسبلة المعروف بسعة علمه في الانساب واطلاعه على اخبار المزارعة ، ان خلف اعتراه شبه جنون فاستلَّ خنجره وطعن عمه ثم دخل بيتا وأقفل على نفسه الباب ، فذهب اليه السيد احمد بن الديوان ابي بكر فناصحه في فتحه ففتحه وقُبض عليه ثم قتل بامر من مسعود بن ناصر ، وهؤلاء ينسبون سبب ذلك الى تأثير السحر الذيَ عمله لهم اهل دُنْغَا من زنجبار ،

وبعد هذه الواقعة المحزنة تشاءم مسعود بن ناصر وكف عن مواصلة القتال ورجع بالجيش الى ممباسة ، ولا يعلم بالتحقيق المدة التي امضوها في زنجبار الى رجوعهم منها ،

وقد استقصينا البحث عن المكان الذي نزل فيه هذا الجيش والذي وقع القتال فيه ، وسألنا عن ذلك كل من توسمنا فيه معرفة لمثل هذه الاخبار من الشيوخ فلم نقف على شيء يطمئن اليه القلب ، غير ان الميجر بيرس ذكر في عرض كلامه عن افريقية الشرقية خبر هجوم المزارعة على زنجبار ، وانا اورد هنا تعريب كلامه كما ترجمه صديقنا صالح بن علي بن صالح في اسبوعية ١٧ أبريل ١٩٢٣ من اسبوعياته التي كان ينشرها ملحقة للجريدة الرسمية بزنجبار ، قال ـ

< ولما آنس والي ممباسة قلة الميل في سياسة الامام الى التدخل في شؤون زنجبار والافريقية الشرقية داخله الطمع وصمم على اخضاع زنجبار ، فتهيأ لها وجرد اسطولا من الخشب الشراعية واتخذ الجزيرة قاعدة لها ، وهاجم زنجبار واحتل البلد ، ولكنه لم يتمكن من اقتحام حصنها ، ثم ان قواده اختلفوا فيما بينهم وانشقوا ووقعت الفتنة بينهم فآلت الى قتل علي بن عثمان المزروعي الذي هو حاكم ممباسة وبقتله وقع الفشل فيهم فاخذوا مراكبهم وتقهقروا الى ممباسة ، >

وقال في موضع آخر عند ذكر قلعة زنجبار هكذا ـ

< ان عرب المزارعة هاجموا تلك القلعة في عام ١٧٥٢ م ولكنهم ارتدوا عنها ولم يفوزوا بطائل > ثم قال < واعتمادا على سجلات البرتغال وروايات الاهالي ، اقول ان موضع بلدة زنجبار كان عند رأس شَنْغَاني > اه ،

وعلى ما ذكر الميجر فيكون المزارعة هاجموا زنجبار من جهة شَنْغَاني التي كان بها القلعة ، وفيها وقع القتال والله اعلم بحقيقة الحال ، وكان علي بن عثمان رحمه الله بطلا شجاعا كبير الآمال بعيد المطامع ، وهذه السجايا هي التي حملته على مهاجمة زنجبار بعد استيلانه على الجزيرة الخضراء ، ولو امدّ الله في عمره لواصل بفتوحاته الى اقصى افريقية الشرقية ، خلف الوالي من الاولاد سالم وسليمان ، وسيأتي ذكر سليمان هذا فيما بعد ان شاء الله ،

****

٢٨

الوالي الرابع

مسعود بن ناصر بن عبدالله بن محمد بن عبدالله بن كهلان

رجوعه بجيش المزارعة من زنجبار ــ بيعته واليا على ممباسة ــ القول بالهجوم على زنجبار ثانيا ــ التحالف المزروعي النبهاني وسببه ــ امارة خلف بن ناصر على الحامية المزروعية في بتة ــ تشجيع الكليفيين لاهل بتة على نصب العداء للمزارعة ــ اغارة اهل بتة على ممباسة ــ الفتنة في بتة واتهام خلف بن ناصر بها ــ قتل اهل بتة لخلف ــ اقتصاص المزارعة من النباهنة في الجزيرة ــ رجوع التحالف المزروعي النبهاني كما كان ــ وفاة الوالي

والينا مسعود هذا هو ابن ناصر بن عبدالله اول ولاة المزارعة من قبل الامام سيف بن ساطان اليعربي الذي تقدم الكلام عنه في ترجمته ، كان مسعود من اكبر قواد علي بن عثمان الذي سافر معه الى محاربة زنجبار ، وبعد ان وقعت تلك الواقعة المحزنة من قتل علي بن عثمان وابن اخيه خلف تشاءم القوم من هذه الغارة وضعفت قلوبهم وفترت هممهم ، ولما رأى منهم مسعود بن ناصر شاور من كان من رؤساء القبائل وامراء الطوائف بين البقاء على الاحتلال وبين الرجوع الى ممباسة ، فاتفق الجميع على الرجوع على ان يستأنفوا القتال مرة اخرى اذا سنحت لهم الفرصة ، فلم يكن لمسعود بد من الاخذ برأيهم فرجع بالجيش الى ممباسة ، وهناك بويع هو واليا عليها خلفا من علي بن عثمان ، وكان ذلك في عام ١١٦٨ ،

القول بالهجوم على زنجبار ثانيا

قيل ان مسعود شرع في اعداد العدة لاستئناف الهجوم على زنجبار ثانيا ، فارسل الخبر بذلك الى واسين فجمع له السيد حسن بن ابي بكر بن شيخ جيشا من شجعان وَديغُو ، وبعث هذا الى كَذِمْبُو رئيس طائفة وَسِغِيجُو يستدعيه ليوافيه بواسين مع جماعته لينتظروا اجتياز الوالي بهم ليسافروا معه الى زنجبار ، خرج الوالي

٢٩

من مبماسة بجيشه ومر بجزيرة وَاسِين وكان السيد حسن وكَذِمْبُو رئيس وَسِغيجُو في انتظارهم مع جم غفير من اهل وَاسِين ووَدِيغُو ووَسِغيجُو ، فابحروا منها الى زنجبار ، هذا ما رويناه من اهل وَاسِين تَكَوْنَغُ وبين الروايتين اختلاف في محل نزول الجيش هذه المرة وفي كيفية القتال ، وينكر كثيرون وقوع هذا الهجوم الثاني وهو الذي اميل اليه لعدم اطلاعنا على شيء مما يدل على ذلك لا في المخطوطات التأريخية التي بايدينا ، ولا في الكتب الافرنجية ، ومن يعرف سيرة الوالي وحرصه على تأمين بلاده وابتعاده عما يثير الفتن والحروب يجزم على عدم صحة هذه الرواية ،

التحالف المزروعي النبهاني

في ايام مسعود بن ناصر تمَّ التحالف المزروعي النبهاني ، فاتفق الفريقان على المعاضدة والمناصرة والمدافعة ، وعدم اعتداء فريق على آخر ، وان يرسل النباهنة حامية مع امير منهم الى الجزيرة ويرسل المزارعة حامية مع امير منهم الى بتة ، ولبيان سبب هذه المحالفة اورد هنا ما دوَّنه اهل بتة في مخطوطاتهم التأريخية ، قالوا ـ

< بين عام ١١٧٠ و ١١٧٧ تولى على بتة السلطان بُوَانَة تَامُ الاصغر ابو بكر بن بُوَانَة مَكُو ، وفي ايامه عزم الامام على اخضاع بتة فارسل اليها جيشا وحارب السلطان وقاتله قتالا شديدا ولكن لم يرجح جانب الامام ، فتقهقر جيشه بعد ان قتل منهم جانب عظيم ، >

فمن هذا يظهر ان السبب في ذلك التحالف وارسال كل فريق الى بلاد الاخر حامية من الجند ، هو التعاون على مدافعة جيش الامام الذي كان يريد الاستيلاء على بلاد الفريقين بقوة ، دام هذا الحال اياما فكان المزارعة يرسلون الى بتة حاميتهم مع امير منهم فيقيم ما شاء الله ثم يرجع ويرسل الاخر كذلك بالتناوب ، وهكذا كان يفعل النباهنة في الجزيرة ،

وكان خلف بن ناذصر بن خلف المزروعي من جملة من ارسل الى بتة اميرا على الحامية المزروعية ، ولم يكن خلف محمود السيرة فابغضه اهل بتة لسوء معاشرته معهم ، وابغضوا المزارعة كلهم بسببه ، فعلم الكليفيون الذين في مبماسة بحال خلف هذا وبمعاملته السيئة ، فصاروا يشجّعون اهل بتة على نصب الاداء للمزارعة ، وكان

من الكليفيين طائفة يقال لهم بنو كِبِنْدا بينهم وبين بعض من اهل بتة رحم وقرابة ، فارسلوا اليهم رسائل تلو رسائل يدعونهم الى محاربة المزارعة في ممباسة ويحثونهم عليها ويعدونهم بمساعدتهم على ذلك هم ومن معهم من الطوائف الاخرى ، وابلغوا ذلك الى سلطان بتة نفسه ، ولكن السلطان لم يلتفت الى هذه المناصبات العدائية ، فلما رأى اقرباء بني كِبِنْدا اهمال السلطان لرأي اقربائهم الذين في ممباسة اغاظهم واتفقوا مع عوام اهل بتة وسفلتهم على الاغارة على ممباسة ، فوصلت سفنهم ورست في مياه كِلِنْدِين ونزلوا وعاثوا في الارض فسادا فقتلوا من لقيهم هناك وقبضوا على النساء والصبيان على قصد اتخاذهم اسرى الحرب ، وحالما بلغ الخبر الى الوالي ارسل اليهم ثلّة من الجند لقتالهم فقتل من اهل بتة كثيرون ، ولما رأى من في السفن ما نزل باصحابهم نشروا الاشرعة ونجوا بانفسهم وهرب آخرون واحتموا باقربائهم بني كِبِنْدا ، وهؤلاء ، عبروا بهم الشط وارسلوهم الى ريبي ، واختفوا هناك ،

ارسل الوالي امره لاهل ريبي بتسليم الجناة ولكن لما كان بين اهل ريبي وبين الكليفيين صلة واتفاق ، أبوا ان يسلموهم ، فاراد الوالي ان يبعث اليهم عسكرا للقبض على الجناة وتأديب اهل ريبي اذا تمادوا في ايوائهم الاعداء ، وكان في ذلك الوقت رجل من الكليفيين اسمه معراج بن مِيرا كان يتظاهر بموالة المزارعة ، فذهب الى الوالي فطلب منه ان يأذن له بالمسير الى ريبي ووعده بالاتيان بالجناة في اليوم الثالث ، فأذن له الوالي وذهب وكلم اهل ريبي في تسليم الجناة وحذرهم من سوء العاقبة ، ولكن لم يصادف قوله اذانا تصغو اليه فرجع الى ممباسة بخفي حنين ، واغتنم البتاويون هذه الفرصة فسافروا برا الى بلادهم ، وهناك نظموا شعرا باللغة السواحلية يحتوي على الطعن في الوالي وفي خلف بن ناصر وبعض اعيان الطوائف الثلاث ذكروهم فيه باسمائهم ويفتخرون في ذلك الشعر بهذه الغارة التي شنوها في كلنديني ، وسنورد هذا الشعر في الترجمة السواحلية لهذا الكتاب ان شاء الله تعالى ،

فتنة بتة واتهام خلف بالمشاركة فيها

في نوبة خلف بن ناصر المذكور وقعت في بتة حادثة فظيعة مؤلمة كادت تقطع الصلة بين المزارعة وبين النباهنة وذلك انه لما كانت سنة ١١٩٠ حدثت هناك فتنة

ضد السلطان بَوَانة مَكُو بن شِيخِي بن بَوَانة تَأُم مَكُو ، لانه كان مبغضا عند رعيته ، وعزم البعض منهم على الدخول عليه والفتك به ، ولكنهم علموا انهم لا يستطيعون الدخول لقفل الابواب دونهم ، وعلموا من جهة اخرى ان خلف له وقت يدخل على السلطان في كل يوم واجتمع رأيهم على ان يكمنوا بمحل ينتظرون هذا الوقت حتى اذا فُتح لخلف الباب دخلوا معه ، وفي ذات يوم ذهب خلف الى السلطان كعادته فجلس على دكة منتظرا الاذن ، فلما فُتح له الباب اذ غوغاء بتة قد خرجوا من مكمنهم يتسابقون الى الدخول على السلطان لقتله فدخلوا مع خلف يتزاحمون ، ولما علم خلف ما جاءوا لاجله بذل جهده في الدفاع عن السلطان ، وبينما هو كذلك اذ تصدّى له احد بني عبدالسلام من بيت وزراء بتة فقتله ظنًا منه انه شريك اولانك السفلة في فعلتهم الشنيعة ، او انه الذي دبر هذه المكيدة ، ثم بعد ذلك خاف النباهنة من اقتصاص المزارعة ممن في الجزيرة من جماعتهم فارسلوا اليهم يخبرونهم بالواقع ليأخذوا حذرهم وينجوا بانفسهم قبل بلوغ الخبر الى المزارعة هناك ، ولكن لم تسمح لهم انفسهم الابية بالفرار فأقاموا في الجزيرة وهم متأهبون للمدافعة عن انفسهم ولما اتصل هذا الخبر بالمزارعة الذين في الجزيرة هجموا عليهم وقتلوهم ، ثم بعد ان وقعت هذه الفظائع اتضح للنباهنة ان التهمة التي وجهوها لخلف لم تكن في محلها ، وان خلف بريء منها فندموا على قتله وارسلوا الى الوالي يعتذرون اليه فعذرهم ،

وكان مسعود بن ناصر من الدهاة المعروفين ، ولم يشاء ان يترك الضغائن تبقى في صدور اهل مباسة وبتة بما حصل بينهم من القتل في الجانبين ، فسعى باجتهاده ودهانه حتى أزال الحقد من قلوب الجميع واجتثه من اصله فرجع المياه الى مجاريها ودام التحالف المزروعي النبهاني كما كان واوثق مما كان ، ولكن النباهنة لم يبعثوا حامية بعد التي قتلت في هذه الفتنة ، ودام المزارعة على ارسالها الى بتة الى ان استولى على بتة السيد سعيد بن سلطان ،

توفي مسعود بن ناصر في قلعة مباسة عام ١١٩٢ بعد ان مكث في الولاية مدة خمس وعشرين سنة ، ودفن داخل القلعة قرب المكان الذي نصب فيه السارية وانمحى اثر قبره لتداول الايدي الاجنبية على القلعة ، وكان مسعود رحمه الله حسن السيرة محبوبا عند عشيرته وعند الناس جميعا مبتعدا كل الابتعاد عن المنازعات

والمحاربات ولاجل ذلك لم يحدث في ولايته الطويلة شيء من حرب ولا قتال سوى ما كان من تأديب اولئك البتاويين الذين اغاروا على ممباسة ، واما ما قيل من هجومه على زنجبار مرة ثانية فلم يثبت عندي ، وكان رحمه الله كثير الاتجار وسهل سبيله للناس مما اتاه من تأمين البلاد ، وكان ايامه ايام رخاً وهناءً وسلام ،

خلف الوالي من الاولاد الذكور ثمانية وهم بدوى وعمران واحمد وعبدالله وراشد وناصر وخميس ومحمد ، والذي اعقب منهم هو احمد بن مسعود وحده ، ومن ذريته فضيلة قاضي ملندي العالم ناصر بن احمد بن محمد كما تقدم بيان ذلك في الفصل الاول من هذا الكتاب والله اعلم ،

****

الوالي الخامس

عبدالله بن محمد بن عثمان بن عبدالله المزروعي

لما توفي مسعود بن ناصر ، اختلف المزارعة فيمن يولُّونه بعده ، ورشح كل واحد من اولاد الولاة نفسه ، وحصل نزاع شديد بينهم ، ثم اصطلحوا اخيرا واتفقوا على تولية عبدالله بن محمد بن عثمان هذا في ذلك اليوم الذي انتقل فيه مسعود بن ناصر الى دار الآخرة في سنة ١١٩٣ ،

وعبدالله بن محمد هو اول وال من المزارعة ولد في السواحل واما الولاة الاربعة المتقدمون فكلهم ولدوا بعمان ، توفي الوالي سنة ١١٩٥ بعد ان امضى في الولاية سنتين تقريبا وكان رحمه الله كسابقه في حسن السيرة والابتعاد عن الحروب ،

وخلف عبدالله من الاولاد اثنين علي ومحمد وانقرض نسله ،

****

الوالي السادس
احمد بن محمد بن عثمان بن عبدالله بن محمد المزروعي

ولايته ـ عصيان موني سمبا سلطان تانغة للوالي ـ الاستعداد للثورة في تانغة ـ بعث
الوالي الجند لاخضاعه ـ اصلاح الديوان حسن بين الوالي وسلطان تانغة ـ وصول السلطان
الى ممباسة لاداء الطاعة ـ فتنة في بتة بين اهلها واهل لاموء وسببها ـ ذهاب الوالي
احمد للاصلاح بينهم ـ اسباب المهاجمة على لاموء ـ ما يقوله اهل لاموء واهل ممباسة
فيها ـ واقعة شيلة ـ انهزام جيش المزارعة والنباهنة وسببه ـ تمليك اهل لاموء بلادهم
للسيد سعيد بن سلطان ـ خروج اولاد مسعود بن ناصر عن الطاعة وسببه ـ الحرب
الاهلية بينهم وبين الوالي ـ فرارهم الى رَياني ودُرُومَة ـ قتل من فر الى رياني ـ اتيان
موني هيجة بن فاكي بمن فر الى درومة منهم ـ وفاء الطوائف الثلاث للمزارعة ـ حظورة
سفك الدماء بينهم ـ عزل شريف سعيد عن المشيخة واقامة احمد بن شيخ
بدلا منه ـ سوء تدبير الامير عبدالله بن احمد ـ وفاة الوالي رحمة الله عليه ،

الوالي احمد بن محمد هو ثاني اولاد محمد بن عثمان ، ولد في ممباسة
وتولى بعد وفاة اخيه عبدالله بن محمد بن عثمان علم ١١٩٠ ﻫ وبايعه جميع عشيرته
واصحاب الحل والعقد في ممباسة ،

قد علمت فيما تقدم ، ان المزارعة بسطوا ايديهم على جميع البلاد الواقعة بين
ملندي وبَنْغانِ ، وكان من عادتهم ان يولوا الولاة من قبلهم على كل بلدة من البلاد
الداخلة في هذه الحدود من غير انيعزلوا سلاطينها عن سلطنتهم ولا رؤساءها عن
ريلستهم ، واتفق في زمان الوالي احمد بن محمد هذا ، ان عصى سلطان تانغة مَوْنِي
سِمْبا (الكبير) فخرج من طاعة المزارعة واستعد للثورة ، فارسل عامل تانغة الى
ممباسة يخبر الوالي بما اتى به موني سمبا وما عزم عليه ، فجهز الوالي جيشا
لمحاربته واخضاعه ، وأمّر على هذا الجيش ولده عبدالله بن احمد فوصلت السفن التي

تقل هذا الجيش الى جزيرة وَاسين والسلطان عليها الديوان حسن بن ناصر المعروف بالديوان شيخ ، وكان بين الديوان وبين مَوْني سِمْبَا صداقة كالصداقة التي بينه وبين المزارعة ، فلم يستحسن الديوان ان يرى صديقيه يتقاتلان على مرأى ومسمع منه فتقدم الى الامير عبدالله بن احمد فطلب منه ان يؤاجل الحرب ريثما يكلم موني سمبا وينصحه في الرجوع الى الطاعة ، فقبل الامير طلبه ، وتوسط الديوان في الاصلاح وازالة ما كان بين الفريقين من سوء التفاهم ، فتم له ذلك واتى بموني سمبا الى مباسة لاداء الطاعة والاعتذار فعذره الوالي وعفا عنه واحسن اليه ،

وحدث في ولاية احمد فتنة عظيمة في بتة بين آل نبهان وبين اهل لاموء ، وسبب هذه الفتنة كما تقول مخطوطا لاموء التأريخية ، ان بوانة بكار بن بوانة مكو احد سلاطين بتة كان قد تزوج في لاموء وامرأة من سراة اهلها ورُزق له منها بنتان حملهما الى بتة ، فتزوجت احداهما من بباي بن شيخي احد العائلة السلطانية فرزق له منها ابن سماه فُومُ لُوطِ ، ولما تولى سلطنة بتة بوانة مادي اوصى السلطنة بعده لفُومُ لُوطِ بن بَباي هذا ، وانما اوصى بذلك رغبة منه في ازالة البغضاء الذي كانت مستحكمة بين اهل لاموؤ وبين النباهنة ، ولما توفي السلطان بْوَاْنَة مَدِي المذكور خالف اقرباؤه وعشيرته هذه الوصية وبايعوا غير الموصى له (والاقرب انه السلطان محمد بن ابي بكر بن بْوَاْنَة مَلُ) فوقعت ثورة عظيمة ضد هذا السلطان ، وتحزب للموصى له بالسلطة جماعة من النباهنة ، كما تحزب آخرون السلطان المبايع ، ولما بلغ اهل لاموء هذا الخبر سافر بعض اهلها الى بتة لنجدة فوم لوط لما بينهم وبينه من رحم وخؤولة ، فاشتدت الفتنة وخاف اولو الرأي منهم من وخيم العاقبة ، ولا يوجد هناك من يقبل الفريقان قوله ، ويستطيع اخماد جذوة هذه الثورة بسديد رأيه ، فسافر الى مباسة طائفة منهم وعرضوا الامر على الوالي راغبين اليه ان يسافر الى بتة لاطفاء تلك الفتنة واصلاح ذات بين الفريقين ، فسافر اليها واصلح بينهم بما ارضى الجميع ، ورجع اهل لاموء الى بلادهم ، وأقام الوالي في بتة اياما بين حفاوة اهلها وأكرامهم ، ثم اقفل راجعا الى مباسة بعد ان ترك هناك حامية ووؤلفة من خمسمائة جندي وأمّر عليهم الامير عبدالله بن احمد ، واجتاز بلاموء فاستقبله اهلها بالاجلال والاكرام ، وعزموا ان يملّكوه بلادهم خوفا من بطش النباهنة ومنعا

لجورهم وتعديهم عليهم ، وشرعوا في بناء قلعتها على ان يسلموها بعد تمام بنايها ، وهناك تعارف الوالي براشد بن دلهم الشكيلي الجد الثاني لراشد بن سعود احد اعيان ممباسة فرغّبه الوالي في استطان ممباسة فرغب فيه وجهز راشد السفر وجاء الى ممباسة واتخذها وطنا له بدلا من لاموء ،

وفي اثناء اقامة الامير عبدالله بتة ، حصلت بينه وبين سلطانها صداقة متينة لما كان بينهما من توافق المشارب ، لان كل واحد منهما كان شجاعا مقداما محبا للحرب ، فاتفق السلطان مع الامير على مهاجمة لاموء والاستيلاء عليها قهراً ، وقد اختلف الروايات في سبب هذه الحرب ، فالذي رأيناه في مخطوطات لاموء التأريخية ، ان السبب فيها هو ان الوالي احمد بن محمد بعد ان اصلح بين اهل لاموء واهل بتة ورجع هو الى ممباسة ، قبض اهل بتة على فُومُ لُوطِ ذلك الذي أُوصي له بالسلطنة وارسلوه الى ممباسة ، وهناك أمر باعدامه ، وأنَّ اهل لاموء بعد ان اتفقوا مع الوالي على الاتحاد معهم ضد اهل بتة ، خلف هو هذا الاتفاق واتحد مع اهل بتة فارسل الى لاموء رجلا من المزارعة يقال له عبدالله بن زاهر لاستطلاع احوال اهله ، ولما وصل هذا الرجل هيأ له اهل لاموء دارا للنزول فيها غير انه أبى ان يبيت في البلد وبات في سفينته ، فاتهمه اهل لاموء بانه مع النباهنة ، ولاجل الاستطلاع على ما في ضميره ، صنع له بُوَانَة زَاهِد مَغُومِي رئيس اهل لاموء طعاما ارسله اليه ليلا مع رسالة بيد نوتي موهّما له انها من سلطان بتة ، وفيها يستبطئ السلطان هجومه على لاموء ويسيغرب منه ذلك ويحثه على المسارعة فيه ، فاغتر عبدالله بن زاهر وحسب ان الطعام والرسالة من صديقه سلطان بتة ، اذ لا يعلم احد هذا السرّ غيرهما ، فكتب جوابا بيده يقول فيه ان اهل لاموء في بناء القلعة والامر يكون بعد انتهاء بنايها ، وسلم الجواب الى النوتي فاوصله هذا الى بُوَانَة زَهِيدِ ، فلما تبين له ما قصده عبدالله بن زاهر جمع مشانخ لاموء ولطلعهم على الرسالة ، ثم ارسل الى عبدالله بن زاهر ليحضر المجلس ، ولما حضر له اخرج له الرسالة فأقرَّ بانها منه وخجل غاية الخجل فغادر المجلس حالا وطلع سفينته راجعا الى بتة ، وهناك تم الاتفاق مع السلطان على محاربة اهل لاموء ، وبعد ذلك جاء عبدالله بن زاهر بجيش عظيم مشتمل على كثيرين من اهل ممباسة واهل بتة ، ولكنهم انكسروا انكسارا

٢٧

عظيما وانهزموا وولوا ادبارهم هاربين ،

هذا ما ذكره كاتب المخطوطات التأريخية ، ولكن اذا نظرنا فيه لا نرى انه يصلح لان يكون سببا يدعو المزارعة والنباهنة الى محاربة اهل لاموء ، بل بالعكس نرى انه يصلح ان يكون سببا لاغارة اهل لاموء على ممباسة وبتة ، ثم يبعد كل البعدان يحمل عبدالله بن زاهر الذي يزعمون انه مع من في سفينته فقط على اهل لاموء مع كثرتهم وبسالتهم ، (وفُومُ لُوطِ الذي يقولون انه قتل في ممباسة ، فقد ذكرت مخطوطات بتة انه رجع منها واشترك المزارعة معه في حرب ضد اهل بتة والسيد سعيد بن سلطان حتى استولى على سيُ) ومع ذلك فان في هذه الرواية خطأ فاحشا لا يتبين الا للمزارعة انفسهم ولمن مثلهم في الالمام بوقائعهم ، والخطأ المذكور هو نسبة هذه الحادثة الى عبدالله بن زاهر مع ان المسمى بهذا الاسم منهم اثنان لا ثالث لهما ، فاما احدهما فتوفي قبل هذه الواقعة بسنين واما الآخر فلم يتول امارة ولا قاد جيشا ، والمعروف عند المزارعة وجميع رواة الاخبار ان صاحب واقعة شيلة هو عبدالله بن احمد بن محمد بن عثمان ،

وهناك قول آخر في سبب هذه الحرب وهو ما ذكره رواة الاخبار من اهل ممباسة وواسين وتَكَوُنْغ ، من ان الامير عبدالله كان تعاهد مع احمد بن شيخ قبل ان يكون سلطانا ، على مساعدة كل واحد منهما للآخر كلما دعت الحاجة الى المساعدة ، وانه بعد ان تولى احمد بن شيخ طلب من اهل لاموء كِكَنْدَ وهو عندهم عبارة عن عشور المحصولات ، فامتنعوا عن دفعه له لان ذلك لم يكون من عوائدهم مع اسلافه الماضين فعزم على محاربتهم وعاهده الامير عبدالله بن احمد على مساعدته بالحامية التي كانت في بتة تحت امارته ، وبعد ذلك ذهب الامير الى لاموء للتطلع على احوالها وكان من امره ما كان من اطلاع اهلها على سوء نيته فغادرهم قاصدا الى بتة ، وهناك استعدوا للهجوم عليها ، وارسل هو الى اهل لاموء ابياتا من الشعر السواحلي يؤذنهم بالحرب ، ورد عليه اهل من الشعر كذلك يشف عن عقل كبير وسياسة سديدة ، وسنورد هذه الابيات بنصها في الترجمة السواحلية لهذا الكتاب ان شاء الله ،

واما مخطوطات بتة فسكتت عن ابداء شيء من اسباب هذه الحرب ،

واقعة شيلة

وبعد ذلك جهز السلطان احمد بالاشتراك مع الامير عبدالله جيشا كثبفا فيه الكفاية لغلبة اهل لاموء وقهرهم والاستلاء على جزيرتهم ، وشحنوهم في عدة سفن مع العدد الكاملة من مؤن الحرب وآلاتها ، وكان بلاموء في ذلك الزمان حِزبان زيني وسعودي ، واما الحزب الزيني فكان مواليا للمزارعة ومحبا لهم فلم يشترك في هذه الحرب من اول الامر ، ولما وصل الامير بجيشه الى لاموء أنزلهم في شيلة چ وكان اهل لاموء مستعدين لمقاتلتهم الى آخر نسمة من حياتهم ، فاشتبك القتال بين الفريقين ودارت رحى الحرب وحمى الوطيس واشتد الامر على اهل لاموء وتقهقروا الى وراً تلّ هِدائو ، ولما رأى الحزب الزيني اشتداد الامر على مواطنيهم خافوا من الانكسار المفضي الى ذلة الجميع فنقضوا عهدهم واشتركوا مع الحزب السعودي في الدفاع عن وطنهم فترجحت كُفَّتهم وخف جانب المزارعة والنباهنة فكانت الغلبة على المهاجمين وانكسروا وقتل في هذه المعركة من اعيان بتة وحدهم ثمانون نفسا ، ورأيت فيما كتبه مؤرخ لاموء بّوَانة مْشَامُ بن كُومْبُو رحمة الله عليه ، ان عدد القتلى من جانب المزارعة والنباهنة كانوا ثلثمانة نفس لو يزيدون ، ولما رأى الامير عبدالله ما حل بجيشه من كثرة القتل وضعف القوة امر الباقين بالنجاة بانفسهم فتسابقوا الى سفنهم هاربين مغلوبين ومع مبالغة الرواة لعدد قتلى هذه الواقعة لم أقف على اسم واحد ممن قتل من الاعيان فضلا عن غيرهم ، ولا يحفظ المزارعة ان واحدا منهم قتل في تلك الحرب ،

وينسب رواة اهل لاموء سبب انهزام جيش المزارعة والنباهنة الى تأثير السحر الذي عمله لهم شيخ علي احد زعماء لاموء في ذلك الوقت ، ويقولون انه لما رأى شيخ علي اشتداد الامر على اهل لاموء ، دعا بطاسة من نحاس وكتب فيها وفقا وطلاسم ، واخذ بيضة دجاج وكتب عليها الاسماء ، فاعطى الطاسة والبيضة رجلا وأمره ان يضرب بالبيضة اول من صادفه من عسكر العدو وبعد ذلك يضرب بالطاسة ويقصد الى البحر الى ان يصل الماء سرته ، ثم يغمس تلك الطاسة فيه ، ففعل الرجل كما امر ، ولم تمض دقائق الا وعم السحب وامطر مطرا غزيرا في الجانب

الذي فيه العدو فأطفأ فتائل بنادقهم ، ولم يتعد المطر الى جانب اهل لامؤ فكانت بنادقهم تعمل عملها في جيش الاتفاق الثناني ،

هذا ليس بالشىء الذي يعتمد عليه في الاستدلال على الوقائع واستنباط اسبابها ، والذي ادى الى الانهزام ـ فيما أراه ـ هو انضمام الحزب الزيني الى السعودي ، وان الاميراغتر قبل الدخول في هذه الحرب بما علمه من حيادة الحزب الزيني عن المحاربة ، فرأى ان جيشه يكفي لغلبة اهل لامؤ وهم في تلك الحالة ـ حالة الانقسام والتفرُّق ، ولكن الله اراد ان ينصر المظلومين فأَلْهَمَهُمُ الاتحاد والاشتراك في مدافعة عدوهم المهاجم ، ولا يخفى ما في الاتحاد من القوة ، وان كان هناك سبب غيبي يصح ان يسند اليه ذلك الانهزام ، فهو نصر الله الذي وعد به المظلومين ، وتختلف الروايات في تأريخ هذه الواقعة ، فاهل بتة يقولون انها كانت سنة ١٢٢٧ ، ويقول اهل لامؤ انها في ١٢٢٣ ، وليس لاهل مباسة شيء في هذا ، وعندي ان رواية اهل بتة اصح بدليل ارسال السيد الى لامؤ عامله في عام ١٢٢٨ ولا يجوز عقلا ان يتأخر السيد عن ذلك مدة خمس سنين على ما ذهب اليه اهل لامؤ ،

وهنا اقول ان الامير عبدالله عفا الله عنه لم يحسن صنعا بالاشتراك مع سلطان احمد في محاربة اهل لامؤ الذين رضوا بانفسهم ان يملّكوا المزارعة بلادهم ، فاضاع بخرقته وسوء تدبيره تلك الجزيرة التي لو ضُمَّت الى ما كان لهم من البلدان لوصلت مملكتهم الى بتة شمالا ، بل لسهل عليهم الاستلاء على البلاد التي بشمالها الى البنادر ، وهذا الذي اتى به الامير هو الذي الجأ لامؤ الى تمليك السيد سعيد بلادهم خوفا من تعدي النباهنة والمزارعة عليهم وخيرا فعلوا ،

وفي عام ١٢٢٨ استولى السيد سعيد على لامؤ وارسل اليها واليا من قبله هو محمد بن ناصر بن سيف المعولي مع حامية وؤلفة من خمسمائة جندي لحمايتها من سطو المزارعة والنباهنة عليها ، ومحمد بن ناصر هذا اول ولاة لامؤ من قبل السيد سعيد ، ثم تولى بعده احمد بن مفتاح الهناني ثم سيف بن احمد البوسعيد ، ثم غيره غيره ، وآخر ولاة لامؤ من قبل اولاد الامام هو عبدالله بن احمد بن سعيد البوسعيد المتوفي عام ؟ ، ولما انتقلت الحكومة الى ايدي الانكليز نصبوا الولاة من قبلهم ، واول وال لهم على لامؤ هو سيف بن سالم بن خلفان ،

الحرب الاهلية بين الوالي وبين اولاد مسعود

كان الوالي ارسل اولاد مسعود بن ناصر الى الجزيرة للقيام بالحامية التي هناك ، ولما رجعوا الى مباسة لقضاء حوائجهم وزيارة اقاربهم ، اتفق ان مروا ذات يوم بنادٍ للكليفيين بمحلة مَجوَكالي فسلموا على اهله وردوا عليهم السلام ، وكان الشريف سعيد بن عمر زعيم الكليفيين حاضرا فقام لهم ورحب بهم ، ثم سألهم عن ميعاد عودهم الى الجزيرة فأجابوه بانه يكون قريبا ، وخاطبهم متعجبا ومظهرا لمحبتهم قائلا < اتتم ابناء الوالي الاسبق واحق الناس بالولاية ، افما كفى هذا الجالس على الكرسي (يعني الوالي احمد بن محمد) استئثاره بالولاية دونكم حتى رمى بكم الى الجزيرة ؟ فانا لله وانا اليه راجعون > فأثر هذا الكلام في نفوس اولاد مسعود وظنوه صادرا من قلب ممتلئ شفقة عليهم وحنانا ، فثارت الحمية من قلوبهم واجمعوا على ان يثوروا على الوالي ثورة تلجوَه الى التنازل عن الولاية لهم ، فقصدوا القلعة ودخلوا عليه وطالبوه بعزل نفسه ، فسألهم الوالي عن سبب ذلك ، فقالوا ان هذه الولاية متناوبة ، فنوبة لاولاد محمد بن عثمان واخرى لاولاد مسعود بن ناصر ، وقد انقضت نوبة اولاد محمد بن عثمان بتولي عبدالله بن احمد ، وهذه الآن نوبتنا ، فنحن اصحابها واولو الحق بها ، فاجابهم الوالي مخاطبا لهم في لطف < الامر ليس كما تقولون ، بل الولاية خاصة لاولاد محمد بن عثمان وحدهم ، وانما تولى مسعود بن ناصر حين كانوا قاصرين لا يصلحون للولاية ولا يستطيعون ادارتها > ، وبعد هذا خرجوا من عنده نابذين طاعته ، واعانهم على هذا البغي اصحاب الدسائس وجمعوا المقاتلين وذهبوا الى كِلِنْديِن وعسكروا بها ، فأرسل الوالي من ينصحهم في ترك القتال والعود الى الطاعة فلم يقبلوا ، فبعث اليهم بثلَّة من العسكر والتقت الفئتان ودارت الحرب بينهما فكانت الهزيمة في اول الامر لعسكر الوالي فقتل منهم جماعة ومن جملتهم قاسم بن جمعة المعمري وفر الباقون ، ثم عزز الوالي عساكره وارسلهم اليهم فقاتلوهم وغُلب الثائرون وألُقي القبض على بعض رؤساء الفتنة ، وفر اولاد مسعود بن ناصر ، فقصد عبدالله بن مسعمد وسالم بن عبدالله بن زاهر الى رَبَايِ ، وآخرون يمموا نحو دُرُومَة ، واصدر الوالي امره الى جميع الجهات للقبض عليهم ،

ولما كانت رَبَايِ تحت الطوائف التسع ورئيسهم الشريف سعيد المعروف بعداوته

للمزارعة ، وجد الشريف الفرصة سانحة للايقاع باولئك الذين فروا الى هناك ، فأرسل الى رؤساء رَبَاي يأمرهم بقتلهم والاتيان برؤوسهم الى ممباسة ، ولكن اهل رَبَاي لعلمهم بشجاعة اولئك الابطال هابهم ، فأرسلوا الى الشريف يقولون بان هؤلاء لا يُغتال بهم لانهم في كل وقت مستعدون للدفاع عن انفسهم ، فرد عليهم الشريف ان ارقبوا حتى اذا دخلوا في الصلاة فاقتلوهم فيها ، فانتظروا حتى اذا كان وقت الصلاة وأحرموا بها هجموا عليهم في الركوع فقتلوهم وارسلوا الى الشريف يخبرهم (يخبرونه ؟) بذلك وبانهم أتون برؤوسهم فما كان من الشريف الا ان هرع الى الوالي وهو خذلان واخبره بان اهل رَبَاي قبضوا على الجماعة وهاهم أتون بهم عصر هذا اليوم ، فخرج الوالي مع عشيرته لملاقاتهم في مكوبة واذا باهل رَبَاي قد وصلوا وبايديهم زنبيل فيه رؤس اولئك المظلومين فوضعوه بين يدي الوالي ، فسألهم ما هذا فقالوا رؤس اخوانكم الذين امرتنا بقتلهم ، وسألهم عمن ابلغهم هذا الامر ، فقالوا الشريف سعيد ، فحوقل الوالي واسترجع ، وقال لو كنت اريد ان اقتل منهم احدا لقتلت الذين هم تحت ايدينا ، ثم غُسلت الرؤس وكُفنت ودُفنت حيث الآن اطلال قلعة مكوبة ،

هذا ما يرويه اهل ممباسة من قصة قتل اولاد مسعود بن ناصر ، واما اولاد زاهر من اهل تَكَوُنْغُ فهم يؤكدون صدور امر قتلهم من الوالي نفسه ، وانما انكر ذلك خوفا من اللوم والعتاب ، وربما يكون ما قاله اهل تَكَوُنْغُ حقا ، ويشهد له امره بقتل من فر الى دُرُومَة كما يجيء ذلك وعدم معاقبة الوالي الشريف سعيد قرينة دالّة على ذلك ،

واما الذين فروا الى دُرُومَة ، فقبض عليهم زعيم الشِنْغَامِيِّين مْوِنْي هِيجَة بن فَاكِ وارسل الى الوالي يخبره بذلك ، فأمره بقتلهم ، ولكن الزعيم مْوِنْي هِيجَة رأى ان في قتلهم نقضا للعهد الذي التزمه الطوائف الثلاث على انفسهم من عدم سفك دماء المزارعة كما التزمت المزارعة مثل ذلك على انفسهم في المعاهدة التي عقدها علي بن عثمان ، وجمع مْوِنْي هِيجَ اقاربه وعشيرته واطلعهم على رأيه فوافقوه عليه ، وجاءوا بالاسرى في جمع عظيم من اهل شَنْغَامْوِي ودُرُومَة وهم ينشدون رجزا سواحليا مفاده ‹ شنغاموي بحرٌ هادئٌ لا تنكسر السفينة بساحله › ولما وصلوا الى القلعة قدم الاسرى الى الوالي قائلا له ‹ هؤلاء عشيرتك جئنا بهم احياء ، فان عفوت عنهم

فاخوانك وان قتلتهم فانت ولي امرهم ، واما نحن الطوائف الثلاث فلا تستطيع ايدينا اراقة دماء المزارعة > ، فاعتقلهم الوالي ثم عفا عنهم ،

ولوفاء الطوائف الثلاث لعدهم (لعهدهم ؟) للمزارعة ، كان الوالي احمد يوصي عشيرته بهم خيرا ، وان يلجؤا الى الجهات التي تحت نفوذهم كلما اضطروا الى الالتجاء ، وكان يحرزهم من الطوائف التسع خصوصا الكليفيين منهم ومن ان يقصدوا الى الجهات التي تحت امرهم ، اقول ــ لقد كان ذلك كذلك في ايام دولة المزارعة ، ولكن بعد ان زالت دولتهم صار الطوائف التسع كالثلاث في موالاة المزارعة ومصادقتهم ، ويدل على ذلك ما اتى به خميس كُومْبُو واولاده وعشيرته من موازرة مبارك بن راشد ومصاحبتهم له في ثورته الاخيرة وتناسوا كل ما جرى بين أبائهم في ايام دولة المزارعة من العداوة والاحن ،

وبعد مدة تبين للوالي ان كل ما فعله اولاد مسعود انما كان بدسائس الشريف سعيد وجماعته ، فعزله عن المشيخة وسحبها من الطوائف التسع وطلب منهم ان يختاروا من غيرهم من يكون زعيما لهم ، فوقع الاختيار على احمد بن شيخ الملندي (الصغير) ، وكان حينئذ في بْوَاغَ مُوْيُو او بَنْغَان ، فذهبوا اليه وجاؤا به فقلده الوالي مشيخة اهل ممباسة ،

توفي الوالي رحمه الله في ربيع الاول عام ١٢٢٩ وخلف من الاولاد الذكور احد عشر وهم سالم ومبارك وعبدالله وصالح وسليمان وخميس وعثمان وعاصم ومحمد وراشد وسعيد ، ومن نسله يتألف بيت احمد من المزارعة الذي منه مبارك بن راشد المشهور بوقائعه ،

****

الوالي السابع

عبدالله بن احمد بن محمد بن عثمان بن عبدالله المزروعي

ولايته ـ قتل كُومْبُو رئيس الوَدِيغُو لسعيد بن عبدالله البحري ـ تجهيز الوالي جيشا
لمحاربة كُومْبُو ـ توسط الديوان السيد احمد بن علوي في الاصلاح بين كُومْبُو والمزارعة
ـ تسليم كُومْبُو دية القتيل واعتذاره الى الوالي ـ حدوث مجاعة في دُرُومَة ـ مساعدة
الوالي لاهلها ـ حكاية المستر هبلي مع شيخ من اهل دُرُومَة ـ ابتداء الحرب بين السيد
سعيد والمزارعة ـ تعيين مبارك بن احمد واليا على بتة ـ تولي فُومُ لُوطِ سلطنة بتة ـ
شكايته من المزارعة الى السيد سعيد ـ رسالة السيد سعيد الى الوالي بالكف عن اهل
بتة ـ ارسال الوالي اليه درعا وقدرا وميقافا ـ الشاعر بْوَانَة مُيَاكَ وتنبؤه للحرب ـ
وصول جيش السيد سعيد الى بتة ـ الحرب بينه وبين المزارعة ـ استيلاء جيش السيد
على بتة ـ اهل لاموء يشيرون على الامير حماد بمهاجمة الجزيرة ـ حرب المزارعة مع
جيش السيد سعيد في بِرْكاو وشْوَاكَة من الجزيرة ـ سقوط الجزيرة في يد السيد
سعيد ـ وفاة الوالي ،

بعد ان توفي الوالي احمد بن محمد في عام ١٢٢٩ ، تولى ابنه عبدالله بن احمد
بن محمد بن عثمان ، ولم يجد من يعارضه في هذه الولاية من اخوته الكثيرين ، لما
كانوا يعرفون فيه من الحنكة والكفاءة ، فولاه اخوته واهل الحل والعقد من عشيرته
وزعماء الطوائف جميعا ، وجاءه الوفود من جميع الجهات يهنئونه بالولاية ويبايعونه على
الطاعة ،

وكان اول ما شرع فيه تقوية الجيش باعداد الاسلحة وتعيين القواد المدرَّبين ،
ونصب الولاة الاكفاء في الاطراف ، وممن نصب من الولاة سعيد بن عبدالله بن
مسعود البُحري الجد الثاني لصديقنا العالم علي بن حميد بن عبدالله البحري صاحب
تاَنْغَة ، فقد عينه الوالي واليا على مَتَنْغَاتَة ، ثم ان هذا الوالي سافر في بعض الايام
من ممباسة قاصدا الى محل ولايته في سفينة صغيرة ، ولما حاذى فُنْزِي حصل

٤٤

بالسفينة تعطيل اضطره الى الدخول الى هناك لاصلاحه ، واتفق ان كان بالقرب من الشاطئ كُوبُو مَوككَنَغَا رئيس الوَديغو وسلطانهم ، وكان كُوبُو هذا مغرما بسفك الدماء ومعجبا بقوته وكثرة اتباعه ، وبينما كان متمشيا مع بعض حاشيته ، اذ ابصر سعيد بن عبدالله من بعد وهو مشتغل مع بحارة السفينة في اصلاحها ، فرماه بسهم فاصاب مقتله وسقط على الارض ، وبذل البحارة الجهد في اسعافه ومعالجته ولكن لم تمض مدة حتى فاضت روحه وقضى نحبه ، واشتغل البحارة في اتمام اصلاح السفينة بسرعة وحملوه الى وَاسِين حيث دفن هناك في احتفال عظيم ،

ورجعت السفينة الى ممباسة واخبر بحارتها الوالي بالامر فحزن عليه واغاظه ما اتى به ذلك الزنجي من الجناية العظيمة وعزم على تأديبه ومعاقبته ، فبعث عسكرا لقتاله امّر عليهم عمّه سليمان بن علي بن عثمان وزوده برسالة الى الديوان السيد احمد بن علوي يأمره فيها بامداد العسكر بالذخيرة ومساعدتهم بكل ما يحتاجون اليه من الادلاء والعيون ، واوصى عمه بدخول وَاسِين اولا وتسليم الرسالة الى الديوان والاخذ برأيه فيما يشير عليه ، ولما وصل الامير الى وَاسِين مع عسكره قدم الرسالة الى الديوان ، وبعدما قرأها وعلم ما عزم عليه الوالي عظم عليه الامر وتحير ولم يدر ماذا يفعل ازاء هذه المعضلة ، لانه رئيس الوَديغُو الروحي من جانب ، وصديق حميم للمزارعة من جانب آخر ، فاذا اعان جيش المزارعة على الوَديغُو اضاع رياسته عليهم ولا يبعد ان يعادوه وهو لا طاقة له عليهم ، واذا خالف امر الوالي خاصمه المزارعة واتهموه بموالاة عدوهم ضدهم ، وهذا اشد عليه من ذلك ، فاستمهل الديوان الامير سليمان بن علي ايّاما ريثما يظهر له من الرأي ما يخلصه من عداوة الجانبين ، وعِيل صبر الامير من طول الامهال وعزم على الاقدام على مهاجمة الوَديغُو ولكنه ادرك خطأً رأيه اذ ربما يكون في اقدامه هذا ما يسيء الديوان فيضيع على نفسه ما يأمله منه من الامداد والمساعدة ، وفوق ذلك يكون مخالفا لامر الوالي ، ثم ظهر له رأي آخر فجمع اعيان البلد في بيت الديوان واطلعهم بالذي جاء من اجله وانه عازم على الاقدام عليه فقال الديوان مخاطبا له < قد علمنا ما عزمت عليه ولكن لا يغب عن ذهنك ان مهاجمتكم لهذه الطائفة غير مضمون النجاح والحرب سجال يوم لك ويوم عليك ولا يدري الانسان عاقبتها ، فاذا فزت فهو المطلوب والا فيزيد اعجاب

هذا الزنجي بنفسه ويحمله ذلك على ازدراءنا جميعا ، والرأي عندي ان نسعى في الاصلاح بينكم وبينه ونرده الى طاعة الوالي فيكون عونا لكم في المستقبل لا عليكم ، وفي ذلك تحصيل لمرادكم منه من دون ايقاد نار الحرب التي لا يعلم الا الله عاقبة امرها › ، فوافقه كل من كان في المجلس على هذا الرأي السديد واستصوبَه الامير سليمان بن علي فافتض المجلس على ذلك ،

ثم خرج الديوان ومعه السيد علي بن احمد بن ابي بكر والسيد ابو بكر بن احمد وغيرهم من رؤساء جزيرة وَأَسِين قاصدين الى كُوبُو ، ولما وصل الديوان هناك استغرب كُوبُو وقومه من وصول هذا الرجل العظيم اليهم وليس من عادة الديوان الخروج من داره فضلا عن الخروج من بلده ، وساله كُوبُو عما جاء لاجله وعن الذي اداه الى تحمل مشقة السفر اليه ، فما كان من الديوان الا ان رمى بعمامته على الارض وجعل يبكي وبكى معه من تبعه من الاشراف ، ثم قال لكُوبُو › انك قد أتيت امرا عظيما بقتلك ذلك العربي والآن قد وصل جيش العرب الى وَأَسِين واتهمونا بالمشاركة معكم في هذه الجناية فألقوا القبض على فلان وفلان وفلان (وعد له رؤساء الاشراف الذين بينه وبينهم صداقة) ولا ينجينا من هذه التهمة ويخلصنا من حرب العرب الا اذا سلمتم دية القتيل واعترفتم بجنايتكم واعتذرتم الى الوالي بما فعلتم ، واذا امتنعتم من هذا فالعرب لا محالة يقتلوننا نحن واياكم جميعا ، فلم يصدق كُوبُو هذا الخبر بادئ ذي بدء وظن ان في الامر خديعة ، فحلف له الديوان بالايمان المغلظة عندهم فدخل في قلبه صِدقه وعلم ان الذي قتله ليس من آحاد الناس ، وحينئذ ندم على ما كان منه وامر بسوق خمسة وعشرين عبدا واثني عشر عاجا يرسل ذلك الى الوالي دية للرجل الذي قتله من غير ان علم انه من اعيان العرب الذين تهتمَّ بامرهم الدولة نفسها ، ولكن الديوان لم يكتفِ بهذا بل ألزمه على الشخوص معه الى وَأَسِين والذهاب مع الامير سليمان بن علي الى مباسة للاعتذار الى الوالي نفسه ، فرضي كُوبُو بذلك وجاءوا الى وَأَسِين وسلم الديوان الدية الى الامير ، والتمس الامير من الديوان ان يرافقهم الى مباسة لما في ذلك من تطمين قلب كُوبُو فوافقه على ذلك وسافروا الى مباسة ، وهناك عرض الديوان الدية على الوالي وأحضر كُوبُو عنده وطلب له العفو منه فعفا عنه ،

في ايام ولاية عبدالله بن احمد هذا ، اصاب ارض دُرُومة مجاعة شديدة أتلفت كثيرين من اهلها ، فنزح الى ممباسة جماعات منهم طلبا لما يسد الرمق من القوت ، فعطف عليهم الوالي ومأنهم وارسل عائلات كثيرة من اهل دُرُومة الى الجزيرة الخضراء وأمر واليها برعايتهم ، فمكثوا في الجزيرة منعمين متمتعين بخيرتها الكثيرة الى ان ذهبت المجاعة من ارضهم فرجعوا الى ممباسة ، هذه الخصلة التي اتى بها الوالي لم يسبق اليها احد من الولاة قبله ، وهي ـ بلا شك ـ منقبة عظيمة في حقه ودليل واضح على عطفه لرعاياه ،

يُحكَى ان المستر هبلي الذي كان واليا على ممباسة كان يجول في ارض دُرُومة ، فلقي في بعض احيانها رجلا طاعنا في السن فجلس اليه وساله ما هي اعدل الحكومتين وأرأفها برعاياها ، اهي الحكومة العربية او انكليزية ؟ فقال له الشيخ ‹ لا ادري اي الحكومة العربية (حكومة عربية ؟) تعنيها لانه قد تعاقبت على هذه البلاد حكومتان عربيتان حكومة المزارعة وحكومة آل بوسعيد › ، فقال هبلي ‹ اعنيهما جميعا عند المقارنة بينهما وبين الحكومة الانكليزية › ، وكان رجؤه ان يسمع من ذلك الشيخ جور العرب وقساوتهم على رعاياهم ، ولكن جاء الامر على خلاف ظنه ، فقال له الشائب ‹ ارأف حكومة من هذه الحكومات هي حكومة المزارعة › ، فساله هبلي ‹ لماذا ؟ › فحكى له حكاية المجاعة المذكورة ، فتعجب المستر هبلي مما اتى به الوالي عبدالله بن احمد وعده من غرائب الامور اذ ما يصدر مثل هذا العطف والحنان ـ على اعتقاده ـ الا من صدور الاورباويين ،

ابتداء الحرب بين السيد سعيد وبين المزارعة

قد علمت من الوقائع التي جرت في ايام الوالي احمد بن محمد ان عبدالله بن احمد هذا كان اميرا على الحامية المزروعية في بتة وقائد للجيش الذي ذهب لمحاربة لاموء ، وصديقا حميما للسلطان احمد بن شيخ النبهاني ، فكان له في صدور اهل بتة اجلال ومهابة ، ولما رجع الى ممباسة وتوفي والده وقام هو خلفا له في الولاية ارسل اخاه مبارك بن احمد الى بتة اميرا على الحامية كالعادة المتَّبعة فيمن كان قبله ، وبقي المزارعة في بتة ولهم ذلك النفوذ الذي خوَّله لهم المعاهدة التي

٤٧

تمت بينهم وبين اهلها من زمان الوالي مسعود بن ناصر ، ولما توفي السلطان احمد بن شيخ وخلفه قُومُ لُوطِ بن بُوَانَة مَدي اساءه نفوذ المزارعة في مملكته واراد التخلص منهم ، وكان في النباهنة حزبان حزب على رأي السلطان ، وآخر موالٍ للمزارعة لا يريد لهم بديلا ، فاتفق السلطان مع من وافقه في رأيه على ان يملكوا السيد سعيد بلادهم اذ هو الرجل الوحيد الذي يقدر على مقاومة المزارعة ، فأرسل اليه يقر له بملك بتة ، ويشتكي اليه تعدي المزارعة عليهم ، فبعث السيد رسالة الى الوالي عبدالله بن احمد يحذّره فيها من تعدّيه على اهل بتة ، فاغاظ الوالي هذا التحذير وتدخل السيد سعيد فيما بينه وبين اهل بتة خُلفاء المزارعة فكان جواب الوالي ان ارسل الى السيد بيد حسين بن علي بن عانش الجنيبي درعا وقدرا وميقافا ، يرمز بذلك الى انه ان كان رجل حرب فليتدرع وينزل في ميدان القتال ، وقيل ارسل اليه شينا من البارود ومُدًا فارغا ،

علم اهل ممباسة بما فعله الوالي فاستاءوا منه وأيقنوا بالحرب العاجلة ، واصبحت هذه الواقعة حديث القوم في انديتهم ، وكان بممباسة في ذلك الوقت بُوَانَة مُيَاكَا بن حاج الغسّاني الشاعر السواحلي المجيد وصاحب الفراسة الصائبة ، وقصد الناس الى ناديه وسألوه عما عسى ان يكون عاقبة تلك الفعلة التي فعلها الوالي ، فأطرق ساعة ثم رفع رأسه وانشد بيتين من الشعر يقول فيها ما ترجمتهما حرفيا ـ

قد غاص الجنيبي ناصب الفخ في البحار
فاذا خرج منها حصل بممباسة أمر عظيم
فأخبروا أهل القرى أن لا يمكثوا معجبين
ففي اول الصيف لتكن قرون البارود في الحصر

_____

ففي اول الصيف حينما يهبّ هبوبه
ترون البزاة اسود رأس الخيمة

_____

وما كاد يدخل صيف عام ١٢٣٨ الا واسطول السيد سعيد قد رسا في مياه مُتَنْغَ وَنْدَ وهو مؤلَّف من ثلاثين سفينة مملوءة باربعة آلاف جندي وعليهم الامير حماد بن احمد البوسعيدي ، وعسكروا هناك ، وأرسل قائد هذا الجيش الى الامير

مبارك بن احمد رسالة يأمره بالتسليم ويؤذنه بالحرب اذا امتنع من ذلك ، ولما وصل الى الامير مبارك هذه الرسالة ، جمع عساكره واستعد للحرب ، ولكن لم يكن لديه من القوة ما يعادل عُشر ما جاء به الامير حماد ، وفضلا عن ذلك فان اكثر الناس قد انحازوا الى جانب السيد لما هالهم من كثرة العَدَد والعدو ، ولم يبق ممن يعتمد عليه من انصاره سوى جنوده المباسيين ، وعلم الامير مبارك انه مغلوب لا محالة ومع ذلك لم ير ان يستسلم للعدو وينقاد له بدون تحكيم السيف بينه وبينهم ، فالتقى الجيشان وخاضَ مبارك غمار تلك الحرب ببسالته المعهودة ، فتقهقر جيش السيد الى الوراء ، ثم اعادوا الكرة عليه فهزمهم ثانيا هزيمة منكرة ، ولما رأى الامير حماد ما حل بجيشه طلب من اهل بتة ان يحتالوا على الامير مبارك حتى يغادر بتة ففعلوا ، وسافر راجعا الى ممباسة هو وعدد لا يزيد على ستين رجلا من جنوده ، وبما أتوه من الحيلة أمكن للامير حماد ان يستولي على بتة بعد انهزام جيشه مرتين في وجه مبارك بن احمد ، ذكر ذلك القبطان فيدال في رحلته نقلا عمن شاهد هذه الوقائع بعيني رأسه ،

ولم يمكث الامير حماد في بتة الا قليلا ثم تهيأ للسفر الى ممباسة ولما اجتاز بلاموء واجتمع بزعماء اهلها اشاروا عليه بمهاجمة الجزيرة الخضراء اولا ، وأخبروه انها المخزن الوحيد لمؤن المزارعة ومصدر ثروتهم ، وانه اذا استولى عليها فتَّ على عضدهم وسهل عليه مهاجمة ممباسة ، اخذ الامير برأيهم الصائب وسافر حتى اذا حاذى ممباسة اطلق مدفعا ، وكان المزارعة يعلمون بامره من قبل وقد استعدوا للمدافعة غاية الاستعداد ، واذا المراكب قد دارت وتوجهت نحو الجزيرة ،

الحرب في الجزيرة الخضراء

وصل اسطول السيد الى الجزيرة على حين غفلة ، ولم يكن المزارعة الذين فيها عالمين بالامر فيستعدوا له ، وكان بها من الامراء سالم بن احمد وعبدالله بن سعيد بن خميس وسعيد بن على الهناوي فأنزل الامير حماد عساكره في بِركَاو وقابلهم عساكر المزارعة ، ودام القتال بينهم اياما وسالت دماء الفريقين انهارا واخيرا انتصر الامير حماد واستولى على الجزيرة ، فبلغ ذلك الوالي عبدالله فجهز جيشا آخر أمَّر

عليه اخاه الامير مبارك بن احمد والي بتة سابقا وسافر بجيشه ومعه السيد احمد بن ابي بكر البَعَلَوي من شجعان سادة اهل وَاسِين ، على رجاء استرداد الجزيرة وانتزاعها من يد الامير حماد ، فنازلوا عساكر السيد في شوَاكَة واتقدت نار الحرب بينهم فخسر الفريقان عددا ليس بالقليل من القتلى والجرحى ، وأبلى الامير مبارك بلاء حسنا وأظهر من الشجاعة ما أثبت له بحق مدح اهل هذه البلاد وثنائهم ، فألفت في مدحه القصائد دامت متداولة بين الاهالي الى مدى غير بعيد ، وذلك ما سلّى هذا الباسل وبرّد أوام قلبه الحزين ، ومع ما أبلاه جيش المزارعة في الدفاع عن جزيرتهم غلب عليهم تلك القوات الهائلة التي جلبها السيد سعيد فانتصر جيشه ثانيا انتصارا باهرا وتملك الجزيرة رغم ايثار اهلها لحكومة المزارعة على حكومة آل البوسعيد ، ورجع الامير مبارك الى مباسة كاسف البال وأخبر اخاه بما جرى من امر الجزيرة فحزن الوالي حزنا عميقا أثر في قلبه فمات كمدا ،

وكان خروج الجزيرة من ايدي المزارعة من اقوى الاسباب التي ساعدت السيد على انتزاع الملك من أيديهم ، وظهر صواب ما أشار به على اهل لاموء على الامير حماد ، توفي الوالي رحمة الله عليه في ١٣ رمضان عام ١٢٣٨ وخلف ابنا واحدا وهو خميس بن عبدالله ،

****

الوالي الثامن

سليمان بن علي بن عثمان بن عبدالله بن محمد المزروعي

ولايته ـ ارساله الوفد الى مُمّبَي لطلب الحماية من الحكومة البريطانية ـ وصول القبطان
فيدال الى مباسة ـ الملازم بوتلر واجتماعه بالوالي ـ المباحثة في سئلة الحماية ـ ضيافة
الوالي للقبطان فيدال ـ رفع العلم الانكليزي على سارية القلعة ـ وصول القبطان اوين ـ
معاهدة الحماية ـ تعيين الملازم الثالث المستر ريتز وكيلا لحكومته في مباسة ـ عبدالله
بن سليم قائد جيش السيد سعيد ونزوله الى مباسة ـ الامير مبارك بن احمد مع
القبطان اوين الى الجزيرة ـ عزل الوالي عن الولاية ،

بعد وفاة الوالي عبدالله بن احمد اختلف اخوته فيمن يكون واليا بعده ، وكل
اراد الولاية لنفسه وكادوا يقتتلون عليها ، ثم اتفقوا اخيرا على تولية عمّهم سليمان
بن علي بن عثمان الذي كان سابقا واليا على الجزيرة الخضراء ، فولُّوه في ١٢
شوال عام ١٢٣٨ ، وكان سليمان عاقلا حاذقا محبا للسلام ، ولما رأى سقوط الجزيرة
في يد السيد سعيد واسداد مخرج المؤن الذي كان المزارعة يعتمدون عليه في
حروبهم ، وشعر بضعف عن مقاومة عدوهم كما ينبغي ، عزم على الاحتماء ببريطانيا
العظمى لمصلحة حفظ النفوس وايقاف الحرب واطفاء الفتنة بينهم ، وبين السيد سعيد
بن سلطان ، شاور الوالي اولي الرأي من جماعته وزعماء الطوائف في هذا الامر
فوافقوه عليه وسددوا رأيه ، وفعلا اختار خميس بن ناصر ومحمد بن عبدالله بن
محمد باشيخ جد آل باشيخ الذين في مباسة وآخرين معهما وارسلهم وفدا الى
مُمّبَي لمفاوضة حكومة الهند في ادخال بلادهم تحت حماية الحكومة البريطانية ، وقابلوا
اولي الامر هناك وعرضوا عليهم المسئلة ووعدوهم بابلاغها الى الدوائر المختصة وارسال
الجواب اليهم فيما بعد ،

بعد سفر الوفد ببضعة اشهر وصل الى مباسة القبطان فيدال في بارجته
< بَرَكُوتَة > ورست في مياه مباسة عشية يوم ٢٧ من ربيع الاول سنة ١٢٣٩ ، ولما

كان الوقت ليلا لم يتمكن القبطان من الاجتماع باهل البلد ، وفي صباح اليوم الثاني ذهب الامير مبارك بن احمد ومعه ست وعشرون رجلا لمقابلة القبطان واداء التحية له باسم عمه الوالي سليمان بن علي ، وفي هذه المقابلة عرض عليه حال البلاد وعزم اهلها على ادخالها في حماية جلالة ملك الانكليز ، ثم طلب منه باسم عمه الاذن في رفع العلم الانكليزي على القلعة ، ولما كانت هذه المسئلة تستلزم التفكر فيها ، اتفقا على تأخيرها الى اليوم الثاني ، ولكن اصبح القبطان فيه مريضا ، فأرسل بالنيابة عنه الملازم بوتلر ، وهنا اترك مجال القول للملازم المذكور ليحكي لنا ما جرى بينه وبين الوالي وما شاهده بعينه حسبما هو مذكور في رحلة القبطان اوين ، قال الملازم ـ

> بعد ما نزلت مكثت قليلا انتظر ابن أخي الشيخ ، واذا هو قد وصل بصحبة جمع من العرب ، وذهبوا بي الى القلعة ، وهناك انتظرنا الشيخ واهل مجلسه ، ولاحظنا صور أولئك العرب فاذا هي تدل على تعب ويؤس وان كانت اسلحتهم محلاة بزينة ، هؤلاء هم الذين استطاعوا ايقاف بلايا البرتغال حين محاولتهم لامتلاك ارض السواحل وهم في كمال قوتهم ، وهم هم الذين يقاومون اليوم قوات امام مسقط ، قوم لا يقصرون في الدفاع عن شرفهم غير انه قد زادت قوة العدو عليهم وأخذت قوتهم في النقصان حتى كادوا يذوقون ذل العبودية ، وهنا اقول ان اهل ممباسة (يعني بهم المزارعة) وان كانوا قد فقدوا قوتهم واغتصبت بلادهم فهم محترمون من جميع من في البلاد السولحلية ،

> دخلنا على الشيخ فرأيته رجلا طويل القامة نحيف الجسم ازدادت شيخوخته من عظم ما تكبَّده من الهموم ، ومع ذلك لم تزل صورته تنم عن لطف ، وقبل ان ننتقل الى خلوة اضطررنا الى انتظار شيخ السواحليين الامير الملندي (لعله احمد بن شيخ الملندي زعيم اهل ممباسة) وبعد مدة يسيرة دخل هذا الشيخ وحياه الحاضرون وصافحني ببشاشة وحياني باللغة البرتغالية المكسَّرة ثم جلس بوقار ، وصورته تدل على ذكاء وعقل وهو في السن الخامسة والستين قصير القامة نحيف الجسم حسن الخلق ، لبس جوخا اخضر ووضع على رأسه عمامة ،

> وبعد ذلك انتقلنا الى غرفة أخرى مع بعض الاعيان وأغلق الباب ووضعت مسئلة الحماية على بساط البحث ، وشرع الشيخ يوضح لي كراهية اهل ممباسة من

امتلاك الاجنبيين لبلادهم وهم اهل أنفة وشرف ، وقال ان مما يؤلم القلب ان يصبحوا مظلومين وتداس حقوقهم تحت الاقدام وتتلف ارواحهم في المدافعة عنها ، لانه ما من قطعة من الارض امتلكها امام مسقط دون ان يدافعوا عنها بكل ما أوتيهم من الشجاعة والاقدام ، والآن بعدما زادت قوة العدو علينا صار الرجاء في حفظ نفوسنا ضعيفا ، وهذا هو السبب الذي دعانا بأجمعنا الى وضع بلادنا هذه تحت ايدي الانكليز ، وهم وان كانوا مخالفين لنا في العادة والعقيدة الا انهم لا يعجزون عن مساعدة المظلومين ورفع شأن الحرية ، >

قال الملازم > اسبابهم كانت جديرة بالالتفات لان طلبهم الحرية كان صادرا من اعماق قلوبهم ، حتى لم اتمالك من الترحم عليهم ، > قال > وبعدما انتهى الشيخ من خطبته طلب مني ان ارفع العلم الانكليزي على سارية القلعة ، فامتنعت من ذلك حسب الامر الذي تلقيته من القبطان فيدال ، ولكن عاهدتهم على ارسال عرائضهم سريعا الى مُمْبَيْ ، وفي اليوم الثاني نزلنا مع القبطان فيدال فقصدنا الى القلعة لزيارة الوالي ، واجتمعنا باعيان البلد هناك ، وبعد انفضاض المجلس دعانا الى منزله لتناول الطعام وكنّا اربعة ، القبطان فيدال وابن أخي الشيخ وزعيم السواحليين وانا الرابع ، ثم ودّعناهم وذهبنا ، >

وبعد ان سافر القبطان فيدال خشي المزارعة ان يفاجئهم مراكب السيد سعيد التي كانت يرجى وصولها عن قريب وهم غير مستعدين لمقاومة تلك القوات الهائلة التي بلغهم خبر اعداد السيد سعيد لها لسحقهم ، وقد اضعفهم خروج الجزيرة من ايديهم ، فرفعوا على القلعة الراية البريطانية وان لم يؤذن لهم في ذلك طلبا لسلامة نفوس كثيرين من رعاياهم ، وبعد مدة وصل جيش السيد بقيادة عبدالله بن سليم ، وتحير لما رأى العلم الانكليزي فكف عن هجومه واكتفى بالحصار البحري ،

وفي ٦ جمادى الآخرة ١٢٣٩ وصل القبطان اوين وأبصر الراية الانكليزية تخفق على سارية القلعة ورأى حول جزيرة مباسة مراكب السيد سعيد محاصرة لها ، وبعد دخوله مباسة ، نزل الملازم الثالث المستر ريتز ، ومعه الترجمان فحُيّي باطلاق خمس مدافع ، وذهب الى القلعة لتحية الوالي ، ثم رجع الى بارجته يشيّعه الامير مبارك بن احمد ، وعلم الملازم من اخبار مباسة ان المزارعة جمعوا نحوا من خمسة وعشرين

الف جندي لاسترداد الجزيرة غير انه لا مراكب في الحال تقل هؤلاء الرجال اليها لغرق اكثر سفنهم في واقعتي الجزيرة ، واستيلاء العدو على باقيها ،

معاهدت الحماية

في صباح اليوم الثاني نزل القبطان اوين واستقبله الرؤساء واعيان البلد وذهبوا به الى القلعة ، وكان في انتظاره اعضاء المجلس ، وبعد مبادلة التحية اعترف الوالي له برفع العلم الانكليزي من دون اذن ، وأبدى له الاسباب الحاملة له على ذلك فأعذره القبطان ، ثم طلب الوالي منه قبول ادخال ممباسة وسائر بلاده الواقعة بين رأسْغُمين ونهر بَنْغان تحت حماية الدولة الانكليزية ، فقبل القبطان اوين ذلك بشرط التزام إبطال النخاسة من جميع هذه البلاد ، فالتزم الوالي هذا الشرط كما التزم القبطان اوين عن دولته ان يرد الى الوالي ما اغتصبه العدو من بلاده ، وحالا أبرمت معاهدة الحماية بين الطرفين وهي مشتملة على ست موادٍ وهي هذه ـ

١ ـ ان تعيد بريطانيا العظمى الى والي ممباسة جميع ما يملكه من البلاد قبل ،

٢ ـ ان يدير السلطنة زعيم المزارعة وتكون وراثية في نسله ،

٣ ـ ان يقيم وكيل الحكومة الحامية مع الوالي ،

٤ ـ ان يقسم العشور بين المتعاهدَيْن على السواء ،

٥ ـ ان يؤذن لرعايا بريطانيا بالاتجار في المالك الداخلية ،

٦ ـ ان تبطل تجارة الرقيق في ممباسة ،

ولتحقيق موادّ هذه المعاهدة أقيم الملازم الثالث لبارجة ليفن المستر جون جمس ريتز وكيلا لبريطانيا العظمى في ممباسة ، وعين المستر جورج فيلبس قائدا للعسكر يعاونه ثلاثة من الانكليز ،

وبعد ان أبرمت هذه المعاهدة ، وعلم بها عبدالله بن سليم قائد جيش البوسعيد ، امر بادخال السفن الى البندر ونزل هو الى البلد وتلقاه اخوانه المزارعة بالترحاب ، وأعجبه ما تم بينهم وبين الانكليز من المعاهدة التي وضعت عن كاهله إصر الحرب وتعباتها ،

وفي ١١ من الشهر المذكور سافر القبطان اوين قاصدا الى الجزيرة يصحبه الامير مبارك بن احمد ومعه خمسون رجلا من رجاله ، هذا كل ما وقفنا عليه من الحوادث التي جرت في زمان سليمن بن علي ذلك الوالي الوديع المحب للسلام ، وفي

السنة الثالثة من ولايته اتفق اولاد احمد بن محمد بن عثمان على خلعه فخلعوه ،
وقصد الجزيرة الخضراء وأقام بها وتوفي فيها رحمة الله عليه ، لم يذكر المتقدمون
سبب خلع الوالي ، ولكن الذي يظهر هو ميله الشديد الى السلام وتهاونه في سبيل
الوصول اليه حتى خشي اولاد احمد بن محمد استسلامه للعدو اذا بقي في الولاية ،
والله اعلم بحقيقة الحال ، خلف الوالي ابنه الوحيد احمد ولم يعقب فانقطع نسله ،

****

الوالي التاسع

سالم بن احمد بن محمد بن عثمان بن عبدالله المزروعي

توليته ــ ميمية العلامة محيي الدين في تهنئته ــ وصول القائد كرستيان واجتماعه باهل البلد في بيت مري الانكليزي ــ انتهاء حماية بريطانيا للمزارعة ــ المستر لين يبدي السبب الحقيقي في تخلص بريطانيا عن هذه الحماية ــ هجوم السيد سعيد لاول مرة على ممباسة ــ بابُ كَافِي بن مَوشَافِي واستثاره الحماسة في القلوب ــ الحرب بين الفريقين ــ المفاوضة السرية بين السيد وعبدالله بن زاهر في شأن الصلح ــ استمالة عبدالله بن زاهر لقلب الوالي الى قبول الصلح ــ معاهدة الصلح ــ نقض السيد سعيد للمعاهدة ــ ناصر بن سليمان واساءته للمزارعة ــ القتال بينه وبينهم ــ حصار المزارعة للقلعة ــ ارسال السيد هلال الميرة لمساعدة من في القلعة ــ شجاعة كِيَاتي بن مَونْي أُوفِي واستيلاؤه على سفينة الميرة ــ ناصر بن سليمان ينادي بالامان ــ القبض عليه وقتله ــ لامية العلامة محيي الدين في واقعة حصار القلعة ــ هجوم السيد للمرة الثانية على ممباسة ــ انهزام جيشه وخسارته ــ بناء سور البلد وقلعة مكوبة ــ الحرب الاهلية في سِيُو ونجدة الوالي لاهلها ضد السيد ــ هجوم السيد للمرة الثالثة على ممباسة ــ واقعة شَاغَة ــ محاولة المزارعة لاسترداد الجزيرة وفشلهم ــ القبض على مَونْي سِمْبَا سلطان تَانْغَة ــ تأسيس راشد بن سالم لبلدة تَكَوُنْغُ ــ وفاة الوالي رحمة الله عليه ،

بعد خلع الوالي سليمان بن علي اختار اولاد احمد بن محمد بن عثمان اخاهم سالما فولوه الحكم وبايعوه في اواسط عام ١٢٤١ وبايعه سائر العرب وزعماء الطوائف الاثنتي عشرة ، وجاءه رؤساء الزنوج يبايعونه على الطاعة ، وبلغ خبر توليته الى العلامة محيي الدين بن شيخ القحطاني وكان في مَتَّنْغَاتَة من اعمال تَانْغَة فارسل اليه قصيدة ميمية يهنّوه فيها بالولاية ، ونحن نورد هاهنا بنصها كما نقلناها من دون تبديل ولا تغيير ، وهي هذه ــ

هذه الابيات نظمها محيي الدين بن الشيخ بن عبدالشيخ القحطاني البراوي في بندر مَتَنْجَاتَة حين جاءه خبر ولاية الشيخ الاجلّ الوالي سالم بن احمد بن محمد بن عثمان المزروعي رحمه الله تعالى آمين ،

باسم الله الرحمان الرحيم

خبرا بغير تكلم يروي الظما	يا مرسلا ابدي العجيب وافهما
فيها البدور مضيئة تلك السم	سر عاجلا حتى الى ممباسة
سادات كهلان وطيبي المنتمى	فيها المشانخ من كهالنة وهم
كالبحر جودا او كغيث قد حما	اسد كرام ولد احمد في الورى
قف ببابها مستأذنا كي تفهما	فاذا أتيت بكوتها مستعجلا
نحو الصباح مقبلا ومسلما	واذا دخلت باذنهم سر عاجلا
ومبلغًا مني السلام معظما	واذا جلست فحاذهم متأدبا
ماذا الجفا بعد الوصال كأنما	سلهم سؤالا بينا يتذلل
فاستنكرت بعد الوضوح كمعلما	طمست رسوم مودة من بيننا
احوالهم وديارهم نعم الحما	ومضى الزمان ولم نجد من مخبر
ماذا لها عجبا فسل مستفهما	ممباسة اخبارها عنا بطت
أم لم تجد كفوأ لها يروي ظما	خلت بها غير الزمان فطلقتأ
حتى ترى كفوأ لها يحمي الحما	فتمانعت وتماطلت خطابها
يروي الصدا ويزيل عن قلب العما	سلها وخذ منها جوابا شافيا
وجبين وجهه بالبهاء ترسما	رجع الرسول مبشرا بسعادة
والنور في جو السماء كأنما	سرعا يحث بسيره مستعجلا
وكأن لمعان البروق تبسما	بدر الدجى ملا الافاق بنوره
متعجبا ما حل في جو السما	فبقيت من تلك المضينة شاخصا
ام ليلة القدر التي ما اعظما	حدثت لنا بحوادث ملكوتها
مستبشر ويقول حين ترنما	فاذا الرسول مبشر بجوابه
طلعت نجوم سعوده وتعظما	بخ بخ تلك البشائر للذي
ممباسة فاستبشرت واستغنما	وهو الذي رضيت به بعلا لها
وتلألأت بسنانه وعلت سما	وتفاخرت وتبخترت لولانها
يسمو بأحمد نسله حين انتما	أعني به والي البرية سالم
نعم الخليفة كفه بحر طما	بدر الكهالنة الكرام وصفوها
عون الضعيف وخيره لن يعدما	عدل حفي للرعية منصف
أم الكريم نواله لن يحرما	كهف الارامل واليتامى والذي
وأبى الظلوم بعدله ان يظلما	غارت أئمة دهرنا من عدله
وأطالها خوف الحسود المرغما	جاوبته لما استطاب نعوته
قد جئتنا بحقيقة تروي الظما	مهلا هداك الله نعم المرسل

٥٧

ونبأتنا نبأ يقينا بينا   يشفي الصدور ويكشف القلب العما

لله درك من نزيل أمنا   نعم النزيل لنا بباب يما

يا اخوة الوالي الولي وحزبه   كونوا جميعا كالثريا أنجما

حذرا تكونوا كالنعوش اجانبا   ما الذلُ الا في الخلاف وطالما

ذلَّ الكثير مع الخلاف وطالما   عز القليل مع الوفاق ترحما

كونوا جميعا ناصريه على العدا   رغما على أنف الحسود ليكظما

فالله ينصركم ونعم نصيركم   يعطي الجزيل ويرتضي بأقل ما

وعليكم مني السلام تحية   من الشيخ محيي الدين نظما تمَّا،

———————

رأينا في المخطوطات التأريخية التي بأيدينا المنقولة من خط العلامة محيي الدين بن شيخ رحمة الله عليه ، انه كان في ممباسة انكليزي يدعى مري ، ففي ٥ ذي الحجة سنة ١٢٤١ دعا هذا الانكليزي جميع مشانخ البلد وزعماء السواحليين الى داره ، ولما اجتمعوا كلهم سألهم قائلا < لمن ولاية ممباسة ؟ اهي لي او للوالي سالم بن احمد ؟ > فأجابوه جميعهم < انها للوالي وما انت الا امانة في يده > ثم خرجوا من عنده ، ولم يروِ لنا الرواة شأن هذا الرجل ولا ما كان له من السلطة حتى سأل الناس هذا السؤال العجيب ، والذي يظهر لي ان هذا الانكليزي كان وكيلا لبريطانيا العظمى مكان المستر ريتز الذي اقامه القبطان اوين بعد ابرام معاهدة الحماية ، اذ لا يليق بالرجل العادي او التاجر مثلا ان يُقْدِم على مثل هذا السؤال ، ولكن ما الداعي لهذا السؤال يا ترى؟ سيظهر لك الجواب فيما يلي ،

في ١٦ ذي الحجة عام ١٢٤١ عقد القبطان كرستيان الذي يسميه مؤرخو ممباسة باسم القبطان أكْلَنْ جلسة عامّة في دار مري المذكور وأرسل الى الوالي يطلب منه حضور هذه الجلسة ، فأرسل بالنيابة عنه أخويه الامير مبارك بن احمد وراشد بن احمد وذهب معهما زعماء السواحليين وأعيان البلد ومنهم

العلامة محيي الدين ، وبعد ان استقرَّ بهم المجلس قال لهم < ان هذه البلدة وما كان تحت حكمها من البلدان الاخرى هي لجلالة ملك بريطانيا ما دام العلم الانكليزي يخفق عليها ، وهذا بحسب المعاهدة التي عقدتموها مع القبطان اوين ، اليس الامر كذلك ؟ > فرد عليه الامير مبارك بن احمد قائلا < لم يكن الامر كذلك ، بل الذي اتفقنا عليه مع القبطان اوين هو ان يكون لحكومة بريطانيا نصف العشور ، وعلى ان ترد هي الينا بلادنا المغصوبة من الجزيرة الخضراء وغيرها ، واما البلاد وحكمها وادارتها فهي للوالي وحده > ، فقال القبطان < اذا كان هكذا فلا مقام لنا معكم ، لانا لا نقيم في بلد لا امر لنا فيه ولا نهي ، وانا ذاهب عنكم مع مري ، > فقال الامير < اذا اخترتم الذهاب عنا برضاكم فلا نمنعكم منه ، ولكن ينبغي ان تعلموا بانا لم نطردكم من بلادنا > ، فقال القبطان < لا لوم عليكم ايها الامير ولكن أتأسَّف على انكم لم تفهموا كلام القبطان اوين ، او لعله لم يفهم كلامكم ويمكن ان يكون الترجمان الذي كان يترجم كلام الطرفين خان في الترجمة وسبَّب ذلك كتابة المعاهدة على خلاف ارادتكم ، واليوم قد اتضح ما كان خفيا من قبل > ، ثم ذهبوا الى القلعة وانزلوا الراية الانكليزية وذهبوا بها وطلعوا على سفينتهم عشية ذلك اليوم واقلعوا صباح يوم ١٧ ذي الحجة ،

من هذا التأريخ انتهى حمايت بريطانيا العظمى لهذه البلاد بعد ان دامت سنتين ونصف سنة ، يقول المستر لين في كتابه < زنجبار> المطبوع بلندن في عام ١٩٠٥ ان تدخل الانكليز في سياسة مباسة أحزن السيد سعيد الذي كان مطيعا لبريطانيا العظمى ، ومحبا للشعب الانكليزي ، فاعترض لدى حكومة مُمْبَي على ما جرى في مباسة ، فردت عليه الحكومة بانها عازمة على نبذ كل ما يخص مباسة في المستقبل وابطال ما اتى به القبطان اوين ، ويقول المستر لين

ايضا انه قد وجه الى بريطانيا العظمى اللوم على تخليها عن ممباسة ، ولكن فاندة ذلك التخلي كانت عظيمة في الخليج الفارسي ، ومراعاة تلك الفائدة استلزمت التحبب الى السيد سعيد ، ولله درُ المستر لين فقد أبدى لنا السبب الحقيقي الذي حمل بريطانيا على رفع حمايتها للمزارعة وتمزيق المعاهدة المبرمة فيما بينها وبينهم ، ولكن هذا السبب اخفاه القبطان كرستيان عليهم ،

هجوم السيد سعيد على ممباسة في المرة الاولى

علمنا بان السيد أحزنه تدخل الانكليز في سياسة ممباسة ، ولا شك انه فرح غاية الفرح بتخليها عنها ، فشرع في اعداد العدة للهجوم على المزارعة وانتزاع املاكهم من ايديهم ، ولما تم له كل شيء خرج من مسقط في تسع سفن ممتلئة بالمدافع الضخمة والاسلحة الكثيرة والالاف من الجنود ، وتولى قيادة هذا الجيش بنفسه ، وكان هو في المركب المسمى ليفابول ، وصل ممباسة بهذه القوة في ١٧ جمادى الآخرة ١٢٤٣ وقصده اخضاع المزارعة وادخالهم في طاعته او ابادتهم عن آخرهم ، وحالما رسى ليفريول والسفن التابعة له في مياه كِلنْدِين ، ارسل السيد رسالتين احداهما الى الوالي والاخرى الى احمد بن شيخ زعيم السواحليين ، وذهب الرسول بالرسالتين الى القلعة ، وكان قد اجتمع في ذلك الوقت رؤساء القباءل واعيان البلد والامراء والقوّاد يتشاورون في قضية هذه الحرب ، واستلم الوالي الرسالتين ، فاخذ ما هي له ودفع الاخرى لصاحبها ، ثم التفت الى الحاضرين وأخبرهم بمضمون الرسالة من ان السيد سعيد يريد منا ان نستلم ونتنازل له عن بلادنا ، والا حاربنا واستولى عليها قهرا ، وطلب من اهل مجلسه ان يشيروا عليه بما يظهر لهم من الرأي ، وكان في المجلس بَابُ كَافي بن مْوشَافي خطيب الكلندينيين وعالمهم وأحد الشجعان المعروفين ،

فقام وخاطب الرسول قائلا ــ ‹ ايها العربي ان هذه البلاد لسالم فان اراد باختياره ان يسلمها لسعيد فلا اعتراض عليه ، وان اراد ان يدافع عنها فنحن معه ، ولكن لا قدرة لنا عليكم وانتم في السفن فانزلوا الى البر › ، وصوَّبه قومه وصاحوا باجمعهم ‹ فلينزلوا! فلينزلوا! › وانشدوا نشائد الحرب ورقصوا برماحهم واقواسهم وبنادقهم فأثاروا حماسة في قلوب الحاضرين ، والتفت الوالي الى عبدالله بن نافع وأمره ان يكتب للسيد سعيد ردا على رسالته بانه لا يستسلم ، وانه مستعد للدفاع عن بلاده ، بعدما ذهب الرسول بالجواب قسم الوالي جيشه الى سرايا وأمر على كل سرية أميرا وارسل بعضهم الى كِلِنْدِين لمواجهة العدو وآخرين الى مَكُوبة وغيرهم الى شِمَنْز ، وأنزل السيد كذلك عساكره والتحم القتال ،

كان السيد سعيد من أفذاذ دهاة العرب لم يكن يعتمد في حروبه على القوة والشجاعة فحسب ، بل كان يؤثر عليهما السياسة بكل ما في هذه الكلمة من المعاني ، والحرب كما قيل خدعة ، وعلم السيد بان اولاد زاهر بن عبدالله يحملون بين جنوبهم ضغينة مما فعله بهم اولاد عثمان بن عبدالله ، فرأى ان يستعين بهم على جماعتهم وما فلَّ الحديد الا الحديد ، فأرسل الى عبدالله بن زاهر ليوافيه في كِلِنْدِين سريعا ،

بينما الحرب قائمة اذ السيد سعيد على ظهر باخرته مختليا مع عبدالله بن زاهر يفاوضه سرا في شأن الصلح مظهرا له رغبته الشديدة فيه ، وافقه عبدالله على ذلك ووعده على السعي في الاصلاح بينه وبين الوالي بما يرضيه ، ففرح السيد سعيد بهذه البشارة وعاهد صاحبه على مكافئته بثلاثة آلاف ريال اذا تم هذا الصلح على يديه ، ولما همَّ عبدالله على النزول من الباخرة قدَّم له السيد ألف ريال مقدمة على ان يدفع له الباقي بعد إتمام عمله ، فقبلها

عبدالله شاكرا ونزل مسرعا الى الوالي فعرض عليه امر الصلح ورغّبه فيه اى ترغيب ، واستمال قلبه اليه بكل ما أوتيه من الدهاء حتى مال اليه قلبه ، ودعا اهل شوراه وأطلعهم على ما جاء به عبدالله فوافقوا على ايقاف الحرب حتى يجتمعوا مع السيد وينظروا في شروط هذا الصلح ،

توقف القتال ودعا السيد الوالي فوافاه هو وأخوه مبارك بن احمد ونفر من جماعته وطائفة من زعماء البلد ، وبعد المناقشة والمباحثة والاخذ والرد تصالحوا وعقدوا بينهم معاهدة صلح وهي هذه ـ

١ ـ تسلم القلعة للسيد سعيد ويترك فيها حامية مؤلفة من خمسين جنديا بشرط ان يكونوا من قبيلة بينها وبين المزارعة موافقة ،
٢ ـ يقيم الوالي وعائلته في القلعة كما كان سابقا ،
٣ ـ يكون الملك للسيد سعيد غير ان الحكومة تكون لسالم في حياته، ولعقبه بعد موته ،
٤ ـ يقسم العشور بين المتعاهدين على السواء ، وللوالي سالم ان يختار من يريده في ادارة الجمارك ،

وبعد ابرامه على هذه الصورة ، تعاهد كل على نفسه الوفاء بما التزمه لصاحبه ، وتحالفا عليه بكل محرّجة من اليمين ، وفعلا سلّم الوالي القلعة للسيد ، فأدخل هذا عساكره فيها وسافر الى زنجبار ومعه كبار المزارعة لتشييعه ، اذا تأملنا في هذه المعاهدة رأيناها في صالح المزارعة لانها لم تفقدهم من الملك الا الاسم فقط ، ولو دامت كما هي لكان حال السيد سعيد معهم كحال ملوك الشرق اليوم مع الدول المستعمرة وهذا يدلّ على ان السيد احسّ بحرج موقفه ازاء قوة المزارعة ، ولو لا ذلك لما قبل هذه الشروط المخلّة بالملك الذي يقاتل عليه ، اللهم الا اذا كان قد اضمر في نفسه عدم الوفاء بها كما هو الواقع وذلك معنى من معاني السياسة ، وسيظهر فيما يلي من القرائن ما يدل على ما ذكرنا ،

بعد مضي شهرين تقريبا من تأريخ هذه المعاهدة ، امدَّ السيد الحامية التي تركها في القلعة بجنود من العرب والبلوشيين أمَّر عليهم الجَمَعْدَار شاهو الزندجالي ، وصلت السفينة التي اقلَّتهم ورست في مَطَابة وجاؤا الى مباسة مشيًا على الاقدام ، ودخلوا القلعة ، لم يعد الوالي سالم يقيم في القلعة من يوم ابرام المعاهدة لانه أنف من الاقامة فيها مع عساكر السيد ، بل اتخذ لنفسه دارًا في نَدِيَ كُو وشرع في بناء مسجد وراءها (هذا المسجد لم يتم بناؤه بسبب ما تخلل ولاية سالم من الحروب ، لكن اطلاله باقية الى الآن ، وهو في الجنوب الشرقي لبيت اسماعيلجي جيونجي) ثم ارسل السيد بعد اولئك الجنود ناصر بن سليمان الاسماعيلي الذي كان واليا من قبله على الجزيرة الخضراء ، ومع كون هذا الامر مخالفا للمادَة الاولى و الثانية من المعاهدة المزروعية السعيدية ، احترم المزارعة واليهم هذا غاية الاحترام ، حذرا من ان يأتوا بشيء فيَتَّهموا بنقض ما تعهَّدوا على انفسهم ،

واقعة حصار القلعة

بعد ان امضى السيد في زنجبار مدة ثلاثة اشهر تقريبا عاد الى عمان فبدأ ناصر بن سليمان يسيء الى الناس ويعاملهم بقسوة ويهين ذوي الاقدار منهم ، فمقتوه وكرهوه ، وأخيرا شرع يطعن في المزارعة وينال من كرامتهم ، فأبلغوه ان يكف عن تعديه عليهم ، ولكن ناصر لم يحسب لامرهم حسابا ، ولما رأى مشانخ البلد وزعماء الطوائف ازدياد الخصام بينه وبين المزارعة وخافوا سِوء العاقبة ، دخلوا في الاصلاح بينهم ، وقبل المزارعة الصلح على ان يكف كل واحد منهم عن التعدّي على الآخر ، وان يرسلوا شكواهم الى عمان وينتظروا ما يأمر به السيد في شأن هذه الحادثة ، لم يقبل ناصر بن سليمان

هذا الصلح وبعد مدة قصيرة ارسل الى الوالي يأمره بتسليم امر البلد اليه ويؤذنه بالحرب ان لم يفعل ، فامتنع الوالي عن ذلك وعده اهانة فظيعة في حقه مع ما فيه من نقض المعاهدة المعقودة بينه وبين السيد ، وتعجب الناس ايضا من فعل ناصر هذا ، وراجعوه في تأخير هذا الامر الى ان يرد جواب السيد من عمان ولكن الوالي الحّ على طلبه وأخبر المشانخ بان هذا الذي يأتي به هو عين ما امر به السيد ، ولا يمكن له ان يتخلف عن امره ،

ولما كان ٥ ذي القعدة عام ١٢٤٣ نشر راية القتال وأمر بالقاء القنابل على البلد واطلاق البنادق على اهله ، فاحترق قسم كبير منه بنيران المدافع ، وخرج ناصر مع عساكره قاصدين الى حيث يسكن الوالي سالم وعشيرته ليلقوا عليهم القبض ويقيدوهم في الحديد، وانتشر آخرون في البلد يعيثون فيه فسادا ، فأراقوا دماء كثيرين من الابرياء ، وما كان من المزارعة الا ان قابلوا هذا الفعلة السيئة بمثلها، فبارزوا عساكر ناصر وأمعنوا فيهم القتال فشتتوا شملهم وفروا هاربين وتبعهم المزارعة يقتلونهم رميا بالرصاص وضربا بالسيوف وطعنا بالخناجر ، فلجأ من بقي منهم الى القلعة وأقفلوا على انفسهم الرتاج وتحصّنوا بها ، وأمر الوالي سالم بحصار القلعة والتشديد عليه ، وكان امام مدخل القلعة من شمالها بيوت قليلة فأمر بهدمها واتخذ مكانها معسكرا ، وكان جدار القلعة الغربي قصيرا ، فخاف من ان يفلت منهم احد من هذه الجهة فأصدر امره بحفر الخندق خارج هذا الجدار فحفروه ،

دام الحصار بشدته حتى نفد ما كان بأيدي من في القلعة من القوت وبلغ منهم الجهد الى ان اكلوا الفيران وخشاش الارض ، ويقال انه بلغ ثمن الصاع من الذرة عشرة ريالات وثمن الفارة الواحدة ريالا كاملا ،

خشي الوالي من حدوث خيانة في حال الحصار تفسد عليه امره ، فجمع

العرب والطوائف الاثنتي عشرة واخذ منهم العهد على الطاعة والوفاء فعاهدوه عليه ، واتفقوا على انه اذا ظهر من احد منهم خيانة ما ، يسلم الى جماعته ليقتلوه بأيديهم جزاء ما اقترفوه من خيانة وطنه ، ولم تمض مدة من اخذ هذا العهد حتى تبين ان كُومْبُو بن خميس وأخاه محمد ونفرا من قومه اتخذوا وسائل جمَّة لمساعدة من في القلعة بارسال الطعام اليهم ، ومن جملة تلك الوسائل انهم كانوا يرمون اليهم ليلا بعرانيس الذرة يعلقونها على المعاريض فيقذفونها بواسطة الاقواس فيحسب الناس انهم يرمونهم بالنبال ليقتلوهم في حين انهم يرمون بالطعام ليحيوا ، اتصل هذا الخبر بالوالي فأخبر زعماء الطوائف بما اتى به كُومْبُو بن خميس من الخيانة فحكموا عليه بالاعدام ، ولكن الوالي أرجأ تنفيذ هذا الحكم الى حصول الفتح خشية الانقسام وهم في حال الحرب ،

بلغ خبر حادثة الحصار الى زنجبار وعليها السيد هلال بن سعيد نائبا عن والده ، فأرسل سفينة مشحونة بالميرة لمساعدة المحصورين ، واتصل نبأ خروج هذه السفينة بالمزارعة فانتظروها ، وما كادت تدخل البندر حتى تعدى لها كِياتي بن مَوئِي أوفِي بن هُنْزِي احد ابطال الطوائف الثلاث فتقلد سيفه السواحلي (سِيمَ) وركب قاربا صغيرا اتخذ جريدة النرجيل مجذافا فجذف بسرعة نحوها حتى ألصقه بها واقتحمها وصال على من فيها فلم ينج منهم الا من القى نفسه في البحر ، وقاد السفينة وأرساها في البندر والناس يهتفون له ويعجبون من قوته وشجاعته ، ولما نزل من السفينة اشهد الحاضرين ان كل ما فيها غنيمة له لا يشاركه فيها احد ، فأقر له الوالي بذلك وابتاعه منه بألفي ريال ولكن هذا الرجل المقدام ، كما كان فريدا في شجاعته ، كان كذلك فريدا في سخائه وسماحته ، فوهب الالفي ريال للجيش المزروعي يستعين بها على شراء معدّات الحرب ، فقبلها الوالي شاكرا مقدرا لعمله العظيم قدره ،

لما ضاق ناصر بن سليمان من الحصار وكاد يموت جوعا هو ومن كان معه في القلعة نادى بطلب الامان ورفع الحصار عنه ، فأجاب سالم نداءه وأمَّنه هو وجنوده على انفسهم وأموالهم فخرجوا من القلعة في ٢٢ جمادى الآخرة عام ١٢٤٤ كأنهم اموات بعثوا من قبورهم ، وسلم ناصر القلعة للوالي بما فيها من الاسلحة ، وأدخل هو عساكره فيها ، وفي اليوم الثاني أذن لجمعدار شاهو بالسفر فسافر هو ومن بقي من عساكره الى زنجبار ، واما ناصر فمكث في ممباسة بضعة ايام ثم طلب الاذن في السفر الى الجزيرة فأذن له ، وفي ١٧ رجب من هذه السنة انتقل الوالي الى القلعة ، وكانت مدة الحصار ثمانية أشهر وسبعة عشر يوما ،

بينما الوالي يستعرض الاسلحة التي تركها العدو اذا وجد في ركن من اركان بعض مخازن القلعة قيودا من الحديد وعلى كل واحد منها اسم من رئيس من رؤساء المزارعة ، وطبعا كان هو من جملتهم ، فازداد الوالي يقينا في ان ما اتى به ناصر كان ولا شك بأمر السيد سعيد ، فأرسل العساكر خلفه يقتفون أثره لحقوه حتى في فُنْزِي فقبضوا عليه وجيء به الى ممباسة وألقي في السجن ثم قتل ،

ويتضح مما ذكرناه بطلان قول الميجر بيرس في كتابه ‹ زنجبار › ان المزارعة اغتنموا فرصة غياب السيد فحاصروا القلعة الى آخر ما قاله ، ولو اطَّلع الميجر على ما أجراه ناصر بن سليمان لظهر له ان المزارعة لم يبدأوا هذه الحرب بل دخلوها مضطرّين ، ولعلم من هو الملوم وأولى بإلقاء تبعتها عليه ، ولا شك في انه لاعذر المزارعة فيما فعلوه من الدفاع عن انفسهم وشرفهم ، ومن تصريح ناصر بن سليمان بانه امتثل امر السيد فيما فعله قرينة دالّة على ان السيد لم يكن ناويا في حال المعاهدة وفاء ما تعهده ولا بر اليمين الذي

٦٦

حلفه ، وكأنه جعل تلك المعاهدة مكيدة يكيد بها المزارعة حتى اذا أمن منهم ونزعوا اسلحتهم وركنوا الى الدعة هاجمهم وقيدهم في الحديد ،

نقلت من المؤرخ النسابة المرحوم عبدالكريم بن طلسم قال ان السر في ارسال ناصر بن سليمان وجعله واليا خلاف نص المعاهدة هو ان يتجسس للسيد احوال المزارعة ويلاحظهم من قرب ، حتى اذا سنحت له الفرصة قيدهم وأرسلهم الى زنجبار ، ولكن ناصر لم يكن سياسيًا كمولاه فلم يتأنَّ في الامر فاستعجل به فعوقب بحرمانه وافتضاح امره ، وأستشهد هنا لما ذكرته من واقعة حصار القلعة من اولها الى آخرها بايراد قصيدة المؤرخ العلامة محيي الدين بن شيخ القحطاني رحمة الله عليه التي ضمنها ذكر هذه الحادثة كما شهدها بعيني رأسه ، وسيقف القارء منها على الحقيقة الناصعة من لسان ذلك الشاهد العدل ونوردها كما نقلناها بعد مقابلتها بعدة نسخ وهي هذه ـ

وحلوها ثوب السموم القتل	يا طالبا لخسيسة بتحيل
ما ذاق منها شربة للجهل	لو انها ساوت جناح بعوظة
أردتهم عجلا بغير تمهل	كم صرعت بغرورها أولو النهى
من عادها وثمودها فتأمل	او ما سمعت بفعلها أمما مضت
دانت لهم امم الزمان الاول	كانوا ملوكا قاهرين على الورى
ظنوا البقاء بها بغير تحول	نحتوا بيوتا من قلال جبالها
صرعي كأعجاز النخيل الطول	حلت بها رسل المنون فأصبحوا
إذ قال ملعون انا الرب العلي	فرعون ذو الاوتاد واخبث كافر
ما كان ينفع قوله حين ابتلي	فأحله بأس الاله لنقله
آمنت به ولقد عصى بالمرسل	آمنت انه لا اله الا الذي
اين الائمة والملوك العدل	يا ايها المغرور كن منتبها
أين الذي يلجأ به في الموهل	أين القضاة وابن ارباب التقى
يجزيك بالحسنى كان لم تفعل	أين الحبيب اذا اكتسبت خطيئة
فكأنهم لم يسكنوا في المنزل	مرت بهم آجالهم فتحولوا
قطعوك عنهم جانبا في المعزل	ويبقى الذين اذا زللت برزة
وعظا ولا تنظر فعال الارذل	يكفيك هذا ان قبلت نصيحتي
حال الخسيسة لا تكن كالغفل	وذكرت احوال القرون لتعتبر
مباسة بين الكرام الفضل	وسأنبيك ما جرى في أرضنا
شمس الملوك ومن صميم الكمل	لما أتاها بالهدى خير الندى
من نسل سلطان الكريم الابطل	أعني بمولانا سعيد سيد
اولاد احمد فاهتدوا بتحمل	ومرآته بالكوت من خدامه
فأنالهم فيها ولاية دول	بذلوا له الكوت المنور بالرضى
من نسل احمد سالم لتأهل	وأقام فيها للبرية واليا

والله يشهد بينهم بتكفل   ما دام او داموا كذاك نسولهم
ومكاتب ما بينهم بمفضل   وجرت على تلك العهود ميامن
نسل الوليد سعيد حامي المعقل   وأقام في الكوت المنور خلفة
ويشاههم وذوي الكموم الطول   وأمده بجنوده من أهله
فكأنها اولاد سيدنا العلي   كانوا جميعا في البلاد محشّما
نحو الزنوج بلاد خير المنزل   وبنصرة الرحمن سيدنا رحل
أهدى الينا ناصرا رجلا خلي   لما اعتنى بعمانه متوجها
وأتى بفعل مثله لم يُفعل   لما أتى غير البلاد بفعله
وقليل صبر لا ينال المأمل   كرهته اصحاب البلاد جميعهم
يا قلة الصبر الخفيف المعقل   وأثار نار فتنة مخمودة
حاسا له بل ذا عليه تقول   ودعي بذلك امرة من سيد
اولاد احمد يا لهم من مرجل   وجرى كلام بينه وشيوخنا
لهيا كأن شرارها قصر علي   لما رأينا ناره موقودة
فكأنها اثواب بأتاوى الخلي   قمنا نرقع لانطفاف لهيبها
ان ينتهي امر الخلاف المؤلي   فتوافقوا توقيف امرهم الى
يستقبلون جميعهم بتذلل   وبكل ما من سيد يأتي لهم
بتحالف والله خير موكل   جرى على هذا التعاهد بينهم
من ناصر ان سلموا البلدان لي   من بعد ذا شفنا خطوطا جملة
وجواب لا الا بخط مفضل   اما فحرب الله واقعة بكم
نشر البيارق فوق كوت تعتلي   لما أتاه جوابهم لخطوطه
فقع الرعود القاصفات الهول   فاذا البنادق والمدافع تفقع
قتل العباد بغير موجب مقتل   حرّق البلاد بنارها مشبوبة
كالصافنات الموريات الصهل   فتشمروا اولاد احمد للوغى
وحمى القبائل من جميع السواحل   وبنوا السيب الحمى العرب أهل الرتب
حتى انتهى خير القتال الاثقل   ما زاد بينهم الحروب مشمر
من نسل مولانا سعيد الاعدل   للبدر سيدنا هلال الاهلة
محصوبة الماس (من ؟) عنده ترسل   فأتاهمو منه الخطوط نصيحة
لكن إبليس الغوي لم يقبل   فأتى وبلغ امره لخطوطه
وأقام كل للوغى متسربل   ناشب نيران الحروب بجهده
ما للانام من القضاء بمؤمل   وقضا الاله على الانام مقدر
ورجال كوت في الحصار مهزل   ما زال بينهم القتال مشددا
شيء لاحياء النفوس النحل   طالت عليهم مدة لم يأتهم
جعلوا جريدة تروسهم من مأكل   صبروا وتموا في الحصار مديدة
لم يبق فيران لهم لم يؤكل   حتى اذا فنيت جميع معاشهم
نفسا ومالا أمنين المقتل   طلبوا الامان ليخرجوا من كوتهم
غير الذي حفر الطوى في مسبل   خرجوا جميعا سالمين وسافروا
الا لصاحبه كما في المنزل   والمكر حقا لا يحيق وباله
سبحان من لا يعتريه تذلل   والارض يورثها لمن يشاء
بعد الطلاق فهل يحل ليسأل   والكوت باق راجعا لبعولها
أن لا والا فالرجوع محلل   وأجيب ان كان الثلاثة او افتدت
بتفكر وتدبر وتأمل   كلمت مقصودي فخذه موعظا
خير الانام شفيعنا عند العلي ،   ثم الصلاة على النبي وآله

قول الناظم رحمه الله < والكوت باق راجعا لبعوله _ > الى آخر البيتين
فيه تشبيه المزارعة ببعل امرأة ، والقلعة بزوج ذلك البعل وخروجهم منها بالطلاق

، ثم كان سائلا سأله هل يعود ملك المزارعة كما كان بعد خروجهم من القلعة هذه مرة ؟ فأجاب أن نعم ، يعود لهم ذلك الى ان يتكرر خروجهم منها ثلاث مرات ، فحينئذ لا عودة لملكهم ، كالزوج اذا طلق امرأته ثلاثا ، وكان الامر كما قال الناظم ، خرج المزارعة من القلعة اول مرة بعد مقتل محمد بن عثمان ، ثم عادوا في ولاية أخيه علي ، وتمت المرة الثالثة بخروج راشد بن سالم كما يأتي فلم يرجعوا اليها ، ولا ادري هل وقع ما قاله الناظم اتفاقا ، او علمه بما أوتيه من البراعة في علم الرمل والتنجم ؟ والله اعلم بحقيقة الحال غير ان ما تنبأ به قد حصل على وفق ما تنبأ ،

بعد حصول الفتح وانتقال الوالي الى القلعة وترتيب امرها ، عزم على انفاذ الحكم على كُومْبُو بن خميس ، ولما علم هذا بالامر فرَّ هاربا متجها نحو جِبَانَة ، فبعث الوالي خلفه نفرا من عبيد الحكومة فأدركوه في محل يقال له مْوَنْزَاي فقبضوا عليه وأتوا به الى ممباسة ، وكان عزمه ــ كما قيل ــ ان يحشد جيشا ويذهب به الى لامُوّ ثم يبحر معه الى زنجبار فيأتي بالسيد هلال مع هذا الجيش لمحاربة المزارعة ،

وبلغ خبر قبضه الى عشيرته فعزموا على ان يعترضوا الطريق الذي يمر فيه فيهجموا على القابضين عليه ويفكوا قيوده ، ولكن لما كانت هذه المغامرة شديدة الخطر عليهم أحجموا عنه ، أحضر كُومْبُو قدام الوالي فوبخه على فعله ، وشفع فيه كثيرون من العرب وغيرهم منهم القاضي احمد بن مسعود بن ناصر المزروعي الذي ألحَّ في شفاعته واستعطاف الوالي عليه ولكن الوالي لم ير ان يقبل فيه شفاعة احد لما في قبوله من تجريء غيره على الاتين بمثل فعله في المستقبل معتمدا على شفاعة الناس فيه ، وهذا الذي فعله الوالي هو ما يقتضيه القوانين الحربية فلا لوم عليه ، بل ينبغي ان يحمد ويشكر على ابداله حكم الاعدام بالحبس مخالفا في ذلك ما قضى به الامة عند اخذهم العهد اثناء الحصار ،

والمستغرب من كُومْبُو بن خميس هذا مضادته للمزارعة وهم اصدقاء والده ، فقد وصل ابوه خميس بن تاني الى ممباسة مستجيرا من النباهنة

٦٩

الذين ارادوا قتله وقصد الى الوالي احمد بن محمد بن عثمان فأجاره وآواه اليه ونصره من اعدائه ، فكان ينبغي لاولاده ان يقدروا هذه المنة قدرها ، وان يوالوا المزارعة لا ان يعادوهم ، ولكن الشيطان لعنه الله وسوس اليهم حتى فعلوا ما لا يليق بهم عفا الله عنهم ،

هجوم السيد سعيد على ممباسة للمرة الثانية

ارسل السيد هلال بن سعيد الى والده بعمان يفيده بما كان من حادثة حصار القلعة ، فجمع السيد الجنود وحشدهم من القبائل المختلفة في عمان فبلغ عددهم ألفي نفس او يزيدون ، وخرج هو نفسه على ظهر الباخرة < ليفربول > ومعه اربعة سفن حربية وست سفن شراعية حاملة للزاد والمؤن ووصل ممباسة في اول صيف عام ١٢٢٥ ،

فبدلا ان يبرىء نفسه مما فعله عامله ناصر بن سليمان وقائد جيشه جمعدار شاهو من الافاعيل المناقضة للمعاهدة التي أبرمها هو نفسه مع المزارعة ويسعى في اعادة الصداقة وتجديد المعاهدة بينهم ، أرسل انذارا الى الوالي سالم وتهديدا بليغا واعلانا له بالحرب ، وهذا دليل آخر على ان السيد لم يكن عازما على وفاء تلك العهود ، ودليل ايضا على ان ما فعله ناصر بن سليمان كان بامر منه لا كما يقول سعيد في الاعتذار رويت له من ان ناصر ادعى الولاية من دون تولية ، وفعل ما فعل من دون امر ، غريب جدا ان يأتي رجل الى بلد ويدَّعي انه واليه من قبل السلطان فيصدقه الناس ويفوضون اليه أمرهم من دون بينة ولا حجة ، ولكن رويت اعتاد ان يقول مثل هذا ، فقد قال في محمد بن عثمان انه لم يولّه الامام بل اغتصب الولاية اغتصابا ، يقول ذلك مع قيام الاجماع على خلافه ، ولو كان ما قاله حقا لسبق الى التنبيه عليه السيد هلال بن سعيد ولحذَّر اهل ممباسة من ذلك الرجل وتصديقه فيما ادعاه ، ولا شك في انه ـ وهو في زنجبار ـ كان ملما بجميع ما أحدثه ناصر بن سليمان في حينه ، وكذلك لتبرأ منه السيد سعيد عند وصوله ممباسة هذه المرة ،

لم يبال المزارعة بذلك التهديد الذي هددهم به السيد ، بل استعدوا لمقاومته بكل ما يستطيعونه من القوة فأنزل السيد عساكره في كِلِنْدِين وآخرين في شَمَانْزِي ، وقسم الوالي جيشه فولَّى على العرب الامير مبارك بن احمد ، وعلى السواحليين كِيَات بن مَوْتِي أُوفِي ، والتحم القتال بين الفريقين ودام ستة ايام وكان سجالا بينهم يوم لهؤلاء ويوم لهؤلاء وفي اليوم السابع حمل عساكر السيد على جيش المزارعة حملة صادقة فتقهقروا الى الوراء وزحف أولئك الى ان دخلوا بلدة كِلِنْدِين واستولوا عليها ، والمراكب تساعدهم باطلاق مدافعها على العدو وهنا قام الامير مبارك بن احمد وخطب في جيشه فنفخ فيهم روحا جديدة استهانوا لها الموت في سبيل الدفاع عن الشرف والحرية ، فكرُّوا على عساكر السيد بشجاعة لا مزيد عليها فهزموهم وفروا يُهَرْوِلون الى الساحل طالبين للنجاة ، ولعظم ما أصابهم من الفزع كانوا يطلعون ثلاثين ثلاثين واربعين اربعين على قوارب لا تحمل أكثر من عشرة او عشرين فيطلق عليهم المزارعة بالرصاصات فتنقلب عليهم القوارب بما حصل من اضطرابهم فيها فيغرقون ، وخسر السيد في هذه المعركة اربعمائة قتيل ما عدى الجرحى والغرقى ، ويقال ان عدد الجميع بلغ زهاء تسعمائة نفس وكانت جيف الغرقى تطفو على وجه الماء وتمر بمركب السيد وهو ينظر اليها فيسترجع ويحوقل ، وكانت بغلتان من بغال السيد (نوع من السفن الشراعية) جرفهما الماء الى مَكُوبة بعد انقطاع المراسي منهما فوقعتا في يد خميس بن احمد الذي كان مرابطا هناك مع ثلة من العسكر فغنمهما مع ما كان فيهما من المؤن وقتل كل من فيهما من الرجال ، وغنم المزارعة في هذه المعركة أشياء كثيرة من الاسلحة وغيرها ،

أبدى الامير مبارك بن احمد وسعيد بن علي الهناوي وكِيَاتِي بن مَوْتِي أُوفِي في هذه الحرب من الشجاعة والاقدام ما صار حديث الناس بعدهم ، يروى ان بضعة وعشرين رجلا من عساكر السيد ابصروا الامير مبارك بن احمد وأطلقوا عليه بنادقهم ، ومن حسن الحظ أخطأته كلها ، فما انقشع الدخان الا وقد تركهم صرعى يتخبطون في دمائهم ، واما سعيد بن علي فانه رأى الاعداء يتسابقون الى دخول مسجد كِلِنْدِين ليتحصَّنوا به ، فانتظر حتى امتلأ المسجد

بهم ، ثم هاجم عليهم فلم ينجُ الا من ألقى بنفسه من الشباك وفرَّ ،

كان في جيش السيد بطل من آل البوسعيد معروف بالشجاعة اشتهر بين اهل مباسة باسم < ولد سعيد مقدر > ، فلم يشأ هذا المغوار ان يلطخ حسامه بدم من دونه في الاقدام فصار يتخلل الصفوف وينادي باسم مبارك بن احمد يطلب مبارزته ، وكان لمبارك علامة يتميز بها في الحرب عن غيره ، وهي ريشة نعامة يغرزها على عمامته ، فلما رآه ولد سعيد مقدر فتصدى له وبارزه فتجاولا جولات كانا فيها كفرسي رهان ، وعلم مبارك انه اليوم بين يدي قرينه ، ان لم يبادر بقتله قتله فاحتال عليه وصاح قائلا < لا تضربه من ورائه > كأنه ينهى شخصا يريد ضرب ولد سعيد من خلفه ، فالتفت الرجل فطعنه مبارك في جنبه بطرف سيفه فألقاه على الارض وأجهز عليه ،

وخسارة المزارعة لم تكن يسيرة ، فقد قتل منهم كثيرون ومن الطوائف الثلاث كذلك ، وقتل في هذه الحرب محمد بن علي البسامي وكِياتي بن مَوْنِي أوفي والعقيد بَوْنِغي وكلهم من الشجعان المعروفين الذين كان اهل مباسة يتباهون بهم ، وأصيب الامير مبارك بن احمد برصاصة في رجله كانت سببا في قضاء اجله فيما بعد ، وجرح سعيد بن علي جراحات كثيرة الا انها لم تكن ذات خطر عليه ،

لما رأى السيد ما حل بجيشه من الانكسار العظيم اقلع قاصدا الى زنجنبار وترك جثث موتى جنوده وراءه ، فاشتغل اهل مباسة مدة اربعة ايام في دفنهم ودفن موتاهم ، وأخبرني الوجيه راشد بن سعود نقلا عن عمّه المعمَّر مطر بن سالم الشكيلي ، انه كان من جملة قتلى عساكر السيد نحو سبعين رجلا من بني الشكيل وعددا عظيما من بني بَحَسَن (با حسن ؟)

فرح اهل مباسة غاية الفرح بما نالوه من النصر المبين في هذه المعركة ، وأدرك الوالي بعد ذلك ما كان يهدده من الخطر ، لو ان جيش السيد وفِّق لمواصلة زحفه حتى وصل بلدة مباسة لسهل عليه الدخول فيها من دون عناء ، لانها غير مسورة ، فجمع العرب وزعماء الطوائف وعرض عليهم مشروع بناء السور حول البلدة فوافقوه عليه ، وحالا شرع في بنانه واشترك في العمل فيه

٧٢

جميع الطوائف بهمّة ونشاط حتى أتموه في مدة ليست بطويلة ، ولراشد بن سالم مؤسّس تَكَوُّنْغ اليد البيضاء في بناء هذا السور فقد تكفل على نفسه بناء جزء كبير منه ، وأتم بماله ما عجز عنه بعض الطوائف الاثنتي عشرة ، جزاه الله عن وطنه خيرا ، وكان سمك هذا السور قريبا من ثلاثة أذرع ، وبني عليه في بعض الجهات أبراج مرتفعة ، هدم هذا البناء لما اتّسعت البلدة ، ولكن بقي من آثاره طلل صغير على الساحل الشرقي شمالي بيت تاريا تُوبِن الذي اتُّخَذ قريبا مستشفى لامراض النساء والاطفال ، ومن الاخباريين من يقول ان بناء السور كان بعد واقعة الحصار لا بعد الهجوم على ممباسة للمرة الثانية ، وعلى كل حال فهو من آثار الوالي سالم ،

محاولة استرجاع الجزيرة الخضراء

لما رأى الوالي انه أفلح كثيرا في مقاومته للسيد سعيد في هجومه الاول والثاني ، طمع في استرجاع الجزيرة الخضراء وانتزاعها من يده ، فجهز جيشا وأمّر عليهم أخيه عبدالله بن مبارك بن احمد وكان عبدالله هذا مثال أبيه في الشجاعة وقوة القلب ، فأنفذه الى الجزيرة عام ١٢٤٨ ، وصل الجيش وبارز عساكر السيد في وَيْشَة (؟) واقتتلوا قتالا شديدا ، لكن قوة المزارعة لم تكن كافية للتغلب على تلك الاستحكامات الحربية التي أعدّها السيد ، ولا لكسر ذلك الجيش الجبار الذي انفذه الى هناك لحماية الجزيرة من سطو المزارعة عليها ، فغلبوا هناك وانقلبوا خائبين ،

الحرب الاهلية في سيو وبتة

في عام ١٢٤٩ وقعت حرب اهلية في سيو وبتة بين السلطان بُوَانَة وَزير بن بُوَانَة تَامُو والسيد سعيد من جهة ، وبين الامير فُومُ لُوطِ بن شيخ والرئيس بُوَانَة مَتَاكَا ، اشتبك القتال بين الفريقين فرجحت كفة السلطان بُوَانَة وَزِير على فُومُو لُوطِ ، وفر هذا هاربا هو وبُوَانَة مَتَاكَا ولحقا الى البادية ، وهناك أرسلا الى الوالي سالم يستنجدانه على عدويهما بُوَانَة وَزِير والسيد سعيد ،

فسافر الوالي لنجدتهما مع ثلة من الجند وخاب السلطان والسيد سعيد فتقهقر جيشهما وانهزموا ، وزحف الوالي بجيشه الى سيو واستولى عليها وسلمها لقُوم لُوطِ وبْوانة مَتَاكَا ، وشكراه على نجدته لهما شكرا جزيلا وقوم لوط هذا كان تولى سلطنة بتة في عام ١٢٣٦ وعزله اهلها وولوا مكانه بْوانة شيخ بن مَدي ، وأصبح حياته في خطر من تعدي الثوار عليه ، فأجاره المزارعة وجاؤا به الى ممباسة وأقام فيها الى قبيل عام ١٢٤٩ فرجع الى بلاده وهناك اتحد مع بْوانة مَتَاكَا ، فكان من امرهما ما ذكرناه ،

اغاظ السيد ما فعله الوالي من مساعدة بْوانة مَتَاكَا وقُومُو لُوطِ ، اذ لولاه لما أصابه تلك الهزيمة العظيمة في هذه الواقعة ، فأراد ان يكيد للوالي ، فأنفذ ثلة من الجند ليكمنوا له في طريقه عند رجوعه الى ممباسة ويقتلوه غيلة ، ولكن الله حفظه وعاد الى بلده سالما ظافرا وقد أدَى واجبه نحو صديقه وحليف صديقه ،

من الحوادث التي جرت بعد الهجوم الثاني للسيد سعيد على ممباسة ما ذكره المستر لين في كتابه < زنجبار > وهو انه لما لحق جيش السيد ذلك القتال الذريع في ذلك الهجوم ، وأصيب كثيرون من عساكره البلوشيين بالحمى ، ولم يعد يقوى على مواصلة قتال المزارعة ، ظهر له ان يصاهر مَدَغَسْكَر رجاً الحصول على جنود يستعين بها في حروبه ، فخطب ملكتها وارسل اليها بمُعَجّل صداقها ، وبعد ذلك ارسل اليها يطلب ان تنجده بألفي رجل ، جاءه الرسول بالجواب وأدركه في لاموء عند منصرفه من حرب سيو ، وقدم اليه رسالة الملكة فاذا فيها ان وزراءها لا يستطيعون زفافها اليه لان قانون بلادهم لا يسمح للملكة ان تقترن بأحد ، ولكن هناك أميرة شابة في البلاط الملكي ، ان اختار ان يِتزوجها فله ذلك ، واما من جهة الرجال ففي استطاعته الحصول على اي عدد يريده منهم ،

هجوم السيد على ممباسة للمرة الثالثة

عند رجوع السيد من حرب سيو ، اجتاز بممباسة فلم ير ان يتخطَاها

من دون (ان) يلحق بها وباهلها ما يقدر عليه من الخسارة ، فأرسى سفينته في مقابلة نِيالِي وأنزل مدافع جرها الى مَكُمان وصوبها نحو القلعة ورمى القلعة والبلد بالقنابر ، وكانت مدافع القلعة تقابلها بالمثل ، وعزم بضعة اشخاص من شجعان الطوائف الثلاث على الاستيلاء على مدافع جيش السيد ، فعبروا الشط الى كِسَوُن وعرجوا الى مَكُمان ، وقبل ان يصلوا الى مكان المدافع أبصرهم العساكر فرموهم بالقنابل وقتلوهم عن آخرهم ، وكان راشد بن محمد بن راشد الشكيلي عم راشد بن مسعود من امهر الطوبجية في الجيش المزروعي ، وبينما هو يطلق مدفعه في البرج المقابل لمَكُمان اذ صوب اليه العجمي طوبخي جيش السيد مدفعه فرماه بقنبلة اطارت رأسه ، هذا كل ما رواه لنا الرواة مما وقع في هذا الهجوم ، ولم يفز السيد بشيء سوى تمتعه برؤية مباسة تحترق بنيران مدافعه ، ولما أيقن انه لا يستفيد شيئا أقلع الى زنجبار ،

واقعة شاغة

مما وقع في زمان الوالي سالم ، انه كانت طائفة من وَشَلغة يغيرون على القرى الواقعة بالقرب من تانغة ويعيثون فيها فسادا فيقتلون وينهبون ، وكان والي تَانْغَة من قبل المزارعة قاسم بن غريب الريامي ، فاستأذن الوالي في محاربة هذه الطائفة فأذن له ، وأرسل اليه من مباسة مددا وأمره على ذلك الجيش ، خرج قاسم بجيشه الى ان وصل رُومْبُو من اراضي شاغة ، فأشهر الحرب عليهم ، واستمر القتال بينهم أياما ، ولكن لم يقدر على فتح هذه البلاد لعسر وصول المدد اليه من بعد الشقة ووعورة الطريق ،

القبض على موني سمبا سلطان تانغة

كان مُوِني سِمْبَا هذا خرج من الطاعة في زمان الوالي احمد بن محمد بن عثمان ، وسعى في ارجاعه اليه الديوان حسن بن ناصر كما تقدم ذكر قضيته في ترجمة الوالي احمد ، وفي هذه الايام تمرد ثانيا وأثار ثورة في تَانْغَة

، فأرسل الوالي اليه جيشا حاربه وقبض عليه وجيء به الى مباسة ، قد شفع في مُوني سِبْبا كثيرون من اهل الوجاهة ، منهم راشد بن سالم مؤسس تَكَوْنُغُ والديوان احمد بن ابي بكر المعروف بالديوان بِنْدو ، ولكن سياسة الوالي هي ان لا يقبل شفاعة احد في الثوار او الساعين في حمل الناس على مخالفة اوامر الحكومة ، فأمر بحبسه ، أغاظ راشد بن سالم ان لا تُقبل شفاعته فعزم على الهجرة من مباسة ، وكان ذلك سببا لتأسيسه بلدة تَكَوْنُغُ ، ويقول بعض الرواة ان الذي اغاظ راشد بن سالم هو عدم قبول الوالي شفاعته في كُومْبُو بن خميس وهذا القول وجيه ودال على عطف اعيان المزارعة على كُومْبُو وعشيرته مع ما اتى به من الخطيئة ،

وفاة الوالي

توفي الوالي رحمة الله عليه في ذي القعدة عام ١٢٥٠ تاركا في قلوب اهل مباسة حزنا عظيما ، وكان رحمه الله أحزم ولاة المزارعة وأسدّهم رأيا وأقواهم بأسا ، لم ينبغ في الولاة مثله ، وكان جميل العشرة حسن السيرة كبير النفس محبا لمعالي الامور ، مؤثرا للشورى في جميع اعماله العمومية ، لم يكن يقدم على أمر الا بعد أخذ رأي أعيان البلد وزعمانه ، ولهذا احبه الناس وأصبح زعماء الطوائف الاثنتي عشرة يحسبون ان الحكومة مشتركة بينهم وبينه ، خصوصا زعماء الطوائف الثلاث الذين كانوا عنده بمنزلة الاخوة الشفقاء ، ولم يكن رحمه الله يرضي ان يأتي احد بما يفسد حكومته او يسبب الثورة او يلجيء على مخالفة الاوامر في بلاده ، ولاجل ذلك ما كان يعذّر المخالفين والعصاة ولا يقبل الشفاعة فيهم ، وما ارشد هذه السياسة ، وخلف الوالي من الاولاد الذكور تسعة وهم راشد وعبدالله وسليمان وضرغام وسبأ وأحمد وزمام وسعيد وكعب ، فالثلاثة الاول من جملة الخمسة والعشرين الذين قبض عليهم السيد ونفاهم الى بندر عباس ، والذين أعقبوا هم راشد واحمد وزمام ، والله اعلم ،

٭٭